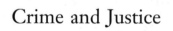

Crime and Justice

Crime and Justice
A Review of Research
Edited by Michael Tonry

VOLUME 25

The University of Chicago Press, Chicago and London

This volume was prepared under Grant Number 92-IJ-CX-K044 awarded to the Castine Research Corporation by the National Institute of Justice, U.S. Department of Justice, under the Omnibus Crime Control and Safe Streets Act of 1968 as amended. Points of view or opinions expressed in this volume are those of the editors or authors and do not necessarily represent the official position or policies of the U.S. Department of Justice.

The University of Chicago Press, Chicago 60637
The University of Chicago Press, Ltd., London

ISSN: 0192-3234

ISBN: 0-226-80847-5

LCN: 80-642217

Contents

Preface

Knowledge has no nationality, but it can be used only if it is shared in a way that can be understood. Crime and punishment are human problems, and it would be astonishing if insights about partial solutions were uniquely applicable only to particular times and places. Until recently, however, limits of language and access made the transmission of criminological knowledge across national borders difficult and erratic, but that is changing. The political will to solve problems sensibly varies widely, but lack of relevant knowledge is not the reason.

The transmission of criminological knowledge across national boundaries has been facilitated over the life of this series, the catalyst having been the acceptance by others of English as the international language of science, economics, and policy analysis. The social science research community is becoming global, as this volume attests.

Two essays, by James B. Jacobs and Lauryn Gouldin on American organized crime and by Roger Lane on the history of murder in America, have by definition an American focus, but the rest draw on literature and practice that transcends national boundaries.

John Braithwaite's overview of restorative justice theory, research, and practice documents developments in North America, Australasia, and Europe and draws on writing from many countries. Whether restorative ideas will someday lead to a paradigm shift as pervasive as the nineteenth-century shift toward individualized sentencing remains to be seen. Evaluations demonstrate that many restorative programs are more satisfying to victims and offenders than the official processes they displace, but it is too soon to tell whether programs will extend to older offenders and more serious offenses than now they typically do and whether positive findings on participants' satisfactions will be paralleled by positive findings on offenders' subsequent behavior.

Josine Junger-Tas and Ineke Haen Marshall's essay on methodological issues in self-report studies likewise discusses issues that have no national identity and literatures from many countries. Pioneering studies in many countries using common instruments and measures have been carried out under the leadership of Dutch researchers and are beginning to provide important cross-national insights.

Jeffrey Fagan and Richard Freeman examine the relations among work, crime, and punishment: the effects of unemployment and underemployment on criminality and the effects of criminality and punishment on employment. The issues are complex, and the literatures are often technical, but many findings are robust. The literature comes from many countries and its implications apply everywhere.

In 1977, Blair Ewing, then acting director of the National Institute of Justice, responding to an initiative from within his department, asked us to convene the first meeting of a group that then created an editorial board. All of the governmental participants in that meeting have retired, as have most of the scholars and practitioners who were there, yet here we are drafting the preface to the twenty-fifth volume.

Like all previous volumes in this series, this one concentrates on the current state of the art of knowledge on important research and policy subjects. We are encouraged to pursue this purpose because a long series of permanent and acting directors of the National Institute of Justice have chosen to support this enterprise, which, whatever its strengths and weaknesses, wins them few political credits. We are grateful for that support and particularly grateful to NIJ's energetic and perceptive current director, Jeremy Travis, and to Mary Graham, director of NIJ's Office of Communications.

Each *Crime and Justice* volume represents much work by many people—authors, referees, editorial board members, even occasionally the editors. However, we know, and authors know, that much of what is good about *Crime and Justice* volumes results from the work of our associate editor, Kate Blake, with whom we have now worked for a decade. We appreciate her talent, her industry, and her patience. Hence we dedicate this book to her.

Michael Tonry
Norval Morris

John Braithwaite

Restorative Justice: Assessing Optimistic and Pessimistic Accounts

ABSTRACT

For informal justice to be restorative justice, it has to be about restoring victims, restoring offenders, and restoring communities as a result of participation of a plurality of stakeholders. This means that victim-offender mediation, healing circles, family group conferences, restorative probation, reparation boards on the Vermont model, whole school antibullying programs, Chinese Bang Jiao programs, and exit conferences following Western business regulatory inspections can at times all be restorative justice. Sets of both optimistic propositions and pessimistic claims can be made about restorative justice by contemplating the global diversity of its practice. Examination of both the optimistic and the pessimistic propositions sheds light on prospects for restorative justice. Regulatory theory (a responsive regulatory pyramid) may be more useful for preventing crime in a normatively acceptable way than existing criminal law jurisprudence and explanatory theory. Evidence-based reform must move toward a more productive checking of restorative justice by liberal legalism, and vice versa.

This essay conceives restorative justice as a major development in criminological thinking, notwithstanding its grounding in traditions of justice from the ancient Arab, Greek, and Roman civilizations that accepted a restorative approach even to homicide (Van Ness 1986, pp. 64–68), the restorative approach of the public assemblies (moots)

John Braithwaite is a professor in the Research School of Social Sciences, Australian National University. My thanks to Stephen Free, Ellen Foulon, Alison Pilger, and Chris Treadwell for their diligent research assistance for this essay. Helpful comments on earlier drafts were provided by many people including Kathy Daly, Carol Heimer, Carol La Prairie, Brenda Morrison, Guy Masters, Christine Parker, Hugh Potter, Kent Roach, Tom Scheff, Lawrence Sherman, Heather Strang, Michael Tonry, and Tom Tyler.

1

of the Germanic peoples who swept across Europe after the fall of Rome (Berman 1983, pp. 53–56), Indian Hindus as ancient as the Vedic civilization (6000–2000 B.C.) (Beck 1997, p. 77) for whom "he who atones is forgiven" (Weitekamp 1989), and ancient Buddhist, Taoist, and Confucian traditions that one sees blended today in North Asia (Haley 1996).

Contemporary Nobel Peace Prize-winning Buddhists, Aug San Suu Kyi of Burma and the Dalai Lama, are reteaching the West that the more evil the crime, the greater the opportunity for grace to inspire a transformative will to resist tyranny with compassion. They follow in the footsteps of Hindus such as Mohandas Gandhi and Christians such as Desmond Tutu. In the words of the Dalai Lama: "Learning to forgive is much more useful than merely picking up a stone and throwing it at the object of one's anger, the more so when the provocation is extreme. For it is under the greatest adversity that there exists the greatest potential for doing good, both for oneself and for others" (Eckel 1997, p. 135). Or as Saint Paul put it, "Where sin abounded, grace did much more abound." The implication of this teaching for criminologists is that preventing crime is an impoverished way of conceiving our mission. Crime is an opportunity to prevent greater evils, to confront crime with a grace that transforms human lives to paths of love and giving.

If we take restorative justice seriously, it involves a very different way of thinking about traditional notions such as deterrence, rehabilitation, incapacitation, and crime prevention. It also means transformed foundations of criminal jurisprudence and of our notions of freedom, democracy, and community.

Restorative justice has been the dominant model of criminal justice throughout most of human history for all the world's peoples. A decisive move away from it came with the Norman Conquest of much of Europe at the end of the Dark Ages (Van Ness 1986, p. 66; Weitekamp 1999). Transforming crime into a matter of fealty to and felony against the king, instead of a wrong done to another person, was a central part of the monarch's program of domination of his people. Interest in restorative justice rekindled in the West from the establishment of an experimental victim-offender reconciliation program in 1974 in Kitchener, Ontario (Peachey 1989). Today, Umbreit (1999) reports that there are at least three hundred of these programs in North America and over five hundred in Europe.

The 1990s have seen the New Zealand idea of family group conferences spread to many countries including Australia, Singapore, the United Kingdom, Ireland, South Africa, the United States, and Canada, adding a new theoretical vitality to restorative justice thinking. Canadian native peoples' notions of healing circles and sentencing circles (James 1993) also acquired considerable influence, as did the Navajo Justice and Healing Ceremony (Yazzie and Zion 1996). Less visible were the rich diversity of African restorative justice institutions such as the Nanante. By the 1990s, these various programs came to be conceptualized as restorative justice. Bazemore and Washington (1995) and Van Ness (1993) credit Albert Eglash (1975) with first articulating restorative justice as a restitutive alternative to retributive and rehabilitative justice. As a result of the popularizing work of North American and British activists such as Howard Zehr (1985, 1990), Mark Umbreit (1985, 1994), Kay Pranis (1996), Daniel Van Ness (1986, 1999), Tony Marshall (1985), and Martin Wright (1982) during the 1980s, and the new impetus after 1989 from New Zealanders and Australians, restorative justice became the emerging social movement for criminal justice reform of the 1990s (Daly and Immarigeon 1998). Since 1995, two organizations, Ted Wachtel's (1997) Real Justice in the United States and John MacDonald's Transformative Justice Australia, have offered training in conferencing to thousands of people worldwide. An evaluation research community also emerged in association with the social movement; this community is dominated by Belgians, Germans, Austrians, and Canadians, though Burt Galaway and Joe Hudson (1975) in Minnesota and Canada were the early and persistent role models of this research community.

During the 1980s, there was also considerable restorative justice innovation in the regulation of corporate crime (Rees 1988; Braithwaite 1995a). Clifford Shearing's (1997) historical analysis is more about governmentalities of post-Fordist capitalism than village moots: "Restorative justice seeks to extend the logic that has informed mediation beyond the settlement of business disputes to the resolution of individual conflicts that have traditionally been addressed within a retributive paradigm . . . In both a risk-oriented mentality of security [actuarialism] and a restorative conception of justice, violence loses its privileged status as a strategy to be deployed in the ordering of security" (p. 12).

Section I of this essay first seeks to conceptualize what restorative justice is against the background of these histories. Sections II–V follow the author's peculiar history of engagement with restorative processes in business regulation (nursing homes, corporate crime) and in Asia and the Pacific. Section VI summarizes fifteen propositions of an Optimistic Account (Sec. VII) and the thirteen propositions of a Pessimistic Account of restorative justice that form the subsections of Section VIII. The Optimistic Account is that each of a number of theories—about shame and shaming, justice, defiance, self-categorization, and deterrence—might have some partial validity. The Pessimistic Account is that restorative justice processes will often fail or backfire, defeating justice. This dialectic leads to a conclusion about how to hedge restorative justice with deterrence, incapacitation, and liberal rights.

I. What Is Restorative Justice, and Why Is It Beginning to Take Off?

Restorative justice is most commonly defined by what it is an alternative to. Juvenile justice, for example, is seen as seesawing back and forth during the past century between a justice and a welfare model, between retribution and rehabilitation. Restorative justice is touted as a long-overdue third model or a new "lens" (Zehr 1990), a way of hopping off the seesaw, of heading more consistently in a new direction while enrolling both liberal politicians who support the welfare model and conservatives who support the justice model. The appeal to liberals is a less punitive justice system. The appeal of restorative justice to conservatives is its strong emphasis on victim empowerment, on empowering families (as in "family group conferences"), on sheeting home responsibilities, and on fiscal savings as a result of the parsimonious use of punishment. When restorative justice is applied to white-collar crime, probusiness politicians also tend to find the approach more appealing than a retributive approach to business wrongdoing. Every one of these bases of political appeal is subject to horrible perversions, as Section VII (The Pessimistic Account) suggests.

In New Zealand, the country with the most developed programmatic commitment to restorative justice, the mainstream conservative and social democratic parties have been joined by Christian profamily parties of the Right in their support for restorative justice. In New Zealand (Maxwell and Morris 1993) and Australia (Moore with Forsythe 1995), the evidence is surprising on how supportive of restorative justice are the police, that traditional ally of law-and-order politicians. The strongest opposition has come from lawyers, including some judges, under the influence of well-known critiques of the justice of informal processing of crime (see Sec. VII). At the same time, in both

New Zealand and Canada, judicial leadership has been at the vanguard, if not the vanguard, of restorative justice reform. In the 1990s, restorative justice became a unifying banner, sweeping up various traditions of justice as "making amends" (Wright 1982), reconciliation (Marshall 1985; Umbreit 1985; Dignan 1992), peacemaking (Pepinsky and Quinney 1991), redress (De Haan 1990), relational justice (Burnside and Baker 1994), transformative justice (Moore with Forsythe 1995, p. 253; Morris 1995), Real Justice (McDonald et al. 1995), and republican justice (Braithwaite and Pettit 1990). During the same period, similar ideas were also being developed by feminist abolitionists (Meima 1990) and in other feminist analyses that emphasized denunciation of the harm and help for victims as more central than punishment (Lacey 1988, pp. 193–94; Harris 1991; Braithwaite and Daly 1994; Roach 1999). Feminist thinking about crime has been a dialectic of Portia (an ethic of justice) and Persephone (an ethic of care) (Heidensohn 1986), out of which some feminists want Portia and Persephone each to check the excesses of the other (Masters and Smith 1998) in a manner rather like that discussed in the conclusion to this essay.

The most influential text of the restorative tradition has been Nils Christie's "Conflicts as Property" (1977), which defined the problem of criminal justice institutions "stealing conflicts" from those affected. Centuries-earlier philosophies of New Zealand Maori (Pratt 1996), North American Indian (Krawll 1994; Aboriginal Corrections Policy Unit 1997*a*), Christian (Van Ness 1986), and Japanese/Confucian/Buddhist (Haley 1996; Masters and Smith 1998) restorative justice have actually been the sources of the deepest influences on the contemporary social movement.

Paul McCold (1997) recently convened a Delphi process on behalf of the Working Party on Restorative Justice of the Alliance of NGOs [Nongovernmental Organizations] on Crime Prevention and Criminal Justice to see if these disparate strands of the emerging alternative might settle on a consensual conception of restorative justice. A Delphi process iteratively solicits expert opinion, in this case on the best way to define restorative justice. The consensus was not overwhelming. The most acceptable working definition was offered by Tony Marshall: "Restorative justice is a process whereby all the parties with a stake in a particular offense come together to resolve collectively how to deal with the aftermath of the offense and its implications for the future" (e-mail, Marshall to McCold, 1997).

This definition does stake out a shared core meaning of restorative justice. Its main limitation is that it does not tell us who or what is to be restored. It does not define core values of restorative justice, which are about healing rather than hurting, moral learning, community participation and community caring, respectful dialogue, forgiveness, responsibility, apology, and making amends (see Nicholl 1998). I take those who have a "stake in a particular offense" to mean primarily victims, offenders, and affected communities (which include the families of victims and offenders). So restorative justice is about restoring victims, restoring offenders, and restoring communities (Bazemore and Umbreit 1994; Brown and Polk 1996). An answer to the "What is to be restored?" question is whatever dimensions of restoration matter to the victims, offenders, and communities affected by the crime. Stakeholder deliberation determines what restoration means in a specific context.

Some have suggested dimensions of restoration that are found to be recurrently important in restorative justice processes. For example, I have defined the following dimensions of restoration as important from a republican perspective: restoring property loss, restoring injury, restoring a sense of security, restoring dignity, restoring a sense of empowerment, restoring deliberative democracy, restoring harmony based on a feeling that justice has been done, and restoring social support (Braithwaite 1996).

All cultures have restorative justice traditions defined in these terms, particularly in their families, schools, and churches, just as they all have retributive traditions. The core belief of the social movement for restorative justice is that all cultures in the circumstances of the modern world will find their restorative traditions a more useful resource than their retributive traditions. Yet all cultures must adapt their restorative traditions in ways that are culturally meaningful to them.

Insufficiently retributive societies were often wiped out in the past by more violent cultures.[1] Punitiveness, however, has less survival value for communities that are more interdependent, a lesson North American states finally learned in their dealings with each other during the nineteenth century and European states in the twentieth. Most of the world continues to live in a zone of violence where international disputes continue to be settled through force of arms; citizens continue to suffer terrible war crimes. However, North America and Western

[1] The most famous example was the razing of Carthage by Rome after Hannibal achieved his tactical objectives and left Rome in peace (when he had it at his mercy).

Europe today constitutes a zone of restorative diplomacy, into which the newly economically interdependent states of Asia are being integrated (cf. Goldgeir and McFaul 1992). Within this zone of restorative diplomacy, democracies do not commit war crimes against one another, indeed do not go to war against one another (Doyle 1983, 1986; Maoz and Abdolali 1989; Burley 1992, pp. 394–95). Rather disputes are mostly settled through conciliation, mediation, conferences, and summits. They are dealt with through processes that fit Marshall's definition of restorative justice (see Laue 1991), albeit processes with huge imbalances of power. According to this analysis, there was a profound difference between Versailles, which was a degradation ceremony intended to humiliate a defeated Germany in 1919 and the Marshall Plan after World War II, which was a restorative approach to reintegrate Germany with respect into the international community (Braithwaite 1991, 1999; Offer 1994; Scheff 1994).

Retributive emotions are things we all experience and things that are easy to understand from a biological point of view. But, on this view, retribution is in the same category as greed or gluttony; biologically they once helped us to flourish, but today they are corrosive of human health and relationships. There is a contrary view that a more rationalist conception of retribution can be reconciled with restoration, however, and indeed must be if restorative justice is to be a pragmatic program (Van Ness and Strong 1997, pp. 27–28; Daly and Immarigeon 1998).

While most of the writing on restorative justice focuses on the comparatively small crimes of juvenile delinquents, in this essay I emphasize its relevance to adult crime as well, including war crimes and crimes at the commanding heights of business power (as in corporate restorative justice) and political power (as in Archbishop Desmond Tutu's Truth and Reconciliation Commission in South Africa, which he explicitly sees as a restorative justice process). On this view, organizations like Transcend that specialize in peacemaking training for international violence are part of the social movement for restorative justice (www.transcend.org).

Reviewers of an earlier version of this essay were wary of the relevance of much of this "noncriminological" material, of the relevance of restorative justice in Africa or Asia to the United States and indeed of my credentials as a restorative justice advocate for undertaking a "dispassionate" criminological review. I am not sure that they are right on three counts. First, regulatory and educative practices and institutions might be better objects of research than criminal justice practices, both because there is enormous selectivity in when we react to regulated phenomena as crime and because regulatory and educational theory deliver superior and more general explanations than criminological theory. Second, my working hypothesis is that better theories of U.S. or Australian crime are likely to be stimulated by broadening our horizons to studying the different patterns of regulatory practices and regulatory outcomes observable in radically different societies. Third, my working hypothesis is that superior explanatory theory (ordered propositions about the way the world is) and superior normative theory (ordered propositions about the way the world ought to be) arise from an explicit commitment to integrating explanatory and normative theory. But for this approach to deliver the goods, what must come with it is a serious commitment to research designed to refute both the normative and explanatory claims. I do not defend this approach here, as Christine Parker and I have done so elsewhere (Braithwaite and Parker 1999). Over time science will judge whether such an approach has marshalled theory and evidence around inferior explanations compared with those advanced by criminologists out of a more standard North Atlantic mold.

Most restorative justice advocates came to the approach through juvenile crime as a result of persistent empirical evidence of the failures of the welfare and justice models. The path that led me and a number of my colleagues who are experts in corporate crime to restorative justice is quite different and instructive. Many young criminologists began to study white-collar crime after Watergate to resurrect Edwin Sutherland's (1983) project. We wanted to document systematically how the crimes of the powerful were unpunished. What we found, in effect, was that the regulation of corporate crime in most countries was rather restorative. The reasons for this were far from ennobling, being about corporate capture combined with high costs of complex corporate crime investigations that states were unwilling to pay. Nevertheless, some of us began to wonder whether we were wrong to see our mission as to make corporate crime enforcement more like street crime enforcement through tougher sanctions.[2] Instead we began to wonder whether street crime enforcement might be more effective if it were more like corporate criminal enforcement.

---

[2] Critics indeed might enjoy the irony that Watergate offender Charles Colson, now of Prison Fellowship Ministries, is a prominent restorative justice advocate.

In my case, engagement with restorative approaches to corporate crime was entangled with my active engagement with social movement politics—particularly the consumer movement, but other social movements as well. In turn, my engagements with regulatory agencies—concerned with nursing homes, occupational health and safety, antitrust, environment, consumer protection, tax, and affirmative action—were as much connected to my history as an NGO activist as with a research background in these domains. For all these reasons I write as a reviewer who "belongs" in the social movement for restorative justice. Normatively serious people who engage with a social movement should not be dispassionate about it; they should have a passion for good science to find where its claims are false. In the following sections I describe four examples of restorative justice praxis to open up an understanding of the interface among activism, theoretical innovation, and evaluation: nursing home regulation, Asian community policing, trade practices enforcement, and restorative justice conferences.

II. Nursing Home Regulation

Valerie Braithwaite, Toni Makkai, Diane Gibson, David Ermann, Anne Jenkins, and I became involved in evaluating nursing home regulation before the Australian federal government took it over from state governments in 1988. Over the next six years we became the government's main consultants in this area. Prior to the change, regulation had consisted of specifying quality of care inputs and prosecuting breaches criminally when enforcement action was required. Since 1988 the move away from the criminal model has been almost total (in our view, it went too far), apart from spectacular cases where multiple deaths from neglect or abuse occurred.

In a radical shift from prescriptive regulation, the old rule books were thrown out and replaced with thirty-one outcome standards (compared with over a thousand standards in most U.S. states) settled consensually between the industry and major stakeholders such as consumer groups, unions, and aged care interests. The new regulatory process was dialogic. While a certain amount of time was spent auditing care plans, quality audit reports, and other records, government inspectors spent more time talking to residents and staff about how the quality of care could be improved. This was a shift to a resident-centered process (victim-centered in criminal justice discourse); an evaluation showed that this could work, residents could be empowered dialogically, even in nursing homes with the sickest residents

(Braithwaite and Makkai 1993). Performance against each of the thirty-one standards was ultimately discussed at a conference of the inspection team and management to which representatives of owners, staff, residents, and relatives were also invited. Occasionally the elected representatives of the residents' committee would invite someone from an outside advocacy group to attend. These functioned in ways quite similar to the family group conferences for juvenile offenders discussed later.

The final evaluation report concluded from a variety of types of data that the new regulatory regime had improved quality of life for Australian nursing home residents and compliance with the law (Braithwaite et al. 1993), notwithstanding the identification of a large number of problems. Action plans agreed at the exit conferences to restore residents' rights to quality of care were overwhelmingly implemented, the most common reason for nonimplementation being coming up with a better plan subsequent to the inspection. More critically to the evaluation of restorative justice, it was also found that inspectors who treated nursing homes with trust (Braithwaite and Makkai 1994), used praise when improvements were achieved (Makkai and Braithwaite 1993a), and had a philosophy of reintegrative shaming (Makkai and Braithwaite 1994), achieved higher compliance with the standards two years later than inspectors who did not. Jenkins (1997) showed that sustaining the self-efficacy of managers for improving quality of care was critical. While defiance (participation in a business subculture of resistance to regulation) did reduce compliance (Makkai and Braithwaite 1991), disengagement was the bigger problem (Braithwaite et al. 1994). Strategies such as praise and avoiding stigmatization were important to sustaining self-efficacy and engagement with continuous improvement. Hence, within a regime that improved regulatory outcomes by shifting from rule-book criminal enforcement to restorative justice, the inspectors who shifted most toward restorative justice improved compliance most (those who used praise and trust more than threat, reintegrative shaming rather than tolerance or stigmatization, those who restored self-efficacy). These results are discussed again when I consider the theories that predict why restorative justice might work better than punitive justice.

The biggest attraction of research in this field was that we could measure compliance with the law with far greater reliability (assessed through independent ratings by two inspectors) than can be obtained with traditional individual criminal offenses or in other areas of business regulation (Braithwaite and Braithwaite 1995). The limited support in this superior data set for some of the criminological theories that had been influential in our thinking to that point about how to design restorative justice—notably control, differential association, and subcultural theories—shaped our subsequent thinking about restorative justice theory (Makkai and Braithwaite 1991).

III. Asian Community Policing

After Brent Fisse and I did some limited fieldwork on how Japanese companies and regulators secured compliance with regulatory laws (Braithwaite and Fisse 1985), I became interested in Japanese social control more broadly. The work of many other scholars suggested that it was based rather heavily on dialogue about collective obligation and relationships as opposed to punishment. This seemed true from social control of the largest corporations (which we were studying) down to the regulation of the petty delinquencies of children in schools. As with nursing homes, Guy Masters's (1995, 1997) work shows that Japanese schools use methods of social control very similar to the family group conferences I discuss later. There was plenty of degradation and punitiveness in Japanese policing as well, especially when cases move from local *koban* policing (Bayley 1976) to policing by detectives and prosecutors (Miyazawa 1992).[3] Yet it seemed to me then, and still does, that the restorative elements of Japanese social control are more influential and sophisticated than in the West. We have much to learn from them (Masters 1997).

In an earlier draft of *Crime, Shame and Reintegration*, I also had a section on Chinese community policing (Braithwaite 1989). I threw it in the bin because Chinese informal justice seemed to involve so much more stigmatization and punitiveness than Japanese justice. Vagg's (1998) Hong Kong data captures well the concerns that beat a path to my wastebasket. Chinese Peoples' Courts, especially as they were projected to us in the cultural revolution, seemed a model of how not to do restorative justice. Yet Hong Lu's (1998) research in Shanghai shows that the most important contemporary restorative justice institution in China, *bang jiao* meetings (*bang* means help, *jiao* means education and admonition) tend to start as rather stigmatizing encounters but to end as reintegrative ones (see also Wong 1996).

---

[3] I am indebted to Christopher Murphy for pointing out that on the basis of his considerable observation of Japanese policing, Bayley and Miyazawa may both be right in this way, like the blind Hindus in the legend, feeling different parts of the elephant.

Chinese restorative justice, in both its positive and negative aspects, deserves more attention because China has by far the largest and most diverse programs, 155,000 local mediation committees, which accounted for over six million cases, compared to under four million cases that went to court in 1994 (Wong 1998). Many of the mediations were of family or neighborhood disputes that were not necessarily criminal. China also is the home of Confucius (551–479 B.C.), arguably the most influential thinker about restorative justice the world has known. Confucius's quest can be read in part as a search for practices of good government that enable people to understand the effects their actions have on one another and that naturally expose the virtue of the virtuous so that others will follow them. Virtue is inculcated by quiet good example rather than by denunciation.

Tsze-kung said, "Has the superior man his hatreds also?" The Master said, "He has his hatreds. He hates those who proclaim the evil of others" (Confucius 1974, p. 143).

From the perspective of a European republican philosophy (Braithwaite and Pettit 1990; Pettit 1997), there is much of value to draw on in Confucian thought but also much that might be dangerous. Confucian communitarianism was patriarchal and hierarchic. Perhaps a settled sense of deference was not so dangerous in a stable world where family, village, and a unitary state were the only institutions that mattered. But in a more complex world where there are many levels of government, up to the International Monetary Fund (IMF) and World Trade Organization, many cross-cutting institutions of civil society to which we belong, a world in which we and our parents are geographically mobile, we need strong, independent individuals as well as strong families and communities. Individuation is vital as a practice of socialization if individuals are to be strong enough to resist tyranny as they move from one site of domination to another in a complex world. Moreover, if we do not move away from the notion of society as a holistic unity to the notion of the separation of powers and an important place for the rule of law, a liberal-republican constitutional order, the lesson of this century's history is that we will get tyranny—"political power out of the barrel of a gun."

Yet we can read the great sweep of Chinese history as a dialectic of learning and unlearning this lesson. I refer in particular to the great historical struggle between the Legalists and the Confucians, and to the dialectic between both legalism and Confucianism and the dialectic of freedom in Taoism, to the disastrous abandonment of the rule of law in the Cultural Revolution and the partial return to it since (Gernet 1982; Huang 1988).

One reason it was an intellectual mistake to scrap the China section of *Crime, Shame and Reintegration* is that the study of Chinese history may hold one key to a macrosociology of restorative justice. In the dialectic of Chinese history between the domination of Confucian and Legalist ideas, a high-water mark of Legalist influence was the Ch'in Dynasty. What brought about the fall of the Ch'in Empire in 211 B.C.

> was not the alienation and hatred of the scholar class, nor the bitter enmity of the surviving remnants of the aristocracy, but the growing popular discontent and mounting outrage over the cruelty of the system of punishments and the intolerable burden of taxes and levies imposed for the massive public works that the emperor commanded. Crime increased as did the number of those condemned, tortured, mutilated, and exiled to labor gangs. As long as the emperor was alive, fear of his powerful and demoniacal personality held the empire together; after his death all the restraints broke, and the empire exploded in rebellion. (Michael 1986, p. 66)

Today the movement of the Confucian-Legalist dialectic is in the reverse direction, with the "rule of law" rebounding as a dominant value. Given the continued trampling of human rights and freedoms in China, this may be a hopeful development, yet part of it is a sharp decline of the proportion of criminal cases dealt with by mediation as opposed to criminal trials. What a pity that so few Western intellectuals are engaged with the possibilities for recovering, understanding, and preserving the virtues of Chinese restorative justice while checking its abuses with a liberalizing rule of law. Whatever the rights and wrongs of it, the legalist-restorative contest is more central to the dynamic of Chinese history than to the histories of other nations and therefore more central to the development of a macrosociology of the fluctuating fortunes of restorative justice.

IV. Trade Practices Enforcement

Between 1985 and 1995, as a part-time commissioner with Australia's national consumer protection and antitrust agency, I attempted with mixed success to persuade my colleagues on the Trade Practices Commission to experiment in an Australian way with the restorative principles I saw as underlying Japanese business regulation. Ironically, when the commission decided to run its boldest restorative justice conference, I made the mistake of voting against it, believing the conduct to be so serious that formal criminal charges should be laid. It involved the most widespread and serious consumer protection frauds ever to come before the agency. They implicated a number of insurance companies systematically ripping off consumers through misrepresentations about policies that in some cases were totally useless. The worst abuses occurred in twenty-two remote Aboriginal communities and these were tackled first. Top management from the insurance company visited these communities for days on end at meetings with the victims, the local Aboriginal community council, the regulators, and local officials of the Department of Social Security in cases where useless policy premiums were being deducted from welfare checks. Some of those executives went back to the city deeply ashamed of what their company had done.

Back in Canberra, meetings were held with insurance regulators and industry associations and even with the prime minister about follow-up regulatory reforms. The plurality of participants led to a plurality of remedies from the first agreement with Colonial Mutual Life (CML), who voluntarily compensated two thousand policyholders and also funded an Aboriginal consumer education fund to "harden targets" for future attempts to rip off illiterate people. It conducted an internal investigation to discover failings in the company's compliance program and to identify officers responsible for the crimes. A press conference was then called to reveal the enormity of the problem. No one realized quite how enormous, until a police union realized that its own members were being ripped off through the practices of another company (in this case, there were 300,000 victims and a payout of at least $50 million and perhaps $100 million by the company). As a result of the CML self-investigation, eighty officers or agents of CML were dismissed, including some senior managers and one large corporate agent, Tri-Global. CML also put in place new internal compliance policies. Some procedures relating to welfare checks changed in the Department of Social Security and there were regulatory and self-regulatory changes concerning the licensing of agents and changes to the law (Fisse and Braithwaite 1993, p. 235). This polycentric problem-solving was accomplished without going to court (except with a couple of individuals who refused to cooperate with the restorative justice process). The disparate array of preventive measures were grounded in the different kinds of theories the rich plurality of players involved in this restorative justice process came up with—theories of education, deterrence, incapacitation, rehabilitation, target hardening, moral hazard, adverse publicity, law, regulation, and opportunity theory.

The cynic about restorative justice will say that the Australian insurance cases were unusually sweeping exercises in crime prevention. True, most crime prevention is more banal. Yet this process was so sweeping in its ramifications precisely because it was restorative. What would have happened if we had prosecuted this case criminally? At best the company would have been fined a fraction of what it actually paid out and there would have been a handful of follow-up civil claims by victims. At worst, illiterate Aboriginal witnesses would have been humiliated and discredited by uptown lawyers, the case lost, and no further ones taken. The industry-wide extensiveness of a pattern of practices would never have been uncovered; that was only accomplished by the communitarian engagement of many locally knowledgeable actors.

V. Restorative Justice Conferences

In *Crime, Shame and Reintegration* I made reference to the desirability of institutionalizing something like the restorative justice conference for criminal offenders (Braithwaite 1989, pp. 173–74). After reading this, John McDonald of the New South Wales Police came to me and said this had already been done in New Zealand. Terry O'Connell showed me videotaped interviews with people such as Maori chief judge of the New Zealand Juvenile Court, Michael Brown. These revealed that one of the rationales for restorative justice in the Maori tradition was the simultaneous communication of "shame" and "healing." It was a depressing revelation that what I thought was the only limited originality in *Crime, Shame and Reintegration* had been preceded by several hundreds of years of Polynesian oral tradition, not just in New Zealand. Indeed, I concluded that Maori ways of thinking about *whakama* or shame were in some important ways an advance on my own thinking. After *Crime, Shame and Reintegration* became a widely read book, many people from Africa, Melanesia, Asia, and the Americas were in touch with me about restorative justice conferences that were part of their tradition. I learned that the Native American healing circle seeks to institutionalize equality rather than hierarchy and "puts the problem in the center—not the person" (Pranis 1996, p. 46, quoting Ada Melton [1995]). These stories challenged assumptions I strongly held until the mid-1990s, for example, that traditional Western criminal process was superior at just fact-finding than restorative justice processes.[4]

Healing circles in the Manitoba First Nation community of Hollow Water began to deal with what many thought of at first as an epidemic of alcohol abuse. As citizens sat in these circles discussing the problems of individual cases, they realized that there was a deeper underlying problem, which was that they lived in a community that was sweeping the sexual abuse of children under the carpet. Through setting up a complex set of healing circles to help one individual victim and offender after another, in the end it had been discovered that a majority of the citizens were at some time in their lives victims of sexual abuse.[5] Forty-eight adults out of a community of six hundred formally admitted to criminal responsibility for sexually abusing children, forty-six as a result of participating in healing circles, two as a result of being referred to a court of law for failing to do so (Lajeunesse 1993; Ross 1996, pp. 29–48). Ross (1996, p. 36) claims that the healing circles have been a success because there have been only two known cases of reoffending. Tragically, however, there has been no genuinely systematic outcome evaluation of Hollow Water.

What is more important than the crime prevention outcome of Hollow Water is its crime detection outcome. When and where has the traditional criminal process succeeded in uncovering anything approaching forty-eight admissions of criminal responsibility for sexual abuse of children in a community of just six hundred? Before reading about Hollow Water, I had always said that the traditional criminal trial process is superior to restorative justice processes for justly getting to the truth of what happened. Restorative justice processes were only likely to be superior to traditional Western criminal process when there was a clear admission of guilt. The significance of Hollow Water is that it throws that position into doubt.

New Zealand remained of preeminent importance, however, because it mainstreamed the conferencing innovation into a Western ju-

---

[4] A conversation with Gale Burford about his work on conferencing family violence with Joan Pennell also has me wondering. In a third of their cases, sexual abuse of children came out during conferences. Gale said: "So violence programs that exclude sexual abuse don't really. They just say if they have sexual abuse don't talk about it or you'll be out of the program."

[5] La Prairie (1994, p. iii) in a sophisticated study of this problem from a restorative justice perspective in another context found that 46 percent of innercity native people in Canada had experienced child abuse. For an outline of the Hollow Water procedures for dealing with sexual abuse, see Aboriginal Corrections Policy Unit (1997, esp. pp. 221–30).

venile justice system (and into the care and protection of abused and neglected children as well). The importance of New Zealand was not because it adopted Maori restorative philosophies; indeed Pakeha (non-Maori) New Zealand tended to reject much of both the restorative and retributive aspects of Maori philosophy, initially justifying the practice of "family group conferences" in terms of a move from the welfare to the Western justice model. When its innovation became internationally celebrated, New Zealand wisely reinterpreted family group conferences as restorative justice. Indeed, for all of us practice was ahead of theory, and it was well into the 1990s before the North American label "restorative justice" subsumed what had been developing elsewhere for a long time.

The way conferences work is very simple. Once wrongdoing is admitted, the offender and his or her family are asked who they would like to have attend a conference as supporters. Similarly, victims are asked to nominate loved ones to attend with them. The conference is a meeting of these two communities of care. First there is a discussion of what was done and what the consequences have been for everyone in the room (the victim's suffering, the stress experienced by the offender's family). Then there is a discussion of what needs to be done to repair those different kinds of harm. A plan of action is agreed and signed by the offender and usually by the victim and the police officer responsible for the case. Asking the offender to confront the consequences of his wrongdoing (and talking them through in the presence of those who have suffered them) is believed by conferencing advocates to have a variety of positive effects in terms of taking responsibility, experiencing remorse, and offering practical help and apology to the victim and the community to right the wrong. Beyond this common core, conferences vary from place to place in how they are run. In Australia, Wagga Wagga was the first conferencing program from 1991 and an important site of early research and development on a culturally pluralized conferencing process suitable for both Western and Australian Aboriginal cases. This research and development is being carried forward by the RISE experiment in Canberra in which thirteen hundred adult and juvenile cases are being randomly assigned to conference versus court by Lawrence Sherman and Heather Strang (Sherman et al. 1998). Drunk driving, property, and violent crimes are covered by the experiment. Only preliminary results are available from the first eleven hundred offenders at the time of writing; RISE is designed to test most of the theories of restorative justice discussed in this essay.

VI. Optimistic and Pessimistic Accounts of Restorative
    Justice

The empirical evidence about restorative justice is organized in this
essay according to the propositions that flow from an optimistic account of restorative justice and a pessimistic one. The propositions of
both accounts are plausible in light of the limited evidence we have at
this time.

The Optimistic Account:

   A. Restorative Justice Practices Restore and Satisfy Victims
      Better than Existing Criminal Justice Practices.
   B. Restorative Justice Practices Restore and Satisfy Offenders
      Better than Existing Criminal Justice Practices.
   C. Restorative Justice Practices Restore and Satisfy Communities
      Better than Existing Criminal Justice Practices.
   D. Reintegrative Shaming Theory Predicts That Restorative
      Justice Practices Reduce Crime More than Existing Criminal
      Justice Practices.
   E. Procedural Justice Theory Predicts That Restorative Justice
      Practices Reduce Crime More than Existing Criminal Justice
      Practices.
   F. The Theory of Bypassed Shame Predicts That Restorative
      Justice Practices Reduce Crime More than Existing Criminal
      Justice Practices.
   G. Defiance Theory Predicts That Restorative Justice Practices
      Reduce Crime More than Existing Criminal Justice Practices.
   H. Self-Categorization Theory Predicts that Restorative Justice
      Practices Reduce Crime More than Existing Criminal Justice
      Practices.
   I. Crime Prevention Theory Predicts That Restorative Justice
      Practices Reduce Crime More than Existing Criminal Justice
      Practices.
   J. Restorative Justice Practices Deter Crime Better than
      Practices Grounded in Deterrence Theories.
   K. Restorative Justice Practices Incapacitate Crime Better than
      Criminal Justice Practices Grounded in the Theory of Selective
      Incapacitation.
   L. Restorative Justice Practices Rehabilitate Crime Better than
      Criminal Justice Practices Grounded in the Welfare Model.
   M. Restorative Justice Practices Are More Cost-Effective than Crimi-
      nal Justice Practices Grounded in the Economic Analysis of Crime.

N. Restorative Justice Practices Secure Justice Better than Criminal Justice Practices Grounded in "Justice" or Just Deserts Theories.

O. Restorative Justice Practices Can Enrich Freedom and Democracy.

The Pessimistic Account:

A. Restorative Justice Practices Might Provide No Benefits Whatsoever to Over 90 Percent of Victims.

B. Restorative Justice Practices Have No Significant Impact on the Crime Rate.

C. Restorative Justice Practices Can Increase Victim Fears of Revictimization.

D. Restorative Justice Practices Can Make Victims Little More than Props for Attempts to Rehabilitate Offenders.

E. Restorative Justice Practices Can Be a "Shaming Machine" that Worsens the Stigmatization of Offenders.

F. Restorative Justice Practices Rely on a Kind of Community that is Culturally Inappropriate to Industrialized Societies.

G. Restorative Justice Practices Can Oppress Offenders with a Tyranny of the Majority, Even a Tyranny of the Lynch Mob.

H. Restorative Justice Practices Can Widen Nets of Social Control.

I. Restorative Justice Practices Fail to Redress Structural Problems Inherent in Liberalism Like Unemployment and Poverty.

J. Restorative Justice Practices Can Disadvantage Women, Children, and Oppressed Racial Minorities.

K. Restorative Justice Practices Are Prone to Capture by the Dominant Group in the Restorative Process.

L. Restorative Justice Processes Can Extend Unaccountable Police Power, Even Compromise the Separation of Powers among Legislative, Executive, and Judicial Branches of Government.

M. Restorative Justice Practices Can Trample Rights because of Impoverished Articulation of Procedural Safeguards.

VII. An Optimistic Account of Restorative Justice

As this essay is about reviewing empirical evidence in a theoretical framework rather than theoretical exegesis, I begin with the three core propositions of the Optimistic Account of restorative justice. These three (A–C) are the corollaries of propositions D–O of the Optimistic

Account. They are that restorative justice does restore victims, offenders, and communities.

A. Restorative Justice Practices Restore and Satisfy Victims Better than Existing Criminal Justice Practices

A consistent picture emerges from the welter of data reviewed in this section: it is one of comparatively high victim approval of their restorative justice experiences, though lower levels of approval than one finds among other participants in the process. So long as the arrangements are convenient, it is only a small minority of victims who do not want to participate in restorative justice processes. Consistent with this picture, the preliminary RISE data in Canberra show only 3 percent of offenders and 2 percent of community representatives at conferences compared with 14 percent of victims disagreeing with the statement: "The government should use conferences as an alternative to court more often." Most of the data to date are limited to a small range of outcomes; we await the first systematic data on some of the dimensions of restoration discussed in Section I. On the limited range of outcomes explored to date, victims do seem to get more restoration out of restorative justice agreements than court orders and restorative justice agreements seem to be more likely to be delivered than court orders even when the former are not legally enforceable.

1. *Operationalizing Victim Restoration.* There is a deep problem in evaluating how well restorative justice restores. Empowerment of victims to define the restoration that matters to them is a keystone of a restorative justice philosophy. Three paths can be taken. One is to posit a list of types of restoration that are important to most victims, such as that discussed in Section I. The problem with this is that even with as uncontroversial a dimension of restoration as restoring property, some victims will prefer mercy to insisting on getting their money back; indeed it may be that act of grace which gives them a spiritual restoration that is critical for them.[6] The second path sidesteps a debate on what dimensions of restoration are universal enough to evaluate. Instead, it measures overall satisfaction of victims with restorative justice processes and outcomes, assuming (without evidence) that satisfaction is a proxy for victims getting restoration on the things that are

---

[6] I am reminded of a village in Java where I was told of a boy caught stealing. The outcome of a restorative village meeting was that the offender was given a bag of rice: "We should be ashamed because one from our village should be so poor as to steal. We should be ashamed as a village."

most important for them. This is the path followed in this review, largely because these are the kind of data available at this stage. The third path is the best one, but the most unmanageable in large quantitative evaluations. It is to ask victims to define the kinds of restoration they were seeking and then to report how much restoration they attained in these terms that matter most to them.

2. *Victim Participation and Satisfaction.* While traditional criminal justice practices are notoriously unsatisfying to victims, it is also true that victims emerge from many restorative justice programs less satisfied than other participants. Clairmont (1994, pp. 16–17) found little victim involvement in four restorative justice programs for aboriginal offenders in Canada. There seems to be a wider pattern of greater satisfaction among aboriginal leaders and offenders than among victims for restorative projects on Canadian aboriginal communities (Obonsawin-Irwin Consulting Inc. 1992a, 1992b; Clairmont 1994; La Prairie 1995).

Early British victim-offender mediation programs reported what Dignan (1992) called sham reparation, for example Davis's (1992) reporting of offers rather than actual repair, tokenism, and even dictated letters of apology. In some of these programs, victims were little more than a new kind of prop in welfare programs: the "new deal for victims" came in Britain to be seen as a "new deal for offenders" (Crawford 1996, p. 7). However, Crawford's conclusion that the British restorative justice programs that survived into the 1990s after weathering this storm "have done much to answer their critics" (Crawford 1996, p. 7) seems consistent with the evidence. Dignan (1992) reports 71 percent satisfaction among English corporate victims and 61 percent among individual victims in one of the early adult offender reparation programs.

In New Zealand, victims attended only half the conferences conducted during the early years of the program,[7] and when they did attend they were less satisfied (51 percent satisfaction) with family group conferences than were offenders (84 percent), police (91 percent), and other participants (85 percent) (Maxwell and Morris 1993, pp. 115,

---

[7] The evidence seems to be that this was mainly due to limitations in the program administration that made it difficult for victims to attend, not due to the fact that most victims did not want to attend; only 6 percent did not want to meet their offender (Maxwell and Morris 1996). It is widely believed that victim attendance is much higher in New Zealand today now that attention has been directed to these administrative problems, but no systematic evidence exists.

120). About a quarter of victims reported that they felt worse as a result of attending the family group conference. Australian studies by Daly (1996) and Strang and Sherman (1997) also find a significant minority of victims who feel worse after the conference, upset over something said or victimized by disrespect, though greatly outnumbered by victims who feel healing as a result of the conference. Similarly, Birchall, Namour, and Syme (1992) report 27 percent of victims feeling worse after meeting their offender and 70 percent better in Western Australia's Midland Pilot Reparation Scheme. The Ministry of Justice (1994), Western Australia, reports 95 percent victim satisfaction with their restorative justice conference program (Juvenile Justice Teams). McCold and Wachtel (1998) found 96 percent victim satisfaction with cases randomly assigned to conferences in Bethlehem, Pennsylvania, compared to 79 percent satisfaction when cases were assigned to court and 73 percent satisfaction when the case went to court after being assigned to conference and the conference was declined. Conferenced victims were also somewhat more likely to believe that they experienced fairness (96 percent), that the offender was adequately held accountable for the offense (93 percent), and that their opinion regarding the offense and circumstances were adequately considered in the case (94 percent). Ninety-three percent of victims found the conference helpful, 98 percent that it "allowed me to express my feelings without being victimized," 96 percent believed that the offender had apologized, and 75 percent that the offender was sincere. Ninety-four percent said they would choose a conference if they had to do it over again. The Bethlehem results are complicated by a "decline" group as large as the control group; either offenders or victims could cause the case to be declined. In the Canberra RISE experiment, victim participation is currently 85 percent. Reports on the Wagga Wagga conferencing model in Australia are also more optimistic about victim participation and satisfaction (Moore and O'Connell 1994), reporting 90 percent victim satisfaction and victim participation exceeding 90 percent (Moore and O'Connell 1994). The highest published satisfaction and fairness ratings (both 98 percent) have been reported by the Queensland Department of Justice conferencing program (Palk, Hayes, and Prenzler 1998).

Umbreit and Coates's (1992) survey found that 79 percent of victims who cooperated in four U.S. mediation programs were satisfied compared to only 57 percent of those who did not have mediation (for earlier similar findings, see Umbreit 1990a). In a subsequent study, Umbreit (1999) found at four combined Canadian sites victim procedural satisfaction at 78 percent, and 62 percent at two combined English mediation sites. Victim satisfaction with outcomes was higher still: 90 percent (four U.S. sites), 89 percent (four Canadian sites), and 84 percent (two English sites). However, victim satisfaction was still generally lower across the sites than offender satisfaction. Eighty-three percent of U.S. mediation victims perceived the outcome "fair" (as opposed to being "satisfied") compared to 62 percent of those who went through the normal court process. Umbreit and Coates (1992) also report reduced fear and anxiety among victims following mediation. Victims afraid of being victimized again dropped from 25 percent prior to mediation to 10 percent after. A survey of German institutions involved in model mediation projects found that the rate of voluntary victim participation generally ranged from 81 percent to 92 percent, and never dropped below 70 percent (Kerner, Marks, and Schreckling 1992).

3. *Honoring of Obligations to Victims.* Haley and Neugebauer's (1992) analysis of restorative justice programs in the United States, Canada, and Great Britain revealed between 64 and 100 percent completion of reparation and compensation agreements. I assume here, of course, that completion of agreements that victims have agreed to is important for victim restoration. Marshall's (1992) study of cases referred to mediation programs in Britain found that over 80 percent of agreements were completed. Galaway (1992) reports that 58 percent of agreements reached through mediation in New Zealand were fully complied with within one year. In a Finnish study, 85 percent of agreements reached through mediation were fully completed (Iivari 1987, 1992). Dignan (1992) reports from England 86 percent participant agreement with mediation outcomes, with 91 percent of agreements honored in full. Trenczek (1990), in a study of pilot victim-offender reconciliation projects in Braunschweig, Cologne, and Reutlingen, West Germany (see also Kuhn 1987), reports a 76 percent full completion rate, and a partial completion rate of 5 percent. Pate's (1990) study of victim-offender reconciliation projects in Alberta, Canada, found a rate of noncompletion of agreements of between 5 and 10 percent, and less than 1 percent in the case of a Calgary program. Wundersitz and Hetzel (1996, p. 133) found 86 percent full compliance with conference agreements in South Australia, with another 3 percent waived for near compliance. Fry (1997, p. 5) reported 100 percent completion of agreements in a pilot of twenty-six Northern Territory police-coordi-

nated juvenile conferences, and Waters (1993, p. 9) reported 91 percent payment of compensation in Wagga Wagga conferences. In another Wagga-style program, McCold and Wachtel (1998, p. 4) report 94 percent compliance with the terms of conference agreements.

Umbreit and Coates (1992) compared 81 percent completion of restitution obligations settled through mediation to 58 percent completion of court-ordered restitution in their multisite study. Ervin and Schneider (1990), in a random assignment evaluation of six U.S. restitution programs, found 89 percent completion of restitution compared with 75 percent completion of traditional programs. Most of these restitution programs, however, were not restorative in the sense of involving meetings of victims and offenders.

4. *Symbolic Reparation.* One reason that the level of satisfaction of victims is surprisingly high in processes that so often give them so little material reparation is that they get symbolic reparation, which is more important to them (Retzinger and Scheff 1996). Apology is at the heart of this: preliminary results from the RISE experiment in Canberra show that 74 percent of victims whose cases were randomly assigned to a conference got an apology compared to 11 percent in cases randomly assigned to court (Strang and Sherman 1997). Sixty percent of victims felt "quite" or "very" angry before the Canberra conferences, 30 percent afterward. Obversely, the proportion of victims feeling sympathetic to the offender almost doubled by the end of the conference (Strang and Sherman 1997). I discuss below a large body of research evidence showing that victims are not as punitive as the rather atypical victims whose bitter calls for brutal punishment get most media coverage. Both the Strang and Sherman (1997) and Umbreit (1992, p. 443) studies report victim fear of revictimization and victim upset about the crime as having declined following the restorative justice process.

In Goodes's (1995) study of juvenile family group conferences in South Australia, where victim attendance ranges from 75 to 80 percent (Wundersitz and Hetzel 1996), the most common reason victims gave for attending their conference was to try to help the offender, followed by the desire to express feelings, make statements to the offender, or ask questions such as "Why me?" (what Retzinger and Scheff (1996) call symbolic reparation) followed by "curiosity and a desire to 'have a look'," followed by "responsibility as citizens to attend." The desire to ensure that the penalty was appropriate and the desire for material reparation rated behind all of the above motivations to attend. The response rate in the Goodes (1995) study was poor and there may be a strong social desirability bias in these victim reports; yet that may be precisely because the context of conference attendance is one that nurtures responsible citizenship cognitions by victims. Eighty-eight percent of Goodes's victims agreed with the conference outcome, 90 percent found it helpful to them, and 90 percent said they would attend again if they were a victim again (Goodes 1995).

With all these quantitative findings, one can lose sight of what most moves restorative justice advocates who have seen restorative processes work well. I am not a spiritual enough person to capture it in words: it is about grace, shalom (which Van Ness [1986, p. 125] characterizes as "peace as the result of doing justice").

Trish Stewart (1993, p. 49) gets near its evocation when she reports one victim who said in the closing round of a conference: "Today I have observed and taken part in justice administered with love." Psychologists are developing improved ways of measuring spirituality—self-transcendence, meaning in life beyond one's self. So in future it will be possible to undertake systematic research on self-reported spirituality and conferences to see whether results are obtained analogous to Reed's (1986, 1987, 1992) findings that greater healing occurred among terminally ill individuals whose psychosocial response was imbued with a spiritual dimension.

For the moment, we must accept an East-West divide in the way participants think about spiritual leadership in conferences. Maori, North American, and Australian Aboriginal peoples tend to think it important to have elders with special gifts of spirituality, what Maori call Mana, attend restorative justice processes (Tauri and Morris 1997, pp. 149–50). This is the Confucian view as well. These traditions are critical of the ethos Western advocates such as myself have brought to conferences, which has not seen it as important to have elders with Mana at conferences. Two years ago in Indonesia I was told of restorative justice rituals in western Sumatra that were jointly conducted by a religious leader and a scholar—the person in the community seen as having the greatest spiritual riches and the person seen as having the greatest riches of learning. My inclination then was to recoil from the elitism of this and insist that many (if not most) citizens have the resources (given a little help with training) to facilitate processes of healing. While I still believe this, I now think it might be a mistake to seek to persuade Asians to democratize their restorative justice practices. There may be merit in special efforts to recruit exemplars of virtue, grace, Mana, to participate. Increasingly, I am tempted to so interpret our experience with RISE in recruiting community representatives with grace to participate in drunk-driving conferences where there is no victim.

B. Restorative Justice Practices Restore and Satisfy Offenders Better than Existing Criminal Justice Practices

This section concludes that offender satisfaction with both corporate and traditional individual restorative justice programs has been extremely high. The evidence of offenders being restored in the sense of desisting from criminal conduct is encouraging with victim-offender mediation, conferencing, restorative business regulatory programs, and whole-school antibullying programs, though not peer mediation programs for bullying. No study has shown restorative justice to make things worse. However, only some of these studies adequately control for important variables and only two randomly assigned cases to restorative versus punitive justice. The business regulatory studies are instructive in suggesting that restorative justice works best when it is backed up by punitive justice in those (quite common) individual cases where restorative justice fails, and that trying restorative justice first increases perceived justice.

1. *Fairness and Satisfaction for Offenders.*   As I show in Section VII*E*, offenders are more likely to respond positively to criminal justice processing when they perceive it as just. Moore with Forsythe's (1995, p. 248) ethnographic work concludes that most offenders, like victims, experienced quite profound "procedural, material, and psychological justice" in restorative justice conferences. Umbreit (1992) reports from his cross-site study in the United States an 89 percent perception of fairness on the part of offenders with victim-offender mediation programs, compared to 78 percent perceived fairness in unmediated cases. Across four Canadian studies, Umbreit (1999) reports 80 percent offender perception of fairness of victim-offender mediation and 89 percent at two combined English sites. The Ministry of Justice (1994), Western Australia, reports 95 percent offender satisfaction with their restorative justice conference program (Juvenile Justice Teams). McCold and Wachtel (1998, pp. 59–61) report 97 percent satisfaction with "the way your case was handled" and 97 percent satisfaction with fairness in the Bethlehem police conferencing program, a better result than in the four comparisons with Bethlehem cases that went to court. Coats and Gehm (1985, 1989) found 83 percent offender satisfaction with the victim-offender reconciliation experience based on a study of

programs in Indiana and Ohio. Smith, Blagg, and Derricourt (1985), in a limited survey of the initial years of a South Yorkshire mediation project, found that ten out of thirteen offenders were satisfied with the mediation experience and felt that the scheme had helped alter their behavior. Dignan (1990), on the basis of a random sample of offenders (n = 50) involved in victim-offender mediations in Kettering, Northamptonshire, found 96 percent were either satisfied or very satisfied with the process. The strongest published result was again on 113 juvenile offenders in the Queensland Department of Justice conferencing program where 98 percent thought their conference fair and 99 percent were satisfied with the agreement (Palk, Hayes, and Prenzler 1998).

2. *Reduced Reoffending as Offender Restoration.*   Pate (1990), Nugent and Paddock (1995), and Wynne (1996) all report a decline in recidivism among mediation cases (as does Neimeyer and Shichor [1995], which is cited in Umbreit [1999]). Umbreit, Coates, and Kalanj (1994) found 18 percent recidivism across four victim-offender mediation sites (n = 160) and 27 percent (n = 160) for comparable nonmediation cases at those sites, a difference that fell short of statistical significance. Similarly, Marshall and Merry (1990, p. 196) report for an even smaller sample that offending declined for victim-offender mediation cases, especially when there was an actual meeting (as opposed to indirect shuttle diplomacy by a mediator), while offending went up for controls. However, the differences were not statistically significant. Schneider (1986, 1990) in an experimental evaluation of six U.S. restitution programs found a significant reduction in recidivism across the six programs. This result is widely cited by restorative justice advocates as evidence for the efficacy of restorative justice. However, all but one of these programs seem to have involved mandated restitution to victims without any mediation or restorative justice deliberation by victims and offenders. The one program that seems to meet the definition of restorative justice here, the Washington, D.C., program, did produce significantly lower rates of reoffending for cases randomly assigned to victim-offender mediation and restitution compared to cases assigned to regular probation. This test is reported in Schneider (1986), but for mysterious reasons Schneider (1990) reports only the nonsignificant differences between before and after offending rates for the control and experimental groups separately, rather than the significant difference between the experimental and control group (which is the relevant comparison).

There is no published evidence on the impact of New Zealand family group conferences on recidivism. Maxwell and Morris (1996, p. 106) conclude that the recidivism of their conference cases is "certainly no worse" than recidivism of like offenders prior to the conferencing reforms, but these are rather speculative data.

The story is similar with Wagga. Forsythe (1995) shows a 20 percent reoffending rate for cases going to conference compared to a 48 percent rate for juvenile court cases. This is a big effect; most of it is likely a social selection effect of tougher cases going to court, as there is no matching, no controls, though it is hard to account for the entire association in these terms given the pattern of the data (see Forsythe 1995, pp. 245–46).

Another big effect with the same social selection worry was obtained with only the first sixty-three cases to go through family group conferences in Singapore. The conference reoffending rate was 2 percent compared to 30 percent over the same period for offenders who went to court (Chan 1996; Hsien 1996).

The most determined attempt to tackle social selection problems through randomization, McCold and Wachtel's (1998) experimental evaluation of Bethlehem, Pennsylvania's Wagga-style police conferencing program, ultimately fell victim to another kind of selection effect. For property cases, there was a tendency for conferenced cases to have higher recidivism than court cases, but the difference was not statistically significant. For violence cases, conferenced offenders had a significantly lower reoffending rate than offenders who went to court. However, this result was not statistically valid because the violent offenders with the highest reoffending rate were those who were randomly assigned to conference but who actually ended up going to court because either the offender or the victim refused to cooperate in the conference. In other words, the experiment failed to deliver an adequate test of the effect of conferences on recidivism both on grounds of statistical power and because of unsatisfactory assurance that the assigned treatment was delivered.

One conferencing program that has dealt convincingly with the social selection problem is in the Canadian coal-mining town of Sparwood, British Columbia, a Royal Canadian Mounted Police program. For almost three years from the commencement of the program in 1995 until late 1997, no young offender from Sparwood went to court.[8]

---

[8] I am indebted to Glen Purdy, a Sparwood lawyer in private practice, for these data. The data until early 1997 are also available at www.titanlink.com.

All were cautioned or conferenced. Three youths who had been conferenced on at least two previous occasions went to court in late 1997. No cases have been to court during 1998 up until the time of writing (October 1998). In the year prior to the program (1994) sixty-four youth went to court. Over the ensuing three years and nine months, this net was narrowed to eighty-eight conferences and three court cases. This was probably not just a net-narrowing effect, however. It may also have been a real reduction in offending. According to police records, compared to the 1994 youth offending rate, the 1995 rate was down 26 percent; the 1996 rate, 67 percent. Reoffending rates for conference cases were 8 percent in 1995, 3 percent in 1996, 10 percent in 1997, and 0 percent for the first nine months of 1998, compared to a national rate of 40 percent per annum for court cases (which is similar in towns surrounding Sparwood). Reoffending rates for Sparwood court cases prior to 1995 have not been collected. While social selection bias is convincingly dealt with here by the universality of the switch to restorative justice for the first three years, eighty-eight conferences is only a modest basis for inference.

Burford and Pennell's (1998) study of a restorative conference-based approach to family violence in Newfoundland found a marked reduction in both child abuse/neglect and abuse of mothers/wives after the intervention. A halving of abuse/neglect incidents was found for thirty-two families in the year after the conference compared to the year before, while incidents increased markedly for thirty-one control families. Pennell and Burford's (1997) research is also a model of sophisticated process development and process evaluation and of methodological triangulation. While sixty-three families might seem modest for quantitative purposes, it is actually a statistically persuasive study in demonstrating that this was an intervention that reduced family violence. This is because within each case a before-and-after pattern is tested against thirty-one different types of events (e.g., abuse of child, child abuses mother, attempted suicide, father keeps income from mother) where events can be relevant to more than one member of the family. Given this pattern matching of families x events x individual family members, it understates the statistical power of the design to say it is based on only sixty-three cases. Burford and Pennell (1998, p. 253) also report reduced drinking problems after conferences, something I doubt is happening after Canberra conferences. The Newfoundland conferences were less successful in cases where young people were abusing their mothers, a matter worthy of further investigation.

Restorative antibullying programs in schools, generally referred to as "whole-school" approaches (Rigby 1996) that combine community deliberation among students, teachers, and parents about how to prevent bullying with mediation of specific cases, have been systematically evaluated with positive results (Farrington 1993; Pepler et al. 1993; Pitts and Smith 1995; Rigby 1996), the most impressive being a program in Norway where a 50 percent reduction in bullying has been reported (Olweus 1993). Gentry and Benenson's (1993) data further suggest that skills for mediating playground disputes learned and practiced by children in school may transfer to the home setting, resulting in reduced conflict, particularly with siblings. The restorative approaches to bullying in Japanese schools, which Masters's (1997) qualitative work found to be a success, can also be read as even more radically "whole school" than the Norwegian innovations.

However, Gottfredson's (1997) and Brewer et al.'s (1995) reviews of school peer mediation programs, which simply train children to resolve disputes when conflicts arise among students, showed nonsignificant or weak effects on observable behavior such as fighting. Only one of four studies with quasi-experimental or true experimental designs found peer mediation to be associated with a decrease in aggressive behavior. Lam's (1989) review of fourteen evaluations of peer mediation programs with mostly weak methods found no programs that made violence worse. It appears a whole-school approach is needed that tackles not just individual incidents but that links incidents to a change program for the culture of the school, in particular to how seriously members of the school community take rules about bullying. Put another way, the school must not only resolve the bullying incident; it must use it as a resource to affirm the disapproval of bullying in the culture of the school.

With the possible exception of McCold and Wachtel's (1998) statistically nonsignificant increase in property reoffending, a point Walgrave (1993, p. 4) made in 1993 remains true today: however widely one defines restorative justice programs, even including his own group's work on court-ordered community service as restorative justice (Walgrave 1999), after more than thirty studies discussed above, "no research shows an increase in recidivism." However, statistical power, randomization, and control have mostly been weak to very weak in this research.

3. *Reduced Reoffending in Corporate Restorative Justice Programs.* In Section I, I recounted how corporate crime researchers like myself be-

gan to wonder if the more restorative approach to corporate criminal law might actually be more effective than the punitive approach to street crime. What made us wonder this? When we observed inspectors moving around factories (as in Hawkins's [1984] study of British pollution inspectors) we noticed how talk often got the job done. The occupational health and safety inspector could talk with the workers and managers responsible for a safety problem and they would fix it. No punishment, not even threats of punishment. A restorative justice reading of regulatory inspection was also consistent with the quantitative picture. The probability that any given occupational health and safety violation will be detected has always been slight and the average penalty for OSHA violations in the post-Watergate United States was $37 (Kelman 1984). So the economically rational firm did not have to worry about OSHA enforcement: when interviewed they would say it was a trivial cost of doing business. Yet there was quantitative evidence that workplace injuries fell after OSHA inspections or when inspection levels increased (Scholz and Gray 1990).

The evidence of the impact of Mine Safety and Health Administration inspections in the United States was even stronger that it saved lives and prevented injuries (Lewis-Beck and Alford 1980; Perry 1981a, 1981b; Boden 1983; Braithwaite 1985, pp. 77–84). Boden's data showed a 25 percent increase in inspections was associated with a 7–20 percent reduction in fatalities on a pooled cross-sectional analysis of 535 mines with controls for geological, technological, and managerial factors; these were inspections at a time when the average penalty for a successful citation was $173 (Braithwaite 1985, p. 3). They were inspections that ended with an "exit conference" that I observed to be often quite restorative. Boden (1983) and the Mine Enforcement and Safety Administration (1977) found no association between the level of penalties and safety improvement, however.

This was just the opposite to the picture we were getting from the literature on law enforcement and street crime. On the streets, the picture was of tough enforcement, more police, and more jails failing to make a difference. In coal mines we saw weak enforcement (no imprisonment) but convincing evidence that more inspectors reduced offending (Braithwaite 1985).

That book was called *To Punish or Persuade: Enforcement of Coal Mine Safety* (Braithwaite 1985) and it concluded that while persuasion works better than punishment, credible punishment is needed as well to back up persuasion when it fails. Writing the book was a somewhat emo-

tional conversion to restorative justice for me as I came to it as a kind
of victim's supporter, a boy from a coal-mining town who wanted to
write an angry book for friends killed in the mines. My research also
found strong empirical evidence that persuasion works better when
workers and unions (representing the victims of the crime) are involved
in deliberative regulatory processes.[9] Nearly all serious mine safety accidents can be prevented if only the law is obeyed (Braithwaite 1985,
pp. 20–24, 75–77); the great historical lesson of the coal industry is
that the way to accomplish this is through a rich dialogue among victims and offenders on why the law is important, a dialogue given a
deeper meaning after each fatality is investigated. The shift from punitive to restorative justice in that industry has been considerable and the
results considerable. During the first fifty years of mine safety enforcement in Britain (until World War I) there were a number of years
when a thousand miners lost their lives in the pits. Fatalities decreased
from 1,484 in 1866 to forty-four in 1982–83, after which the British
industry collapsed. In the years immediately prior to World War I, the
average number of annual criminal prosecutions for coal mine safety
offenses in the United Kingdom was 1,309. In both 1980 and 1981,
there were none (Braithwaite 1985, p. 4).

The qualitative research doing ride-alongs with mine safety inspectors in several countries resolved the puzzle for me. Persuasion worked
much of the time; workers' participation in a dialogue about their own
security worked. However, the data also suggested that persuasion
worked best in the contexts where it was backed by the possibility of
punishment.

In the United Kingdom during the 1970s, fifty pits were selected
each year for a special safety campaign; these pits showed a consistently
greater improvement in accident rates than did other British pits (Collinson 1978, p. 77). I found the safety leaders in the industry were companies that not only thoroughly involved everyone concerned after a
serious accident to reach consensual agreement on what must be done
to prevent recurrence, they also did this after "near accidents" (Braithwaite 1985, p. 67) and they discussed safety audit results with workers

---

[9] For example DeMichiei et al.'s (1982, p. i) comparison of mines with exceptionally
high injury rates with matched mines with exceptionally low injury rates found that at
the low-injury mines: "Open lines of communication permit management and labor to
jointly reconcile problems affecting safety and health; Representatives of labor become
actively involved in issues concerning safety, health and production; and Management
and labor identify and accept their joint responsibility for correcting unsafe conditions
and practices."

even when there was no near-accident. In a remarkable foreshadowing of what we now believe to be reasons for the effectiveness of whole-school approaches to bullying and family group conferences, Davis and Stahl's (1967, p. 26) study of twelve companies who had been winners of the industry's two safety awards, found one recurring initiative was a "safety letter to families of workers enlisting family support in promoting safe work habits." That is, safety leaders engaged a community of care beyond the workplace in building a safety culture. In *To Punish or Persuade*, I shocked myself by concluding that after mine disasters, including the terrible one in my home town that had motivated me to write the book, so long as there had been an open public dialogue among all those affected, the families of the miners cared for, and a credible plan to prevent recurrence put in place, criminal punishment served little purpose. The process of the public enquiry and helping the families of the miners for whom they were responsible seemed such a potent general deterrent that a criminal trial could be gratuitous and might corrupt the restorative justice process that I found in so many of the thirty-nine disaster investigations I studied.

Joe Rees (1988, 1994) is the scholar who has done most to work through the promise of what he calls communitarian regulation, which we might read as restorative regulatory justice. First Rees (1988) studied the "Cooperative Compliance Program" of the Occupational Safety and Health Administration between 1979 and 1984. OSHA essentially empowered labor-management safety committees at seven Californian sites to take over the law enforcement role, to solve the underlying problems revealed by breaches of the law. Satisfaction of workers, management, and government participants was high because they believed it "worked." It seemed to. Accident rates ranged from one-third lower to one-fifth as low as the Californian rate for comparable projects of the same companies, as the rate in the same project before the cooperative compliance program compared with after (Rees 1988, pp. 2–3).

Rees's next study of communitarian regulation was of U.S. nuclear regulation after Three Mile Island. The industry realized that it had to transform the nature of its regulation and self-regulation from a rule book, hardware orientation to one oriented to people, corporate cultures, and software. The industry's CEOs set up the Institute of Nuclear Power Operations (INPO) to achieve these ends. Peers from other nuclear power plants would take three weeks off their own jobs to join an INPO review team that engaged the inspected facility in a dialogue about how they could improve. Safety performance ratings were also issued by the review team; comparative ratings of all the firms in the industry were displayed and discussed at meetings of all the CEOs in the industry and at separate meetings of safety officers. Rees (1994) sees these as reintegrative shaming sessions. Here is an excerpt from a videotape of a meeting of the safety officers:

> It's not particularly easy to come up here and talk about an event at a plant in which you have a lot of pride, a lot of pride in the performance, in the operators . . . It's also tough going through the agonizing thinking of what it is you want to say. How do you want to confess? How do you want to couch it in a way that, even though you did something wrong, you're still okay? You get a chance to talk to Ken Strahm and Terry Sullivan [INPO Vice Presidents] and you go over what your plans are, and they tell you, "No, Fred, you've got to really bare your soul.." . . It's a painful thing to do. (Rees 1994, p. 107)

What was the effect of the shift in the center of gravity of the regulatory regime from a Nuclear Regulatory Commission driven by political sensitivities to be tough and prescriptive to INPO's communitarian regulation (focused on a dialogue about how to achieve outcomes rather than rule book enforcement)? Rees (1994, pp. 183–86) shows considerable improvement across a range of indicators of the safety performance of the U.S. nuclear power industry since INPO. Improvement has continued since the completion of Rees's study. For example, more recent World Association of Nuclear Operators data show scrams (automatic emergency shutdowns) per unit declined in the United States from over seven per unit in 1980 to one by 1993.

In Section II, I showed that shifting nursing home regulation from rule-book enforcement to restorative justice improved regulatory outcomes and that the inspectors who shifted most toward restorative justice improved compliance most (those who used praise and trust more than threat, reintegrative shaming rather than tolerance or stigmatization, those who restored self-efficacy). These results are discussed again when I consider the theories that predict why restorative justice might work better than punitive justice. For the moment, I simply note that communitarian regulation has had considerable documented success in restoring coal mining firms, nuclear power plants, and nursing homes to a more responsible approach to compliance with the law.

Equally, writers such as Gunningham (1995) and Fiona Haines (1997) have shown that there are serious limits to communitarian regulation—rapacious big firms and incompetent little ones who will not or cannot respond responsibly. Deterrence and incapacitation are needed, and needed in larger measure than these regimes currently provide, when restorative justice fails (see also Ayres and Braithwaite 1992; Gunningham and Grabosky 1998).

Carol Heimer pointed out in comments on a draft of this essay that "if high-level white collar workers are more likely to get restorative justice, it may be because their corporate colleagues and other members of the society believe that their contributions are not easily replaced, so that offenders must be salvaged" (see Heimer and Staffen 1995). This is right, I suspect, and a reason why justice is most likely to be restorative in the hands of communities of care who can see the value of salvaging the offender and the victim.

C. Restorative Justice Practices Restore and Satisfy Communities Better than Existing Criminal Justice Practices

In every place where a reform debate has occurred about the introduction of family group conferences, two community concerns have been paramount: while victims might be forgiving in New Zealand, giving free reign to victim anger "here" will tear at our community; while families may be strong elsewhere, "here" our worst offenders are alienated and alone; their families are so dysfunctional and uncaring that they will not participate meaningfully. But as Morris et al. (1996, p. 223) conclude from perspectives on this question summarized from a number of jurisdictions: "Concerns about not being able to locate extended family or family supporters, to engage families or to effectively involve so-called 'dysfunctional' families, about families forming a coalition to conceal abuse and about families' failing to honour agreements do not prove to have been well-founded in any of the jurisdictions reported in this book."

In his discussion of the Hollow Water experience of using healing circles to deal with rampant sexual abuse of children in a Canadian First Nations community, Ross (1996, p. 150) emphasizes the centrality of restoring communities for restoring individuals: "If you are dealing with people whose relationships have been built on power and abuse, you must actually show them, then give them the experience of, relationships based on respect . . . [so] . . . the healing process must involve a healthy group of people, as opposed to single therapists. A single therapist cannot, by definition, do more than talk about healthy relationships."

The most sophisticated implementation of this ideal that has been well-evaluated is Burford and Pennell's (1998) Family Group Decision Making Project to confront violence and child neglect in families. Beyond the positive effects on the direct objective of reducing violence, the evaluation found a posttest increase in family support, concrete (e.g., babysitting) and emotional, and enhanced family unity, even in circumstances where some conference plans involved separation of parents from their children. The philosophy of this program was to look for strengths in families that were in very deep trouble and build on them.

Members of the community beyond the offender and the victim who attend restorative justice processes tend, like offenders, victims and the police, to come away with high levels of satisfaction. In Pennell and Burford's (1995) family group conferences for family violence, 94 percent of family members were "satisfied with the way it was run"; 92 percent felt they were "able to say what was important," and 92 percent "agreed with the plan decided on." Clairmont (1994, p. 28) also reports that among native peoples in Canada, the restorative justice initiatives he reviewed have "proven to be popular with offenders . . . and to have broad, general support within communities." The Ministry of Justice (1994), Western Australia, reports 93 percent parental satisfaction, 84 percent police satisfaction, and 67 percent judicial satisfaction, plus (and crucially) satisfaction of Aboriginal organizations with their restorative justice conference program (Juvenile Justice Teams). In Singapore, 95 percent of family members who attended family group conferences said that they benefited personally from the experience (Hsien 1996). For the Bethlehem police conferencing experiment, more parents of offenders were satisfied (97 percent) and likely to believe that justice had been fair (97 percent) than in cases that went to court (McCold and Wachtel, 1998, pp. 65–72).

A study by Schneider (1990) found that completing restitution and community service was associated with enhanced commitment to community and feelings of citizenship (and reduced recidivism). While the evidence is overwhelming that where communities show strong social support, criminality is less (Cullen 1994; Chamlin and Cochran 1997), it would be optimistic to expect that restorative justice could ever have sufficient impacts in restoring microcommunities to cause a shift in the macro impact of community on the crime rate (cf. Brown and Polk 1996).

But building the microcommunity of a school or restoring social bonds in a family can have important implications for crime in that school or that family. Moreover, the restoring of microcommunity has a value of its own, independent of the size of the impact on crime. In the last section I showed how whole-school approaches to bullying can halve bullying in schools. There is a more important point of deliberative programs to give all the citizens of the school community an opportunity to be involved in deciding how to make their school safer and more caring. It is that they make their schools more decent places to be in while one is being educated. There is Australian evidence suggesting that restorative sexual harassment programs in workplaces may reduce sexual harassment (Parker 1998). Again the more important value of these programs than the improved compliance with the law may be about more general improvements in the respect with which women are treated in workplaces as a result of the deliberation and social support integral to such programs when they are effective.

I have known restorative justice conferences where supporters of a boy offender and a girl victim of a sexual assault agreed to work together to confront a culture of exploitative masculinity in an Australian school that unjustly characterized the girl as "getting what she asked for" (Braithwaite and Daly 1994). Conversely, I have seen conferences that have missed the opportunity to confront homophobic cultures in schools revealed by graffiti humiliating allegedly gay men and boys (Retzinger and Scheff 1996). After one early New Zealand conference concerning breaking into and damaging the restaurant of a refugee Cambodian, the offender agreed to watch a video of *The Killing Fields* and "pass the word on the street" that the Cambodian restaurateur was struggling to survive and should not be harassed. A small victory for civil community life perhaps, but a large one for that Cambodian man.

One of the most stirring conferences I know of occurred in an outback town after four Aboriginal children manifested their antagonism toward the middle-class matriarchs of the town by ransacking the Country Women's Association Hall. The conference was so moving because it brought the Aboriginal and the white women together, shocked and upset by what the children had done, to talk to each other about why the women no longer spoke to one another across the racial divide in the way they had in earlier times. Did there have to be such an incivility as this to discover the loss of their shared communal life? Those black and white women and children rebuilt that communal life as they restored the devastated Country Women's Association Hall, working together, respectfully once more (for more details on this case, see the Real Justice website http://www.realjustice.org/).

One might summarize that the evidence of restorative justice restoring communities is of very small accomplishments of microcommunity building and of modest numbers of community members going away overwhelmingly satisfied with the justice in which they have participated. Maori critics of Pakeha restorative justice such as Moana Jackson (1987) and Juan Tauri (1998) point out that it falls far short of restoring Maori community control over justice. Neocolonial controls from Pakeha courts remain on top of restorative justice in Maori communities. This critique seems undeniable; nowhere in the world has restorative justice enabled major steps toward restoring precolonial forms of community among colonized peoples; nowhere have the courts of the colonial power given up their power to trump the decisions of the indigenous justice fora.

At the same time, there is a feminist critique of this indigenous critique of community restoration. I return later to at least one case where male indigenous elders in Canada used control over community justice as a resource in the oppression of women complaining of rape by dominant men. In this case the community was torn asunder to the point of a number of women leaving it.

With all the attention given to the microcommunity building of routine restorative justice conferences, we must not lose sight of historically rare moments of restorative justice that reframe macrocommunity. I refer, for example, to the release of IRA terrorists from prison so that they could participate in the IRA meetings of 1998 that voted for the renunciation of violent struggle. I refer to much more partially successful examples, such as the Camp David mediations of President Carter with the leaders of Egypt and Israel (more partially successful because it excluded the Palestinians themselves), and to more completely successful local peacemaking such as that of the Kulka Women's Club in the Highlands of New Guinea (Rumsey 1999).

D. Reintegrative Shaming Theory Predicts That Restorative Justice Practices Reduce Crime More than Existing Criminal Justice Practices

> ma te whakama e patu!
> "Leave him alone, he is punished by shame." (Maori saying)

Crime, Shame and Reintegration (Braithwaite 1989) gives an account of why restorative justice processes ought to prevent crime more effectively than retributive practices. The core claims are: tolerance of crime makes things worse; stigmatization, or disrespectful, outcasting shaming of crime, makes crime worse still; while reintegrative shaming, disapproval within a continuum of respect for the offender, disapproval terminated by rituals of forgiveness, prevents crime.

In developing the theory, I was much influenced by the restorative nature of various Asian policing and educational practices, by what I saw as the effectiveness of restorative regulatory processes for dealing with corporate crime both in Asia and the West, and by the restorative nature of socialization in Western families that succeed in raising law-abiding children. That child development literature is not reviewed again here. Essentially, what it shows is that both laissez-faire parenting that fails to confront and disapprove of children's misconduct and punitively authoritarian parenting both produce a lot of delinquents; delinquency is less likely when parents confront wrongdoing with moral reasoning (Braithwaite 1989). One implication for restorative justice advocates of this substantial body of empirical evidence is that the justice system will do better when it facilitates moral reasoning by families over what to do about a crime as an alternative to punishment by the state.

Restorative justice conferences work by inviting victims and supporters (usually family supporters) of the victim to meet with the offender and the people who care most about the offender and most enjoy the offender's respect (usually including both the nuclear and extended family, but not limited to them). This group discusses the consequences of the crime, drawing out the feelings of those who have been harmed. Then they discuss how that harm might be repaired and any steps that should be taken to prevent reoffending. Attendance of over forty people can occur, but average attendance (beyond the offender) reported is six in New Zealand (Robertson 1996), six in Victoria (Ban 1996), five in Bethlehem (McCold and Wachtel 1998, p. 30), eight in Canberra (unpublished RISE data), and twenty-three in Manitoba (Longclaws, Galaway, and Barkwell 1996). Wachtel (1997, p. 73) reports a five-hour conference in Pennsylvania with an attendance of seventy-five.

In terms of reintegrative shaming theory, the discussion of the consequences of the crime for victims (or consequences for the offender's family) structures shame into the conference; the support of those who enjoy the strongest relationships of love or respect with the offender structures reintegration into the ritual. It is not the shame of police or judges or newspapers that is most able to get through to us; it is shame in the eyes of those we respect and trust. These are not new ideas. They have existed for hundreds of years in Maori philosophies of justice. Maori thought about *whanau* conferences repeatedly use the words shame (*whakama*) and healing in equivalent ways to my use of shaming and reintegration. In Maori thinking, it is the shame of letting one's extended family down that is a particularly important type of shame to discuss. The advantage of this sort of shame over the individual guilt/shame one is expected to experience as one stands alone in the dock of Western justice is that it is readily transcended when family members extend forgiveness to the offender.

Evidence from 548 adult and juvenile cases randomly assigned to court versus conference in Canberra, Australia, is that offenders both report and are observed to encounter more reintegrative shaming in conferences than in court, that conference offenders experience more remorse and more forgiveness than court offenders, and are more likely to report that they have learnt from the process that there are people who care about them (Sherman and Strang 1997*a*). Eighty percent of conference offenders compared to 40 percent of court offenders said after the process that they felt they had repaid their debt to victims and to society. Another two years of data collection are required in this study before we know whether reoffending was less in the cases where reintegrative shaming was experienced. Harris and Burton's (1997) work at least shows that reliable observational measurement of reintegrative shaming is possible: ratings of how much reintegrative shaming occurred in forty-five conferences and court cases by independent raters agreed between 67 percent and 93 percent of the time.

Makkai and Braithwaite's (1994) test of the theory in the domain of compliance of Australian nursing homes with quality of care standards has the attraction of test-retest reliabilities of the measure of compliance with the law between .93 and .96, obtained by having an independent inspector check compliance. Makkai and Braithwaite found that homes checked by inspectors with a reintegrative shaming philosophy experienced improved compliance with the law in a follow-up inspection two years later. Nursing homes inspected by stigmatizing inspectors suffered an equivalent drop in compliance two years later, while homes checked by tolerant and understanding inspectors suffered an intermediate fall in compliance. Lu (1998) has produced a different kind of encouraging data on the validity of the theory of reintegrative shaming in the very different context of community justice in Shanghai.

E. Procedural Justice Theory Predicts That Restorative Justice Practices Reduce Crime More than Existing Criminal Justice Practices

The idea of reintegrative shaming is that disapproval is communicated within a continuum of respect for the offender. A key way to show respect is to be fair, to listen, to empower others with process control, to refrain from bias on the grounds of age, sex, or race. More broadly, procedural justice communicates respect (Lind and Tyler 1988; Tyler 1990). Conferences do not have all the procedural safeguards of court cases; yet the Optimistic Account predicts offenders and victims will find them fairer. Why? Conferences are structurally fairer because of who participates and who controls the discourse. Criminal trials invite along those who can inflict maximum damage on the other side; conferences invite those who can offer maximum support to their own side, be it the victim side or the offender side. In other words those present are expected to be fair and therefore tend to want to be fair. They tend not to see their job as doing better at blackening the character of the other than the other does at blackening theirs.

Citizens are empowered with process control, rather than placed under the control of lawyers. In the study of nursing home regulation discussed above, Makkai and Braithwaite (1996) found that of the various facets of procedural justice, perceived process control on the part of citizens is the one that predicts subsequent compliance with the law. Other research suggests other dimensions of procedural justice may be important, however. For example, in the Milwaukee domestic violence experiment (Bridgeforth 1990, p. 76), "arrestees who said (in lockup) that police had not taken the time to listen to their side of the story were 36 percent more likely to be reported for assaulting the same victim over the next 6 months than those who said the police had listened to them" (Sherman 1993, p. 463; see also Paternoster et al. 1997). More broadly, in Why People Obey the Law, Tyler (1990) found that citizens were more likely to comply with the law when they saw themselves as treated fairly by the criminal justice system. Sherman (1993) has reviewed further more recent supportive evidence on this question.

The key questions are whether citizens feel they are treated more fairly in restorative justice processes than in courts and whether they are more likely to understand what is going on. The answer seems clearly to be yes. Early results from the Canberra conferencing experiment show that offenders are more likely to understand what is going on in conferences than in court cases, felt more empowered to express their views, had more time to do so, were more likely to feel that their rights were respected, to feel that they could correct errors of fact, and to feel that they were treated with respect, and were less likely to feel in conferences that they were disadvantaged due to "age, income, sex, race, or some other reason" (Sherman and Barnes 1997; Sherman et al. 1998). Without the randomized comparison with court, a number of other studies have shown absolutely high levels of citizen satisfaction with the fairness of restorative justice processes (Sec. VIIA–C).

Given that there is now strong evidence that restorative justice processes are perceived to be fairer by those involved and strong evidence that perceived procedural justice improves compliance with the law, the Optimistic prediction follows that restorative justice processes will improve compliance with the law.

F. The Theory of Bypassed Shame Predicts that Restorative Justice Practices Reduce Crime More than Existing Criminal Justice

Scholars working in the affect theory tradition of Sylvan Tomkins (1962), most notably Donald Nathanson (1992) and David Moore (with Forsythe 1995), have a theoretical perspective on why restorative justice should reduce crime based more on the nature of shame as an affect than on shaming, reintegration, and stigmatization as practices. According to this perspective, shame can be a destructive emotion because it can lead one to attack others, attack self, avoid, or withdraw (Nathanson's [1992] compass of shame). All of these are responses that can promote crime. A profound deficiency of Braithwaite's (1989) theory is that it is just a theory of shaming, with the emotion of shame left undertheorized.

From this perspective, therefore, a process is needed that enables offenders to deal with the shame that almost inevitably arises at some level when a serious criminal offense has occurred. Denial, for example being "ashamed to be ashamed," in Scheff's words, is not an adaptive response. Shame is a normal emotion that healthy humans must experience; it is as vital to motivating us to preserve social bonds essential to our flourishing as is fear to motivating us to flee danger. Indeed Scheff (1990, 1994), Retzinger (1991), and Scheff and Retzinger (1991) finger bypassed shame as the culprit in the shame-rage spirals that characterize our worst violence domestically and internationally.

The evidence these authors offer for the promotion of anger through bypassed shame is voluminous but of a quite different sort from the more quantitative evidence adduced under the other propositions in this section of the essay. It consists primarily of collections of clinical case notes (preeminently Lewis's 1971 research) and microanalyses of conversations (preeminently Retzinger's 1991 marital quarrels). Yet the thrust of this work is also supported by Tangney's (1995) review of quantitative studies on the relationship between shame and psychopathology: Guilt about specific behaviors, "uncomplicated by feelings of shame about the self," is healthy. The problem is "chronic self-blame and an excessive rumination over some objectionable behavior" (Tangney 1995, p. 1141). Scheff and Retzinger take this further, suggesting that shame is more likely to be uncomplicated when consequences that are shameful are confronted and emotional repair work is done for those damaged. Shame will become complicated, chronic, more likely to descend into rage if it is not fully confronted. If there is nagging shame under the surface, it is no permanent solution to lash out at others with anger that blames them. Then the shame and rage will feed on each another in a shame-rage spiral. Consistent with this analysis, Ahmed (1999) has shown in a study of bullying among twelve hundred Canberra schoolchildren that bullies deal with shame through bypassing it, victims acknowledge and internalize shame so that they suffer persistent shame, while children who avoid both bullying and being victimized by bullies have the ability to acknowledge and discharge shame so that shame does not become a threat to the self.

According to Retzinger and Scheff's work, if we want a world with less violence and less dominating abuse of others, we need to take seriously rituals that encourage approval of caring behavior so that citizens will acquire pride in being caring and nondominating. With dominating behavior, we need rituals of disapproval and acknowledged shame of the dominating behavior, rituals that avert disapproval-unacknowledged shame sequences. Retzinger and Scheff (1996) see restorative justice conferences as having the potential (a potential far from always realized) to institutionalize pride and acknowledged shame that heals damaged social bonds. Circles in this formulation are ceremonies of constructive conflict. When hurt is communicated, shame acknowledged by the person who caused it, respect shown for the victim's reasons for communicating the hurt, and respect reciprocated by the victim, constructive conflict has occurred between victim and offender. It may be that in the "abused spouse syndrome," for example, shame is bypassed and destructive, as a relationship iterates through a cycle of abuse, manipulative contrition, peace, perceived provocation, and renewed abuse (see Retzinger 1991). Crime wounds, justice heals; but only if justice is relational (Burnside and Baker 1994).

Moore with Forsythe (1995, p. 265) emphasize that restorative justice should not, in the words of Gypsy Rose Lee, accentuate the positive and eliminate the negative; rather it should accentuate the positive and confront the negative. Tomkins (1962) adduces four principles for constructive management of affect: "(1) That positive affect should be maximized. (2) That negative affect should be minimized. (3) That affect inhibition should be minimized. (4) That power to maximize positive affect, to minimize negative affect, and to minimize affect inhibition should be maximized." Nathanson (1998, p. 86) links this model to an hypothesized capacity of restorative justice processes to build community, where community is conceived as people linked by scripts for systems of affect modulation. Community is built by: "(1) Mutualization of and group action to enhance or maximize positive affect; (2) Mutualization of and group action to diminish or minimize negative affect; (3) Communities thrive best when all affect is expressed so these first two goals may be accomplished; (4) Mechanisms that increase the power to accomplish these goals favor the maintenance of community, whereas mechanisms that decrease the power to express and modulate affect threaten the community."

In the most constructive conflicts, shame will be acknowledged by apology (reciprocated by forgiveness) (Tavuchis 1991). Maxwell and Morris (1996) found in New Zealand family group conferences that the minority of offenders who failed to apologize during conferences were three times more likely to reoffend than those who had apologized. Interpreting any direction of causality here is admittedly difficult.

Moore (1994, p. 6) observes that in courtroom justice shame is not acknowledged because it is "hidden behind impersonal rhetoric about technical culpability."

Both Moore with Forsythe (1995) and Retzinger and Scheff (1996) have applied their methods to the observation of restorative justice conferences, observing the above mechanisms to be in play and to be crucial to shaping whether conferences succeed or fail in dealing with conflicts in ways that they predict will prevent crime. For Retzinger and Scheff (1996), conferences have the ostensible purpose of material reparation; but underlying the verbal and visible process of reaching agreement about material reparation is a more nonverbal, less visible process of symbolic reparation. It is the latter that really matters according to their theoretical framework, so the emphasis in the early restorative justice literature on how much material reparation is actually paid becomes quite misguided.

The evidence now seems strong that bypassed shame contributes to violence; Sherman and Barnes's (1997) and Sherman et al.'s (1998, pp. 127–29) admittedly preliminary evidence suggests that in conferences offenders may accept and discharge shame more than when they go through court cases. If both propositions are correct, conferences might do more to reduce crime than court cases.

G. Defiance Theory Predicts that Restorative Justice Practices Reduce Crime More than Existing Criminal Justice Practices

"Disrespect begets disrespect," claims Howard Zehr (1995), and few things communicate disrespect as effectively as the criminal exploitation of another human being. Sherman (1993) has woven the propositions from Subsections *D–F* about procedural justice, the social bonds that render shaming reintegrative and bypassed shame into an integrated theory of defiance. It has three propositions:

1. Sanctions provoke future defiance of the law (persistence, more frequent or more serious violations) to the extent that offenders experience sanctioning conduct as illegitimate, that offenders have weak bonds to the sanctioning agent and community, and that offenders deny their shame and become proud of their isolation from the sanctioning community. 2. Sanctions produce future deterrence of law-breaking (desistance, less frequent or less serious violations) to the extent that offenders experience sanctioning conduct as legitimate, that offenders have strong bonds to the sanctioning agent and community, and that offenders accept their shame and remain proud of solidarity with the community. 3. Sanctions become irrelevant to future law breaking (no effect) to the extent that the factors encouraging defiance or deterrence are fairly evenly counterbalanced. (Sherman 1993, pp. 448–49)

Sherman hypothesizes that restorative justice processes are more likely to meet the conditions of proposition 2 than traditional punitive processes. The evidence to date supports this. We have already seen that restorative processes are accorded high legitimacy by citizens, that they are better designed to empower those with strong bonds with the of-

fender, and that they outperform court in inducing the acknowledge-
ment and discharging of shame for wrongdoing.

While Sherman (1993) reviews some suggestive evidence that law
breaking might vary under the conditions that are hypothesized to vary
defiance, a systematic test of defiance theory remains to be undertaken.
Results from the RISE experiment are still very preliminary here, only
laying the foundations for the test of this theory. One published result
encouraging to defiance theory, however, is that while 26 percent of
drunk drivers randomly assigned to court felt bitter and angry after
court, only 7 percent of offenders felt bitter and angry after a conference (Sherman and Strang 1997b).

Hagan and McCarthy (1997, pp. 191–97) have tested Sherman's defiance theory against the prediction that children who have been humiliated, treated unfairly, and had bonds severed by virtue of being victims of sexual abuse or physical violence (with bruising or bleeding)
will have their criminal behavior amplified by traditional criminal justice processing more than offenders who have not been abused. Their
data, collected among homeless children in Toronto and Vancouver,
supported the defiance theory prediction.

H. Self-Categorization Theory Predicts that Restorative Justice Practices Reduce Crime More than Existing Criminal Justice Practices

Self-categorization theory (Turner et al. 1987) explains the conditions under which a social self-concept or social identity becomes salient through individuals categorizing their self as having a similar
identity to that shared by various social groups. These emergent identities shape what we are and how we act. I act the way I do because I
am an Australian, male, a criminologist, a consumer advocate, a republican, and so on. According to self-categorization theory, it is group
identities that matter more than group interaction. I do not have to
spend time going to Australian Republican Movement meetings for my
identity as a republican to affect how I act.

The notion of group influence is therefore different in emphasis
from that proposed in the theory of reintegrative shaming, which emphasizes interdependence. Like most criminological theories, Braithwaite's (1989) is sloppily theorized on this question, slipping back and
forth between interaction-based and identity-based accounts of how
criminal subcultures influence action. This is true of Sutherland's
(1983) theory as well, headlined as a theory of differential association,
it actually defines differential association cognitively rather than inter-

actively: "An excess of definitions favorable to violations of law over definitions unfavorable to violation of law" (Sutherland and Cressey 1978, p. 81).

Albert Cohen's (1955) subcultural theory is more incipiently a self-categorization theory than other classic criminological theories. For Cohen, children who fail in the status system of the school have a status problem. They can solve that status problem by identifying with other groups that invert the values of the school. If the school values being "square," there is attraction to being "cool," feeling membership in a cool group. If the school values control of aggression, then there is attractiveness in a group that values free expression of aggression. While there is evidence that children experience Cohen's reaction formation (Koh 1997), there is more evidence in more contexts for Matza's (1964) view that delinquents drift between law-supportive and law-neutralizing identities, though some studies do not find a lot of drift away from law-supportive identities among delinquents (Box 1981, pp. 107–8; Ball 1983; Thurman 1984; Agnew and Peters 1986; Anderson 1999; Koh 1997). Sykes and Matza (1957) have suggested five techniques of neutralization that make drift possible: denial of victim ("We weren't hurting anyone"); denial of injury ("They can afford it"); condemnation of the condemners ("They're crooks themselves"); denial of responsibility ("I was drunk"); and appeal to higher loyalties ("I had to stick by my mates").

Restorative justice conferences may prevent crime by facilitating a drift back to law-supportive identities from law-neutralizing ones. How might they accomplish this? At a victim-offender mediation or conference when the victim is present, it is hard to sustain denial of victim and denial of injury. In contrast, these techniques of neutralization are fostered by criminal justice institutions that sustain separations of victims and offenders. Admittedly, victims often do not convince the offender in a conference that they were hurt in a way they could ill afford. Yet when this occurs, victim supporters will often move offenders through the communicative power, the authenticity, that comes from their love of the victim. An upset daughter explaining how frightened her mother now is in her own house can have a more powerful impact on the offender than direct expressions of concern by the victim.

Condemnation of the condemners is also more difficult to sustain when one's condemners engage in a respectful dialogue about why the criminal behavior of concern to them is harmful. Katz, Glass, and Cohen's (1973) research shows that outgroup derogation is the preferred way of handling shame when the victim is a member of an outgroup. Conferences and healing circles are designed to make the condemners members of an in-group rather than an outgroup by two moves: inviting participants from all the in-groups that matter most to offenders; encouraging victims and victim supporters to be respectful, even forgiving, of them as a person thus rendering their outgroup location more ambiguous. One of the advantages of the presence of victim supporters is that if the victim is irrevocably a member of an outgroup, the consequences of the crime might be effectively communicated by a victim supporter who happens to be a member of an in-group.

The evidence is that the transience of in- and outgroup categorizations is contextually responsive to variables like politeness and respectfulness, the very modes of interaction restorative justice processes seek to nurture (Turner et al. 1987, pp. 55–56). From a self-categorization perspective, an advantage of Chinese social structuring is the relative lack of clear boundaries in defining an in-group, for example in the elastic definition of Chia or family, depending on the problems at issue (Bond and Wang Sung-Hsing 1983, p. 68).

Denial of responsibility is tested at a conference. The presence of supporters who know and care for an offender risk that a denial of responsibility like "I was drunk" might lead to a discussion of his responsibility for recurrent drunkenness that has induced irresponsible behavior in the past. Obversely, criminal trials only test those denials of responsibility legally relevant to mitigating guilt. Even for that legally relevant subset of the psychologically relevant denials, they are tested in ways that are least likely to be persuasive to the offender—by attacking his credibility as a person in the eyes of a judge or jury. The restorative conference supports him as a person while questioning the usefulness of his denials to him as a person and to clearing things up for those who have been hurt. The restorative process, by showing a path to redemption, provides an alternative to denial. This contrasts with the two paths the court proffers—guilt and punishment or innocence and impunity—a choice that makes denial an attractive posture.

Criminal offenders are criminal offenders partly because they are good at denial. When a shaft of shame is projected across the room from victim to offender, the offender may have a shield that deflects the shame, only to find the deflected shame spears through the heart of his mother who quietly sobs beside him. What I have observed in many conferences is that it may then be mother's or father's or sister's shame that gets behind his shield of denial. This only happens, of course, when he loves one of these intimates.

Appeals to higher loyalties like loyalties to one's mates is the technique of neutralization of greatest interest from a self-categorization perspective. Emler and Reicher's (1995) interviews with delinquents reveal that they are simultaneously concerned about having a reputation for whatever it is their delinquent group values (say toughness) while being concerned about maintaining a different reputation with their families. Their delinquents worked hard at keeping families unaware of the different values and conduct they manifest in the delinquent group. Delinquents' parents rarely met their peers. Delinquents were more likely than nondelinquents to keep peers and parents apart (Emler and Reicher 1995, p. 204). Koh (1997, p. 376) found that incarcerated Singaporean delinquents endorsed neutralization techniques to a lesser extent when their family identity was salient and when confrontation with authority was seen to be public rather than private.

Goffman (1956) is the preeminent theorist of what he calls strategies for matching audience segregation to role segregation. In the nineteenth century village, all our roles were played out for the same audience. The condition of modernity, however, is of a proliferation of group identities—mother, criminologist, golfer, Christian, cat breeder—but where those groups are scattered across global space. Most of us are actually not more alone in the modern city; but our togetherness is not unified with place (Braithwaite 1993*a*). This means, as Benson (1989) shows empirically, that the white-collar criminal in the contemporary world is peculiarly vulnerable to shame if only his business activities might be revealed to his church group. Restorative justice conferences are designed to do just this—to bring together the audiences the criminal would most want to be segregated.

This design can and does backfire. On rare occasions, we have had restorative justice conferences in Australia where a delinquent gang, or two rival gangs on the victim and offender sides, have dominated the conference numerically and persuasively (in neutralizing shame). On many occasions, we have observed adult restorative justice conferences for drunk driving where the offender's drinking group has dominated the conference with denials of victim, of injury, of responsibility (Mugford and Inkpen 1995).

Overall, my observation from sitting through more than a hundred conferences of different types is that such cases are in the minority. Why? One reason is Matza (1964) was right that drift toward and away from rejection of the law's moral bind is more common than outright rejection of moral commitment to the law. For example, while parents of serious delinquents are more likely to have been delinquents themselves (Wilson and Herrnstein 1985, pp. 95–103), they are not Fagins. Criminal parents almost always disapprove of their children's delinquency (West and Farrington 1973, p. 116). Even when we put together a conference dominated by multiproblem families concerning a violent offense, we find empirically that very few of the utterances are approving of violence. One reason for this is that philosophers in the Aristotelian tradition of truth-finding through undominated dialogue, like Habermas (1996), are right that the closer we get to conditions of undominated speech, the more overwhelmingly it will turn out to be the case that evils such as violence will be near-universally condemned. That is, there is a moral fact of the matter that gratuitous violence is wrong and undominated dialogue will converge on consensus about contextual judgments of the wrongness of specific violent acts.

A nice moral feature of restorative justice from this perspective is that restorative justice might only work with crimes that ought to be crimes. If a group of citizens cannot agree in an undominated conference that an act of obscenity is wrong, then the obscenity should not be a crime; and the conference will fail in controlling obscenity. But the fact of the matter is that most criminal offenses brought to justice in democratic societies are more like the violence case than the obscenity case: they are unambiguously wrong to most citizens attending a conference.

Put another way, when a victim comes to a conference with a broken nose, denial of victim and denial of injury are likely to be revealed as bad arguments. From a Habermasian perspective, techniques of neutralization for violence can only be sustained by avoiding undominated dialogue about their justice. Restorative justice breaks through that avoidance. The social psychological research literature supports the interpretation that self-interested egotistical neutralizations are vulnerable to group dialogue: "In situations without strong social bonds [courtrooms?], people are egotistical. Once a group identity is created, however, people are increasingly responsive to group-centered motives" (Tyler and Dawes 1993, p. 102). The challenge for circles is to forge a common group identity in the face of the other identities that divide them; they are a group committed to achieving restoration.

Of course, circles are never free of domination, so the degree of truth of the Habermasian analysis is contingent. However, some of the ineradicable dominations of social life systematically conduce to law-abiding in-groups having more power in the long haul than law-neutralizing ones, at least with juveniles. It is well documented that delinquency declines beyond a certain age; one reason is that collective support for delinquency declines from about age sixteen (Emler and Reicher 1995). However much delinquent peer groups dominate a young person, she is not unaware that these peers are not going to be around forever; she knows that when they go off the scene, family will still be there lending money, caring, giving emotional support. At least she knows this in those cases where the conference facilitator has succeeded in getting to the conference communities of care (including nonfamily ones) beyond the delinquent peer group who will stick by the offender in the long haul.

Where the offender is so dominated by a delinquent peer group that the longer term nature of family bonds does not trump this domination, a restorative justice strategy still has time on its side. Empirically, the peer group is more likely to disintegrate between ages thirteen and twenty than the family. Very few of the gang members in Esbensen and Huizinga's (1993) Denver survey reported being in a delinquent gang for more than one year. Many members indicated that they would like not to be members and expected to leave the gang in future. If we just hang in with one unsuccessful conference after another in which delinquent peers dominate family, eventually the balance will shift in the other direction. Restorative justice rewards the patient. As Siti Hamidah of the Association of Muslim Professionals said of Singaporean conferences: "Many want to change but don't know how, so it's a time to make concrete plans, like returning to school or finding a job" (Hsien 1996).

It is often the case in the short term that peer influences dominate family influence because though the delinquent group "is characterized by a lack of intimacy or affection, there is a strong sense of belongingness" (Koh 1997, p. 201). Yet where that belongingness is grounded in its provision of an alternative status system to the status system of a school that fails them, removal of the original cause by dropping out of school may undermine a belongingness so grounded. Indeed, there is evidence of reduced delinquency following school drop-out (Elliott and Voss 1974).

An unattractive way of applying the lessons of self-categorization theory to restorative justice would be to exclude delinquent peers from the conference, or to exclude drinking mates in the difficult case of the shameless Aussie drunk driver. There is little point persuading a delinquent during an hour stacked with the law abiding when she will spend the next thousand hours in a world surrounded by the law violating. Better to confront the whole delinquent group or the whole drinking group with the indefensibility of their techniques of neutralization. Better to win the conscience of the delinquent in the presence of his delinquent peers than to win a Pyrrhic victory in their absence. What one must guard against, however, is allowing a law-neutralizing group to dominate a conference. Where the law-neutralizing group is strong, a lot of work is needed to balance them with a plurality of law-abiding citizens who also enjoy the respect and trust of the offender (Mugford and Inkpen 1995). Ross (1996, p. 182) finds special virtue in the participation of healed victims and healed victimizers of sexual abuse who can cut through the (often shared) neutralizations that they had to cut through in confronting their own abuse:

> In Hollow Water, ex-offenders are not shunned forever, but seen as important resources for getting under the skin of other offenders and disturbing the webs of lies that have sustained them. Better than anyone, they understand the patterns, the pressures and the ways to hide. As they tell their personal stories in the circle, they talk about the lies that once protected them and how it felt to face the truth about the pain they caused. It is done gently but inflexibly, sending signals to offenders that their behaviour has roots that can be understood, but that there are no such things as excuses. (Ross 1996, p. 183)

Indeed, at Hollow Water, before they met their own victim in a healing circle, sexual abusers met other offenders and other offenders' victims, who would simply tell their stories as a stage in a process toward breaking down the tough-guy identity that pervaded the dominating relationship with their own victim. Note what an interesting strategy this is from a defiance theory perspective as well. Averting defiance is about getting offenders to put their caring identity rather than their defiant self in play.

I can summarize by suggesting that self-categorization theory might be read to make the following predictions about restorative justice:

1. Restorative justice prevents crime when (*a*) justice rituals are structured so that condemners are harder to condemn because they are members of an in-group, (*b*) if condemners are irrevocably members

of an outgroup, condemnation still influences intermediaries who are in-group members present at the conference (who can pass that influence on to the offender), (c) discussion of consequences reveals that denial is a coping strategy that blocks in-group acceptance, (d) justice rituals break down the segregation of law-abiding and law-neutralizing in-groups in circumstances where the law-abiding groups will (i) have more persuasive arguments to the extent that speech is undominated and (ii) be more dominant to the extent that speech is dominated.

2. Restorative justice will more often achieve conditions a–d than traditional trials because trial lawyers have a trained competence at exaggerating evil, condemning condemners, denying victim, denying injury, and denying responsibility, at blackening grey and whitening brown, in short in consolidating offenders and victims into opposed out-groups.

I. Crime Prevention Theory Predicts That Restorative Justice Practices Reduce Crime More than Existing Criminal Justice Practices

Lon Fuller (1964, p. 33) suggests that only two types of problems are suited to full judicial-legal process: yes-no questions such as "Did she do it?" and more-less questions such as "How much should be paid?" Polanyi (1951, pp. 174–84) distinguishes polycentric problems from these. They require reconciliation of complex interacting consequences of multidimensional phenomena. Polycentric problems are not well suited to the judicial model. Because most crime problems beyond the determination of guilt are polycentric, courts are rather ineffective at preventing crime.

In response to the recognition that courts cannot be expected to be competent at crime prevention, crime prevention has expanded as a largely police-facilitated alternative to expending criminal justice resources on dragging cases through the courts. From a restorative justice perspective, an uncoupling of crime prevention from case processing amounts to lost opportunity in two ways. First, every police officer knows that the best time to persuade a householder to invest in security is after a burglary; every business regulator knows the best time to persuade a company to invest in a corporate compliance system is after something goes wrong and someone gets into trouble. They also know that they do not have the resources to get around and persuade all households and all businesses to invest in security or compliance systems. Given that the police or the regulator must make contact with victims and offenders when an offense is cleared, it is a suboptimal use of resources not to seize that opportunity for crime prevention. Moreover, it brings finite crime-prevention resources to bear at the moment when motivation for implementing demanding preventive measures is at its peak and at its peak for good reason: one study has shown prospects of another burglary four times as high as in houses that had not been burgled before (Bridgeman and Hobbs 1997, p. 2). Hence, a project in Huddersfield that focused resources such as temporary alarms on prior victims reduced domestic burglary by 24 percent; in a Rockdale project by 72 percent (Bridgeman and Hobbs 1997, p. 3). Focusing crime prevention on existing cases of victimization (Pease 1998) also mainstreams crime prevention to where the resources are—street-level enforcement—rather than leaving crime prevention ghettoized in specialist areas. This of course is not to deny that there will always be circumstances where crime prevention is best deployed before any offense occurs.

Restorative justice resolves the tension between the incapacity of the court for polycentric problem-solving and the imperatives for mainstreaming crime prevention into case management. It also resolves the most fundamental tension between crime prevention theory and practice. The theory says "involve the community"; the practice says "citizens don't turn up to neighborhood watch meetings except in highly organized communities that don't need them." I don't go to neighborhood watch meetings, even though I think I should. But if the kid next door gets into trouble, if my secretary is a victim, and they ask me to attend to support them, I attend. I am touched by the invitation, that they have chosen me as one whose support they value in a time of stress.

Corruption and capture are worries with problem-oriented policing that leaves discretion totally with law enforcement agencies to decide the preventive measures required. This is especially true with business regulation—be it police regulating prostitution or drug markets or antitrust agencies regulating competition policy. Ayres and Braithwaite (1992, chap. 3) have shown game-theoretically and in terms of republican theory how transforming the crime prevention game from a bipartite game between state and business into a tripartite state-business-community game prevents corruption and capture. "Community" is the ingredient needed to prevent the crimes that arise from crime prevention; and restorative justice may deliver community to deliberative forums better than any strategy yet attempted. At the same time, abuse of police powers in mainstream processes of arrest is rendered accountable to community when a mother complains during a conference that the police used unnecessary force on her son. I have observed mothers do this in conferences (because they are polycentric) but not in court-rooms (because they are not).[10]

Crime prevention is a preeminently important area of criminal justice practice and evaluation research, but a theoretical backwater. In some respects this is a good thing because one should want prevention practitioners not to be theoretically committed, to be interpretively flexible, searching to read situations from the different angles illuminated by multiple theories. Plural understandings of a crime problem stimulate a disparate range of action possibilities that can be integrated into a hedged, mutually reinforcing package of preventive policies (Braithwaite 1993b). Plural understandings are best generated out of a dialogue between crime prevention professionals, such as police, and community members with disparate perspectives from their direct experience with the problem phenomenon.

In the discussion of the CML case in Section IV, a disparate array of preventive measures was discovered grounded in the different kinds of theories the rich plurality of players involved in this restorative justice process came up with—theories of education, deterrence, incapacitation, rehabilitation, target hardening, moral hazard, adverse publicity, law, regulation, and opportunity theory.

Restorative justice rituals can be a lever for triggering prevention of the most systemic and difficult-to-solve crimes in contemporary societies, like sexual abuse in families (Hollow Water), like the crimes of finance capital (CML). We should take seriously the possibility of family group conferences with leaders of Colombian cocaine cartels. How do we know they are beyond shame? How do we know that they would not like to retire at seventy instead of fear violent usurpation by a rival. Even common thieves retire because they find managing a criminal identity takes its toll: "You get tired. You get tired trying to be a tough guy all the time. People always expecting this and that" (Shover 1996, p. 137). How do we know that organized crime bosses might not find very attractive an agreement that allowed them to pass on some of their wealth to set up legitimate businesses for their children so they did not need to bequeath to them the life they had led (see Rensselaer

---

[10] There is another reason. Mothers do not complain in court against the police for the same reason their sons do not—because legal aid lawyers in Australia are fairly systematic in warning clients that complaining about the police is likely to backfire in a way that leads to a longer sentence.

1992)? How do we know that they do not actually hate killing other human beings in order to survive themselves? An incipient and only very partially successful model here is the Raskol gang surrenders and gang retreats in Papua New Guinea that have involved surrenders of up to four hundred alleged gang members (Dinnen 1996).

In summary, restorative justice can remove crime prevention from its marginal status in the criminal justice system, mainstreaming it into the enforcement process. It can deliver the motivation and widespread community participation crime prevention needs to work and to protect itself against corruption and capture by organized interests (including the crime prevention industry itself). It can sometimes deliver the political clout to crime prevention that it needs to tackle systemic problems systemically.

J. Restorative Justice Practices Deter Crime Better than Criminal Justice Practices Grounded in Deterrence Theory

Bentham would be disappointed at the current state of the evidence on how well deterrence works (Sherman et al. 1997). I do not review here the vast literature on the limited effectiveness of criminal punishments as deterrents. In another essay (Braithwaite 1997), I have reviewed some of the reasons why deterrence does not work as well as it ought. Deterrence is shown to fail as a policy not so much because it is irrelevant (though it is for many) but because the gains from contexts where it works are cancelled by the losses from contexts where it backfires.

Evidence surrounding Brehm and Brehm's (1981) theory of psychological reactance is particularly instructive. The theory of reactance asserts that intentions to control are reacted to as attempts to limit our freedom, which lead us to reassert that freedom by acting contrary to the direction of control. Reactance is found to be greatest for those who care most about the freedom. This insight motivates a fundamental reframing of deterrence theory. Because deterrence works well (without reactance) for people who care little about the freedom being regulated, what we need to do is search for such people who are in a position to prevent the crime.

In Braithwaite (1997) it is argued that for most crimes there are many actors with the power to prevent it. The victimization of a child by a fourth-grade bully can be prevented by the intervention of every child in the playground in grade five or above who observes it. This may be why whole-school approaches to bullying work, while peer mediation programs that target only the bully do not (see Sec. VII*B*). The sanctioning that counts is not that directed at the bully, but the softer sanctions of disapproval directed at those who fail to intervene to prevent bullying before it gets out of hand.[11]

When Canberra drunk-driving conferences work best, loved ones, drinking mates, and friends from work become key players in suggesting preventive agreements that draw on the capacity of many hands to prevent. Drinking mates may sign a designated driver agreement. Bar staff at the drinker's pub may undertake to call a taxi when the offender has had too much and make him take it. Uncle Harry may undertake to ensure that the car is always left in the garage on Friday and Saturday nights. Even with an offense as seemingly solitary as drunk driving, often there are many with preventive capabilities who can be rendered responsible for mobilizing those capabilities through a restorative justice dialogue. While reactance may be strong with the young male drink-driver who is a "petrol head," proud of his capacity to hold his drink, there may be no reactance from any of the other targets at a restorative justice conference. Indeed, when there is a collective reaction of nonreactance, we observe this to calm the anger of a young offender. Common garden varieties of juvenile crime are even more collective, proffering more soft targets, than drunk driving (Zimring 1981).

Again, it was my empirical work with Fisse on corporate crime that led to the conclusion that the way to deter crime was not to seek to deter the criminal who benefits most from the crime, but to look for a softer target who has preventive capabilities. The paradigm-transforming moment in our praxis with this insight was the Solomons Carpet case (Fisse and Braithwaite 1993). Solomons had committed a false advertising offense. There were problems of proof and the penalty likely to be imposed by the courts was light. At the Trade Practices Commission we conferenced it without success. Involving even the CEO in successive conferences did not work; he was a hard target for deterrence, calling our bluff to take the case to court. In a final attempt, when we involved Mr. Solomon, the chairman of the board, he turned out to be a soft target who was ashamed that his company was flouting its legal obligations. He sacked the CEO and put in place a

---

[11] It is common for other children to be involved in "holding" the victim for the bully or preventing him from getting away (Rigby 1996, p. 151). Victims themselves have preventive capacities that research evidence shows can be developed to protect them from bullying (Rigby 1996, p. 226).

remarkable program of compensation for consumers and industry-wide preventive (self-regulatory) measures. So we learned that a good regulatory strategy was to conference, conference again, and conference again with ever wider circles of executives with preventive capabilities until we found the soft target. Move up the organization until we found the soft target who could be moved by reason or deterred by fear of a personal sense of shame.

We have applied this strategy in nursing-home regulation as well. Dialogue proceeds for about an hour among the stakeholders at the end of an inspection on the positive things that have been accomplished, what the problems are, and who will take responsibility for what needs to be done. In this process, most participants turn out to be soft targets, wanting to put their responsible self forward, volunteering action plans to put right what has been found wrong. This is why it succeeds in improving compliance with the law (Braithwaite et al. 1993).

At the same time, it is clear from our data that there are cases where dialogic regulation fails—where the hardest of targets are in charge, dominating, and intimidating softer targets who work under them. Empirical experience gives good reasons for assuming that even the worst of corporate malefactors has a public-regarding self that can be appealed to, a self-categorization as "responsible businessman," for example (Ayres and Braithwaite 1992). However, when trust is tried and found to be misplaced, there is a need to escalate to deterrence as a regulatory strategy. When deterrence fails—because of reactance, or simply because noncompliance is caused by managerial incompetence rather than rational calculation of costs and benefits—then there is a need to move higher up an enforcement pyramid to an incapacitative strategy. Incapacitation can mean withdrawing or suspending a license for a nursing home that has proved impregnable to both persuasion and deterrence.

Hence, there are increasingly solid empirical grounds for suspecting that we can often reduce crime by replacing narrow, formal, and strongly punitive responsibility with broad, informal, weak sanctions—by making the many dialogically responsible instead of the few criminally responsible. By dialogically responsible I mean responsible for participating in a dialogue, listening, being open to accountability for failings and to suggestions for remedying those failings. The theory I have advanced (Braithwaite 1997) is that this is more likely when there are many actors with causative or preventative capability with respect to that abuse. Where we can engage all of those actors in moral reasoning and problem-solving dialogue, the more of them there are, the more likely one or more will be a soft target. When just one player with causative responsibility or with a powerful preventative capability turns, empirical experience shows that many other actors who had hitherto been ruthlessly exploitative suddenly find a public-regarding self that becomes surprisingly engaged with a constructive process of righting the wrong.

The implication of the analysis in this section of the essay is that punishing crooks is a less efficient deterrence strategy than opening up discussion with a wide range of actors with preventive capabilities, some of whom might be motivated by a raised eyebrow to change their behavior in ways that prevent reoffending. It is to keep expanding the number of players involved in a restorative justice process until we find someone who surprises us by being influenced through the dialogue to mobilize some unforeseen preventive capability. The hypothesis is that creative restorative processes have enormous potential to surprise us as Mr. Solomon did. You do not give up after a first conference because no one turns up who can deliver that surprise. You keep convening new conferences with new carers, new stakeholders, new resource people until someone walks through the door who can pull one of the levers to prevent a criminality that is almost always "overdetermined" (Lewis 1986). Again, restorative justice rewards the patient.

Parker, in commenting on a draft of this essay, pointed out that I think this because of my view (some would say naive view) of human beings as social beings that are almost always enmeshed in multiple communities: "The Braithwaite argument is that there almost always are many with that capacity [to prevent] because we all live in a community wherein many individuals can pull strings of informal control and evoke bonds of responsibility" (see also Parker 1999a). The argument draws sustenance from empirical findings such as those of Pennell and Burford (1996, p. 218) in their Canadian study of family violence conferences: the conferences "generated a sense of shame across the extended family for not having acted in the past to safeguard its relatives as well as a sense of shared identity because often the problems which their relatives experienced were common in their own lives."

It also draws sustenance from that other Canadian experience at Hollow Water. How can we understand the accomplishment of no fewer than forty-eight child abusers brought to justice in such a small

Canadian community? Without the restorative process, could we have expected Western punitive justice to have convicted even three or four, or any? Probably not. It was the restorative process that flushed out those with knowledge of the evil. The fact is that for any kind of crime, communities know about and are concerned about countless crimes of which the police are ignorant. Karstedt-Henke and Crasmoller (1991) showed in Germany that for every juvenile crime the police detect, parents detect at least four, teachers detect about two, and peers detect more than five. Given the stronger evidence for an effect of certainty of punishment on crime than an effect of severity of punishment (Braithwaite 1997, n. 47), "soft" restorative justice for forty might just accomplish more general deterrence than tough incarcerative justice for four.

With respect to knowledge, restorative justice is a virtuous circle, retributive justice a vicious circle. When the community knows about many crimes and reacts to them restoratively, the benefits of restoration motivate others to speak up, increasing community knowledge of crimes they will want to do something about. When the police know about few crimes and respond punitively, the collateral costs of punishment silence citizens into minding their own business, reducing reporting of crime. Again, in a world where certainty of sanctions matters more than severity of sanction and where informal sanctions deter more than formal ones, the corollary is that virtuous circles of restorative justice deter more than vicious circles of punitive justice.

So the process implication of our analysis is dialogic regulation of social life of the sort we get in a family group conference or a restorative exit conference such as we see with nursing home or nuclear safety (Rees 1994) inspection. There is a structural implication as well, which is developed in Braithwaite (1997): more robust separations of powers within and between the private and public sectors. The number of third-party enforcement targets is greater to the extent that we have richer, more plural, separations of power in a polity.

Dialogue among a wider range of citizens beyond the offender himself means that ripples of general deterrence spread out more widely. When many different types of subcriminal responsibility are known to be at risk of exposure to people we care about in restorative justice conferences, we are all deterred in our many roles. This is why Australian nursing home regulation has worked reasonably well. Whether we are the responsible nurse, the aide, the chaplain, the gardener, or the man who visits the lady in the next bed, if no one raises the alarm about a resident who is being abused, we know that our inaction might be disapproved in a conference. Restorative justice in other words is not just about specific deterrence of the offender: it also widens the scope of general deterrence (albeit a more benign general deterrence).

The benign nature of this general deterrence will be seen by most critics as the greatest weakness of restorative justice. The crunch is that restorative justice sets free many whom deterrence or desert theories say should go to jail—like the insurance executives from CML. While it is clear that offenders and others who attend restorative justice processes do not view them as a soft option but rather as a difficult and demanding experience (Umbreit and Coates 1992; Sherman and Strang 1997c; Schiff 1998), of course the agreements reached are softer than prison.

A final qualification about general deterrence arises from the assumption that restorative justice will often fail and fail again and again until deterrent justice must be tried in an attempt to protect the community. Since, for the reasons outlined in Braithwaite (1997), deterrence will also often fail, we will sometimes need to escalate our response to incapacitation. Figure 1 represents this articulation of restorative justice to deterrence and incapacitation. The idea of the pyramid, which is justified in detail in Ayres and Braithwaite (1992, chap. 2), is that we start with the restorative strategy at the base of the

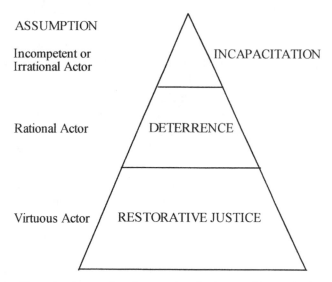

ASSUMPTION

Incompetent or
Irrational Actor   INCAPACITATION

Rational Actor   DETERRENCE

Virtuous Actor   RESTORATIVE JUSTICE

Fɪɢ. 1.—Toward an integration of restorative, deterrent, and incapacitative justice pyramid. The possibility of escalation channels regulatory activity down to the base of the pyramid. This model transcends the limitations of passive deterrence in criminology by learning from the shift to active from passive deterrence in international relations theory. With passive deterrence, one simply calculates the probability of compliance on the basis of the expected size and risk of punishment. Active deterrence, in contrast, is dynamic, open to escalating threats in response to moves by the other player, as well as to graduated reduction in tension strategies.

The pyramid dynamically meets the challenge that unless the threat of punishment lingers in the background, there will be a class of ruthless criminals who will exploit the opportunity of restorative justice with a deceitful pretence of cooperation. Where restorative justice for a first or second offense is backed up by a passive deterrent tariff for a third, the rational actor will cheat for one or two free throws. If enforcement is the product of restorative justice negotiation, Langbein and Kerwin (1985) show game-theoretically that rational actors will avoid immediate compliance. Langbein and Kerwin's model is only true, however, if deceit, holding back on compliance, does not cause an escalation of penalties. In practice it does; deterrence is active rather than passive, which is why Langbein and Kerwin's prediction is false as a description of most regulatory activity (see, e.g., Bardach and Kagan 1982; Braithwaite 1985).

The reality of active deterrence as a strategy that works, at least in the business regulatory domain, where it has been more systematically studied and theorized than with common crime, commends Fisse's (1983) suggestion of giving it a jurisprudentially principled foundation through implementing "reactive fault" as the core criterion of criminal fault. In its most radical version, this would mean in a case of assault, the alleged assailant would go into a circle not on the basis of an admission of criminal guilt, but on the basis of admitting responsibility for the *actus reus* of an assault ("I was the one who punched her"). Functionally, New Zealand law already accomplishes this result by putting cases into family group conferences not on the basis of an admission of criminal guilt, but on the basis of formally "declining to deny" criminal allegations. Whether the mental element required for crime was present would be decided reactively, on the basis of the constructiveness and restorativeness of his reaction to the problem caused by his act (Braithwaite 1998*b*). If the reaction were restorative, the risk of criminal liability would be removed; only civil liability would remain. However, if reactive criminal fault were found by a court to be present, that would be insufficient for a conviction; the mental element for the crime would also have to be demonstrated before or during its commission.[12] But it would be the reactive fault that would be the more important determinant of penalty than the concurrent fault. In practice, criminal justice systems vary enormously in the reactiveness versus proactiveness of their criminal law in action: Japan being unusually strong on reactive fault, the United States on proactive or causal fault (Haley 1996; Braithwaite 1998b). According to this analysis, this helps Japan enjoy lower crime rates than the United States in a way that has a profound jurisprudential justification.

Encouraging findings on deterrence are emerging as the surprising positive result of the RISE experiment on restorative conferencing in Canberra. Preliminary data reveal a modest "Sword of Damocles" effect, something actually revealed in previous criminological research (Sherman 1992). For example, Dunford's (1990) study suggests that a warrant for arrest may deter domestic violence better than either actual arrest or nonarrest. To date, offenders randomly assigned to conferences in Canberra are coming out somewhat more fearful that they will be rearrested if they offend again, more fearful of family and friends finding out about rearrest, more fearful of a future conference, more fearful of at least one other consequence of a court case than those assigned to court (Sherman and Strang 1997b; Sherman et al. 1998). In this variety of ways, conferences may sharpen our perceptions of how bad the punitive consequences would be if we were caught again. This is a somewhat unusual result because what much criminological research shows is that actual experience of the justice system reduces its terrors. For example, tax audits can have counterproductive effects by teaching many of those who are audited that they can cheat on their tax without going to jail and teaching them "how to avoid being caught when they evade taxes" (Kinsey 1986, p. 416).

What the preliminary RISE data suggest is that changes at the margin to send increasing numbers of offenders to conferences may simultaneously increase the deterrent power of both conferences and court. From the deterrence perspective against which I am measuring restorative justice in this section, this is good news. The problem is that if deterrent threats cause defiance and reactance, restorative justice may

[12] Brent Fisse takes the more radical view that if criminal liability is about punishing conduct known to be harmful and if failure to respond responsibly is harmful, then such reactive fault can be sufficient to establish criminal liability.

be compromised by what sits above it in a dynamic pyramidal strategy of deterrence and incapacitation. For Ayres and Braithwaite (1992), this is the greatest challenge facing responsive regulatory institutions. The challenge is to have the Sword of Damocles always threatening in the background but never threatened in the foreground. The criminal justice system must have an image of invincibility at the same time as it has an image of mercy and forgiveness. Police have a lot to learn here from the wisdom of business regulatory inspectors, such as Hawkins's British pollution inspectors: "Negotiating tactics are organized to display the enforcement process as inexorable, as an unremitting progress, in the absence of compliance, towards an unpleasant end" (Hawkins 1984, p. 153). Here is a New York nursing home inspector's account of how their surprisingly restorative regulatory system keeps cooperation in the foreground while coercion looms in the background:

> You can maintain the same demeanor when confronted with tension and stress, when the facility gets aggressive and unpleasant [in one case this involved putting a gun on the table]. You can be friendly if they don't correct. You just pass it on. You never have to be anything but assured and friendly. The enforcement system will take on the battle . . . The team leader just tells them [the nursing home] what the repercussions are if you don't correct. You just let the system take over. That's all you have to do. A good team leader is confident, friendly, and explains consequences. She never uses a standover approach. (Braithwaite 1994, p. 30)

Part of the trick of deterrence that is always threatening but never threatened (Ayres and Braithwaite 1992, pp. 44–53) is to enculturate trust in regulatory interactions (Braithwaite and Makkai 1994), while institutionalizing distrust through an enforcement system (Braithwaite 1998a). It is to surprise the very worst of people by treating them as trustworthy; because if we can persuade them to put their best self forward (in the presence of people whose respect they crave) we will regularly be surprised to find that the most socially responsible of their many selves is restorative. Restorative justice is not about picking good apples for reconciliation and bad apples for deterrence; it is about treating everyone as a good apple as the preferred first approach.

This implies that to be effective restorative justice requires considerable nuance in administration, yet a nuance most human beings have at their disposal. Just as they know from experience with life that it is better to discuss consequences, allowing the offenders to discover their own shame, than to say "shame on you," they also know that direct threat engenders defiance in a way an image of invincibility does not. The prediction here, that will be tested in the RISE experiment, is that conferences will fail if they are either "shaming machines" (Retzinger and Scheff 1996) or threat machines. The widespread understanding of this wisdom in the community is reflected in the fact that the majority of parents of children in societies such as the United States succeed in raising nondelinquent children because they do have an "authoritative" rather than an "authoritarian" parenting style (Baumrind 1973, 1978). Durkheim (1961, p. 10) understood it as well when he said: "Punishment does not give discipline its authority, but it prevents discipline from losing its authority."

K. Restorative Justice Practices Incapacitate Crime Better than Criminal Justice Practices Grounded in the Theory of Selective Incapacitation

Incapacitation means removing an offender's capacity to reoffend; there are many ways to do this beyond incarceration, execution, and cutting off the hands of pickpockets. A useful feature of restorative justice is that it empowers communities of care to be creative about how to incapacitate. The empirical evidence on selective incapacitation in criminology is almost exclusively limited to a consideration of selecting the most dangerous criminals for incarceration. That evidence suggests that we are not very good at getting the selection right (Gottfredson and Gottfredson 1994; MacKenzie 1997, p. 9). Failures to incapacitate those who commit serious further offenses tend to be well publicized. Less well publicized is the likely more serious problem of false positives whose criminal career might have ended had we not thrust them into daily interaction with criminals in a prison where they learn new skills in the illegitimate labor market or suffer demeaning experiences that engender defiance, shame, and rage.

Through using incarceration much more selectively, restorative justice should be able to avert a lot of damage that makes our crime problems worse. That is mere speculation, however, as there is no empirical evidence to support such a hope. At the same time, the pyramidal theory of restorative justice outlined in the last section means that there is a willingness to resort to incapacitation when both restorative justice and deterrence repeatedly fail to protect the community from a serious risk.

However, imprisonment is not the principal method of incapacitation to which restorative justice would want to resort. Again there is much that criminology can learn from business regulation here. When a company continually creates a serious risk to the community, a common alternative to putting the company in jail is to put the jailer into the company. An example was the "resident inspector" program run by the Mine Safety and Health Administration in the United States for repeat offending high-accident mines. The presence of the inspector in these mines stopped certain unsafe practices from being contemplated, substantially reducing deaths and injuries to well below the national average in mines that had been the least safe in the country (Braithwaite 1985, p. 83). Similar resident inspector programs have been applied in the nuclear industry, the nursing home industry, and more recently in relation to the environmental compliance problems of Consolidated Edison in New York. Braithwaite and Daly (1994, p. 200) have outlined how successive restorative justice conferences might escalate incapacitative response for domestic violence: for example, there could be escalation from weekly reporting by all family members of any violent incidents to the man's aunt or brother-in-law (conference 1), to a relative or other supporter of the woman moving into the household (conference 2), to the man moving to a friend's household (conference 3).

That essay also makes much of flipping the incapacitation target—incapacitating the male offender by assuring the female victim of the resources and guaranteed shelter to walk out, leaving the offender alone in a house without a victim and therefore without a capacity to victimize.

In cases such as the Aboriginal insurance scandals discussed earlier, agents who make fraudulent claims can be incapacitated by licensing schemes that deny them a license for this kind of work. Doctors, lawyers, and company directors can be delicensed through either positive or negative licensing schemes.

Drunk drivers can also be deprived of a license to drive, a form of incapacitation that works badly in Australia, where drunks driving without licenses is pandemic. More social and less legal assurances of incapacitation may sometimes have more promise and restorative justice conferences can deliver these. Drinking mates can sign undertakings that they will prevent him from driving after drinking and will make him comply with a designated driver agreement. Uncle Harry can incapacitate him from drinking and driving on Friday and Saturday nights when he goes out with the boys by taking ownership of the car and its keys on those nights. Such incapacitation can be escalated by a conference in response to noncompliance by agreement up front that the consequence of failure to hand over the car at these times is that Uncle Harry will take permanent possession of the car for a year.

The theory of restorative justice here is that Uncle Harrys have a more plural range of incapacitative keys they can turn than a prison guard who can turn just one key. Uncle Harry can respond dynamically when his incapacitative ideas backfire. But they are less likely to backfire when the offender voluntarily commits to them. As we have seen, unenforceable restorative justice agreements enjoy higher compliance than enforceable court agreements (see Sec. VIIA). Beyond the greater commitment we all have to undertakings we choose ourselves, the further reasons for superior compliance are that the Uncle Harrys of this world come up with ideas more attuned to the reality of the offender's circumstances than can a judge, and are better monitors of their implementation than police officers because one Uncle Harry might have more contacts with the offender in a month than all the police in the city during a year. Intimates, in short, can incapacitate more intensively, more creatively, more sensitively, more consensually, and in a more dynamically responsive way than the criminal justice system. At this stage, the Optimistic Account of Incapacitation lacks systematic support, but does map a promising new research agenda for the possibilities of restorative justice.

L. Restorative Justice Practices Rehabilitate Crime Better than Criminal Justice Practices Grounded in the Welfare Model

In Section VIIB I showed that there is some evidence that, while limited, all suggests that restorative justice processes may prevent reoffending better than traditional criminal justice processing. The qualitative literature on restorative justice is certainly littered with case studies of offenders who have been rehabilitated as a result of the deliberation at conferences.

What is clear from the criminological literature is that when rehabilitation of criminal behavior does occur, it is at the hands of families more than any other institution. Obversely, family dysfunction correlates as consistently with delinquency as any variable. Hence, the Maori critiques of the Western justice system that led to the restorative justice reforms of 1989 have a strong empirical foundation: Western justice weakens families because it takes away their responsibility for dealing with crime and preventing recurrence. Weaken family responsibility, especially for cultures with deeply embedded traditions of family responsibility, and you destroy the fabric of crime control (Hassall 1996). Some Australian Aboriginal peoples articulate a similar critique—in a culture where the father of an adolescent's future wife has the primary role in social control, a justice system that wrenches young offenders away from any influence by that person or other relevant elders will destroy, has destroyed, the basis for social control.

One reason why restorative justice ought to do better at rehabilitation than rehabilitative justice is that it does not have rehabilitation as its aim. Rehabilitation is like spontaneity as an objective: when you try to be spontaneous you are not very spontaneous. When the criminal justice system is seen as setting out to change people, even by offering rewards, that engenders reactance, though reactance to reward does not seem as great as to punishment (Brehm and Brehm 1981, p. 229).

The practical focus on the consequences of the crime and the needs this creates for victims and the community, more act focused and less focused on the offender as a person, more victim focused and less offender focused, means that the process is less stigmatizing and more dignified for the offender. It is hard for the communication of disapproval to be respectful when the focus is on the twisted psyche of the offender or his defective conscience. By definition, stigmatic labeling is not averted when words such as sociopath are bandied around with the family.

However good the diagnosis, however good the rehabilitation program it commends, the very fact that it comes out of a program designed to deliver a diagnosis and a treatment renders the process stigmatic. This means that the crime-reduction effects of the rehabilitative program have to be very strong before they can outweigh the crime-instigating effects of the stigmatization. Any program where social workers, psychologists, or psychiatrists come in to do things to or for people risks stigmatization by the very fact of professionalized doing or helping. Retributivist critics of rehabilitation are right when they say rehabilitation strips the offender of dignity in this way (Murphy and Hampton 1989); they are wrong to suggest that punishment confers dignity; a space that gives the offender an opportunity to choose to put things right is what restores dignity. It is such a choice to put things right that most nurtures a continuing commitment to keep things right, that nurtures rehabilitation.

Of course offenders are often desperately in need of a drug rehabilitation program, face-to-face counseling, job training, remedial education, all manner of rehabilitative programs. If that need is desperate, citizens should speak up for the need in a restorative justice program and the offenders should see committing to it as part of putting things right. This empowerment of the offender, together with their community of care, to choose from rehabilitative programs offered by health and welfare professionals in the state, private, and voluntary sectors is different from state monopolies of social work and health care provision in the traditional welfare model.

I must confess to seeing these as empty ideals in all the restorative justice programs of which I have experience. I have seen many drunk-driving conferences where the offender is a tottering alcoholic, but where no one in the community of care raises the need for a drug treatment program, sometimes because most supporters are also excessive drinkers. In New Zealand, the rhetoric of citizens being empowered to choose rehabilitation programs without having them forced down their throat by the state is impressive; yet this occurs in a context where the retrenchment of the once exemplary New Zealand welfare state by successive conservative governments means there are no programs left to choose (cf. Maxwell and Morris 1996). Australia is almost as bad in this respect.

It therefore seems highly doubtful that restorative justice conferences are having major rehabilitative effects at this time. They may, however, be averting some of the disempowerment of traditional "corrections," the stigmatization of rehabilitation oriented to changing pathology. Two of the things we know from the vast literature on the effectiveness of programs for the rehabilitation of criminals are that voluntarily chosen programs outperform enforced rehabilitation, and that programs that strengthen community support for the offender outperform those that wrench offenders out of communities of care into the hands of professionals who offer individual treatment (Cullen 1994). In sum, what should make restorative justice more effective at rehabilitation than rehabilitative justice has historically been are its empowering, communitarian, dignifying, and victim-centered characteristics. Delivering on this potential is unlikely to be demonstrated at the moment when the welfare state is being dismantled, even as it requires the dismantling of welfarist justice monopolized by state correctional professionals.

M. Restorative Justice Practices Are More Cost Effective than Criminal
   Justice Practices Grounded in the Economic Analysis of Crime

The economic analysis of law (e.g., Posner 1977) provides a more theoretically sophisticated, though transparently false explanatory structure than the other utilitarian analyses in deterrence, rehabilitation, and incapacitation theory. It makes false predictions because it is myopic. Its models assume that rational choosing of costs and benefits provides a total explanation of compliance when emotions and twisted cognition's play havoc with the reality (see Braithwaite 1997). Makkai and Braithwaite (1993*b*) found that actual costs of compliance with nursing home laws explained only 19 percent of the variance in the subjectively expected costs that should inform rational choices. While there is a powerful effect of expected cost of compliance on compliance, this is not a monotonically increasing effect. There is a turning point in the relationship explained by the behavior of "disengagers." Their behavior is not to be understood in terms of rational game-playing but in terms of dropping out of the enforcement game. Regulatory disengagers, rather like many heroin addicts, are in the regulatory system but not of it and certainly not economically calculative about it.

All this means that the underspecification in economic analyses of law is of a fatal sort. It is not that the models are basically right and can be improved by tinkering that includes more of the excluded variables. When a variable like reactance can reverse the direction of a deterrence coefficient, when disengagers come into play in a way that turns an increasing relationship into a decreasing one, advice on the optimal level of deterrence will be not only wrong, but very wrong. Moreover, these influences mean it will be wrong in a way that assumes increasing deterrence will deliver more economic benefits than it ever in fact does (to the extent that defiance and disengagement neutralize or reverse deterrence). Finally, even if an empirically correct economic analysis of the optimal level of penalties were discovered, its implementation would lead us into a deterrence trap that would create economic chaos in respect of some of our most serious crimes (Braithwaite 1997). For example, if the probability of detection for insider trading is one in a hundred and the expected returns are a million dollars, fines for insider trading will have to exceed $100 million to deter the average insider trader, and be much higher to deter the biggest sharks. Coffee's (1981) deterrence trap is that fines of this magnitude will cause bankruptcies, punishing innocent workers who are retrenched.

It is difficult therefore to imagine the construction of a purely economic model of crime that will not set deterrence at a counterproductively high level. The responsive theory of regulatory deterrence in Ayres and Braithwaite (1992) certainly draws heavily on economic analysis, but it uses the economic analysis as an element in the design of a dynamic model that moves from restorative justice when experience proves it a failure and then moves from deterrent justice when experience proves that a failure. That is, there should be no reliance on a statically optimal level of deterrence. We do not want to rely on that because, for the reasons adduced, it will always be wrong.

A dynamic model based on a regulatory pyramid where restorative justice is privileged at the base of the pyramid is more likely to get it right, albeit clumsily. It iterates through one failed strategy after another until contextual deliberation declares one effective. It should also be cheaper because it averts maximally expensive options like imprisonment and courts staffed by highly paid judges, prosecutors, and other professionals as it privileges the efforts of volunteers from the citizenry.

Systematic evidence on the costs of restorative justice compared to punitive justice is scarce, though Peter Reuter has a study underway as his contribution to the RISE experiment in Canberra. Claims are regularly made about multimillion dollar savings in New Zealand, particularly as a result of closure of juvenile institutions. While the number of residential places has dropped by almost two-thirds since 1989 (Maxwell and Morris 1996), this seems plausible, but no published studies exist of the magnitude of the claimed savings. It certainly is true that nations such as Germany, Austria, New Zealand, and China, which are vigorously committed to restorative programs for juveniles, pay for extremely modest numbers of institutional beds per capita compared to nations like the United States, the United Kingdom, and Australia. However, to be maximally effective in the terms of the last subsection, restorative justice requires a more credible investment in the welfare state and this does not come cheap. Of course, the benefits of a decent welfare state should not be measured primarily in terms of crime prevention.

The most thorough study is of Scottish mediation of disputes largely among neighbors, family, and friends (Knapp and Netten in Warner 1992, pp. 105–37). Theoretically, these were supposed to be cases that otherwise would have been prosecuted. In the comparison group, nineteen of the forty-four cases were not prosecuted. Across the two programs, when prosecutions did occur, the average prosecution case costs were just over £200, compared with about £300 for mediation and reparation cases, leading Knapp and Netten to conclude that for comparatively simple matters that would not lead to either a not guilty plea or imprisonment, mediation and reparation was rather more expensive than prosecution.

N. Restorative Justice Practices Secure Justice Better than Criminal Justice Practices Grounded in "Justice" or "Just Deserts" Theories

> Allowing offenders to buy their way out of prison with monetary and nonmonetary compensation to victims unacceptably confounds the private goals of mediation and the public goals of criminal law (Brown 1994, p. 1253).

For "just deserts" theorists, it is unjust that offenders get unequal treatment depending on whether they have a merciful or a punitive victim, a poor one who needs compensation or a rich one who does not, a victim who will cooperate in the diversion from court or one who will not. Some restorative justice advocates turn this around by saying that it is morally wrong to privilege equality of treatment for offenders over "equality of justice [which] means equal treatment of victims" (Barnett 1981, p. 259). Or equal justice might mean equality of opportunity for victims with known offenders to pursue the forms of restoration most important to them in the way of their choosing (see generally Roach 1999). Because equality for victims and equality for offenders are utterly irreconcilable, the more practical justice agenda is to guarantee victims a minimum level of care and to guarantee offenders against punishment beyond a maximum limit. The normative theory of restorative justice illuminates a practical path to those guarantees.

The fundamental problem restorative justice advocates have with the justice model has been most eloquently captured by Martin Wright (1992, p. 525): "Balancing the harm done by the offender with further harm inflicted on the offender only adds to the total amount of harm in the world." As with previous sections of this essay, the analysis of the justice of restorative justice compared with the so-called justice or just deserts model is influenced by a consideration of white-collar crime that is so often lacking in the work of desert theorists.

There is now, as we have seen, a good deal of evidence that citizens are more likely to feel that restorative processes are just and respect their rights after they have experienced them than are citizens who have experienced the justice of courts (see Subsecs. *A–C* above). Desert theorists have to respond to this by saying that citizens in a democracy do not understand what justice entails, do not understand what their own interests in justice should cause them to want. While this response may be largely false, given the worries we ought properly to have about tyrannies of the majority, we must recognize it can sometimes be true. The systematic evidence we have from judicial oversight of New Zealand conferences is not consistent with any widespread tyranny of the majority. Maxwell and Morris (1993) report that 81 percent of family group conference plans were approved without modification by courts, with the overwhelming majority of changes (in 17 percent of cases) being to make orders at a higher level rather than at a lower level (a lower level being what one would expect to see if there were a tyranny of the majority to be checked). Almost identical results have been obtained in the Restorative Resolutions project for adult offenders in Manitoba (83 percent judicial ratification of plans, with five times as much modification by addition of requirements as modification by deletion) (Bonta, Rooney, and Wallace-Capretta 1998, p. 16).

There is no consensus within the social movement for restorative justice on what should count as unjust outcomes. Most advocates want it to be a more modest philosophy than to aspire to settle this question. Rather, restorative justice should settle for the procedural requirement that the parties talk until they feel that harmony has been restored on the basis of a discussion of all the injustices they see as relevant to the case. Within that dialogue about justice, Braithwaite and Pettit (1990) and Braithwaite and Parker (1999) have made the case for a republican conception of justice. Most restorative justice advocates do not know or care what is involved in a republican rationale for restorative justice, let alone subscribe to it. The most popular philosophical foundations among advocates for the justice of restorative justice are spiritual (e.g., Van Ness 1986). Yet civic republicanism is one secular philosophical foundation that has a critique of the just deserts model enjoying some support among restorative justice theorists. One of the virtues of republican theory is that its justification of restorative justice does not depend on all those involved in restorative justice processes subscribing to a republican conception of justice, in the way that just deserts does depend on a consistent commitment of judges and juries to the conception of justice in its justice model.

In considering the Pessimistic Account of restorative justice, Section VIII of this essay assesses a number of concerns about the injustice of restorative justice, both procedurally and in terms of outcomes. I conclude that the propositions of the Pessimistic Account about the injustices of restorative justice are true insofar as we can judge from the current state of the evidence. The truth of that critique, I want to contend, is consistent with the conclusion in this section that restorative justice is more just than just deserts.

Following Campbell (1988, pp. 3–4), Parker (1999*b*, pp. 45–47) makes a Rawlsian distinction between the concept and the conception of justice in her republic of justice. Parker's concept of justice is: "Those arrangements by which people can (successfully) make claims against individuals and institutions in order to advance shared ideals of social and political life" (Parker 1999, p. 46). A concept of justice thus conceived as means, formal and informal, by which people seek to secure social and individual relations they think are right will yield different views (conceptions) of rightness. Parker's (1999) republican conception of substantive justice is of freedom as nondomination (following Skinner 1984; Pettit 1993, 1997). The just society then institutionalizes processes of disputing that will maximize freedom as nondomination. So Parker (1999, p. 49) integrates concept and conception in a definition of justice that I will adapt only slightly here: Justice is "that set of arrangements that allow people to make claims against other individuals and institutions in order to secure freedom against the possibility of domination."

Freedom as nondomination is the same republican conception of freedom as a citizenship status that Braithwaite and Pettit (1990) called dominion. Freedom as nondomination is contrasted with freedom as noninterference, which is at the core of the liberal tradition. Republicans from Rome to Montesquieu, Madison, and Jefferson wanted more than liberty in the impoverished individualistic sense favored by the liberals who came to dominate Western political discourse through the nineteenth century. Resilient liberty required community assurance against domination through the guarantees of a rule of law, a separation of powers, uncoerced deliberation in governance, welfare policies that guarantee protection from the dominations of poverty, and norms of civic virtue. It required liberty, equality, and fraternity/sorority.

Braithwaite and Pettit (1990) have sought to rework what they consider all the key normative questions in the criminal justice system in accordance with the maximization of freedom as nondomination. They also compare a full retributivist position with a full republican position and conclude that a full just-deserts policy would increase injustice while a republican policy would reduce it. This results from certain facts about complex modern societies. These are mostly facts about the distribution of power, which prevent punishment from being imposed on those most deserving of it. A policy of attempting punishment of all those who deserve it (and who can be caught) has the effect of increasing injustice, worsening tendencies to punish most where desert is least. This is because of a tendency for the law to be "the most powerful where the least needed, a sprinkler system that turns off when the fire gets too hot" (Geertz 1983, p. 217).

Braithwaite and Pettit (1990, chap. 9) argue that a number of bureaucratic realities about criminal justice systems conduce to the theorem that where desert is greatest, punishment will be least. One is the problem of system capacity (Nagin 1978; Pontell 1978). Braithwaite and Pettit rely on this literature to show that those locations in time and space where crime is greatest, and those types of crime where offending is most widespread and serious, are precisely where the criminal justice system resorts to leniency in order to keep cases flowing and avert system overload. But bureaucratic pressures are not the main reason for the truth of the theorem. Structural realities of power are more important. Braithwaite and Pettit (1990) argue that in the terms of just deserts theory, there are more white-collar criminals deserving severe punishment in any society than blue-collar criminals deserving severe punishment. Attempts to give deserved punishment to all who are guilty, however, successfully impose desert on blue-collar offenders while being systematically unsuccessful with white-collar offenders.

The white-collar crime enforcement system in every country operates on comparatively restorative principles. Braithwaite and Pettit (1990) argue this is sociologically inevitable as well as desirable. Retributive corporate crime prevention would fail because of deterrence traps, formidable defiance, and the superior capacity of the powerful to deploy rational countermeasures against deterrence—like the appointment of "vice presidents responsible for going to jail" (Braithwaite 1984). The best path to equal justice for equal wrongs is therefore to move blue-collar criminal enforcement down the same restorative path that white-collar enforcement has long followed.

The injustice of the justice model arises from its reactive quality in a world where equal reactions produce unequal results. Parker (1999) works through the proactive reforms required for republican access to justice. She suggests, for example, that all organizations above a certain size have access to justice plans that, through consultation with stakeholders, identify the various types of injustices (to consumers, workers, minorities, creditors, and so on) that are common consequences of its activities; set up restorative justice fora to correct these injustices when they arise; and deploy preventive law measures to ensure compliance with the law and remove blockages to access to justice. Performance indicators would be required under these plans to demonstrate improved access to justice this year compared to last year (continuous improvement). The results of independent audits against these performance indicators would be made public. Responsively regulated access to restorative justice plans in the large organization sector then frees up more finite legal aid resources for injustices inflicted in small organizations like families and by individuals.

Parker's imagined world of access to restorative justice is one where most victims of the most serious crimes (organizational crimes) that currently get no justice are given access to corporate restorative justice. It is a world of profoundly greater justice than the "justice" model imagines. Of course justice imagined is not justice accomplished. It can be said, however, that the justice model skew of our present system, a skew toward just deserts for the poor and impunity for the powerful, accomplishes profound injustice. Moves in the direction of restorative justice for poor offenders and restorative justice for more victims of corporate offenders are the practical moves toward an amelioration of that injustice.

O. Restorative Justice Practices Can Enrich Freedom and Democracy

Christie's (1977) claim is that the king's justice stole conflicts from citizens; it was a significant accomplishment in the progressive consolidation of the domination of monarchs over their people in Europe from the eleventh to the nineteenth centuries. For much of Europe, justice was centralized under state control and local restorative justice was substantially extinguished by 1200 (Weitekamp 1999). Yet restorative justice as mainstream disputing between and within clans was not extinguished by the English in Scotland until well into the nineteenth century; it was never extinguished by the Dutch in Indonesia, where *Adat* (local) criminal laws work in parallel with a dominant Dutch criminal law of the Indonesian state. Elsewhere, Cree, Navajo, and Maori restorative justice survived, though barely. Even in England and France, the greatest imperial extinguishers of restorative justice, restorative justice practices remain profoundly influential in civil society, in schools, for example. The globalized centrality of the prison and professional police forces in the statist revolution's new justice model actually came quite late.

While the story of our criminal law is a story of imperial oppression to extinguish restorative justice, its major victories are historically recent enough across most of the globe for there to be substantial residues of more democratic modes of doing justice available to be revitalized. Recent empirical experience in places like New Zealand is that the flames of restorative justice can be rekindled surprisingly quickly because citizens find that they like restorative justice and popular demand for it spreads.

Control over punishment systems (combined with discretion to issue royal or presidential pardons) strengthened the power and legitimacy of rulers (see, e.g., Foucault 1977; Garland 1985, 1990). The new democratic rulers of the past two centuries continued to see their control of the secret police as vital to combating organized threats to their monopoly on the legal use of violence, the control of the regular police as vital to their control of disorganized threats. Yet abuse of that power (executing someone popular and innocent; the Guilford four) proved at times such a threat to their legitimacy that rulers were forced by political opponents to institutionalize certain principles of fairness and consistency into the state system. That process started with Magna Carta. These are accomplishments of liberalism that are worth preserving in a civic republican justice system.

At the same time, the pretence that the state punishes crime in a consistent, politically evenhanded way, so vital to the legitimation of statist criminal justice, is seen by citizens as a pretence. One law for the rich, another for the poor. That is the reality that seems transparent to citizens in totalitarian and democratic states alike. This is another dimension of the democratic appeal of shifting the control over mercy from the monarch back to the people affected, while using state law to constrain excesses of community through defining maximum punishments, rights, and procedural requirements. The theme of how to set up a just interaction between the peoples' justice and the law's justice is one to which I return in the conclusion of the essay.

There is more to the democratic virtue of restorative justice than returning conflicts to the citizens from whom they have been stolen. Western democratic institutions were planted in the shallow soil of societies where disputing had been taken over by the king. Disputing over daily injustices is where we learn to become democratic citizens. And the learning is more profound when those daily injustices reveal deeply structured patterns of injustice. Engagement with them is de Tocqueville's apprenticeship of liberty. In Benjamin Barber's terms, democratic disputing is educative, central to learning to be free:

> While we root our fragile freedom in the myth that we are born free, we are in truth born dependent. For we are born fragile, born needy, born ignorant, born unformed, born weak, born foolish, born unimaginative—born in chains . . . Our dependency is both physical—we need each other and cannot survive alone—and psychological; our identity is forged through a dialectical relationship with others. We are inescapably embedded in families, tribes, and communities. As a consequence, we must learn to be free. That is to say, we must be taught liberty. We are born small, defenseless, unthinking children. We must be taught to be thinking, competent, legal persons and citizens. We are born belonging to others; we have to learn how to sculpt our individuality from common clay. (Barber 1992, pp. 4–5)

I remember in 1991, in the early days of restorative justice conferencing in Australia, suggesting to Sergeant Terry O'Connell that it was a mistake to allow young children to attend and participate in conferences. Sometimes it is, but basically empirical experience has proved me wrong. In conferences, children are learning to be democratic citizens. The adults are mostly wise enough to make allowance for the unsophistication of much of what they say and to support them, help them establish the relevance of their point of view. Often it is the very unsophistication of the child's legitimate perspective that is so moving: "I've listened to what you've said about [my big brother]. It's not true. He is always kind to me; he helps me when I don't know what to do. I don't know any boy who is kinder than my brother."

We might hope for the town we love (I do) that the thousands of children who have now experienced participatory antibullying programs in our schools, the thousands of adults who have experienced restorative justice conferences in our police stations or community halls, will learn how to do justice restoratively and apply those lessons in the families, clubs, and workplaces where they face their sharpest conflicts. Most especially we might hope conferences are educating the police for democracy. Experience is the best educator, more so the more nuanced the skills required. We hope that citizens are learning in conferences how to deliberate respectfully in the face of the greatest of the provocations of daily life. If they can learn to deliberate wisely and respectfully in the most provocative contexts, then they are citizens well educated for democracy. My observation is that the citizens of my town are learning, however disappointed I become at the slowness of the learning and at the many setbacks restorative justice has suffered in Canberra. The hope is that the seeds of our democratic institutions will be planted in slightly deeper soil in the next century as a result.

VIII. A Pessimistic Account of Restorative Justice

My disposition is transparently optimistic about restorative justice. Partly this manifests a bias, a personality that suffers pathological optimism. But it also represents a considered belief that the criminal justice system needed a new and positive vision, that criminologists had become depressingly nihilistic in the 1970s and 1980s. The optimistic bias that gives pessimists something better to shoot at can yet be the kind of optimism that we see among the best natural scientists—the medical researcher whose very optimism about a new theory of disease motivates extraordinary rigor in putting in place randomized controlled trials to refute it. But that is not enough. The scientific optimist is also required to develop and test ideas about the side effects and the contraindications of her new drug. The adverse side effects and contraindications of restorative justice are numerous. Many have already been introduced in the course of qualifying the Optimistic Account. In this section, I rework the concerns into a systematic Pessimistic Account with thirteen propositions.

A. Restorative Justice Practices Might Provide No Benefits Whatever to over 90 Percent of Victims

Most victims of crime are victims of white-collar crimes without ever coming to realize this. They pay higher prices every day for products whose prices have been fixed by criminal price-fixing conspiracies. Even for offenses like burglary, where the victim is acutely aware of victimization, in every country in the world it is only a small minority of cases that are cleared by arrest. Even for offenses like domestic violence, where the victim knows she has been victimized and by whom, reports to the police followed by admissions of guilt are extremely rare. Of course, if restorative justice does reduce the crime rate, many people who would otherwise have been victimized get a benefit. But restorative justice has nothing to offer the overwhelming majority of citizens who are actually victimized by crime. The documented volume of unapprehended white-collar crime and domestic violence alone (Braithwaite and Pettit 1990, chap. 9) makes it easy to demonstrate that it would be foolishly optimistic to believe that the criminal justice system could do something for the known victims of known criminals for even 10 percent of our crime.

While there are limits on what the state can do to heal when there is no known criminal, these limits are less for organizations in civil society. The women's shelter movement can help to heal survivors who will not lay a complaint; circles can and do heal victims in the absence of offenders. There can and should be a level of state funding for victim support groups that allows them to provide professional, material, and emotional support at least to all victims of violence who request it.

B. Restorative Justice Practices Have No Significant Impact on the Crime Rate

Because more than 90 percent of victimizations will always be untouched by state restorative justice processes, preventive effects of restorative justice interventions would have to be massive to register any measurable impact on the overall crime rate. It would take a much bigger conferencing program than exists anywhere in the world to conference one percent of all (detected and undetected) criminal offenders. In the unlikely circumstance that conferences halved their reoffending, that would reduce the crime rate by half a percent.

Yet no one thinks that the effects of an eighty-minute conference on days, months, and years of competing influences will be massive. Many of the pessimists reasonably say that even if restorative justice theory is right (which they doubt), the impact of transitory restorative justice interventions are sure to be so small as to be detectable only on a massive (unaffordable) sample. The theory is therefore useless because its benefits (if true) could never be demonstrated by economically feasible scientific research.

Consider the Canberra drunk-driving restorative justice experiment being conducted by Sherman and Strang. For every officially recorded drunk-driving offense that comes into the experiment, the offenders are reporting eighteen other undetected drunk drives during that year. Add to that all the undetected drunk drives of those who are never caught and it is clear that the 450 RISE drunk-driving conferences touch only a tip of the iceberg. However it is the really serious repeat offenders who are most likely eventually to be caught. So at least the restorative justice process might eventually get a shot at a good proportion of the worst offenders (one would hope so in Canberra with as many as fifteen hundred drunk-driving convictions every year in a city of just 310,000). Furthermore, if the Optimistic Account's analysis of the general deterrent and crime prevention (e.g., culture changing) superiority of restorative justice over punitive justice is right, then there might be a measurable impact on the overall crime rate.

Even if not, the economic and protective value to the community of reducing reoffending for that minority of offenders who do find their way into the criminal justice system should not be discounted. But this is a much more modest claim than the claim that restorative justice can significantly reduce the crime rate. It may be made more modest by the fact that restorative justice processes cause crime as well as prevent them. Offenders learn the identity of their victim as a result of meeting them in a restorative justice process, or learn some other fact of their lifestyle that makes it easier to revictimize them. Offenders who experience heightened rather than reduced anger over what the victim says may revictimize, for example, through intimidating speech or threats during the conference. These concerns will be explored systematically in the RISE experiment.

C. Restorative Justice Practices Can Increase Victim Fears of Revictimization

The studies reported in Section VII.A clearly establish that this can happen. However, they also establish that reduction of victim fears of revictimization appears to be about twice as common. While victims are mostly surprised to learn how shy, ashamed, and inadequate offenders are, some offenders are formidable and scary. Such cases can destabilize restorative justice programs in the media. Our worst case in Canberra involved an offender who threatened a woman with a syringe filled with blood. The conference was not well run and feelings between offender and victim deteriorated. Subsequently, the victim found a syringe left on the dashboard of her car, which she took to be a threat from the offender (though this allegation was never proved). The case was covered by a local television station. Out of two thousand Canberra conferences (some with no victims, some with twenty), this is the only case of escalated victim fear that hit the media. But one can be enough. Restorative justice programs need to offer much more comprehensive support to the victims who face such traumas.

D. Restorative Justice Practices Can Make Victims Little More than Props for Attempts to Rehabilitate Offenders

This concern became acute with a number of British mediation programs during the 1980s where it was common for the offender and victim not to meet face-to-face, but rather for the mediator to be a go-between. Where no meeting occurs, Retzinger and Scheff's (1996) symbolic reparation, which we have seen is more important to most victims than material reparation, is more difficult. In these circumstances we can expect the dissatisfaction of victims to focus on the limits of the material reparation they get, "projects which claim to provide reparation for victims actually operating to maximise the potential for diversion of children from prosecution" (Haines 1999, p. 6). The British concern about victims being no more than props has not been a major issue in the debate in Australia and New Zealand about the pluses and minuses of restorative justice conferences. This is not to deny that victims used as props by a youth lobby who are concerned only to get a kinder deal for young offenders does not emerge as a deficiency in particular cases.

Jennifer Brown (1994, p. 1274) is concerned that victim anger may be redirected in ways that may be destructive for victims by mediation ground rules that "forbid blaming and extended discussion of past events " in favor of "a more forward-looking, problem-solving outlook." A connected concern is that approaches by state officials, perhaps particularly if they are police, may create pressure on victims to take part in a restorative justice process when they would rather cut their emotional and material losses. Brown (1994, p. 1266) is probably right that at least for a subset of victims, "the very rhetorical appeal of the program may induce a sense of guilt in a reluctant victim." Indeed, the same point might be made of the moral obligation imposed on victim and offender supporters by restorative justice processes. That is the inevitable fallout of a program that seeks to get things done by nurturing citizenship obligations; it comes with a cost.

E. Restorative Justice Practice Can Be a "Shaming Machine" that Worsens the Stigmatization of Offenders

The "shaming machine" concern has been well articulated in Retzinger and Scheff's (1996) essay, "Strategy for Community Conferences: Emotions and Social Bonds," written after their observation of a number of Australian conferences, from which they came away concerned about the damaging effects of sarcasm, moral superiority, and moral lecturing in particular:

> The point about moral indignation that is crucial for conferences is that when it is repetitive and out of control, it is a defensive movement in two steps: denial of one's own shame, followed by projection of blame onto the offender. . . . For the participants to identify with the offender, they must see themselves as like her rather than unlike her (There but for the grace of God go I). Moral indignation interferes with the identification between participants that is necessary if the conference is to generate symbolic reparation. In our judgement, uncontrolled repetitive moral indignation is the most important impediment to symbolic reparation and reintegration. But on the other hand, to the extent that it is rechannelled, it can be instrumental in triggering the core sequence of reparation . . . Intentional shaming in the form of sustained moral indignation or in any other guise brings a gratuitous element into the conference, the piling of shame on top of the automatic shaming that is built into the format. This format is an automatic shaming machine . . . in a format that is already heavy with shame, even small amounts of overt shaming are very likely to push the offender into a defensive stance, to the point that she will be unable to even feel, much less express, genuine shame and remorse. (P. 13)

Restorative justice processes are "already heavy with shame" as a result of the simple process of victims and their supporters talking about the consequences of the crime. In effect, that is all one needs. Umbreit (1994, p. 4) makes a similar point on victim defensiveness: "For individual victims, use of such terms as 'forgiveness' and 'reconciliation' is highly judgmental and preachy, suggesting a devaluing of the legitimate anger and rage the victims may be feeling at that point."

Braithwaite and Mugford (1994) think that the best protection against the vices of moral lecturing and sarcasm is to do a good job of inviting a large number of caring supporters for both the victim and the offender, a point also discussed by Retzinger and Scheff (1996). If these invitees really do care about the offender, they will counter moral lecturing with tributes to the sense of responsibility and other virtues of the offender. Then, even if the sort of connection with the moral

lecturer that would allow productively reparative communication is
severed, the bond with the other participant who comes to her defense
is strengthened in the same sequence. For Braithwaite and Mugford
(1994) this is the genius in the design of a Maori conference, a Cree
healing circle, or Japanese school discipline, that is absent in the design
of dyadic Western victim-offender mediation.[13] Of course, training of
facilitators to intervene against moral lecturing and ask for respectful
discussion of consequences and solutions is also a remedy. Training of
citizens through learning how to do restorative justice in school disputes is even more important: reason is more likely to prevail in democratic deliberation when citizens are educated to reasonableness (Barber 1992). Over the next few years there will be a flood of research
coming out of the RISE experiment on what predicts the degeneration
of conferences into defensive self-righteousness and their elevation
into the symbolic reparation Retzinger and Scheff want.

F. Restorative Justice Practices Rely on a Kind of Community That Is Culturally Inappropriate to Industrialized Societies

The most common assertion of critics of restorative justice, even in
the face of thriving programs in large multicultural cities like Auckland, Minneapolis, Adelaide, and Singapore, is that it might work well
in rural contexts but not in the metropolises of industrialized societies.
The theory outlined in Section VII really makes a different kind of
prediction, however:

> In our cities, where neighborhood social support is least, where the
> loss from the statist takeover of disputing is most damaging, the
> gains that can be secured from restorative justice reform are
> greatest. When a police officer with a restorative justice ethos
> arrests a youth in a tightly knit rural community who lives in a
> loving family, who enjoys social support from a caring school and
> church, that police officer is not likely to do much better or worse
> by the child than a police officer who does not have a restorative
> justice ethos. Whatever the police do, the child's support network
> will probably sort out the problem so that serious offending does

---

[13] As Mark Umbreit has pointed out to me, much victim-offender mediation is not
dyadic. Other participants are often involved. He also rightly points out that dyadic encounters have their advantages too. Some things might be said one-on-one that could
never be drawn out in front of the wider group. In short, some of the most successful
conferences may adjourn for dyadic mediations; some of the most successful mediations
may expand into conferences.

not occur. But when a police officer with a restorative justice ethos arrests a homeless child in the metropolis like Sam, who hates parents who abused him, who has dropped out of school and is seemingly alone in the world, it is there that the restorative police officer can make a difference that will render him more effective in preventing crime than the retributive police officer. (Braithwaite 1998a, pp. 18–19)[14]

Hagan and McCarthy's (1997, p. 163) research shows that homeless youth in Toronto and Vancouver were far from alone. A majority speak of their "street families" who look out for them: "you really learn what friendship is. . . . If I need them, they're there for me." In other words, part of our stigmatization of the homeless is to view them as somehow asocial, noncommunal.

Certainly the restorative justice movement could be more conscious of helping other peoples to recover their own restorative traditions rather than showing them our own. I have suggested (Braithwaite 1996) the need for culturally specific investigation of how to save and revive the restorative justice practices that remain in all societies. Thence the following two elements for a research agenda: helping indigenous community justice to learn from the virtues of liberal statism—procedural fairness, rights, protecting the vulnerable from domination; and helping liberal state justice to learn from indigenous community justice—learning the restorative community alternatives to individualism (Braithwaite 1996).

The design of restorative justice institutions can be rather minimalist. A conference, for example, can be defined by a strategy for who is invited and a small number of procedural rules about advising the defendant of a right to leave and take their chances in court, speaking in turn, and so on. Even "speaking in turn" may be too Eurocentric to be a minimal requirement as in some cultures it shows polite engagement to finish another person's sentence or to speak at the same time. Perhaps the ideal is undominated speech. The ideal is certainly not to be culturally prescriptive: to allow participants to begin and end

[14] Put another way, the kind of theory I favor does not have a structurally or culturally determinate explanation of crime: low Japanese crime rates are not about village culture or Japanese culture; to understand them we look to Japanese regulatory practices and Japanese provision of opportunities for human development. Changing regulatory practices and development opportunities can explain why Japanese crime rates fell from World War II in a way that it is hard for changing Japanese culture or the demise of village life to explain (Masters 1997).

a conference with a prayer if that is their wish, to include noisy babies if they wish or exclude them if they wish, to allow Samoan offenders to kneel at the feet of victims and First Nations Canadians to wash the feet of victims (Griffiths and Hamilton 1996), to communicate by a storytelling that may appeal to less formally educated members of a community (Young 1995) more than by a deductive reasoning that appeals to certain dominant men, or to lawyers. The sad fact is that this ideal is often not realized in restorative justice processes. Cunneen (1997), Findlay (1998), and Blagg (1998), for example, are right to point out that the interest of Australian Aboriginal people in participating in restorative justice alternatives was often assumed rather than discovered by reformers through an empowering dialogue with Aboriginal people (and other silenced minorities). Sometimes, we even inflict Maori process on young Maori who say they don't believe in "too much shit about the Maori way" (Maxwell and Morris 1993, p. 126).

For all these failings, the design of restorative justice processes is for participant ownership and adaptation whereas the design of the Western criminal trial is for consistency—to be determinedly unicultural— one people, one law. The complex challenge for restorative justice is to improve the match between aspirations of design and reality of accomplishment.

G. *Restorative Justice Practices Can Oppress Offenders with a Tyranny of the Majority, Even a Tyranny of the Lynch Mob*

Empowering indigenous justice in many parts of the world can and does at times empower communities to kill offenders and more commonly to punish them corporally. Police in outback Australia are not coy to confess to criminologists that they allow the latter to happen; they would never let themselves be seen to allow the former. Liberal justice regimes that turn a blind eye to violent indigenous justice succumb to a dangerous kind of cultural relativism. It is one thing to accept the legitimacy of traditional forms of social control in a unicultural traditional society. In a multicultural society where all people learn to count on the state for protection of their rights, without state oversight of respect for fundamental human rights there is no way of being sure that those punished really are members of the traditional society, or even if they are, that they are not cultural dissidents who wish to call on the protections afforded to all citizens by the state regardless of race. Without state oversight, there is no way of assuring that the rights of a victim from a different cultural group than the offender will be protected. Moreover, as Ross (1996, p. 234) points out: "In many communities, the overnight withdrawal of the Western justice system would not be followed by the immediate substitution of effective aboriginal approaches, but by significant violence."

Some Australian outback police, black and white, show considerable wisdom in communicating the message that traditional justice processes are encouraged to run their course so long as they do not cross certain lines. "If you do that, blackfella law will be pushed aside by whitefella law." Put another way, what such police do is encourage Aboriginal restorative traditions, but when they want to exercise their retributive traditions with any vigor, require them to put their case to a court of law. No citizens can feel secure in their rights when in some contexts the state is willing to sacrifice them to the tyranny of the lynch mob.

This is not to say that courts have generally been less tyrannous than the mob. On the contrary, public executions stopped because the mob booed and pelted executioners as they carried out the horrors ordered by the courts (Hay 1975, pp. 67–68; Foucault 1977, pp. 61–67) and because juries refused to convict for minor offenses that would lead to the gallows (Trevelyan 1978, p. 348). Courts around the world still order executions (in private) in numbers that surely exceed those imposed by popular justice tribunals. Today, no popular justice fora impose other sanctions as barbarous as imprisonment, which Graeme Newman (1983) points out in practice can be considerably more barbarous than corporal punishment. Certainly, contemporary liberal courts have some upper limits on the barbarism they can indulge. However, it seems empirically wrong, both as a matter of attitude and practice, that courts are less punitive than victims and restorative justice fora.

In practice, if courts in New Zealand were less punitive than family group conferences, they would be cutting conference agreements for community work and other sanctions on a regular basis, but we have seen that increments are much more common than cuts (Maxwell and Morris 1993). The Clotworthy case before the Court of Appeal of New Zealand, for example, has been challenging to the principles of restorative justice.[15]

Mr. Clotworthy inflicted six stab wounds, which collapsed a lung and diaphragm of an attempted robbery victim. Justice Thorburn of

---

[15] *The Queen v. Patrick Dale Clotworthy*, Auckland District Court T. 971545, Court of Appeal of New Zealand, CA 114/98.

the Auckland District Court imposed a two-year prison sentence, which was suspended, a compensation order of $15,000 to fund cosmetic surgery for an "embarrassing scar," and two hundred hours of community work. These had been agreed at a restorative conference organized by Justice Alternatives. The judge found a basis for restorative justice in New Zealand law and placed weight on the wish of the victim for financial support for the cosmetic surgery and emotional support to end through forgiveness "a festering agenda of vengeance or retribution in his heart against the prisoner." The Court of Appeal allowed the victim to address it, whereupon the victim "reiterated his previous stance, emphasizing his wish to obtain funds for the necessary cosmetic surgery and his view that imprisonment would achieve nothing either for Mr. Clotworthy or for himself" (p. 12). The victory for restorative justice was that "substantial weight" was given by the court to the victim's belief that expiation had been agreed; their honors accepted that restorative justice had an important place in New Zealand sentencing law. The defeat was that greater weight was given to the empirical supposition that a custodial sentence would help "deter others from such serious offending" (p. 12). The suspending of the two-year custodial sentence was quashed in favor of a sentence of four years and a $5,000 compensation order (which had already been lodged with the court); the community service and payment of the remaining compensation were also quashed. The victim got neither his act of grace nor the money for the cosmetic surgery.

At the level of attitudes, Sessar (1998) has shown that judges and prosecutors in Germany have more punitive attitudes than the general public. In the United States, Gottfredson and Taylor (1987) found the general public to be no more retributive than correctional policy makers. Doob and Roberts's (1983, 1988) research shows that the more information the public has about particular cases, the less punitive they become. Hough and Roberts (1998) use data from the British Crime Survey to suggest that citizens derive their information about punishment primarily from the mass media, underestimate the severity of sentences actually imposed, and approve penalties lower than those actually imposed. Kerner, Marks, and Schreckling (1992) show that while a majority of Cologne victims who had been through victim-offender mediation felt the German justice system was too lenient, only 28 percent felt the treatment of "their" offender was too lenient. When citizens of most Western democracies answer opinion polls, they support capital punishment; when they sit on juries, they are much less supportive. Roberts and Stalans's (1997) literature review suggests that while in response to opinion polls citizens support tougher sentencing in the abstract, on more specific judgments about appropriate punishment they are not more punitive than the status quo and are very supportive of restitution as an alternative (when it is brought to their attention as an alternative). A number of studies find victims to be considerably less punitive than popular stereotypes would have it (Kigin and Novack 1980; Novack, Galaway, and Hudson 1980; Heinz and Kerstetter 1981; Shapland, Willmore, and Duff 1985; Sessar, Beurskens, and Boers 1986; Weitekamp 1989, pp. 83–84; Sessar 1990; Youth Justice Coalition 1990, pp. 52–54; Umbreit 1990b, 1994, pp. 9–13). McCold and Wachtel (1998, p. 35) found victims to be less punitive than victim supporters in Bethlehem conferences and much less punitive than offender supporters (though more punitive than the offenders themselves). This evidence is one reason the social movement for restorative justice has generally moved from seeing victims of crime movements as potential sources of resistance (see Scheingold, Pershing, and Olson 1994) to tangible sources of support.

All of this serves to keep the problem of the tyranny of the majority in perspective. While it is extremely rare for victims to fly into rages of abuse, it does happen in restorative justice processes: and when it does, justice can be compromised. The remedy has to be an absolute right of the accused to walk out of the restorative justice process and try their chances in a court of law.

H. Restorative Justice Practices Can Widen Nets of Social Control

Polk (1994, p. 134) and Minor and Morrison (1996), among others, have expressed concern about the net-widening potential of conferencing and other restorative justice programs. Systematic data to test such concerns are scarce. Maxwell and Morris (1996) do not find evidence of net widening as a result of the New Zealand restorative justice reforms of 1989. This is most particularly true at the most intensive end of intervention, with the number of places in residences for young offenders falling from two hundred to seventy-six and sentences that involve custody declining from an average of 374 a year prior to the juvenile justice reforms to 112 in 1990 (Maxwell and Morris 1996, p. 94). Forsythe (1995) found no net widening in the Wagga Wagga juvenile conferencing program; indeed found a small decrease in juvenile cases being processed by the justice system after the program's introduction. The Sparwood, British Columbia, police conferencing program discussed in Section VIIB was unique in terms of the net-widening hypothesis because it completely abolished court in favor of conferences that were held much less frequently than court cases had been held in the past. Yeats (1997, p. 371) associates the introduction of restorative justice conferences and an expanded cautioning program for juveniles in Western Australia with more than a halving of the number of charges heard in the children's court in the mid-1990s. Dignan (1992, p. 462) found quite modest net widening in the Kettering evaluation of a British adult victim reparation program; while some experienced higher levels of intervention than they might otherwise have experienced, more experienced lower levels of intervention that they would otherwise have encountered. The John Howard Society's Restorative Resolutions project in Manitoba was designed to be confined to adult cases where the Crown had already recommended a prison sentence of six months or more (this being true in 90 percent of the cases) (Bonta, Rooney, and Wallace-Capretta 1998). This approach to restorative probation builds in strong guarantees of net narrowing and has considerable promise for reducing minority overrepresentation in prison.

Net widening is most likely to occur with programs the police do not take seriously and which depend on referrals from the police. The police then refer cases they would not normally be bothered doing much about and the restorative justice program is motivated to get more cases by proving to the police that they are a tough option. A reverse of this situation is the New Zealand program. Here police support for conferencing is strong and in any case the police cannot send a juvenile to court without a youth justice coordinator having the chance to opt for a family group conference (with the offender's consent).[16]

It is worth considering why net widening is believed to occur in critiques of the welfare model of criminal justice, and whether these factors might not be so worrying in a restorative justice program aimed at securing freedom as nondomination (Walgrave 1995). Walgrave makes the point: "Educative and clinical arguments within a legal system imbue subjective and speculative approaches of the clinical practitioner with the coercive power of justice" (p. 230). With restorative justice, educative and clinical services are options selected by the joint deliberation of offenders and their community of care, who enjoy an absolute right of veto over them. Welfare professionals actually suffer a diminution in coercive state backing of their discretion to intervene

---

[16] The New South Wales Young Offenders Act 1997 empowers a "specialist youth officer" to opt for a conference against the advice of the police and precludes police commencement of proceedings before giving the specialist youth officer an opportunity to consider the conference option.

under the restorative justice model. As Walgrave (1995, p. 233) puts it, the restorative model is a move from "the state of power" and "the welfare state" to "the empowering state."

On the present limited evidence, restorative justice more often narrows than widens nets of formal state control; but it does tend to widen nets of community control. Whether the nets that are widened are state or community nets, an assumption that net widening is a bad thing seems wrong. From a republican normative perspective, net widening that increases freedom as nondomination is a good thing (Braithwaite and Pettit 1990). From this republican perspective, it is important to widen nets of social control over white-collar crime and domestic violence. Even with juveniles, we need to widen nets of community control over school bullying because this so demonstrably is oppressive of the freedom of victims, because restorative justice programs aimed at reducing bullying work (Olweus 1993), and because bullying is connected to other problems—victims being more susceptible to suicide than nonvictims and offenders being more supportive of adult wife abuse than children who are not bullies (Rigby, Whish, and Black 1994).

If it is true that restorative justice narrows nets of judicial control and widens nets of community control, then another kind of critique of restorative justice swings into play. Brown (1994, p. 129) quotes Barbara Babcock who in turn is referring to an argument by Thurman Arnold: "The trial is an important occasion for dramatic enactment, the symbolic representation of the community's most deeply held values." Restorative justice advocates see this as the romantic vision of the law of trial lawyers (and Hollywood). The guilty plea cases that are the bread and butter of both criminal courts and restorative justice programs are devoid of courtroom drama; on average, Canberra RISE cases that go to court are over in about ten minutes and very few people are present to observe the "drama." Yes, then, the Pessimistic Account is right that restorative justice programs can widen nets of community control and even nets of state control for some types of crime. The question is whether they should.

I. Restorative Justice Practices Fail to Redress Structural Problems
Inherent in Liberalism Like Unemployment and Poverty

Critics correctly point out that there is little evidence of restorative justice programs conquering not just unemployment and poverty, but family breakdown and other problems that underlie offending (Waters

1993). There is little doubt about the validity of this criticism. Even from the perspective of theories that motivate restorative justice, like the theory of reintegrative shaming (see Braithwaite 1995*b*), the main implications for crime control policy of the theories are not about the redesign of the criminal justice system. From my theoretical perspective, the low-crime society will be one with redemptive schooling (Knight 1985), a jobs compact that guarantees a job or training to all long-term unemployed (Braithwaite and Chappell 1994), vigorous social movement politics (Braithwaite 1995*b*), robust separations of private and public powers (Braithwaite 1997), a strong welfare state, strong markets, and strong plural communities (which include strong families that constitute independent individuals, and vigorous social movement politics) (Braithwaite 1998*b*). It will also be one that shames domination and denial of human rights as it promotes restorative justice. In short, it will be a civic republican society with a citizenry that takes seriously the virtues of liberty, equality, and fraternity/sorority. More abstractly, the low-crime society will be one whose citizens enjoy republican freedom as nondomination, with the rich panoply of institutional implications that follow from it (Pettit 1997).

For republicans, it is therefore important that restorative justice not undercut other elements vital for progress toward a republican polity. It is hard to see in the literature evidence of it doing this. We do see retributive justice wrench young people away from loving families, give them criminal records that destroy their employability (Hagan 1991); restorative justice does not seem very guilty of this. At its best, it heals families, extends their bonds of care, gets young people who have been expelled back into school, or helps them find jobs. But restorative justice does not normally accomplish these things and it does not, cannot, have any substantial effect on unemployment and educational disadvantage. An entirely different institutional agenda is required for that. One of the things about the social movement for restorative justice is that the people in it are active in other arenas of struggle for justice— in the women's movement, aboriginal rights movements, the peace movement, churches, the consumer movement, the environment movement, the development movement, the labor movement. They are not so naive as to believe that restorative justice as an alternative disputing philosophy can be the primary vehicle for securing the transformative changes they seek. Elections need to be won, constitutions rewritten, economies restructured, the World Trade Organization and the IMF reformed. Wearing the hat "criminologist" would make them look silly as they engage in those other struggles.

It would be a mistake to skew any of these political agendas toward a preoccupation with crime control; they are much more important than that (see Crawford 1997). This is not to deny the importance of pointing out that it is harder for restorative justice programs to restore when they are not surrounded by the infrastructure of a decent welfare state and a vigorous civil society. Ken Polk (1994; see also White 1994) is right to emphasize the greater importance of "developmental institutions" of family, school, work, and recreation that confer positive identities. Developmental institutions are more important than disputing institutions (regardless of whether they are restorative or punitive). Shearing's Community Peace Foundation in South Africa is doing exciting work to transform the relationship between (restorative) justice and developmental institutions in circumstances so challenging that it may show us a new path.

George Pavlich (1996) has a concern that runs deeper. It is that restorative justice restores individuals as subjects of liberal legality. It becomes "fundamentally implicated in the identity of liberal law" (Pavlich 1996, p. 714), which implies that "in the West popular justice, as it is currently understood, is impossible" (Fitzpatrick 1992, p. 199). Again restorative justice is pretty much guilty as charged here (see Shearing's (1995) appropriation of neoliberal discourses). As argued in Section VII.N and the conclusion, like the analysis in Habermas (1996), my analysis of restorative justice sees much that is worth preserving in liberal legalism. This analysis finds virtue in the institutionally specific kind of interplay between popular justice and the law bequeathed by the liberal tradition described in the conclusion. Liberal legalism is not the right culprit if we want to tackle unemployment, homelessness, educational disadvantage, sexism, racism, and the like. Without it, these problems would likely be even worse. We need to engage with other forms of social movement politics besides the social movement for restorative justice to tackle seriously the economic institutions that are the deeper villains here. At the same time, a republican justice that connects more of our private troubles to public issues will enable the law to be a slightly more useful tool against scourges like racism.

J. Restorative Justice Practices Can Disadvantage Women, Children, and Oppressed Racial Minorities

Disadvantaging of the powerless can occur through treating them harshly or through silencing them. On the latter, Gabrielle Maxwell (1993, p. 292) actually concludes that restorative justice conferences are "places where women's voices are heard" (see also Burford and

Pennell's [1998] findings). Similarly, Rigby (1996, p. 143) with data from eighty-five hundred students shows that at all ages girls are more interested than boys in talking through bullying problems in school programs. Daly (1996) reports that while a minority (15 percent) of offenders were women in her study of Australian conferences, 54 percent of victims, 58 percent of victim supporters, and 52 percent of offender supporters were women. In Canberra, offenders randomly assigned to conferences are considerably less likely than offenders assigned to court to say that they were disadvantaged in proceedings due to "age, income, sex, race, or some other reason" (Sherman and Barnes 1997). While there was no comparison with court, Joe Hudson's (1998) study of Canadian family group conference participants found 80 percent to be "very satisfied" with the way all conference participants were treated as equals. Morris et al. (1996, p. 224) conclude from the consideration of the issue across the set of contributions to their volume: "Fears raised by commentators about the disempowerment of women have not been supported by observers and researchers who note their active participation in the process in contrast with their nonparticipation in judicial processes." Our research group's qualitative observations of restorative justice at various sites is that women's voices in restorative justice conferences are often extremely influential; in juvenile conferences if we were to nominate one type of actor who is more likely to be influential in the outcome than any other, it might be the mother of the offender.

This may be a good thing from the perspective of empowerment of women in a deliberative democracy. It constitutes a kind of empirical response to feminist critics of republicanism and deliberative democracy who fear the pursuit of communitarian consensus that may be a male consensus (Phillips 1991; Young 1995). At the same time, it opens up another feminist concern about restorative justice. It is that women again bear the burden of all the unpaid caring (Daly 1996). The potential fiscal benefit of conferences that they may be cheaper than courtroom justice is a benefit likely to be carried on women's backs. Hughes (1996) explores this concern through considering Campbell's (1993) analysis that in "Britain's dangerous places," it is women who are the "community builders," while men deal with unemployment by indulging a cult of selfish irresponsibility and brute force. In Britain's high-crime communities: "Crime and coercion are sustained by men. Solidarity and self-help are sustained by women. It is as stark as that" (Campbell 1993, p. 319). No, the data do not suggest it is as stark as that. Yet there seems little doubt that women do more of the restoring than men in restorative justice processes. The price tag for communitarian empowerment (that most women say they want in all the interview-based research) is a gendered burden of care.

A related worry about restorative discourses is that they may domesticate violence. Sara Cobb (1997, p. 414) finds that "the morality of mediation itself" can frame the interpretation of action, subsuming, taming the morality of right and wrong so that "the category 'victim' dissolves" (p. 436). Some restorative justice advocates view it as a good thing for the category victim to dissolve, indeed for the category "crime" to dissolve. There is a divide between some mediation advocates who believe the mediator should be "neutral" and some conferencing advocates who see a conference beginning from an assumption that a crime has been admitted about which the facilitator is not neutral, but disapproving. Rights are not necessarily domesticated to needs (Minow 1990) by a justice that "erases any morality that competes with the morality of mediation." The right kind of interplay between the justice of the law and the restorative justice of the people might secure rights as trumps against the morality of mediation, a topic I return to in the conclusion.

An opposite kind of claim about disadvantage sometimes made about restorative justice programs is that they are a benefit granted disproportionately to Caucasians. It is not an allegation I have seen made in New Zealand and Canada where so many of the leading programs have been run by and for First Nation peoples. However, there have been some worrying suggestions of the validity of such a concern in the United States (Gehm 1990; Brown 1994; Schiff 1998) and Australia (Daly 1996; Wundersitz and Hetzel 1996; Blagg 1997).

K. Restorative Justice Practices Are Prone to Capture by the Dominant Group in the Restorative Process

Restorative business regulatory practices are frequently captured by business (Clinard and Yeager 1980, pp. 106–9). As Dingwall, Eekelaar, and Murray (1983) have shown, child protection practice is liable to "family capture." As with business regulation, Dingwall, Eekelaar, and Murray show that a "rule of optimism" prevails among family regulators who have a bigger caseload than they can manage. Sandor (1993) even worries that family group conferences might ignite episodes of physical abuse, so common in the lives of serious juvenile offenders. This is a worry that deserves testing by a major empirical study. Indigenous justice can empower elders to tyrannize the young of their tribe. Critics have alleged this in a most alarming way in Canada through allegations by women from a reserve that project leaders of a program of indigenous justice administered by a panel of elders "manipulated the justice system to protect family members who had committed violent rapes, had intimidated victims and witnesses into withdrawing charges, had perjured themselves during the trial of the project leader's son (for rape), had slashed tyres of community members who tried to speak out and sent the alleged 'rape gangs' to their homes, and generally had used the project to further their strangle-hold on the community and the justice system."[17]

In New Zealand, I saw one tragic conference where the state funded the travel of an offender to another community because his *whanau* (extended family) wanted to separate him from a liaison with a girlfriend it did not want. In pushing for this, the Youth Justice Advocate was not an advocate for the youth, who was heartbroken by this outcome, but was captive of the *whanau*, which was the repeat player in the use of his legal services. Observational work on juvenile justice conferences quite regularly reports lower levels of offender involvement than involvement by their family members. Maxwell and Morris's (1993, pp. 110–12) interviews found fully 45 percent of young offenders, compared to 20 percent of family members saying they were not involved in making the conference decision. In Canberra and South Australia, Daly (1996) reported 33 percent of offenders not to be engaged with the process. The Maxwell and Morris (1993) data showed family members of the offender having by far the largest influence on the decision, followed by professionals who were present, the young offender, and the victim (not surprising since the victim was absent from a majority of the conferences in this study). Kevin Haines's (1999) critique of conferences as a "room full of adults" who dominate a child is therefore often correct. All such failures are relative, however: the RISE experiment in Canberra shows that young offenders are considerably more likely to believe that they could express their views when they went to a conference than when they went to court (Sherman and Barnes 1997; Sherman et al. 1998, pp. 121–22).

The best remedy to this problem is systematic attention in the restorative justice preparatory process to empowerment of the most vul-

[17] This is a quote that I treat as anonymous with respect to person and place. I was able to confirm the same broad story from two other sources.

nerable parties—individual victims and offenders—and systematic disempowerment of the most dominant parties—the police, school authorities, state welfare authorities, sometimes large business corporations. How is this accomplished? The most critical thing is to give the individual offender and the individual victim the one-on-one power in a meeting in advance of the conference to decide who they do and do not want to be there to support them. Unfortunately, the practice is often to empower the parents of young offenders to decide who should be there. They can certainly have a legitimate say; but on the offender side it is only the offender who should make the final decision about who will make her most comfortable, whom she most trusts. To the extent that one is concerned here with imbalances of power between children and adults, men and women, major corporations and consumers, dyadic victim-offender mediation cements an imbalance. Imbalances are muddied, though hardly removed, by conferences between two communities of care, both of which contain adults and children, men and women, organized interests (like Aboriginal Community Councils in the CML case) and disorganized individuals.

Simple rules of procedure can privilege less dominant voices over state voices. The police should never be allowed to give their version of what happened in advance of the offender's version. The New Zealand and South Australian practice of giving attending police a right of veto over the conference agreement is a bad practice from this perspective. The victim and the offender should have a right of veto, and should be formally reminded of it at the start of the conference, but perhaps no agent of the state should have such a right as a conference participant. On this view, if the police feel a victim has dominated an offender by requiring excessive punishment, their approach should be to advise the offender of their right to walk away from the agreement and have the matter heard by a court. Against this view is a non-RISE case we had in Canberra where the police did not veto an agreement, enthusiastically crafted by the victim and the mother of the offender, to have a child wear a T-shirt emblazoned with "I am a Thief." Certainly, formal negative performance indicators for facilitators should include how much they talk,[18] dominating proceedings, and participation in setting the terms of the conference agreement.

[18] Perhaps I am partially wrong here, however, if the more general literature on the effectiveness of problem solving in mediation is a guide. Carnevale and Pruitt's (1992, p. 565) review concludes that when disputants are able to resolve the dispute themselves, mediator intrusiveness gets in the way, but when conflict intensity or hostility are high, interventionist mediation can improve outcomes.

With restorative business regulation, Ayres and Braithwaite (1992) have shown game-theoretically the importance of having third parties present during regulatory negotiation to protect against corporate capture. With nursing home regulation, for example, this can mean representatives of the residents' committee, supported by advocacy groups where they want this, relatives, staff and their unions, and outside board members as well as management meeting with the regulators.

While there are such measures we can take to counterbalance capture, there can be no doubt the Pessimistic Account is right that the risk of capture by dominant groups is an ineradicable reality of restorative justice (just as it is of state justice).

L. Restorative Justice Processes Can Extend Unaccountable Police Power, Even Compromise the Separation of Powers among Legislative, Executive, and Judicial Branches of Government

Critics such as Danny Sandor (1993) and Rob White (1994) are particularly concerned about conferences facilitated by the police, something now happening in Australia, the United Kingdom, the United States, and Canada, and being advocated elsewhere. It is all very well to reply that facilitation is not control, that police should not have a veto power over decisions, but no one can deny that good facilitators have "dramatic dominance" (to use Stephen Mugford's Goffmanesque characterization) even if they exert little direct control. This dramatic dominance ensures among other things that the conference is orderly, that everyone has their turn to speak without interruption, that civility triumphs over abuse. Supporters of police conferencing in police stations, such as the Police-Citizens Consultative Committee in Wagga Wagga, claim this lends "gravitas" to proceedings. These citizens and police also argue that police facilitation, indeed the presence of the police uniform, helps victims feel secure, a critical problem given the evidence that victims often come away from criminal justice processes, including restorative ones, feeling more afraid of their offender (see Sec. VIIA). Interesting and important speculations, but there is no evidence to support the importance of such alleged advantages. Conversely, there is no evidence to support counterclaims that offenders are intimidated by the presence of a police uniform during a conference or by the police station as a venue. It seems unlikely that either is totally false; many young people do distrust the police and many crime victims distrust "do-gooder social workers" and trust the police.

What does seem true, by definition, is that hard-line views on either side of this debate do disempower and disadvantage participants. A rule that police must or must not facilitate conferences has unfortunate consequences when it precludes someone from taking the facilitator role who is the most gifted person who most enjoys the confidence of the disputants. It has perhaps even more unfortunate consequences when it forces police officers to facilitate conferences when they do not believe this is "police work" (see Hoyle and Young 1998). In New Zealand, where police do not facilitate conferences, I saw one conference where a Pakeha official facilitator handed over the effective facilitation of the conference to a police officer because the police officer was Maori and all the participants Maori. A rule that Maori conferences must be held on the traditional Marae might be most unwise if that would terrify a Samoan victim. A rule that it be held on neutral ground is sad if one party is quite stipulative about where she will feel safe about the conference and the other party does not care. In my unsystematic observation on this question, most parties do not seem to care greatly about where conferences are held; but when they do express a strong preference, why not yield to them?

The more fundamental question is whether there is something wrong in principle with police facilitating a conference. Does it make the police investigator, prosecutor, judge, and jury? It is only a very partial answer to reply that the investigator is never the police facilitator in such programs. Even if the police have no veto over the conference decision, they can still dominate it and become a de facto judge and jury. At least a lay facilitator who dominates a conference process does not add that domination to institutional domination over the decision to proceed with the matter. At a lower level, this is also a separation of powers argument against facilitation control in the hands of any state agency that already has control over another part of the process--such as control by the courts (as in South Australia) or a juvenile justice or welfare agency. It is not an argument against a prosecutor or judge having a right of veto over the outcome of a conference.

Is there therefore any case for control of facilitation by a state agency rather than facilitator recruitment by an institution in civil society, especially when that civilian facilitator has the power to co-opt a police facilitator if that is what the parties want? There are two cases for state control. One is simply politically pragmatic. Restorative justice reform requires enormous energy and political will to struggle against retributivism and vested interests, not least within police forces. My own position has been politically pragmatic in just this way: to admire those with the courage to take on the battle, wherever they pop up institutionally—in civil society, the police, the courts, prosecutors, state welfare agencies. During the research and design era of restorative justice, so long as the activists are sensible and competent as well as committed, let us encourage openness to research results from their innovation. We really have so little data on who is right about these questions of comparative advantage in institutional location. My own suspicion is to think that success is 70 percent driven by attention to getting implementation detail right and only 30 percent by getting the institutional infrastructure right. Gifted people can run wonderful restorative justice programs in an open field with no infrastructure whatsoever. They seem to have done so for millennia. But that suspicion is itself something that must be open to empirical refutation.

A second argument for institutional location of conferencing in a police service is about the transformation of police cautioning and police culture more broadly. Even in New Zealand, with the largest juvenile conferencing program anywhere, for every juvenile case dealt with by a conference, more than five are dealt with by a police caution. Rendering police cautioning more restorative is more important than rendering conference or court processing more restorative. From the perspective of the theory of reintegrative shaming, if, as seems to be the case (Braithwaite 1995c), stigmatizing interactions do more to increase crime than reintegrative ones do to reduce it, five stigmatizing police cautions will do more damage than any good from one reintegrative conference. Not just in formal cautioning but in daily interaction on the street, the challenge of transforming police culture from a stigmatizing to a restorative style is important. In a place like Wagga Wagga, the openness to inviting critics from the community, prosecutors, and the like to sit in on the sergeants' committee, where decisions were made to encourage constables to send cases to conference rather than court, constituted an interesting moment in the history of police accountability and culture change. The hope of the leading police reformers in this area, like Terry O'Connell in Australia, has been that police "ownership" of conferencing will imbue police commitment to restorative justice in wider arenas, including their own internal affairs (corruption, sexual harassment). At this stage, however, I doubt if anyone could plausibly demonstrate that any police service has experienced a major change of corporate culture as a result of restorative justice innovation. Perhaps Thames Valley, England, is beginning to approach this situation. The evidence is clear that significant police cultural change has not occurred in Bethlehem, Pennsylvania (McCold and Wachtel 1998, p. 3), though the individual police most exposed to conferences did move toward a more restorative and less crime-control oriented philosophy of policing. But then cultural change is never rapid and always resisted.

If the relationship of any restorative justice program with the police is not well managed, disaster is courted. The police are the gatekeepers to the criminal justice system and if they shut the gate to restorative justice, it is nigh impossible to push it open against their resistance. All manner of hybrids are possible. One is for a conferencing unit to be located in police stations, pushing internally to divert cases as they come through the station door, caressing and cajoling police cooperation, but with the facilitators actually being employees of an institution in civil society contracted by the justice minister or other government agency to deliver the service. Some of these facilitators could be respected businesspeople who would have the sophistication to run conferences for complex white-collar crimes, others could have special language skills, others special gifts in gaining the confidence of young people, others could be elders of a local indigenous group.

More broadly, from a republican perspective, one wants to see most restorative justice conferencing transacted in civil society without ever going through the police station door—in Aboriginal communities, schools, extended families, churches, sporting clubs, corporations, business associations, and trade unions. Equally, one wants to see those community justice processes subject to state oversight for breaches of citizens' rights and procedural fairness. In such a world, restorative justice would contribute to the building of a republican democracy with a much richer separation of powers. That is not the world we live in yet. For the moment, the restorative justice debate is debilitated by excessively statist preoccupations to the point where the reforms in place do raise some legitimate worries about impoverishing rather than enhancing the separation of powers in our democracies.

M. *Restorative Justice Practices Can Trample Rights because of Impoverished Articulation of Procedural Safeguards*

Robust critiques of the limitations of restorative justice processes in terms of protection of rights have been provided by Warner (1994), Stubbs (1995), Bargen (1996), and Van Ness (1999). There can be little doubt that courts provide superior formal guarantees of procedural fairness than conferences.

At the investigatory stage, Warner (1994, p. 142) is concerned: "Will police malpractice be less visible in a system which uses FGCs [family group conferences]? One of the ways in which police investigatory powers are scrutinized is by oversight by the courts. If the police act unlawfully or unfairly in the investigation of a case, the judge or magistrate hearing the case may refuse to admit the evidence so obtained or may criticize the police officer concerned. Allegations of failure to require parental attendance during questioning, of refusal to grant access to a lawyer, of unauthorized searches and excessive force could become hidden in cases dealt with by FGCs."

These are good arguments for courts over restorative justice processes in cases where guilt is in dispute. But the main game is how to process that overwhelming majority of cases where there is an open and shut admission of guilt. Here no such advantage of court over conference applies, quite the reverse. As Warner herself points out, a guilty plea "immediately suspends the interests of the court in the treatment of the defendant prior to the court appearance" (Hogg and Brown 1985). In the production line for guilty pleas in the lower courts there is not time for any of that. In restorative justice conferences there is. Mothers in particular do sometimes speak up with critical voices about the way their child has been singled out, has been subject to excessive police force, and the like. Police accountability to the community is enhanced by the conference process. And such deterrence of abuse of police power that comes from the court does not disappear since the police know that if relations break down in the conference, the case may go to court as well.

Police therefore have reason to be more rather than less procedurally just with cases on the conference track than with cases on the court track. The preliminary RISE data from Canberra suggest they are. In about 90 percent of cases randomly assigned to a conference, offenders thought the police had been fair to them ("leading up to the conference" and "during"); but they only thought this in 48–78 percent (depending on the comparison) of the cases randomly assigned to court (Sherman et al. 1998). Offenders were also more likely to say they trusted the police after going through a conference with them than after going through a court case with them.

At the adjudicatory stage, Warner (1994) is concerned that restorative justice will be used as an inducement to admit guilt. In this, restorative justice is in no different a position than any disposition short of the prospect of execution or life imprisonment. Its proffering can induce admissions. Systemically though, one would have thought that a shift from a punitive to a restorative justice system would weaken the allure of such inducements. In the preliminary data from the four RISE experiments in Canberra, there is a slight tendency for court offenders to be more likely than conference offenders to agree that, "The police made you confess to something which you did not do in this case." But this difference is only statistically significant in the Juvenile Personal Property experiment (Sherman et al. 1998, pp. 123–24).

Warner (1994) is right, however, to point out that guilt is not always black and white. Defendants might not understand self-defense, intoxication, and other defenses that might be available to them. Even so, it remains the case that such matters are more likely to be discussed in a conference lasting about eighty minutes (Canberra data) than in a court case averaging about ten minutes (Canberra data). This may be a simple reason why Canberra offenders who go through a conference are more likely to believe that the proceedings "respected your rights" than offenders who went through court (Sherman and Barnes 1997; Sherman et al. 1998).

At the dispositional or sentencing stage, Warner (1994) makes some good points about the care needed to ensure that sentences reflect only offenses the evidence in this case has shown to have been committed and only damage the evidence shows to have been done. We have had conferences in Canberra where victims have made exaggerated claims of the damage they have suffered, in one case many thousands of dollars in excess of what more thorough subsequent investigation proved to be the truth. Warner (1994) and Van Ness (1999) are both concerned about double jeopardy when consensus cannot be reached at a conference and the matter therefore goes to court, though Warner (1994) concedes it is not "true double jeopardy." Indeed it is not. The justice model analogue would seem to be to retrial after a hung jury (which no one would call double jeopardy) rather than retrial after acquittal. Moreover, it is critical that defendants have a right to appeal in court an unconscionable conference agreement they have signed, to have lawyers with them at all stages of restorative justice processes if that is their wish, and that they be proactively advised of these rights.

Most restorative justice programs around the world do not legally guarantee the American Bar Association's (1994) guideline that "statements made by victims and offenders and documents and other materials produced during the mediation/dialogue process [should be] inadmissible in criminal or civil court proceedings." This is a problem that can and should be remedied by appropriate law reform.

Van Ness (1999) has systematically reviewed the performance of restorative justice programs for juveniles against the United Nations Standard Minimum Rules for the Administration of Juvenile Justice ("The Beijing Rules"). Restorative justice programs are certainly found wanting in the review though he concludes that they often tend to outperform traditional court processes on rules such as right to a speedy trial. For example, the New South Wales Young Offenders Act 1997 has the following requirement: "Time Limit Holding Conferences: A conference must, if practical, be held not later than twenty-one days after the referral for the conference is received." While Van Ness's work certainly affirms our hypothesis that restorative justice processes can trample on rights, where rights will be better or worse protected after the introduction of a restorative justice program is a contextual matter. For example, when in South Africa prior to the Mandela Presidency thirty thousand juveniles a year were being sentenced by courts to flogging, who could doubt that the institutionalization of restorative justice conferences might increase respect for children's rights, as Sonnekus and Frank (1997, p. 7) argue: "[Under Apartheid] the most common sentence given was corporal punishment and children often preferred a whipping instead of residential care in a reformatory or school of industry. The time children spent in prison while awaiting trial and placement was not applied toward their sentence, thus a child may have served double and even triple sentences."

Nevertheless, our Pessimistic Account is correct that rights can be trampled because of the inferior articulation of procedural safeguards in restorative justice processes compared to courts. The conclusion grapples with how justice might be enhanced in the face of this critique by a creative interplay between restorative fora and traditional Western courts.

IX. Conclusion

There are good preliminary theoretical and empirical grounds for anticipating that well-designed restorative justice processes will restore victims, offenders, and communities better than existing criminal justice practices. More counterintuitively, a restorative justice system may deter, incapacitate, and rehabilitate more effectively than a punitive system. This will be especially so if restorative justice is embedded in a responsive regulatory framework that opts for deterrence when restoration repeatedly fails and incapacitation when escalated deterrence fails. We find active deterrence under a dynamic regulatory pyramid to be more powerful than passive deterrence in a sentencing grid; community incapacitation is more variegated and contextually attuned than clumsy carceral incapacitation.

In the face of all the discretion that community responsiveness implies, most surprising of all is the conclusion that restorative justice is more just than the justice of the justice model. Empirical evidence of community perceptions of justice under the two models strongly supports this. Normative theory of a republican cast explains why we should get this result. Restorative justice delivers freedom as nondomination in a way just deserts cannot and citizens in democracies have profoundly deep aspirations to freedom and deep distrust of domination. Restorative justice confronts the dilemma that equal justice for offenders is utterly incompatible with equal justice for victims. I have argued that a greater degree of equality for both is delivered by rejecting equality as a goal, guaranteeing victims a minimum level of care, and guaranteeing offenders against punishment beyond a maximum.

For all of this hope about the advantages of restorative justice over the models with which it must compete, restorative justice offers limited prospects of a revolutionary improvement in the circumstances of victims or the control of crime. The primary reason for this is that the most fundamental things we must do to control crime and thereby improve the lot of victims are not reforms to the justice system. They are reforms about liberty, equality, and community in more deeply structural and developmental senses.

Even so, just disputing processes have an important role to play in connecting private troubles to public issues. When communities start taking responsibility for the vulnerabilities of their young offenders and start talking about these vulnerabilities at and after conferences, of course they become more engaged with the deeper institutional sources of the problems.[19] When communities begin taking responsibility for family violence, as at Hollow Water, a profoundly institutional debate is triggered (Lajeunesse 1993; Ross 1996; Aboriginal Corrections Policy Unit 1997a, 1997b; Green 1998). When communi-

---

[19] For the profoundly institutional way the citizens of Wagga did this, see City of Wagga Wagga (1993).

ties engage with their victimization by powerful corporations, as with the Aboriginal insurance cases, the imagination of prime ministers can be caught up in the aspirations for restructuring the regulation of finance capital.

Restorative justice can trample the rights of offenders and victims, dominate them, lack procedural protections, and give police, families, or welfare professionals too much unaccountable power. Braithwaite and Parker (1998) suggest three civic republican remedies to these problems: contestability under the rule of law, a legal formalism that enables informalism while checking the excesses of informalism; deindividualizing restorative justice, muddying imbalances of individual power by preferring community conferences over individual-on-individual mediation; and vibrant social movement politics that percolates into the deliberation of conferences, defends minorities against tyrannies of the majority, and connects private concerns to campaigns for public transformation.

Lawyers who work for advocacy groups—for indigenous peoples, children, women, victims of nursing home abuse—have a special role in the integration of these three strategies. Lawyers are a strategic set of eyes and ears for advocacy groups that use specific legal cases to sound alarms about wider patterns of domination. When appropriate public funding is available for legal advocacy, advocates can monitor lists of conference outcomes and use other means to find cases where they should tap offenders or victims on the shoulder to advise them to appeal the conference agreement because they could get a better outcome in the courts. They thus become a key conduit between rule of law and rule of community deliberation. It is a mistake to see their role as simply one of helping principles of natural justice and respect of rights to filter down into restorative justice. It is also to assist movement in the other direction—to help citizens to percolate up into the justice system their concerns about what should be restored and how. A rich deliberative democracy is one where the rule of law shapes the rule of the people and the concerns of the people reshape the rule of law. Top-down legalism unreconstructed by restorative justice from below is a formula for a justice captured by the professional interests of the legal profession (the tyranny of lawyers). Bottom-up community justice unconstrained by judicial oversight is a formula for the tyranny of the majority. When law and community check and balance each other, according to Braithwaite and Parker (1998), prospects are best for a rich and plural democracy that maximizes freedom as nondomination.

Communitarianism without rights is dangerous. Rights without community are vacuous. Rights will only have meaning as claims the rich can occasionally assert in courts of law unless community disapproval can be mobilized against those who trample the rights of others. Restorative justice can enliven rights as active cultural accomplishments when rights talk cascades down from the law into community justice.

None of the problems in the Pessimistic Account is satisfactorily solved. None of the claims in the Optimistic Account is satisfactorily demonstrated. Decades of research and design on restorative justice processes will be needed to explore my suspicion that the propositions of both the Optimistic and Pessimistic Accounts are right. For the moment, we can certainly say that the literature reviewed here does demonstrate both the promise and the perils of restorative justice. It is, however, an immature literature, short on theoretical sophistication, on rigorous or nuanced empirical research, far too dominated by self-serving comparisons of "our kind" of restorative justice program with "your kind" without collecting data (or even having observed "your kind" in action). That disappoints when the panorama of restorative justice programs around the globe is now so dazzling, when we have so much to learn from one another's contextual mistakes and triumphs.

REFERENCES

Aboriginal Corrections Policy Unit. 1997a. *The Four Circles of Hollow Water.* Aboriginal Peoples Collection. Ottawa: Solicitor General Canada.
———. 1997b. *Responding to Sexual Abuse: Developing a Community-Based Sexual Abuse Response Team in Aboriginal Communities.* Ottawa: Solicitor General Canada.
Agnew, R., and A. A. Peters. 1986. "The Techniques of Neutralization: An Analysis of Predisposing and Situational Factors." *Criminal Justice and Behavior* 13:81–97.
Ahmed, Eliza. 1999. "Shame Management and Bullying." Ph.D dissertation, Australian National University, Department of Psychology.
American Bar Association. 1994. "Victim-Offender Mediation/Dialogue Pro-

gram Requirements." Resolution adopted by the American Bar Association House of Delegates.

Anderson, Elijah. 1999. *Code of the Streets*. New York: Norton.

Ayres, I., and J. Braithwaite. 1992. *Responsive Regulation: Transcending the Deregulation Debate*. New York: Oxford University Press.

Ball, R. A. 1983. "Development of Basic Norm Violation: Neutralization and Self-Concept within a Male Cohort." *Criminology* 21:75–94.

Ban, Paul. 1996. "Implementing and Evaluating Family Group Conferences with Children and Families in Victoria Australia." In *Family Group Conferences: Perspectives on Policy and Practice*, edited by Joe Hudson, Allison Morris, Gabrielle Maxwell, and Burt Galaway. Sydney: Federation Press and Criminal Justice Press.

Barber, Benjamin R. 1992. *An Aristocracy of Everyone: The Politics of Education and Future of America*. New York: Oxford University Press.

Bardach, E., and R. A. Kagan. 1982. *Going by the Book: The Problem of Regulatory Unreasonableness*. Philadelphia: Temple University Press.

Bargen, J. 1996. "Kids, Cops, Courts, Conferencing and Children's Rights—a Note on Perspectives." *Australian Journal of Human Rights* 2(2):209–28.

Barnett, Randy E. 1981. "Restitution." In *Perspectives on Crime Victims*, edited by Burt Gallaway and Joe Hudson. St. Louis: Mosby.

Baumrind, D. 1973. "The Development of Instrumental Competence through Socialization." In *Minnesota Symposium of Motivation*, vol. 7, edited by A. D. Pick. Minneapolis: University of Minnesota Press.

———. 1978. "Parental Disciplinary Patterns and Social Competence in Children." *Youth and Society* 9:239–76.

Bayley, David H. 1976. *Forces of Order: Police Behavior in Japan and the United States*. Berkeley: University of California Press.

Bazemore, G., and M. Umbreit 1994. *Balanced and Restorative Justice: Program Summary: Balanced and Restorative Justice Project*. Washington, D.C.: U.S. Department of Justice, Office of Juvenile Justice and Delinquency Prevention.

Bazemore, G., and C. Washington. 1995. "Charting the Future of the Juvenile Justice System: Reinventing Mission and Management." *Spectrum* (Spring), pp. 51–66.

Beck, Guy L. 1997. "Fire in the Atman: Repentance in Hinduism." In *Repentance: A Comparative Perspective*, edited by Amitai Etzioni and David E. Carney. New York: Rowman & Littlefield.

Benson, M. L. 1989. "Emotions and Adjudication: A Study of Status Degradation among White-Collar Criminals." Unpublished manuscript. Knoxville: University of Tennessee, Department of Sociology.

Berman, Harold J. 1983. *Law and Revolution: The Formation of the Western Legal Tradition*. Cambridge, Mass.: Harvard University Press.

Birchall, P., S. Namour, and H. Syme. 1992. "Report on the Midland Pilot Reparation Scheme." Unpublished manuscript. Perth: independently prepared.

Blagg, Harry. 1997. "A Just Measure of Shame? Aboriginal Youth and Conferencing Australia." *British Journal of Criminology* 37:481–501.

———. 1998. "Restorative Visions and Restorative Justice Practices: Conferencing, Ceremony and Reconciliation in Australia." *Current Issues in Criminal Justice* 10:5–14.

Boden, Leslie I. 1983. "Government Regulation of Occupational Safety: Underground Coal Mine Accidents, 1973–1975." Unpublished manuscript. Boston: Harvard School of Public Health.

Bond, Michael H., and Wang Sung-Hsing. 1983. "China: Aggressive Behavior and the Problem of Maintaining Order and Harmony." In *Aggression in Global Perspective*, edited by Arnold P. Goldstein and Marshall H. Segall. New York: Pergamon.

Bonta, James, Jennifer Rooney, and Suzanne Wallace-Capretta. 1998. *Restorative Justice: An Evaluation of the Restorative Resolutions Project.* Ottawa: Solicitor General Canada.

Box, S. 1981. *Deviance, Reality and Society.* London: Holt, Rinehart & Winston.

Braithwaite, John. 1984. *Corporate Crime in the Pharmaceutical Industry.* London and Boston: Routledge & Kegan Paul.

———. 1985. *To Punish or Persuade: Enforcement of Coal Mine Safety.* Albany, N.Y.: SUNY Press.

———. 1989. *Crime, Shame and Reintegration.* Cambridge: Cambridge University Press.

———. 1991. "Thinking about the Structural Context of International Dispute Resolution." In *Whose New World Order: What Role for the United Nations?* edited by M. R. Bustelo and P. Alston. Sydney: Federation Press.

———. 1993a. "Shame and Modernity." *British Journal of Criminology* 33:1–18.

———. 1993b. "Beyond Positivism: Learning from Contextual Integrated Strategies." *Journal of Research in Crime and Delinquency* 30:383–99.

———. 1994. "The Nursing Home Industry." In *Beyond the Law: Crime in Complex Organizations*, edited by Michael Tonry and Albert J. Reiss, Jr. Vol. 18 of *Crime and Justice: A Review of Research*, edited by M. Tonry. Chicago: University of Chicago Press.

———. 1995a. "Corporate Crime and Republican Criminological Praxis." In *Corporate Crime: Ethics, Law and State*, edited by F. Pearce and L. Snider. Toronto: University of Toronto Press.

———. 1995b. "Inequality and Republican Criminology." In *Crime and Inequality*, edited by J. Hagan and R. Peterson. Palo Alto, Calif.: Stanford University Press.

———. 1995c. "Reintegrative Shaming, Republicanism and Policy." In *Crime and Public Policy: Putting Theory to Work*, edited by Hugh Barlow. Boulder, Colo.: Westview.

———. 1996. "Restorative Justice and a Better Future." *Dalhousie Review* 76(1):9–32.

———. 1997. "On Speaking Softly and Carrying Sticks: Neglected Dimensions of Republican Separation of Powers." *University of Toronto Law Journal* 47:1–57.

———. 1998a. "Institutionalizing Distrust, Enculturating Trust." In *Trust and Democratic Governance*, edited by V. Braithwaite and M. Levi. New York: Russell Sage Foundation.

————. 1998*b*. "Repentance Rituals." Unpublished manuscript. Canberra: Australian National University.

————. 1999. "Domination, Quiescence and Crime." Unpublished manuscript. Canberra: Australian National University.

Braithwaite, John, and Valerie Braithwaite. 1995. "The Politics of Legalism: Rules versus Standards in Nursing-Home Regulation." *Social and Legal Studies* 4:307–41.

Braithwaite, J., and D. Chappell. 1994. "The Job Compact and Crime." *Current Issues in Criminal Justice* 5:295–300.

Braithwaite, John, and K. Daly. 1994. "Masculinities, Violence and Communitarian Control." In *Just Boys Doing Business*, edited by T. Newburn and E. Stanko. London and New York: Routledge.

Braithwaite, John, and Brent Fisse. 1985. "Varieties of Responsibility and Organizational Crime." *Law and Policy* 7(3):315–43.

Braithwaite, J., and T. Makkai. 1993. "Can Resident-Centred Inspection of Nursing Homes Work with Very Sick Residents?" *Health Policy* 24:19–33.

————. 1994. "Trust and Compliance." *Policing and Society* 4:1–12.

Braithwaite, J., T. Makkai, V. Braithwaite, and D. Gibson. 1993. *Raising the Standard: Resident Centred Nursing Home Regulation in Australia.* Canberra: Australian Government Publishing Service.

Braithwaite, John, and S. Mugford. 1994. "Conditions of Successful Reintegration Ceremonies: Dealing with Juvenile Offenders." *British Journal of Criminology* 34:139–71.

Braithwaite, John, and Christine Parker. 1999. "Restorative Justice Is Republican Justice." In *Restorative Juvenile Justice: Repairing the Harm of Youth Crime*, edited by G. Bazemore and L. Walgrave. Monsey, N.Y.: Criminal Justice Press.

Braithwaite, John, and Philip Pettit. 1990. *Not Just Deserts: A Republican Theory of Criminal Justice.* Oxford: Oxford University Press.

Braithwaite, V., J. Braithwaite, D. Gibson, and T. Makkai. 1994. "Regulatory Styles, Motivational Postures and Nursing Home Compliance." *Law and Policy* 16:363–94.

Brehm, Sharon S., and Jack W. Brehm. 1981. *Psychological Reactance: A Theory of Freedom and Control.* New York: Academic Press.

Brewer, D. D., J. D. Hawkins, R. F. Catalano, and H. J. Neckerman. 1995. "Preventing Serious, Violent, and Chronic Juvenile Offending: A Review of Evaluations of Selected Strategies in Childhood, Adolescence, and the Community." In *A Sourcebook: Serious, Violent, and Chronic Juvenile Offenders*, edited by J. C. Howell, B. Krisberg, J. D. Hawkins, and J. J. Wilson. Thousand Oaks, Calif., and London: Sage.

Bridgeforth, Carol A. 1990. "Predicting Domestic Violence from Post-arrest Suspect Interviews." Master's dissertation, University of Maryland, Institute of Criminal Justice and Criminology.

Bridgeman, C., and L. Hobbs. 1997. *Preventing Repeat Victimisation: The Police Officers' Guide.* London: Police Research Group.

Brown, Jennifer Gerada. 1994. "The Use of Mediation to Resolve Criminal Cases: A Procedural Critique." *Emory Law Journal* 43:1247–1309.

Brown, M., and K. Polk. 1996. "Taking Fear of Crime Seriously: The Tasmanian Approach to Community Crime Prevention." *Crime and Delinquency* 42:398–420.

Burford, G., and J. Pennell. 1998. "Family Group Decision Making Project: Outcome Report, Volume I." St. John's: Newfoundland Memorial University.

Burley, A. 1992. "Toward an Age of Liberal Nations." *Harvard International Law Journal* 33:393–405.

Burnside, Jonathan, and Nicola Baker, eds. 1994. *Relational Justice: Repairing the Breach.* Winchester: Waterside.

Campbell, Bea. 1993. *Goliath: Britain's Dangerous Places.* London: Methuen.

Campbell, Tom. 1988. *Justice.* London: Macmillan.

Carnevale, Peter J., and Dean G. Pruitt. 1992. "Negotiation and Mediation." *Annual Review of Psychology* 43:531–82.

Chamlin, M. B., and J. K. Cochran. 1997. "Social Altruism and Crime." *Criminology* 35:203–28.

Chan, Wai Yin. 1996. "Family Conferences in the Juvenile Justice Process: Survey on the Impact of Family Conferencing on Juvenile Offenders and Their Families." Subordinate Courts Statistics and Planning Unit Research Bulletin, Singapore, February.

Christie, Nils. 1977. "Conflicts as Property." *British Journal of Criminology* 17:1–26.

City of Wagga Wagga. 1993. "Wagga Wagga's Communitarian Response to the Juvenile Justice Advisory Council's Green Paper 'Future Directions for Juvenile Justice in New South Wales.'" Wagga Wagga: City of Wagga Wagga.

Clairmont, Donald. 1994. "Alternative Justice Issues for Aboriginal Justice." Paper prepared for the Aboriginal Justice Directorate. Ottawa: Department of Justice.

Clinard, Marshall, and Peter C. Yeager. 1980. *Corporate Crime.* New York: Free Press.

Coats, R., and J. Gehm. 1985. *Victim Meets Offender: An Evaluation of Victim Offender Reconciliation Programs.* Valparaiso, Ind.: PACT Institute of Justice.

———. 1989. "An Empirical Assessment." In *Mediation and Criminal Justice*, edited by M. Wright and B. Galaway. London: Sage.

Cobb, Sara. 1997. "The Domestication of Violence in Mediation." *Law and Society Review* 31:397–440.

Coffee, J. C., Jr. 1981. "No Soul to Damn, No Body to Kick: An Unscandalized Essay on the Problem of Corporate Punishment." *Michigan Law Review* 79:413–24.

Cohen, A. K. 1955. *Delinquent Boys: The Culture of the Gang.* Glencoe, Ill.: Free Press.

Collinson, J. L. 1978. "Safety: Pleas and Prophylactics." *Mining Engineer* (July), pp. 73–83.

Confucius. 1974. *The Philosophy of Confucius*, trans. James Legge. New York: Crescent Books.

Crawford, Adam. 1996. *Victim/Offender Mediation and Reparation in Compara-*

tive European Cultures: France, England and Wales. Paper presented at the Australian and New Zealand Society of Criminology Conference, Wellington, January/February.

———. 1997. *The Local Governance of Crime: Appeals to Community and Partnerships.* Oxford: Clarendon.

Cullen, Francis T. 1994. "Social Support as an Organizing Concept for Criminology: Presidential Address to the Academy of Criminal Justice Sciences." *Justice Quarterly* 11:527–59.

Cunneen, C. 1997. "Community Conferencing and the Fiction of Indigenous Control." *Australian and New Zealand Journal of Criminology* 30:292–312.

Daly, K. 1996. "Diversionary Conferences in Australia: A Reply to the Optimists and Skeptics." Paper prepared for presentation at the annual meeting of the American Society of Criminology, Chicago, November.

Daly, K., and R. Immarigeon. 1998. "The Past, Present, and Future of Restorative Justice: Some Critical Reflections." *Contemporary Justice Review* 1(1): 21–46.

Davis, G. 1992. *Making Amends: Mediation and Reparation in Criminal Justice.* London: Routledge.

Davis, Robert T., and R. W. Stahl. 1967. "Safety Organization and Activities of Award-Winning Companies in the Coal Mining Industry." Bureau of Mines Information circular 8224. Washington, D.C.: Bureau of Mines.

De Haan, W. 1990. *The Politics of Redress: Crime, Punishment and Penal Abolition.* London: Unwin Hyman.

DeMichiei, John M., John F. Langton, Kenneth A. Bullock, and Terrance C. Wiles. 1982. *Factors Associated with Disabling Injuries in Underground Coal Mines.* Washington, D.C.: Mine Safety and Health Administration.

Dignan, J. 1990. *An Evaluation of an Experimental Adult Reparation Scheme in Kettering, Northamptonshire.* Sheffield: University of Sheffield, Centre for Criminological and Legal Research.

———. 1992. "Repairing the Damage: Can Reparation Work in the Service of Diversion?" *British Journal of Criminology* 32:453–72.

Dingwall, Robert, J. Eekelaar, and T. Murray. 1983. *The Protection of Children: State Intervention and Family Life.* Oxford: Blackwell.

Dinnen, Sinclair. 1996. "Challenges of Order in a Weak State." Ph.D. dissertation, Australian National University.

Doob, A., and J. Roberts. 1983. *Sentencing: An Analysis of the Public's View of Sentencing. A Report in the Department of Justice, Canada.* Ottawa: Department of Justice.

———. 1988. "Public Attitudes towards Sentencing in Canada." In *Public Attitudes to Sentencing,* edited by N. Walker and M. Hough. Aldershot: Gower.

Doyle, M. 1983. "Kant, Liberal Legacies and Foreign Affairs," pts. 1 and 2. *Philosophy and Public Affairs* 12(3):205–35; 12(4):323–53.

———. 1986. "Liberalism and World Politics." *American Political Science Review* 80(4):1151–69.

Dunford, F. 1990. "System-Initiated Warrants for Suspects of Misdemeanour Domestic Assault: A Pilot Study." *Justice Quarterly* 7:631–53.

Durkheim, E. 1961. *Moral Education: A Study in the Theory and Application of the Sociology of Education*, trans. E. K. Wilson and H. Schnurer. New York: Free Press.

Eckel, Malcolm David. 1997. "A Buddhist Approach to Repentance." In *Repentance: A Comparative Perspective*, edited by Amitai Etzioni and David E. Carney. New York: Rowman & Littlefield.

Eglash, Albert. 1975. "Beyond Restitution: Creative Restitution." In *Restitution in Criminal Justice*, edited by J. Hudson and B. Galaway. Lexington, Mass.: Lexington Books.

Elliott, D. S., and H. L. Voss. 1974. *Delinquency and Dropout*. Lexington, Mass.: Lexington Books.

Emler, N., and S. Reicher. 1995. *Adolescence and Delinquency: The Collective Management of Reputation*. Oxford: Blackwell.

Ervin, L., and A. Schneider. 1990. "Explaining the Effects of Restitution on Offenders: Results from a National Experiment in Juvenile Courts." In *Criminal Justice, Restitution and Reconciliation*, edited by B. Galaway and J. Hudson. New York: Willow Tree.

Esbensen, Finn-Aage, and David Huizinga. 1993. "Gangs, Drugs and Delinquency in a Survey of Urban Youth." *Criminology* 31:565–87.

Farrington, David P. 1993. "Understanding and Preventing Bullying." In *Crime and Justice: A Review of Research*, vol. 17, edited by M. Tonry. Chicago: University of Chicago Press.

Findlay, Mark. 1998. "Decolonising Restoration and Justice." *Current Issues in Criminal Justice* 10:85–88.

Fisse, B. 1983. "Reconstructing Corporate Criminal Law: Deterrence, Retribution, Fault, and Sanctions." *Southern California Law Review* 56:1141–1246.

Fisse, B., and J. Braithwaite. 1993. *Corporations, Crime and Accountability*. Cambridge: Cambridge University Press.

Fitzpatrick, Peter. 1992. "The Impossibility of Popular Justice." *Social and Legal Studies* 1:199–215.

Forsythe, Lubica. 1995. "An Analysis of Juvenile Apprehension Characteristics and Reapprehension Rates." In *A New Approach to Juvenile Justice: An Evaluation of Family Conferencing in Wagga Wagga*, edited by David Moore, with Lubica Forsythe and Terry O'Connell. A report to the Criminology Research Council. Wagga Wagga: Charles Sturt University.

Foucault, Michel. 1977. *Discipline and Punish: The Birth of the Prison*. London: Pantheon.

Fry, Don. 1997. "A Report on Diversionary Conferencing." Alice Springs: Northern Territory Police.

Fuller, Lon. 1964. *The Morality of Law*. New Haven, Conn.: Yale University Press.

Galaway, B. 1992. "The New Zealand Experience Implementing the Reparation Sentence." In *Restorative Justice on Trial: Pitfalls and Potentials of Victim-Offender Mediation—International Research Perspectives*, edited by H. Messmer and H. U. Otto. Dordrecht and Boston: Kluwer.

Galaway, Burt, and Joe Hudson, eds. 1975. *Considering the Victim*. Springfield, Ill.: Charles C. Thomas.

Garland, D. 1985. *Punishment and Welfare*. Aldershot: Gower.

——. 1990. *Punishment and Modern Society*. Oxford: Clarendon.

Geertz, Clifford. 1983. *Local Knowledge*. New York: Basic Books.

Gehm, John. 1990. "Mediated Victim-Offender Restitution Agreements: An Exploratory Analysis of Factors Related to Victim Participation." In *Criminal Justice, Restitution, and Reconciliation*, edited by B. Galaway and J. Hudson. Monsey, N.Y.: Willow Tree.

Gentry, Deborah B., and Wayne A. Benenson. 1993. "School-to-Home Transfer of Conflict Management Skills among School-Age Children." *Families in Society* 74(February):67–73.

Gernet, Jacques. 1982. *A History of Chinese Civilization*. Cambridge: Cambridge University Press.

Goffman, E. 1956. "Embarrassment and Social Organization." *American Journal of Sociology* 62:264–71.

Goldgeir, James, and Michael McFaul. 1992. "A Tale of Two Worlds: Core and Periphery in the Post–Cold War Era." *International Organization* 46:467–92.

Goodes, T. 1995. "Victims and Family Conferences: Juvenile Justice in South Australia." Adelaide: Family Conferencing Team.

Gottfredson, Denise. 1997. "School-Based Crime Prevention." In *Preventing Crime: What Works, What Doesn't, What's Promising: A Report to the United States Congress*, edited by Lawrence Sherman, Denise Gottfredson, Doris MacKenzie, John Eck, Peter Reuter, and Shawn Bushway. Washington, D.C.: National Institute of Justice.

Gottfredson, S. D., and D. M. Gottfredson. 1994. "Behavioral Prediction and the Problem of Incapacitation." *Criminology* 32:441–74.

Gottfredson, Stephen D., and Ralph B. Taylor. 1987. "Attitudes of Correctional Policymakers and the Public." In *America's Correctional Crisis: Prison Populations and Public Policy*, edited by Stephen D. Gottfredson and Sean McConville. New York: Greenwood.

Green, Ross Gordon. 1998. *Justice in Aboriginal Communities*. Saskatoon: Purich.

Griffiths, Curt Taylor, and Ron Hamilton. 1996. "Sanctioning and Healing: Restorative Justice in Canadian Aboriginal Communities." In *Restorative Justice: International Perspectives*, edited by Burt Galaway and Joe Hudson. Monsey, N.Y.: Criminal Justice Press.

Gunningham, Neil. 1995. "Environment, Self-Regulation and the Chemical Industry: Assessing Responsible Care." *Law and Policy* 17:57–109.

Gunningham, Neil, and Peter Grabosky. 1998. *Smart Regulation: Designing Environmental Policy*. Oxford: Clarendon.

Habermas, Jürgen. 1996. *Between Facts and Norms: Contributions to a Discourse Theory of Law and Democracy*. London: Polity.

Hagan, J. 1991. "Destiny and Drift: Subcultural Preferences, Status Attainments, and the Risks and Rewards of Youth." *American Sociological Review* 56:567–82.

Hagan, John, and Bill McCarthy. 1997. *Mean Streets: Youth Crime and Homelessness*. Cambridge: Cambridge University Press.

Haines, Fiona. 1997. *Corporate Regulation: Beyond "Punish or Persuade."* Oxford: Clarendon.

Haines, Kevin. 1999. "Some Principled Objections to a Restorative Justice Approach to Working with Juvenile Offenders." In *Restorative Juvenile Justice: Repairing the Harm of Youth Crime*, edited by G. Bazemore and L. Walgrave. Monsey, N.Y.: Criminal Justice Press.

Haley, John. 1996. "Crime Prevention through Restorative Justice: Lessons from Japan." In *Restorative Justice: International Perspectives*, edited by Burt Galaway and Joe Hudson. Monsey, N.Y.: Criminal Justice Press.

Haley, John, assisted by A. M. Neugebauer. 1992. "Victim-Offender Mediations: Japanese and American Comparisons." In *Restorative Justice on Trial: Pitfalls and Potentials of Victim-Offender Mediation—International Research Perspectives*, edited by H. Messmer and H. U. Otto. Dordrecht and Boston: Kluwer.

Harris, M. K. 1991. "Moving into the New Millennium: Toward a Feminist Vision of Justice." In *Criminology as Peacemaking*, edited by H. E. Pepinsky and R. Quinney. Bloomington: Indiana University Press.

Harris, Nathan, and Jamie Burton. 1997. *The Reliability of Observed Reintegrative Shaming, Shame, Defiance and Other Key Concepts in Diversionary Conferences*. RISE Working papers. Canberra: Australian National University.

Hassall, Ian. 1996. "Origin and Development of Family Group Conferences." In *Family Group Conferences: Perspectives on Policy and Practice*, edited by Joe Hudson, Allison Morris, Gabrielle Maxwell, and Burt Galaway. Sydney: Federation Press and Criminal Justice Press.

Hawkins, Keith. 1984. *Environment and Enforcement: Regulation and the Social Definition of Pollution*. Oxford: Clarendon.

Hay, D. 1975. "Property, Authority and the Criminal Law." In *Albion's Fatal Tree*, edited by D. Hay, P. Linebaugh, J. G. Rule, E. P. Thompson, and C. Winslow. London: Allen Lane.

Heidensohn, Frances. 1986. "Models of Justice: Portia or Persephone? Some Thoughts on Equality, Fairness and Gender in the Field of Criminal Justice." *International Journal of the Sociology of Law* 14:287–98.

Heimer, Carol A., and Lisa R. Staffen. 1995. "Interdependence and Reintegrative Social Control: Labeling and Reforming 'Inappropriate' Parents in Neonatal Intensive Care Units." *American Sociological Review* 60:635–54.

Heinz, A., and W. Kerstetter. 1981. "Pretrial Settlement Conference: Evaluation of a Reform in Plea Bargaining." In *Perspective on Crime Victims*, edited by B. Galaway and J. Hudson. St. Louis: Mosby.

Hogg, Russel, and David Brown. 1985. "Reforming Juvenile Justice: Issues and Prospects." In *Juvenile Delinquency in Australia*, edited by A. Borowski and J. Murray. Sydney: Methuen Australia.

Hough, Michael, and Julian Roberts. 1998. "Attitudes to Punishments: Findings from the British Crime Survey." Home Office Research Study no. 179. London: H. M. Stationery Office.

Hoyle, Carolyn, and Richard Young. 1998. "A Survey of Restorative Cautioning with the Thames Valley Police." Oxford: University of Oxford, Centre for Criminological Research.

Hsien, Lim Li. 1996. "Family Conferencing Good for Young Delinquents: Report." *Straits Times* (March 6).

Huang, Ray. 1988. *China: A Macro History.* Armonk, N.Y.: M. E. Sharpe.

Hudson, Joe. 1998. "Conducting the Family Group Conference Process: An Overview." Paper presented at "Conferencing: A New Response to Wrongdoing," Minneapolis, August.

Hughes, Gordon. 1996. "Convergent and Divergent Discourses of Communitarian Crime Prevention: A Meditation on Current Developments in Europe, the USA, Australia and New Zealand." Paper presented to the annual conference of the Australian and New Zealand Society of Criminology, January/February, Wellington.

Iivari, J. 1987. "Mediation as a Conflict Resolution: Some Topic Issues in Mediation Project in Vantaa." Paper presented to the International Seminar on Mediation, Finland, September. Cited in *Crime and Accountability: Victim Offender Mediation in Practice*, edited by T. Marshall and S. Merry. 1990. London: Home Office.

———. 1992. "The Process of Mediation in Finland: A Special Reference to the Question 'How to Get Cases for Mediation.' " In *Restorative Justice on Trial: Pitfalls and Potentials of Victim-Offender Mediation—International Research Perspectives*, edited by H. Messmer and H. U. Otto. Dordrecht and Boston: Kluwer.

Jackson, Moana. 1987. "The Maori and the Criminal Justice System: A New Perspective—He Whaipaanga Hou." Report for New Zealand Department of Justice. Wellington: Department of Justice, Policy and Research Division.

James, T. M. 1993. "Circle Sentencing." Yellowknife: Supreme Court of the Northwest Territories.

Jenkins, Ann L. 1997. "The Role of Managerial Self-Efficacy in Corporate Compliance with Regulatory Standards." Ph.D. dissertation, Australian National University.

Karstedt-Henke, Susanne, and Bernhard Crasmoller. 1991. "Risks of Being Detected, Chances of Getting Away." In *The Future of the Juvenile Justice System*, edited by J. Junger-Tas, L. Boendermaker, and P. van der Laan. Leuven: Acco.

Katz, I., D. Glass, and S. Cohen. 1973. "Ambivalence, Guilt and the Scapegoating of Minority Group Victims." *Journal of Experimental Social Psychology* 9:423–36.

Kelman, Steven. 1984. "Enforcement of Occupational Safety and Health Regulations: A Comparison of Swedish and American Practices." In *Enforcing Regulation*, edited by Keith Hawkins and John M. Thomas. Boston: Kluwer-Nijhoff.

Kerner, H., E. Marks, and J. Schreckling. 1992. "Implementation and Acceptance of Victim-Offender Mediation Programs in the Federal Republic of Germany: A Survey of Criminal Justice Institutions." In *Restorative Justice on Trial: Pitfalls and Potentials of Victim-Offender Mediation—International Research Perspectives*, edited by H. Messmer and H. U. Otto. Dordrecht and Boston: Kluwer.

Kigin, R., and S. Novack. 1980. "A Rural Restitution Program for Juvenile Offenders and Victims." In *Victims, Offenders and Alternative Sanction*, edited by J. Hudson and B. Galaway. Lexington, Mass.: Lexington Books.

Kinsey, Karyl A. 1986. "Theories and Models of Tax Cheating." *Criminal Justice Abstracts* (September), pp. 402–25.

Knight, T. 1985. "Schools and Delinquency." In *Juvenile Delinquency in Australia*, edited by A. Borowski and J. M. Murray. Melbourne: Methuen.

Koh, Angeline Cheok Eng. 1997. "The Delinquent Peer Group: Social Identity and Self-Categorization Perspectives." Ph.D. dissertation, Australian National University.

Krawll, M. B. 1994. *Understanding the Role of Healing in Aboriginal Communities*. Ottawa: Solicitor General Canada, Ministry Secretariat.

Kuhn, A. 1987. "Koperverletzung als Konflikt, Zwischenbericht 1987 zum Project Handschlag." Unpublished paper cited in T. Trenczek, "A Review and Assessment of Victim-Offender Reconciliation Programming in West Germany." In *Criminal Justice, Restitution and Reconciliation*, edited by B. Galaway and J. Hudson. Monsey, N.Y.: Willow.

Lacey, N. 1988. *State Punishment: Political Principles and Community Values*. London: Routledge.

Lajeunesse, T. 1993. *Community Holistic Circle Healing: Hollow Water First Nation, Aboriginal Peoples Collection*. Ottawa: Solicitor General, Canada, Ministry Secretariat.

Lam, J. A. 1989. *The Impact of Conflict Resolution Programs on Schools: A Review and Synthesis of the Evidence*. Amherst, Mass.: National Association for Mediation in Education.

Langbein, L., and C. M. Kerwin. 1985. "Implementation, Negotiation and Compliance in Environmental and Safety Regulation." *Journal of Politics* 47:854–80.

La Prairie, C. 1994. *Seen but Not Heard: Native People in the Inner City*. Report 3, *Victimisation and Domestic Violence*. Ottawa: Ottawa Department of Justice.

———. 1995. "Altering Course: New Directions in Criminal Justice and Corrections: Sentencing Circles and Family Group Conferences." *Australian and New Zealand Journal of Criminology* ("Special Issue: Crime, Criminology, and Public Policy," edited by David Dixon) 28(December):78–99.

Laue, James H. 1991. "Contributions of the Emerging Field of Conflict Resolution." In *Approaches to Peace: An Intellectual Map*, edited by W. S. Thompson, K. M. Jensen, Richard N. Smith, and Kimber M. Schraub. Washington, D.C.: U.S. Institute of Peace.

Lewis, David. 1986. "Causation" and "Postscript: Redundant Causation." In *Philosophical Papers*, vol. 2. Oxford: Oxford University Press.

Lewis, Helen B. 1971. *Shame and Guilt in Neurosis*. New York: International Universities Press.

Lewis-Beck, Michael S., and John R. Alford. 1980. "Can Government Regulate Safety: The Coal Mine Example." *American Political Science Review* 74:745–56.

Lind, E. Allan, and Tom R. Tyler. 1988. *The Social Psychology of Procedural Justice*. New York: Plenum.

Longclaws, Lyle, Burt Galaway, and Lawrence Barkwell. 1996. "Piloting Family Group Conferences for Young Aboriginal Offenders in Winnipeg, Canada." In *Family Group Conferences: Perspectives on Policy and Practice*, edited by Joe Hudson, Allison Morris, Gabrielle Maxwell, and Burt Galaway. Sydney: Federation Press and Criminal Justice Press.

Lu, Hong 1998. "Community Policing—Rhetoric or Reality? The Contemporary Chinese Community-Based Policing System in Shanghai." Ph.D. dissertation, Arizona State University.

MacKenzie, D. L. 1997. "Criminal Justice and Crime Prevention." In *Preventing Crime: What Works, What Doesn't, What's Promising: A Report to the United States Congress*, edited by Lawrence Sherman, Denise Gottfredson, Doris MacKenzie, John Eck, Peter Reuter, and Shawn Bushway. Washington, D.C.: National Institute of Justice.

Makkai, T., and J. Braithwaite. 1991. "Criminological Theories and Regulatory Compliance." *Criminology* 29:191–220.

———. 1993*a*. "Praise, Pride and Corporate Compliance." *International Journal of the Sociology of Law* 21:73–91.

———. 1993*b*. "The Limits of the Economic Analysis of Regulation." *Law and Policy* 15:271–91.

———. 1994. "Reintegrative Shaming and Regulatory Compliance." *Criminology* 32:361–85.

———. 1996. "Procedural Justice and Regulatory Compliance." *Law and Human Behavior* 20:83–98.

Maoz, Z., and N. Abdolali. 1989. "Regime Types and International Conflict, 1816–1976." *Journal of Conflict Resolution* 33:3–36.

Marshall, T. F. 1985. *Alternatives to Criminal Courts*. Aldershot: Gower.

———. 1992. "Restorative Justice on Trial in Britain." In *Restorative Justice on Trial: Pitfalls and Potentials of Victim-Offender Mediation—International Research Perspectives*, edited by H. Messmer and H. U. Otto. Dordrecht and Boston: Kluwer.

Marshall, T. F., and S. Merry. 1990. *Crime and Accountability: Victim Offender Mediation in Practice*. London: Home Office.

Masters, Guy. 1995. "The Family Model of Social Control in Japanese Secondary Schools." Unpublished manuscript. Lancaster: Lancaster University, Department of Applied Social Science.

———. 1997. *Reintegrative Shaming in Theory and Practice*. Ph.D. dissertation, Lancaster University.

Masters, Guy, and David Smith. 1998. "Portia and Persephone Revisited: Thinking about Feeling in Criminal Justice." *Theoretical Criminology* 2:5–28.

Matza, D. 1964. *Delinquency and Drift*. New York: Wiley.

Maxwell, Gabrielle M. 1993. "Arrangements for Children after Separation? Problems and Possibilities." In *Women's Law Conference Papers: 1993 New Zealand Suffrage Centennial*. Wellington: Victoria University of Wellington.

Maxwell, Gabrielle M., and Allison Morris. 1993. *Family, Victims and Culture: Youth Justice in New Zealand*. Wellington: Victoria University of Wellington, New Zealand Social Policy Agency and Institute of Criminology.

———. 1996. "Research on Family Group Conferences with Young Offenders in New Zealand." In *Family Group Conferences: Perspectives on Policy and Practice*, edited by Joe Hudson, Allison Morris, Gabrielle Maxwell, and Burt Galaway. Sydney: Federation Press and Criminal Justice Press.

McCold, Paul. 1997. "Restorative Justice Variations on a Theme." Paper presented at the international conference "Restorative Justice for Juveniles—Potentialities, Risks and Problems for Research," Leuven, Belgium, May 12–14.

McCold, Paul, and Benjamin Wachtel. 1998. "Restorative Policing Experiment: The Bethlehem Pennsylvania Police Family Group Conferencing Project." Report. Pipersville, Pa.: Community Service Foundation.

McDonald, J., D. Moore, T. O'Connell, and M. Thorsborbe. 1995. *Real Justice Training Manual: Coordinating Family Group Conferences.* Pipersville, Pa.: Pipers Press.

Meima, M. 1990. "Sexual Violence, Criminal Law and Abolitionism." In *Gender, Sexuality and Social Control,* edited by B. Rolston and M. Tomlinson. Bristol: European Group for the Study of Deviance and Social Control.

Melton, Ada Pecos. 1995. "Indigenous Justice Systems and Tribal Society." *Judicature* 79:126.

Michael, Franz. 1986. *China through the Ages: History of a Civilization.* Taipei: SMC.

Mine Enforcement and Safety Administration. 1977. *A Report on Civil Penalty Effectiveness.* Washington, D.C.: Mine Enforcement and Safety Administration.

Ministry of Justice, Western Australia. 1994. "Juvenile Justice Teams: A Six Month Evaluation." Perth: Ministry of Justice.

Minor, Kevin I., and J. T. Morrison. 1996. "A Theoretical Study and Critique of Restorative Justice." In *Restorative Justice: International Perspectives,* edited by Burt Galaway and Joe Hudson. Monsey, N.Y.: Criminal Justice Press.

Minow, Martha. 1990. *Making All the Difference: Inclusion, Exclusion and American Law.* Ithaca, N.Y.: Cornell University Press.

Miyazawa, Setsuo. 1992. *Policing in Japan: A Study on Making Crime.* Albany, N.Y.: SUNY Press.

Moore, David B. 1994. "Public Anger and Personal Justice: From Retribution to Restoration—and Beyond." Paper to the Silvan S. Tomkins Institute Colloquium "The Experience and Expression of Anger," October, Philadelphia.

Moore, David B., with L. Forsythe. 1995. *A New Approach to Juvenile Justice: An Evaluation of Family Conferencing in Wagga Wagga.* Wagga Wagga: Charles Sturt University.

Moore, David B., and Terry O'Connell. 1994. "Family Conferencing in Wagga Wagga: A Communitarian Model of Justice." In *Family Conferencing and Juvenile Justice,* edited by Christine Alder and Joy Wundersitz. Canberra: Australian Studies in Law, Crime, and Justice, Australian Institute of Criminology.

Morris, Allison, Gabrielle Maxwell, Joe Hudson, and Burt Galaway. 1996. "Concluding Thoughts." In *Family Group Conferences: Perspectives on Policy and Practice*, edited by Joe Hudson, Allison Morris, Gabrielle Maxwell, and Burt Galaway. Sydney: Federation Press and Criminal Justice Press.

Morris, Ruth. 1995. "Not Enough!" *Mediation Quarterly* 12(3):285–91.

Mugford, S., and N. I. Inkpen. 1995. *The Implementation of Shaming Conferences as a New Policy Strategy: The Case of Drink Drivers*. Paper presented at the forty-seventh American Society of Criminology Conference, Boston, November.

Murphy, Jeffrie, G., and Jean Hampton. 1989. *Forgiveness and Mercy*. New York: Cambridge.

Nagin, Daniel. 1978. "Crime Rates, Sanction Levels and Constraints on Prison Population." *Law and Society Review* 12:341–66.

Nathanson, Donald. L. 1992. *Shame and Pride: Affect, Sex and the Birth of the Self*. New York: Norton

———. 1998. "From Empathy to Community." Paper presented at "Conferencing: A New Response to Wrongdoing," August, Minneapolis. Available on the Real Justice website: www.realjustice.org.

Newman, Graeme. 1983. *Just and Painful*. London: Macmillan.

Nicholl, Caroline G. 1998. *Implementing Restorative Justice*. Washington, D.C.: U.S. Department of Justice, Office of Community Oriented Policing Services.

Novack, S., B. Galaway, and J. Hudson. 1980. "Victim and Offender Perceptions of the Fairness of Restitution and Community-Service Sanctions." In *Victims, Offenders and Alternative Sanctions*, edited by J. Hudson and B. Galaway. Lexington, Mass.: Lexington Books.

Nugent, W. R., and J. B. Paddock. 1995. "The Effect of Victim-Offender Mediation on Severity of Reoffense." *Mediation Quarterly* 12:353–67.

Obonsawin-Irwin Consulting, Inc. 1992*a*. "An Evaluation of the Sandy Lake First Nation Justice Project." Ontario: Ministry of the Attorney General.

———. 1992*b*. "An Evaluation of the Attawapiskat First Nation Justice Project." Ontario: Ministry of the Attorney General.

Offer, A. 1994. "Going to War in 1914: A Matter of Honour?" Paper presented at the Australian War Memorial Conference.

Olweus, Dan. 1993. "Annotation: Bullying at School: Basic Facts and Effects of a School Based Intervention Program." *Journal of Child Psychology and Psychiatry* 35:1171–90.

Palk, Gerard, Hennessey Hayes, and Timothy Prenzler. 1998. "Restorative Justice and Community Conferencing: Summary of Findings from a Pilot Study." *Current Issues in Criminal Justice* 10:138–55.

Parker, Christine. 1998. "Public Rights in Private Government: Corporate Compliance with Sexual Harassment Legislation." *Australian Journal of Human Rights* 5(1):159–93.

———. 1999*a*. "Compliance Professionalism and Regulatory Community: The Australian Trade Practices Regime." *Journal of Law and Society* 26:215–39.

———. 1999*b*. *Just Lawyers*. Oxford: Oxford University Press.

Pate, K. 1990. "Victim-Offender Restitution Programs in Canada." In *Crimi-*

nal Justice, Restitution and Reconciliation, edited by B. Galaway and J. Hudson. New York: Willow Tree.

Paternoster, Raymond, Robert Brame, Ronet Bachman, and Lawrence W. Sherman. 1997. "Do Fair Procedures Matter? The Effect of Procedural Justice on Spouse Assault." *Law and Society Review* 31:163–204.

Pavlich, George. 1996. "The Power of Community Mediation: Government and Formation of Self-Identity." *Law and Society Review* 30:707–33.

Peachey, D. E. 1989. "The Kitchener Experiment." In *Mediation and Criminal Justice: Victims, Offenders and Community*, edited by M. Wright and B. Galaway. London: Sage.

Pease, Ken. 1998. "Repeat Victimisation: Taking Stock." Crime Detection and Prevention Series Paper no. 90. London: Police Research Group.

Pennell, Joan, and Gale Burford. 1995. *Family Group Decision Making: New Roles for "Old" Partners in Resolving Family Violence*. Implementation Report, vol 1. St. John's: University of Newfoundland, School of Social Work, Family Group Decision Making Project.

———. 1996. "Attending to Context: Family Group Decision Making in Canada." In *Family Group Conferences: Perspectives on Policy and Practice*, edited by Joe Hudson, Allison Morris, Gabrielle Maxwell, and Burt Galaway. Sydney: Federation Press and Criminal Justice Press.

———. 1997. "Family Group Decision Making: After the Conference—Progress in Resolving Violence and Promoting Well-Being." St. John's: University of Newfoundland, School of Social Work, Family Group Decision Making Project.

Pepinsky, H. E., and R. Quinney, eds. 1991. *Criminology as Peacemaking*. Bloomington: Indiana University Press.

Pepler, Debra J., Wendy Craig, Suzanne Ziegler, and Alice Charach. 1993. "A School-Based Antibullying Intervention." In *Understanding and Managing Bullying*, edited by Delwin Tattum. London: Heinemann.

Perry, Charles S. 1981a. "Safety Laws and Spending Save Lives: An Analysis of Coal Mine Fatality Rates, 1930–1979." Unpublished manuscript. Lexington: University of Kentucky, Department of Sociology.

———. 1981b. "Dying to Dig Coal: Fatalities in Deep and Surface Coal Mining in Appalachian States, 1930–1978." Unpublished manuscript. Lexington: University of Kentucky, Department of Sociology.

Pettit, P. 1993. "Liberalism and Republicanism." *Australian Journal of Political Science* 28:162–89.

———. 1997. *Republicanism*. Oxford: Clarendon.

Phillips, A. 1991. *Engendering Democracy*. Cambridge: Polity.

Pitts, John, and Philip Smith. 1995. "Preventing School Bullying." Police Research Group Crime Detection and Prevention Series Paper no. 63. London: Home Office.

Polanyi, Michael. 1951. *The Logic of Liberty*. Chicago: University of Chicago Press.

Polk, Ken. 1994. "Family Conferencing: Theoretical and Evaluative Questions." In *Family Conferencing and Juvenile Justice*, edited by Christine Alder and Joy Wundersitz. Australian Studies in Law, Crime, and Justice. Canberra: Australian Institute of Criminology.

122   John Braithwaite

Pontell, Henry. 1978. "Deterrence: Theory versus Practice." *Criminology* 16:3–22.
Posner, Richard A. 1977. *Economic Analysis of Law*. 2d ed. Boston and Toronto: Little, Brown.
Pranis, K. 1996. "A State Initiative toward Restorative Justice: The Minnesota Experience." In *Restorative Justice: International Perspectives*, edited by B. Galaway and J. Hudson. Monsey, N.Y.: Criminal Justice Press.
Pratt, John. 1996. "Colonization, Power and Silence: A History of Indigenous Justice in New Zealand Society." In *Restorative Justice: International Perspectives*, edited by Burt Galaway and Joe Hudson. Monsey, N.Y.: Criminal Justice Press.
Reed, P. 1986. "Developmental Resources and Depression in the Elderly." *Nursing Research* 36:368–74.
———. 1987. "Spirituality and Well-Being in Terminally Ill Hospitalized Adults." *Research in Nursing and Health* 10:335–44.
———. 1992. "An Emerging Paradigm for the Study of Spirituality in Nursing." *Research in Nursing and Health* 15:349–57.
Rees, Joseph V. 1988. *Reforming the Workplace: A Study of Self-Regulation in Occupational Safety*. Philadelphia: University of Pennsylvania Press.
———. 1994. *Hostages of Each Other: The Transformation of Nuclear Safety since Three Mile Island*. Chicago: University of Chicago Press.
Rensselaer, W. L., III. 1992. "Colombia's Cocaine Syndicates." In *War on Drugs: Studies in the Failure of U.S. Narcotics Policy*, edited by A. McCoy and A. Block. Boulder, Colo.: Westview.
Retzinger, Suzanne. 1991. *Violent Emotions*. Newbury Park, Calif.: Sage.
Retzinger, Suzanne, and Thomas J. Scheff. 1996. "Strategy for Community Conferences: Emotions and Social Bonds." In *Restorative Justice: International Perspectives*, edited by Burt Galaway and Joe Hudson. Monsey, N.Y.: Criminal Justice Press.
Rigby, Ken. 1996. *Bullying in Schools and What to Do about It*. Melbourne: Australian Council for Educational Research.
Rigby, Ken, Alison Whish, and Garry Black. 1994. "School Children's Peer Relations and Wife Abuse." *Criminology Australia* (August), pp. 8–12.
Roach, Kent. 1999. *Due Process and Victims' Rights: The New Law and Politics of Criminal Justice*. Toronto: University of Toronto Press.
Roberts, Julian V., and Loretta J. Stalans. 1997. *Public Opinion, Crime, and Criminal Justice*. Boulder, Colo.: Westview.
Robertson, Jeremy. 1996. "Research on Family Group Conferences in Child Welfare in New Zealand." In *Family Group Conferences: Perspectives on Policy and Practice*, edited by Joe Hudson, Allison Morris, Gabrielle Maxwell, and Burt Galaway. Sydney: Federation Press and Criminal Justice Press.
Ross, Rupert. 1996. *Returning to the Teachings: Exploring Aboriginal Justice*. London: Penguin.
Rumsey, Alan. 1999. "Women as Peacemakers in the New Guinea Highlands: A Case from the Nebilyer Valley, Western Highlands Province?" In *Reflections on Violence in Melanesia*, edited by Sinclair Dinnen and Allison Ley. Sydney: Federation Press.

Sandor, Danny. 1993. "Juvenile Justice: The Thickening Blue Wedge." *Alternative Law Journal* 18:104–8.

Scheff, Thomas J. 1990. *Microsociology: Discourse, Emotion, and Social Structure.* Chicago: University of Chicago Press.

———. 1994. *Bloody Revenge: Emotions, Nationalism and War.* Boulder, Colo.: Westview.

Scheff, Thomas J., and Suzanne M. Retzinger. 1991. *Emotions and Violence: Shame and Rage in Destructive Conflicts.* Lexington, Mass.: Lexington Books.

Scheingold, Stuart A., Jana Pershing, and Toska Olson. 1994. "Sexual Violence, Victim Advocacy, and Republican Criminology: Washington State's Community Protection Act." *Law and Society Review* 28(4):501–33.

Schiff, Mara F. 1998. "The Impact of Restorative Interventions on Juvenile Offenders." In *Restoring Juvenile Justice*, edited by Lode Walgrave and Gordon Bazemore. Monsey, N.Y.: Criminal Justice Press.

Schneider, A. 1986. "Restitution and Recidivism Rates of Juvenile Offenders: Results from Four Experimental Studies." *Criminology* 24:533–52.

———. 1990. *Deterrence and Juvenile Crime: Results from a National Policy Experiment.* New York: Springer-Verlag.

Scholz, John T., and Wayne B. Gray. 1990. "OSHA Enforcement and Workplace Injuries: A Behavioral Approach to Risk Assessment." *Journal of Risk and Uncertainty* 3:283–305.

Sessar, Klaus. 1990. "Tertiary Victimisation: A Case of the Politically Abused Crime Victims." In *Criminal Justice, Restitution and Reconciliation*, edited by B. Galaway and J. Hudson. Monsey, N.Y.: Willow Tree.

———. 1998. "Punitive Attitudes of the Public: Reality and Myth." In *Restoring Juvenile Justice*, edited by Lode Walgrave and Gordon Bazemore. Amsterdam: Kugler.

Sessar, K., A. Beuerskens, and K. Boers. 1986. "Wiedergutmachung als Konfliktregelungsparadigma?" *Kriminologisches Journal* 18:86–105.

Shapland, J., J. Willmore, and P. Duff. 1985. *Victims in the Criminal Justice System.* Cambridge Studies in Criminology. Brookfield, Vt.: Gower.

Shearing, Clifford. 1995. "Reinventing Policing: Policing as Governance." In *Privatisierung staatlicher Kontrolle: Befunde, Konzepte, Tendenzen. Interdisziplinare Studien zu Recht und Staat* 3:69–88.

———. 1997. "Violence and the Changing Face of Governance: Privatization and Its Implications." Cape Town: Community Peace Foundation.

Sherman, L. W. 1992. *Policing Domestic Violence.* New York: Free Press.

———. 1993. "Defiance, Deterrence and Irrelevance: A Theory of the Criminal Sanction." *Journal of Research in Crime and Delinquency* 30:445–73.

Sherman, L. W., and G. Barnes. 1997. "Restorative Justice and Offenders' Respect for the Law." RISE Working Paper no. 3. Canberra: Australian National University, Research School of Social Sciences, Law Program.

Sherman, Lawrence, Denise Gottfredson, Doris MacKenzie, John Eck, Peter Reuter, and Shawn Bushway. 1997. *Preventing Crime: What Works, What Doesn't, What's Promising: A Report to the United States Congress.* Washington, D.C.: National Institute of Justice.

Sherman, L. W., and H. Strang. 1997*a*. "The Right Kind of Shame for Crime

124   John Braithwaite

Prevention." RISE Working Paper no. 1. Canberra: Australian National University, Research School of Social Sciences, Law Program.

———. 1997b. "Restorative Justice and Deterring Crime." RISE Working Paper no. 4. Canberra: Australian National University, Research School of Social Sciences, Law Program.

———. 1997c. "Community Policing and Restorative Justice." Press Release, Australian National University, April 21.

Sherman, L. W., H. Strang, G. C. Barnes, J. Braithwaite, N. Inkpen, and M. M. Teh. 1998. "Experiments in Restorative Policing: A Progress Report." Canberra: Australian National University, Research School of Social Sciences, Law Program.

Shover, Neal. 1996. *Great Pretenders: Pursuits and Careers of Persistent Thieves.* Boulder, Colo.: Westview.

Skinner, Q. 1984. "The Idea of Negative Liberty: Philosophical and Historical Perspectives." In *Philosophy in History: Essays on the Historiography of Philosophy,* edited by R. Rorty, J. Schneewind, and Q. Skinner. Cambridge: Cambridge University Press.

Smith, D., H. Blagg, and N. Derricourt. 1985. "Victim-Offender Mediation Project." Report to the Chief Officers' Group, South Yorkshire Probation Service. Cited in *Crime and Accountability: Victim-Offender Mediation in Practice,* edited by T. Marshall and S. Merry. 1990. London: Home Office.

Sonnekus, Eon, and Cheryl Frank. 1997. "Reconstructing and Developing Juvenile Justice in the New South Africa: Towards Restorative Juvenile Justice." Paper presented to the conference on Restorative Justice for Juveniles, Leuven, Belgium, April.

Stewart, Trish. 1993. "The Youth Justice Co-ordinator's Role—a Personal Perspective of the New Legislation in Action." In *The Youth Court in New Zealand: A New Model of Justice,* edited by B. J. Brown and F. W. M. McElrea. Auckland: Legal Research Foundation.

Strang, H., and L. W. Sherman. 1997. "The Victim's Perspective." Working Paper no. 2. Canberra: Australian National University, Research School of Social Sciences, Law Program.

Stubbs, J. 1995. "'Communitarian' Conferencing and Violence against Women: A Cautionary Note." In *Wife Assault and the Canadian Criminal Justice System,* edited by Mariana Valverde, Linda MacLeod, and Kirsten Johnson. Toronto: University of Toronto, Centre of Criminology.

Sutherland, E. H. 1983. *White Collar Crime: The Uncut Version.* New Haven, Conn.: Yale University Press.

Sutherland, E. H., and D. R. Cressey. 1978. *Criminology.* 10th ed. New York: Lippincott.

Sykes, G., and D. Matza. 1957. "Techniques of Netralization: A Theory of Delinquency." *American Sociological Review* 22:664–70.

Tangney, June Price. 1995. "Recent Advances in the Empirical Study of Shame and Guilt." *American Behavioral Scientist.* 38:1132–45.

Tauri, Juan. 1998. "Family Group Conferencing: A Case Study of the Indigenisation of New Zealand's Justice System." *Current Issues in Criminal Justice* 10:168–82.

Tauri, Juan, and Allison Morris. 1997. "Re-forming Justice: The Potential of Maori Processes." *Australian and New Zealand Journal of Criminology* 30:149–67.

Tavuchis, N. 1991. *Mea Culpa: A Sociology of Apology and Reconciliation.* Stanford, Calif.: Stanford University Press.

Thurman, Q. C. 1984. "Deviance and the Neutralization of Moral Commitment: An Empirical Analysis." *Deviant Behavior* 5:291–304.

Tomkins, Sylvan. 1962. *Affect/Imagery/Consciousness.* New York: Springer.

Trenczek, T. 1990. "A Review and Assessment of Victim-Offender Reconciliation Programming in West Germany." In *Criminal Justice, Restitution and Reconciliation,* edited by B. Galaway and J. Hudson. Monsey, N.Y.: Willow Press.

Trevelyan, G. M. 1978. *English Social History: A Survey of Six Centuries from Chaucer to Queen Victoria.* London: Longman.

Turner, John C., with Michael A. Hogg, Penelope J. Oakes, Stephen D. Reicher, and Margaret S. Wetherell. 1987. *Rediscovering the Social Group: A Self-Categorization Theory.* London: Blackwell.

Tyler, Tom. 1990. *Why People Obey the Law.* New Haven, Conn.: Yale University Press.

Tyler, Tom, and Robyn M. Dawes. 1993. "Fairness in Groups: Comparing the Self-Interest and Social Identity Perspectives." In *Psychological Perspectives on Justice: Theory and Applications,* edited by Barbara A. Mellers and Jonathan Baron. Cambridge: Cambridge University Press.

Umbreit, Mark. 1985. *Crime and Reconciliation: Creative Options for Victims and Offenders.* Nashville: Abingdon.

———. 1990a. "Mediation in the Nineties: Pushing Back the Boundaries." *Mediation* 6:27–9.

———. 1990b. "The Meaning of Fairness to Burglary Victims." In *Criminal Justice, Restitution and Reconciliation,* edited by B. Galaway and J. Hudson. Monsey, N.Y.: Willow Tree.

———. 1992. "Mediating Victim-Offender Conflict: From Single-Site to Multi-Site Analysis in the U.S." In *Restorative Justice on Trial: Pitfalls and Potentials of Victim-Offender Mediation—International Research Perspectives,* edited by H. Messmer and H. U. Otto. Dordrecht and Boston: Kluwer.

———. 1994. *Victim Meets Offender: The Impact of Restorative Justice and Mediation.* Monsey, N.Y.: Criminal Justice Press.

———. 1999. "Restorative Justice through Juvenile Victim-Offender Mediation." In *Restorative Juvenile Justice: Repairing the Harm of Youth Crime,* edited by G. Bazemore and L. Walgrave. Monsey, N.Y.: Criminal Justice Press.

Umbreit, M., and R. Coates. 1992. *Victim-Offender Mediation: An Analysis of Programs in Four States of the U.S.* Minneapolis: Citizens Council Mediation Services.

Umbreit, M., with R. Coates and B. Kalanj. 1994. *Victim Meets Offender: The Impact of Restorative Justice and Mediation.* Monsey, N.Y.: Criminal Justice Press.

Vagg, Jon. 1998. "Delinquency and Shame: Data from Hong Kong." *British Journal of Criminology* 38:247–64.

Van Ness, Daniel. 1986. *Crime and Its Victims: What We Can Do*. Downers Grove, Ill.: Intervarsity Press.

———. 1993. "New Wine and Old Wineskins: Four Challenges of Restorative Justice." *Criminal Law Forum* 4:251–76.

———. 1999. "Legal Principles and Process." In *Restorative Juvenile Justice: Repairing the Harm of Youth Crime*, edited by G. Bazemore and L. Walgrave. Monsey, N.Y.: Criminal Justice Press.

Van Ness, Daniel, and Karen Heetderks Strong. 1997. *Restoring Justice*. Cincinnati: Anderson.

Wachtel, Ted. 1997. *Real Justice: How We Can Revolutionize Our Response to Wrongdoing*. Pipersville, Pa.: Piper's Press.

Walgrave, Lode. 1993. "In Search of Limits to the Restorative Justice for Juveniles." Paper presented at the International Congress on Criminology, Budapest, August 23–27.

———. 1995. "Restorative Justice for Juveniles: Just a Technique or a Fully Fledged Alternative?" *Howard Journal* 34:228–49.

———. 1999. "Community Service as a Cornerstone of a Systematic Restorative Response to (Juvenile) Crime." In *Restorative Juvenile Justice: Repairing the Harm of Youth Crime*, edited by G. Bazemore and L. Walgrave. Monsey, N.Y.: Criminal Justice Press.

Warner, K. 1994. "The Rights of the Offender in Family Conferences." In *Family Conferencing and Juvenile Justice: The Way Forward or Misplaced Optimism?* edited by C. Alder and J. Wundersitz. Canberra: Australian Institute of Criminology.

Warner, S. 1992. *Making Amends: Justice for Victims and Offenders*. Aldershot: Avebury.

Waters, Andrew. 1993. "The Wagga Wagga Effective Cautioning Program: Reintegrative or Degrading?" Bachelor's thesis, University of Melbourne, Department of Criminology.

Weitekamp, E. 1989. "Restitution: A New Paradigm of Criminal Justice or a New Way to Widen the System of Social Control?" Ph.D. dissertation, University of Pennsylvania.

———. 1999. "The History of Restorative Justice." In *Restorative Juvenile Justice: Repairing the Harm of Youth Crime*, edited by G. Bazemore and L. Walgrave. Monsey, N.Y.: Criminal Justice Press.

West, D. J., and D. P. Farrington. 1973. *Who becomes Delinquent? Second Report of the Cambridge Study in Delinquent Development*. London: Heinemann Educational.

White, Rob. 1994. "Shame and Reintegration Strategies: Individuals, State Power and Social Interests." In *Family Conferencing and Juvenile Justice*, edited by Christine Alder and Joy Wundersitz. Canberra: Australian Institute of Criminology, Australian Studies in Law, Crime, and Justice.

Wilson, J. Q., and R. Herrnstein. 1985. *Crime and Human Nature*. New York: Simon & Schuster.

Wong, Dennis. 1996. "Paths to Delinquency: Implications for Juvenile Justice in Hong Kong and China." Ph.D. dissertation, University of Bristol.

———. 1998. "Juvenile Justice in China: The Quest for a Just Restorative Approach." Paper presented at the twelfth International Congress on Criminology, Seoul, August.

Wright, M. 1982. *Making Good: Prisons, Punishment and Beyond.* London: Hutchinson.

———. 1992. "Victim-Offender Mediation as a Step towards a Restorative System of Justice." In *Restorative Justice on Trial: Pitfalls and Potentials of Victim-Offender Mediation—International Research Perspectives,* edited by H. Messmer and H. U. Otto. Dordrecht and Boston: Kluwer.

Wundersitz, Joy, and Sue Hetzel. 1996. "Family Conferencing for Young Offenders: The South Australian Experience." In *Family Group Conferences: Perspectives on Policy and Practice,* edited by Joe Hudson, Allison Morris, Gabrielle Maxwell, and Burt Galaway. Sydney: Federation Press and Criminal Justice Press.

Wynne, Jean. 1996. "Leeds Mediation and Reparation Service: Ten Years Experience with Victim-Offender Mediation." In *Restorative Justice: International Perspectives,* edited by Burt Galaway and Joe Hudson. Monsey, N.Y.: Criminal Justice Press.

Yazzie, Robert, and James W. Zion. 1996. "Navajo Restorative Justice: The Law of Equality and Justice." In *Restorative Justice: International Perspectives,* edited by Burt Galaway and Joe Hudson. Monsey, N.Y.: Criminal Justice Press.

Yeats, Mary Ann. 1997. " 'Three Strikes' and Restorative Justice: Dealing with Young Repeat Burglars in Western Australia." *Criminal Law Forum* 8:369–85.

Young, Iris. 1995. "Communication and the Other: Beyond Deliberative Democracy." In *Justice and Identity: Antipodean Practices,* edited by Margaret Wilson and Anna Yeatman. Wellington: Bridget Williams Books.

Youth Justice Coalition. 1990. *Kids in Justice: A Blueprint for the 90s.* Sydney: Law Foundation of New South Wales.

Zehr, Howard. 1985. *Retributive Justice, Restorative Justice.* New Perspectives on Crime and Justice. Occasional Papers of the MCC Canada Victim Offender Ministries Program and the MCC, U.S. Office of Criminal Justice, vol. 4. Elkhart, Ind.: Mennonite Central Committee; Kitchener, Ontario: Canada Victim Offender Ministries Program.

———. 1990. *Changing Lenses: A New Focus for Criminal Justice.* Scottsdale, Pa.: Herald Press.

———. 1995. "Rethinking Criminal Justice: Restorative Justice." Unpublished manuscript of a conference paper presented in Auckland.

Zimring, F. E. 1981. "Kids, Groups and Crime: Some Implications of a Well-Known Secret." *Journal of Criminal Law and Criminology* 72:867–85.

James B. Jacobs and Lauryn P. Gouldin

Cosa Nostra: The Final Chapter?

ABSTRACT

An unprecedented law enforcement attack, coupled with new civil and regulatory organized crime control strategies, leaves the survival of the Italian organized crime families in doubt. Although the families in different cities operate, for the most part, independently, their internal composition is consistent. They are characterized by a rigid hierarchical structure and an extreme emphasis on secrecy. Cosa Nostra can be distinguished from other organized crime groups, including recently developing Asian and Russian gangs in the United States and most domestic youth gangs, by its focus on infiltration of businesses and domination of such legitimate enterprises over sustained periods, in addition to its involvement in various illicit activities and markets. However, in some countries, including Russia and parts of Eastern Europe, where organized crime participates in both legal and criminal markets, the U.S. experience with Cosa Nostra may offer clues to promising control techniques. First, it is imperative to act quickly in response to developing organized crime syndicates. Second, electronic surveillance, both wiretaps and bugs, is a necessary and serious impediment to the operation of organized crime groups. Third, a successful attack on organized crime cannot be a short-term campaign.

Since the late 1970s, a presidential commission, numerous congressional hearings, mobsters' testimony in legal proceedings and autobiographical accounts, and hundreds of criminal and civil cases have unearthed a wealth of information about the structure and activities of the Italian organized crime families known as the Mafia, the mob, the

James B. Jacobs is professor of law at New York University School of Law. Lauryn P. Gouldin has a bachelor of arts degree from Princeton University (1995) and is a student at New York University School of Law.

outfit, or Cosa Nostra.[1] This information offers scholars an unprecedented opportunity to assess how these organized crime families achieved and maintained their dominance. Since the late 1970s, the federal, state, and local government attack on Cosa Nostra, using criminal, civil, and regulatory strategies, has been one of the most successful law enforcement campaigns in U.S. history. Its documentation is important so that future generations of scholars as well as policy makers and policy implementers in the United States and in other countries will have a model for dealing with sophisticated organized crime.

Section I of this essay provides a note on sources and data on Cosa Nostra. Section II describes the structure of Cosa Nostra families. Section III examines the range of Cosa Nostra's operations. Section IV deals with Cosa Nostra's links to the political system and to its role as a power broker. Sections V and VI document the effective law enforcement strategies and other legal resources wielded by federal, state, and local governments against Cosa Nostra in the last two decades of the twentieth century. Claims of success in the war on organized crime, as elaborated in Section VII, derive from the imprisonment of hundreds of Cosa Nostra members and associates, the purge of Cosa Nostra from certain unions and industries, and the significant organizational deterioration of the crime families. This essay concludes by identifying the lessons to be drawn from the U.S. experience with Cosa Nostra and their applicability to future domestic, foreign, and international organized crime control.

I. Note on Sources and Data

With the exception of Ianni and Reuss-Ianni (1972), sociologists and criminologists have not been able to carry out case studies of Cosa Nostra; nor does the subject lend itself to quantitative analysis (Reuter 1994). Until the 1970s, although Cosa Nostra was a fixture in American popular culture, many academics regarded it as a myth (e.g., Smith 1975). That position was substantially undermined by the release in trial proceedings of the famous "DeCavalcante tapes" in the mid-1960s. The FBI recorded hundreds of conversations in which Sam De-Cavalcante, the head of a minor New Jersey Cosa Nostra family, and

[1] The term "Cosa Nostra" was revealed by Joseph Valachi in 1963 and subsequently confirmed by electronic surveillance and the testimony of organized crime figures who became government witnesses.

various colleagues discussed the structure, organization, history, and politics of Cosa Nostra (see Zeiger 1973, 1975). Even though the defections and prosecutions of 1980s and 1990s have proved the existence of Cosa Nostra beyond any shadow of doubt, the "Mafia as myth" literature remains on the shelves of libraries and is sometimes perpetuated in the contemporary scholarship of academic writers whose eyes and ears seemingly remain closed to the mass of information on Cosa Nostra that is now available.

There have been dozens of major criminal trials of Cosa Nostra bosses since the late 1970s and more than a thousand prosecutions (Jacobs, Panarella, and Worthington 1994). Practically all of the trials have relied on extensive electronic eavesdropping based on "bugs" that the FBI and various state and local law enforcement agencies planted in Cosa Nostra members' cars, homes, and social clubs. The overheard conversations, which have been made public through their presentation in civil and criminal cases, provide extremely reliable information about the nature of organized crime and its activities.

Until Joseph Valachi went public in 1963 (Maas 1968), no Cosa Nostra member had ever been willing to testify about Cosa Nostra. Beginning in the 1970s, however, Cosa Nostra's much vaunted code of *omerta* began to disintegrate and, by the late 1980s and early 1990s, many high-ranking organized crime figures agreed to testify for the government in exchange for leniency and placement in the federal Witness Security Program, which, for the first time, offered a Cosa Nostra figure who turned against his comrades hope of survival.

The defectors have provided a wealth of information about Cosa Nostra's membership, organizational hierarchy, rules, and criminal activities. One of the first Cosa Nostra members to "flip" was Aladema "Jimmy the Weasel" Fratianno, acting boss of the Los Angeles crime family; he testified for the government in the first Racketeer Influenced and Corrupt Organizations (RICO) prosecution against a Cosa Nostra boss (*United States v. Tieri*, Ind. 80–381 [SDNY, June 15, 1980]) and later in the "commission" case brought against the leaders of the New York families (*United States v. Salerno*, 868 F.2d 524 [2d Cir. 1989]). In the famous "pizza connection" case (*United States v. Badalamenti*, 84 CR 236 [SDNY 1987], convictions aff'd, *United States v. Casamento*, 887 F.2d 1141 [2d Cir. 1989]), Tomasso Buscetta provided extensive information about a cooperative drug-trafficking relationship between Mafia groupings in Italy and the Bonanno family in New York City. Salvatore "Sammy the Bull" Gravano, a former underboss of the Gambino crime family, provided rich descriptions of that crime family's operations in the prosecution of John Gotti and in several other cases. For the government's civil racketeering suit against the International Teamsters Union and its executive board, Angelo Lonardo, former underboss of the Cleveland crime family, provided an extraordinary deposition detailing Cosa Nostra's role in designating the president of the Teamsters Union and in controlling that union. Vincent Cafaro has likewise been extensively debriefed and used in many prosecutions. The defectors' testimony in many cases has passed through a number of screens that ought to assure a high degree of reliability: savvy prosecutors believe the testimony to be truthful as do grand juries and trial juries (beyond a reasonable doubt); the latter even after such testimony has been exposed to extensive cross-examination by skilled defense lawyers.

The information that emanates from electronic eavesdropping and the live testimony of defectors is confirmed and supplemented by the testimony of other witnesses, including FBI and other law enforcement agents, labor union officials, and private citizens who have done business with or been victimized by the mob. The most famous law enforcement witness is Joe Pistone (Donnie Brasco), the only FBI agent ever to infiltrate Cosa Nostra. For six years (1976–82), Pistone hung out with organized crime members and their associates based in New York City, in effect conducting a participant observation study unparalleled in the history of criminology. Throughout this period, Pistone passed vital information about the mob along to the top echelons of the FBI. Pistone's observations have been thoroughly presented and cross-examined in court and published as a narrative (Pistone and Woodley 1987). In 1997, Pistone's exploits were dramatized in the popular film *Donnie Brasco*.

Much less reliable than the electronically seized conversations and the cross-examined court testimony of former Cosa Nostra members, but still valuable, are a number of autobiographies and biographies. Among the most prominent are Joseph Bonanno's (with Sergio Lalli) memoir *A Man of Honor* (1983), Ovid Demaris's *The Last Mafioso: The Treacherous World of Jimmy Frattiano* (1980), Nick Pileggi and Henry Hill's *Wiseguy: Life in a Mafia Family* (1985), Vincent Teresa's *My Life in the Mafia* (1973), and Peter Maas's *Underboss: Sammy the Bull Gravano's Story of Life in the Mafia* (1997).

In addition to primary sources, there are many reports by special commissions, the U.S. General Accounting Office, the U.S. Department of Justice, and congressional committees. Taken together, these reports, based to a significant extent on live testimony, provide a wealth of information about the activities of Cosa Nostra and of the law enforcement agencies most significantly involved in investigations and prosecutions. The 1967 President's Commission on Law Enforcement and Administration of Justice published a Task Force Report on Organized Crime (written by criminologist Donald Cressey in close collaboration with New York City Police Department organized crime specialist Ralph Salerno). While the task force report, which also formed the basis for Cressey's *Theft of The Nation* (1969), probably exaggerated the formal organizational structure of Cosa Nostra and the authority of its "ruling commission," it constitutes a very useful source. Two decades later, the President's Commission on Organized Crime (1986*a*) published a series of volumes on various organized crime matters, including important analyses of labor racketeering and the role of organized crime in legitimate industry (1986*b*).

A great deal of important information about organized crime can be found in congressional hearings beginning with Senator Estes Kefauver's hearings (Special Committee on Organized Crime in Interstate Commerce) in 1950–51 (see Kefauver 1951; Moore 1974). The committee took testimony from more than six hundred witnesses in hearings around the country. The most dramatic moment in the hearings was the committee's grilling of New York city mob boss, Frank Costello, whose rambling, evasive, and disingenuous answers spoke volumes. Perhaps the committee's main contribution was exposing the ties between corrupt political machines (such as Tammany Hall) and organized crime bosses (such as Frank Costello) in many cities (see Peterson 1983).

In 1956, Senator John McClellan began a series of hearings for the Senate Select Committee on Improper Activities in the Labor or Management Field (McClellan 1962). Robert Kennedy served, for a period, as chief counsel to this committee and, before a national television audience, engaged in an angry exchange with Jimmy Hoffa whose activities in the Teamsters Union the committee was investigating (Kennedy 1960). The McClellan Committee's findings led, in 1959, to passage of the Landrum-Griffin Act, which was an attempt to bolster union members' rights vis-à-vis their own unions. In 1963, with Attorney General Kennedy's support and assistance, Senator McClellan and his colleagues on the Permanent Subcommittee on Investigations publicly questioned Joseph Valachi about his thirty-three years in the Genovese crime family. Valachi had decided to go public when, while serving a prison term, he learned that he had been marked for execution.

In the 1980s, the U.S. Senate Permanent Subcommittee on Investigations, under Senator Sam Nunn's chairmanship, convened hearings on various organized crime issues and elicited testimony from hundreds of witnesses, including former Sicilian Mafia boss Tomasso Buscetta and Cosa Nostra defectors Vincent Cafaro and Angelo Lonardo (see, e.g., U.S. Senate Permanent Subcommittee on Investigations 1981, 1983).

Among the state crime commission reports on organized crime, the New York State Organized Crime Task Force's *Corruption and Racketeering in the NYC Construction Industry* (1990) stands out. This report provides an in-depth examination and analysis of Cosa Nostra's involvement in labor unions and construction and supply companies in the New York City metropolitan area. It shows how Cosa Nostra, through its labor power, established and policed employer cartels and how it converted power and influence in a major industry into cash. Another outstanding government report is the Pennsylvania Crime Commission's *Organized Crime in Pennsylvania: A Decade of Change* (1990), which covers Cosa Nostra's extensive operations in traditional rackets and the legitimate economy throughout Pennsylvania, in small cities as well as in Philadelphia and Pittsburgh. Crime commissions in New Jersey and Illinois have also provided many useful reports on organized crime operations in those states.

There is also a rich scholarly literature on organized crime, beginning perhaps with John Landesco's classic *Organized Crime in Chicago* (1968), originally published in 1929. An outstanding introduction to scholarship in the field is Howard Abadinsky's text *Organized Crime* (1994); see also Sifakis (1987). Excellent histories include Virgil Peterson's *The Mob: 200 Years of Organized Crime in New York* (1983) and Stephen Fox's *Blood and Power: Organized Crime in the Twentieth Century* (1989); see also Block (1994). Peter Reuter has produced valuable economic analysis, based on empirical study of organized crime's role in establishing and maintaining cartels in legitimate industry (Reuter 1983, 1987, 1993; see also Florentini and Peltzman 1995; Kleinknecht 1996). In addition, there are a number of excellent biographies of organized crime figures (Al Capone, Meyer Lansky, Arnold Rothstein, Frank Costello, Vito Genovese) and law enforcement officials (e.g., Harry J. Anslinger, Thomas Dewey, J. Edgar Hoover).

II. The Structure of Cosa Nostra

As of the mid-1980s, twenty-four Italian organized crime families had been identified as active in the United States (there were fewer in 1998; several have effectively been dismantled). FBI Director William Webster testified before the President's Commission on Organized Crime (PCOC) in 1983 that there were approximately 1,700 "made members" of Cosa Nostra and perhaps ten times that number of associates (President's Commission on Organized Crime 1983).

A. The National Perspective

Although there has been a good deal of debate about the degree of coordination among the different organized crime families (cf. Cressey 1969 and Smith 1975), it is best to think of Cosa Nostra as a melange of locally based crime families, each with exclusive jurisdiction in its own geographic area. The report of the Task Force on Organized Crime of the 1967 President's Crime Commission, chiefly drafted by noted criminologist Donald Cressey and New York City detective and organized crime expert Ralph Salerno, claimed that Cosa Nostra was a nationwide syndicate governed by a ruling commission comprised of bosses of the nation's most powerful families. In his 1983 autobiography, Joseph Bonanno also spoke about a nationwide commission (Bonanno and Lalli 1983). However, other than a mysterious and bungled 1956 conference in Appalachian, New York (see *United States v. Bufalino*, 285 F.2d 408 [2d Cir. 1960]), which was attended by Cosa Nostra figures from all over the country, there is no empirical evidence to support that claim. Perhaps a loose commission, with representatives from various crime families, did at one time exist, and subsequently lapsed. Unfortunately, the exaggerated Cressey/Salerno account prompted equally exaggerated rebuttals, some claiming that organized crime was a myth (see Smith 1975) reflecting anti-Italian prejudice.

Electronic surveillance (wiretaps and bugs) in the early 1980s revealed a certain degree of collaboration among various crime families. For example, several mob leaders from around the country came to New York City to consult with Genovese crime family boss Tony Salerno (Bonavolonta and Duffy 1996). Angelo Lonardo, representing the Cleveland Cosa Nostra family, was overheard briefing Salerno. Later, Lonardo, at that point a cooperating witness for the government, told the PCOC that the Chicago crime family ("the Outfit") dominates the Midwestern Cosa Nostra families, except for Cleveland's, which reports to New York City's Genovese family. Ken Eto, a former associate of the Chicago family, verified that the Cleveland family is subordinate to the Genovese family (PCOC 1985). Louis Sunshine, a Cleveland organized crime associate, came to New York City specifically to seek Salerno's support for Roy Williams's bid to become president of the Teamsters. Williams' own deposition in *United States v. International Brotherhood of Teamsters* (708 F.Supp. 1388 [SDNY 1989]) outlined how, since the 1950s, organized crime families negotiated among themselves in determining the president and other top officers for the Teamsters Union (Jacobs, Panarella, and Worthington 1994). Carlos Trafficante (Florida) also came to New York City to consult with Salerno. In addition, defectors have revealed close co-operation between the Gambino family (New York) and the Bruno-Scarfo family (Philadelphia) (Fresolone and Wagman 1994; Maas 1997).

There is evidence of a New York City-based commission of Cosa Nostra crime families.[2] In the "commission case" (*United States v. Salerno*), the U.S. Attorney for the Southern District of New York indicted four of the five crime family bosses (the boss of the Bonanno family, in disgrace with the other families and, thus ostracized from "commission" proceedings, was not indicted) and a number of other powerful capos and soldiers. They were charged with participating in the affairs of an enterprise (the Cosa Nostra commission) through a pattern of racketeering activity (including operating a concrete cartel in violation of the antitrust laws). The prosecutors alleged that the commission's purpose was to "regulate and facilitate the relationships between and among La Cosa Nostra Families." More specifically, the government charged the commission with "promoting and carrying out joint ventures . . . ; resolving actual and potential disputes . . . ; extending formal recognition to newly elected Bosses of La Cosa Nostra families and, from time to time, resolving leadership disputes within a Family; . . . approving the initiation or 'making' of new members or soldiers . . . ; . . . keeping persons inside and outside La Cosa Nostra in fear of the Commission . . . with threats, violence and murder" (*United States v. Salerno*, indictment; see Jacobs, Panarella, and Worthington 1994).

---

[2] The PCOC (1986*a*) cites Lucky Luciano as having founded the commission in 1931. The PCOC also claimed that there was a commission in 1986 that consisted of the five New York bosses and bosses from Buffalo, Chicago, Detroit, and Philadelphia.

Though successful, the commission case left much uncertainty about the precise jurisdiction and authority of Cosa Nostra's commission. Clearly, it did not operate as a day-to-day executive board. It apparently functioned intermittently, like a court called on to solve occasional disputes. The fact that all the members of this commission were leaders of New York City crime families throws doubt on the claim that, at present, there is a commission that represents and centrally commands Cosa Nostra families throughout the country. It does stand to reason, though, that the New York City Cosa Nostra crime families needed a commission to solve disputes and facilitate the cooperation necessary for five families to coexist in a single metropolitan area. The infrequency of interfamily violence, given that the five families are involved in the same rackets and legitimate industries, implies the existence of this type of problem-solving and coordinating entity. The commission clearly allocated to each family interests and revenues from various construction industry rackets. In addition, in his personal account of the FBI's massive decade-long investigation of the New York City organized crime families, Jules Bonavolonta describes how electronic eavesdropping revealed the commission deadlocked 2-2 on Gambino family boss Paul Castellano's proposal to assassinate one of his associates (Little Pete Tambone) for drug trafficking (Bonavolonta and Duffy 1996).

B. Family Structure

Each of the Cosa Nostra families is headed by a "boss" who exercises virtually unchallenged authority (within the family) and whose position entitles him to a generous cut of all the members' revenues. The boss provides resources, including defense lawyers, for members and their families when they are in need. He also takes care of a good deal of the payoffs to politicians, police, and other officials necessary for keeping the family's operations running smoothly. In addition, the boss can approve or veto the proposal of one of his family's crews or individuals to embark on a new criminal venture. Of course, the boss also represents the family in interfamily "sit-downs" and negotiations.

The second in command, acting as a deputy for the boss, is the "underboss." The third position in the family's ruling triumvirate is a senior advisor known as "consigliere" or counselor. The boss chooses a limited number of "capos" (caporegimes), each with authority over a "crew" comprised of "soldiers" ("made members" of Cosa Nostra who have also, traditionally, been referred to as "good fellows" or "wise guys"). All made members of Cosa Nostra are of Italian descent and all are male. Cosa Nostra crews also include large numbers of associates who work for but are not members of the family. A 1998 estimate of the size and composition of New York's Genovese family calculated that for every made member (approximately 250), there were four or five associates (Raab 1998*b*).

The families operate as patriarchal organizations, not as bureaucracies. Each crew, in effect, has a franchise to engage in diverse criminal ventures, as long as the family's boss approves and is given the appropriate percentage of the proceeds. Cosa Nostra soldiers and crews must be entrepreneurs in crime, seeking out profitable opportunities in both the underworld and the upperworld (Jacobs and Panarella 1998).

Traditionally, the strength of Cosa Nostra families was predicated on the absolute loyalty of its members. Before Senator McClellan's Permanent Subcommittee on Investigations, Valachi described the secret induction ceremony into Cosa Nostra families and the code of *omerta* (silence) to which all members swear fealty (McClellan 1962). Valachi's depiction has been confirmed by subsequent defectors including Salvatore "Sammy the Bull" Gravano (Gambino family), and Philip Leonetti (Scarfo family) (Maas 1968, 1997; *United States v. Leonetti* 1988 WL 61738 [EDPA 1988]). In his testimony in *United States v. Salerno*, former Cleveland family underboss Angelo Lonardo described the same initiation ceremony. In 1989, in Medford, Massachusetts, authorities recorded, with the aid of an eavesdropping device, the initiation of four men into New England's Patriarca family (*United States v. Bianco*, 998 F.2d 1112 [2d Cir. 1993]). The following year, as part of the FBI's Operation Broadsword investigation of the Bruno-Scarfo family in Philadelphia, turncoat George Fresolone wore a recording device that allowed FBI agents to record his initiation into that family (Fresolone and Wagman 1994).

All these accounts reveal a ritual that involves the prospective member being asked a series of questions to confirm his loyalty, including his willingness to kill on behalf of the family. All members must take the oath of *omerta*, swearing fealty to the family. The initiate's hand (usually the trigger finger) is pinpricked until blood is drawn and a picture of a saint is then burned in the initiate's hand (Maas 1997; Fresolone and Wagman 1994, *United States v. Bianco, United States v. Salerno* [testimony of Angelo Lonardo]).

III. Cosa Nostra Operations

Cosa Nostra's longevity can be attributed to the ability of each family to seek out, develop, and exploit a range of criminal opportunities, including but not limited to the corruption and control of national and local labor unions, the creation and enforcement of cartels, supplying illicit goods and services, and carrying out thefts, frauds, and hijackings. Cosa Nostra's foothold in both the criminal underworld and the upperworld of legitimate businesses, unions, and politics distinguishes Cosa Nostra from other U.S. organized crime groups that may participate successfully in illicit markets but have been uninterested or unable to become power brokers in labor, business, and politics (Jacobs 1999).

Many other organized crime groups have operated in the United States and other countries. In the 1920s and 1930s there were very strong Jewish, Irish, and German organized crime groups in New York City and elsewhere (Peterson 1983; Fox 1989). There have been black organized crime groups throughout the twentieth century active in numbers, prostitution, and other rackets in the black neighborhoods of American cities (e.g., Schatzberg 1993). In the waning years of the twentieth century, we have seen the emergence of Russian organized crime groups (Finckenauer 1994; Handelman 1995), Chinese triads or tongs (Chin 1990, 1994), Colombian drug traffickers, Jamaican posses, and other groups (Kenny and Finckenauer 1995). In New York City, an Irish gang called the "Westies" (English 1990) has attracted a good deal of attention because of its extreme and savage violence, often carried out at the behest of a Cosa Nostra crime family. Crime groups like these clearly have the capacity to mount sophisticated criminal operations and scams and to use deadly violence when necessary to further their goals. None of them, however, has so far shown anything like the sophistication and acumen necessary to fill Cosa Nostra's shoes. More specifically, none of these groups has shown that it can control labor unions, much less play the role of influence peddler, cartel enforcer, and "fixer" for whole industries. None of these groups has shown the ability to become a significant political force through control of grassroots party organization and campaign contributions. In other words, what makes Cosa Nostra distinctive, even unique, is its successful penetration of labor unions, legitimate industry, and politics and its simultaneous power and influence in both the underworld and the upperworld. These activities, and the resulting power and prestige, justify treating Cosa Nostra as a criminological topic in its own right. Indeed, a comprehensive urban history of the United States in the twentieth century would have to devote considerable attention to the role of Cosa Nostra.

In conducting all of its operations, Cosa Nostra relies on and exploits its reputation for ruthless violence (Reuter 1987). Actual violence is rarely necessary to obtain the compliance of businessmen and others who are not professional criminals. Reuter explains that the industry presence of organized crime figures who "have a reputation for being able to execute threats of violence . . . and to suppress the course of justice when complaints are brought against them" means that actual violence is rarely necessary (Reuter 1985, p. 56).

A. Labor Racketeering

Since the beginning of this century, labor racketeering has provided Cosa Nostra with power, status, legitimacy, and financial reward (see Seidman 1938; Hutchinson 1969; Taft 1970). Organized crime involvement with the unions began in the 1910s and 1920s when companies recruited mob assistance in strike breaking. The mobsters turned the situation to their advantage by infiltrating the unions and establishing a connection with the labor movement that has propelled Cosa Nostra's economic success (Jacobs and Panarella 1998). For decades, Cosa Nostra controlled the International Longshoremen's Association, the Laborers Union, the Hotel Employees and Restaurant Employees Union, and the International Brotherhood of Teamsters (IBT). It also controlled dozens of union locals (PCOC 1986b; Abadinsky 1994; Jacobs and Panarella 1998). Cosa Nostra turned union power into profit by embezzling and defrauding the unions and their pension and welfare funds, selling labor peace, and taking payoffs in exchange for sweetheart contracts and for turning a blind eye to violations of collective bargaining agreements. Cosa Nostra has also used its labor power to obtain ownership interests in businesses and to establish and police business cartels (New York State Organized Crime Task Force 1990).

Beginning in the 1940s and 1950s, power over the International Longshoremen's Union enabled Cosa Nostra to wield unfettered control over shipping through New York City's ports (Bell 1964). Cosa Nostra (primarily the Gambino and Genovese families) determined who worked on the docks and decided the order for unloading cargo ships. Shippers, at the mercy of the mob because of the immediacy of their needs, paid bribes to forestall labor unrest and to get their ships promptly loaded and unloaded (Abadinsky 1994). As a matter of course, the shippers suffered additional losses from theft of freight. The mob's role in the Longshoremen's Union and control of unloading and loading was analyzed by Daniel Bell in his classic essay "The Racket-Ridden Longshoremen" (1964). In the 1970s, the FBI's massive UNIRAC investigation of the Longshoremen's Union revealed that the Gambino and Genovese families' influence extended over East Coast ports from New York to Miami (see *United States v. Local 1804–1, International Longshoremen's Association*, 812 F.Supp. 1303 [SDNY 1993]).

Cosa Nostra treated the nation's largest labor union, the International Brotherhood of Teamsters, as a racketeering enterprise. According to the PCOC, the Teamsters Union "was firmly under the influence of organized crime" since the 1950s (1986). In return for supporting Jimmy Hoffa for the Teamsters presidency, the mob bosses were, in effect, given control of Teamster locals, access to the Teamster pension funds, and influence over matters in which the Teamsters played a role. By the late 1980s, when the U.S. Department of Justice brought a civil RICO suit against members of the Teamsters General Executive Board, Cosa Nostra members, and the IBT itself, organized crime was entrenched in at least thirty-eight of the largest Teamster locals (PCOC 1986*b*). In effect, bosses from different parts of the country promoted their own candidates for the Teamsters presidency. This history is very effectively told by Teamsters president Roy Williams and by former Cleveland crime family underboss Angelo Lonardo in their depositions in *United States v. International Brotherhood of Teamsters* and in a number of books about the Teamsters and Jimmy Hoffa (Brill 1978; Moldea 1978; Crowe 1993).

Cosa Nostra influence in the Laborer's International Union of North America guaranteed a powerful presence in the construction industry. The DeCavalcante tapes revealed boss Sam DeCavalcante speaking of his family's control of a laborer's union local (Zieger 1973). For years, the Chicago crime family strategically positioned Cosa Nostra members in the laborers' locals in that city (Abadinsky 1994). The clear connection between New York City's various laborers' locals and the Lucchese and Genovese families was documented by the PCOC (1986*b*) and by several major civil RICO suits that resulted in Local

6A and the District Council being placed under a court-appointed trusteeship (New York State Organized Crime Task Force 1990).

The Hotel Employees and Restaurant Employees International Union has also suffered from Cosa Nostra corruption. Control of the Hotel Employees Union Local 54 (in New Jersey) enabled Philadelphia's Bruno-Scarfo family to dictate the purchasing decisions of Atlantic City hotels (Abadinsky 1994). In Chicago, Cosa Nostra control of an HEU local gave the mob power over the restaurant industry (McClellan 1962). In New York City, the Colombo and Gambino families, for many years, directed Hotel Employees Locals 6 and 100 (PCOC 1986*b*).

Cosa Nostra, especially the Lucchese crime family, has been firmly entrenched in many New York City building trades local unions including painters, carpenters, mason tenders, and plumbers (New York State Organized Crime Task Force 1990). Nepotistic succession of mob leaders and the strategic positioning of a corps of supporters within the organization firmly established Cosa Nostra in the building trades. Union officials who were members or associates of Cosa Nostra effectively ran patronage systems in their locals. Cosa Nostra's ability to sustain its control over these unions was bolstered by the status conferred by other labor leaders, some political officials, and other members of the "establishment" (New York State Organized Crime Task Force 1990). For example, Cosa Nostra figures such as John Cody (Teamsters), Ralph Scopo (Laborers), Anthony Scotto (Longshoremen), and associate Harry Davidoff (Teamsters) were some of the most powerful labor figures in the second half of the century. The formation of viable opposition groups within the building trades unions was deterred by threats of blacklisting and personal violence. Union dissidents were beaten and even murdered.

Union control translated into economic gain. Mob bosses exchanged their support of particular union officials for opportunities to siphon money from the union. As union pension funds grew, Cosa Nostra-dominated unions placed their members and associates as trustees of these funds and then plundered them at will. Indeed, organized crime used the massive Teamsters Central States Pension Fund as a kind of mob bank for bosses in Chicago, Kansas City, Milwaukee, and Cleveland (*United States v. Dorfman*, 470 F.2d 246 [2d. Cir. 1996]). Generous loans from this fund (controlled by Cosa Nostra associate Allen Dorfman) financed Cosa Nostra's operations in Las Vegas (Skolnick 1978).

Control over unions enabled Cosa Nostra members to extort payoffs from businesses for labor peace and to solicit bribes in exchange for sweetheart contracts (Jacobs and Panarella 1998). Cosa Nostra-dominated unions regularly turned a blind eye to violations of collective bargaining agreements by ignoring employers' failures to make required payments to pension and welfare funds, by overlooking the bad-faith operation of "double-breasted" shops (staffed by both union and nonunion workers), and by facilitating other employer practices in violation of their contractual obligations. The mob also siphoned money from employers by forcing them to put no-show employees (Cosa Nostra members, friends, or associates) on their payrolls.

Cosa Nostra also benefited indirectly from its entrenched position in the unions because control of the unions and pension funds extended Cosa Nostra influence into peripheral spheres. For example, Cosa Nostra could dictate who the union hired for dental and medical plans, insurance, and other goods and services (New York State Organized Crime Task Force 1990). Sometimes these goods and services were also provided by firms controlled by mob associates, but even legitimate providers had to make kickbacks to the mob.

B. Business Racketeering and Cartels

Cosa Nostra bosses and soldiers have also exercised control over many businesses and, in some cases, entire industries. In New York City, the five organized crime families have traditionally exerted strong influence in the construction industry, the garment center, the Fulton Fish Market, and sea cargo operations on the docks. Since the 1950s, these families have been entrenched in the Javits Exhibition Center, air cargo operations at John F. Kennedy airport, and commercial waste hauling and disposal. They have also been active in such industries as moving and storage, securities, linen businesses, food processing, importation and retail distribution, and even in homeless shelters (Kwitny 1979; Jacobs and Hortis 1998; Jacobs 1999).

In some cases, Cosa Nostra control of an industry derived from a family's direct ownership of a participating business. In his 1970s expose of organized crime's infiltration of legitimate business, *Wall Street Journal* investigative journalist Jonathan Kwitny documented the effect of this type of business racketeering, particularly with respect to Cosa Nostra's ownership or control of firms in the meat processing and cheese industries (Kwitny 1979). Gambino family boss Paul Castellano founded Dial Meat Purveyors, which distributed poultry to three hundred butchers, grocers, and supermarkets in the New York metropolitan area (Cook 1987) and ultimately to two national supermarket chains (Maas 1997). If the supermarkets complained, Castellano used his influence to orchestrate labor problems. Small butchers' objections to Dial's high prices resulted in empty shelves (Maas 1997). Even chicken industry magnate Frank Perdue recognized that entry into the New York poultry market required negotiation with Castellano (PCOC 1986b; Cook 1987; O'Brien and Kurins 1991; Maas 1997).

The investigations and prosecutions of the 1980s revealed many examples of organized crime figures holding ownership interests in trucking, carting, and garment manufacturing firms. For example, Thomas Gambino (a capo in the Gambino crime family) amassed a $100 million fortune mostly through ownership of trucking companies.

Mob ownership of a business within a particular industry was often complemented by corruption of unions that represented workers in that industry's union. Cosa Nostra's control of the labor supply enabled it, in effect, to direct the industries in which the mob-dominated unions functioned (Reuter 1985; see also PCOC 1986b). In New York City, for example, there were mob-sponsored cartels in concrete production and pouring, dry wall, waste hauling, garment industry trucking, and window replacement (Jacobs 1999). Only firms that were owned by or that made payoffs to Cosa Nostra could do business. The privileged firms could count on the "enforcement power" of the Cosa Nostra-corrupted unions. They were able to restrict access to the industry and could fix prices and allocate contracts. "Outside" firms could not operate because they could not get union labor and if they tried to work without union labor they would be picketed, disrupted, and attacked. The cartel members inflated prices, essentially charging a "cartel tax" or "mob tax" that industry participants and consumers had to pay in order to obtain the good or service controlled by the cartel (Jacobs and Hortis 1998).

In the "commission case" (*United States v. Salerno*), federal prosecutors proved that four of New York City's five Cosa Nostra crime families controlled a cartel of concrete contractors. S & A Concrete, owned in part by Anthony Salerno (boss of the Genovese family) and Paul Castellano (boss of the Gambino family), was the only company permitted to bid on contracts valued in excess of five million dollars (Jacobs, Panarella, and Worthington 1994). S & A Concrete profits were allocated to each family. The concrete club assigned middle-sized contracts (i.e., $2–5 million) to one of a half-dozen cartel members in which Cosa Nostra families held interests. Other companies were permitted to bid on and carry out smaller contracts but had to pay 2 percent of the contract price to the Colombo crime family. Control of this cartel was grounded both in Cosa Nostra's manipulation of the industry's labor supply (Cement Workers Local 6A and Teamsters Local 282) and Genovese family associate Edward "Biff" Halloran's partial ownership of the city's three largest concrete producers (Jacobs 1999). Through this cartel, for more than a decade the mob controlled every concrete contract in the city (Jacobs and Panarella 1998).

The mob exerted similar influence in the New York City drywall industry through Vincent DiNapoli, a Genovese capo. While Cosa Nostra did not control the manufacture of drywall (as it did concrete), the families (particularly the Genovese family) did infiltrate the carpenters' union, hold ownership interests in several of the city's drywall contractors, and run the industry's employers' association, the Metropolitan New York Dry Wall Contractors Association (Jacobs 1999). Much like its concrete counterpart, the drywall cartel allocated bids and took 2 percent of the contract price as a kickback. Those firms that were not members of DiNapoli's cartel could expect to pay an additional $1,000 per week to assure labor peace (Jacobs 1999).

For years, two powerful Cosa Nostra-sponsored cartels allocated contracts and fixed prices in the New York City and Long Island waste hauling industry (Jacobs and Hortis 1998). In his analysis of the New York City, Long Island, and New Jersey waste hauling cartel, Peter Reuter (1993) explains that the cartel operated smoothly for years in part because a Cosa Nostra member sat on the grievance committee of the New York Trade Waste Association. For two decades, there were no examples of any carters refusing to accept the committee's resolution of a dispute over "ownership" of a customer (Jacobs 1999). A similar organized crime cartel operated in Westchester County, just north of New York City. There is also evidence that organized crime families in Chicago and Los Angeles ran waste hauling cartels.

Thomas and Joseph Gambino gained control of New York City's garment district through their ownership of several trucking companies on which the industry was dependent and their control of International Ladies Garment Workers Union Local 102 (Jacobs 1999). Similar schemes were created by the Lucchese crime family around New York City's window replacement and painting industries.

C. Criminal Rackets

Traditionally, Cosa Nostra has also profited tremendously from black-market trafficking in illegal goods and services, including loan-sharking, gambling, and drug trafficking.

1. *Loan-sharking.* For Cosa Nostra, an organization with stores of capital and the power of intimidation, loan-sharking (the provision of high interest loans in violation of usury laws) has traditionally represented easy money (Goldstock and Coenen 1978). Cosa Nostra's involvement in illicit industries provides a ready client base for black-market banking, because drug dealers and bookies generally have no alternative source of credit (Kenney and Finckenauer 1995). Cosa Nostra also makes loans to legitimate businesses that may be too risky for banks or that are simply unwilling or unable to wait for a standard application to be processed. The cost of this immediate availability is exorbitant; some estimates of average Cosa Nostra interest rates range as high as 250 to 1,000 percent per annum (Kenney and Finckenauer 1995). Cosa Nostra loan sharks often specialize in particular categories of borrowers and repeat clients (Reuter and Rubinstein 1978). Members of the family at all levels are involved in loan-sharking, but those who deal at lower levels tend to attract the more risky ventures and have to chase down repayments more often.

Defector Sammy "The Bull" Gravano explained that family members regularly lend money to one another (Maas 1997). When Gravano was first associated with the Colombo family, he was arrested in connection with an armed robbery. Carmine "The Snake" Persico, at the time a captain in the Colombo family agreed to loan Gravano bribe money on a "vig" arrangement whereby Gravano would owe $300 a week in interest on his $10,000 loan.[3]

More frequently, subordinate Cosa Nostra members borrow from capos and bosses in order to loan the money out on the street. Gravano explained that street-level loan sharks lend to less dependable borrowers (Maas 1997). Former FBI agent Jules Bonavolonta recounted the story of Frankie Ancona, who was married to the daughter of a Gambino family capo (Bonavolonta and Duffy 1996). Ancona borrowed $250,000 (at extremely high interest) from the family for his own loan-sharking schemes. When he was unable to repay the Gambino family, he received threats that his family would be assaulted and his home

[3] See Abadinsky for a description of the different types of repayment arrangements and schedules that Cosa Nostra loan sharks typically invoke.

burned. When Ancona failed to repay a loan from Gerry Lang, acting Colombo family boss, Lang took the deed to Ancona's house and immediately evicted him (Bonavolonta and Duffy 1996).

Because of their control over the investment of union pension and welfare funds, Cosa Nostra members could persuade bankers to approve loans to Cosa Nostra members and associates, including those who wanted the money for loan-sharking (Kwitny 1979). In some cases, a mobster would arrange bank loans for his clients so they could repay him (Kwitny 1979).

One of the predicate racketeering offenses for the 1986 RICO prosecution of the commission case was a conspiracy to allocate loan-sharking territories on Long Island (*United States v. Salerno*). The prosecution charged the defendant commission members with facilitating loan-sharking by resolving a territorial dispute between the Lucchese and Gambino crime families (Jacobs, Panarella, and Worthington 1994). Loan-sharking was also one of the predicate offenses in the 1992 prosecution of Gambino family boss John Gotti. Among other offenses, Gotti was convicted of making extortionate extensions of credit and extortionate collections of credit (*United States v. Gotti*, aff'd, 6 F. 3d 924, *United States v. Locascio* [2d Cir. 1993]).

In a 1994 case, *United States v. DiSalvo* (34 F.3d 1204 [3d Cir. 1994]), two Scarfo family associates, DiSalvo and Simone, were convicted of loan-sharking offenses. Turncoat Philip Leonetti (former Scarfo family underboss) described the intrafamily payoff arrangement with respect to loan-sharking schemes. "When Scarfo became the family boss, Simone asked Scarfo not to extract money from DiSalvo's loanshark business, i.e. to exempt him from the 'elbow'" (34 F.3d 1204, 1206). However, this was only a temporary arrangement; later DiSalvo, like everyone else, was expected to share his loan-sharking profits with Scarfo and at least two other superiors in the family. In exchange, DiSalvo received Scarfo family assistance when he faced problems getting repayment of a $200,000 loan (*United States v. DiSalvo*).

The factual basis for the more recent loan-sharking conviction of Gambino family associate Norman Dupont illustrates the connection between loan-sharking and extortion (*United States v. Dupont*, 112 F.3d 506 [2d Cir. 1996]). Dupont loaned $17,800 to an individual named Friedman, a Manhattan car service owner who was charged $400 per week in interest. The jury found that when Friedman fully paid his debt, Dupont insisted that he continue paying him between $200 and

$300 per week in "protection money." When Friedman failed to pay, Dupont had him assaulted (*United States v. Dupont*).

2. *Gambling.* Since the 1940s, gambling has been important for Cosa Nostra, because of its profitability and because, relative to other illicit activities, gambling enjoys a greater degree of social acceptability (Bell 1964). Gambling replaced prostitution as Cosa Nostra's moneymaker. Explanations for Mafia abandonment of prostitution emphasize that it simply did not pay as well as gambling. In addition, Daniel Bell argues that Mafia involvement in prostitution "threatened the tacit moral acceptance and quasi-respectability that gamblers and gambling have secured in the American way of life" (Bell, p. 130). Cosa Nostra's involvement in the industries of prostitution and pornography, while arguably at one time an integral part of their criminal operations, has waned considerably since the first half of the century. In 1936, Lucky Luciano and several codefendants, targeted by investigators for their efforts to centralize control of New York City brothels, were successfully prosecuted for sixty-two counts of compulsory prostitution (Block 1983). (Luciano's sentence, thirty to fifty years, would later be cut short by a grant of clemency by Governor Dewey in exchange for his assistance during the Second World War; Kenney and Finckenauer 1995). By the time of Luciano's conviction, most other Cosa Nostra families had largely extricated themselves from the business, although some organized crime figures continued to extort protection payoffs from independent brothels (Abadinsky 1994). In the area of pornography, as well, organized crime has in most areas (perhaps excluding Chicago) failed or, at least, opted not to dominate non-Mafia "amateurs" (Abadinsky 1994).

Bookmaking for races and sporting events, placing and laying off bets for numbers, pools, and lotteries have proven lucrative for Cosa Nostra (of these, PCOC [1985] identified sports betting as the biggest revenue source). Some of the mid-century titans of organized crime, including Arnold Rothstein, and later Meyer Lansky and Bugsy Siegel (both of whom were closely allied with Cosa Nostra), were bosses of huge gambling operations. Frank Costello became a millionaire many times over through his gambling interests, especially slot machines. Indeed, his gambling machine partnership with Louisiana political boss Huey Long is one of the best examples of the alliance between organized crime figures and politicians (Hanna 1974).

The development of Las Vegas is a critical chapter in Cosa Nostra gambling history. With financial backing from Meyer Lansky, Frank

Costello, and other Cosa Nostra figures, Bugsy Siegel projected organized crime into Las Vegas. Through control of the wire service in Las
Vegas, he directed Las Vegas's bookmaking operations (Skolnick
1978). With mob financing, Siegel also built the Flamingo, the first of
the huge Las Vegas gambling hotels. Over time, Cosa Nostra bosses
obtained interests in many of the largest casinos in Las Vegas (Skolnick
1978). At one point, approximately a quarter of a billion dollars of the
Teamsters central states pension funds were invested in the mortgages
of those casinos (PCOC 1985). In effect, this huge Teamsters fund
functioned as a bank for the mob. In addition, Cosa Nostra bosses enjoyed huge returns on their Las Vegas investments by skimming
money from casino profits (PCOC 1983). In 1986, with the aid of the
testimony of Angelo Lonardo, a Cleveland underboss turned government witness, a number of Midwest mobsters were sentenced to prison
for tax evasion emanating from the Las Vegas operations (e.g., *United
States v. Spinale*, no. 86–95, D.Nev., July 15, 1986).

Because the 1968 President's Commission's Task Force on Organized Crime theorized that gambling was the main money maker for
Cosa Nostra, the FBI's first real antiorganized crime thrust in the early
1970s focused on gambling. While the gambling program ultimately
was regarded as unsuccessful, it did generate dozens of prosecutions
and, more important, extensive intelligence information on organized
crime.

In the 1980s, the PCOC directed much of its attention to Cosa Nostra gambling operations. According to the 1985 PCOC estimate, in the
tristate New York area alone, $1.5 billion is spent each year on num-
bers games, sports bookmakers, and other forms of illegal wagering
controlled by organized crime (PCOC 1985, p. 3). FBI agent Frank
Storey, Jr. told the PCOC that, by a conservative estimate, more than
one-half of Cosa Nostra revenues came from gambling (p. 57), but he
did not provide any documentation to show how he arrived at this estimate.

The PCOC (1985, p. 637) articulated the special problems of gambling regulation, including the distinction between gambling, which is
not popularly viewed as harmful, and drug trafficking, which is "uni-
versally condemned." Michael DeFeo, U.S. Department of Justice
Deputy Chief of the Organized Crime and Racketeering Section,
Criminal Division, explained to PCOC that these perceptions ultimately influenced the allocation of law enforcement efforts (PCOC
1985, p. 184). During the early 1970s, over 50 percent of federal orga-

nized crime law enforcement efforts were directed at gambling, but three-quarters of those convicted were sentenced to mere probation. Because "the game was not worth the candle" (p. 184), by 1986 only 10 percent of law enforcement investigations were directed at gambling (maybe 25 percent if the number includes cases where gambling is one of many predicate racketeering acts [e.g., *United States v. Salerno; United States v. Gotti*]). This phenomenon, according to PCOC, makes "illegal gambling the 'highest profit-lowest risk' business in which organized crime groups can involve themselves" (p. 637).

FBI investigators indicate that a typical sports bookmaking operation may be arranged like one that was videotaped in the Northeast:

> There are a total of six telephones in use, five of which are visible. The sixth one is at the end of the table at the bottom of the screen. The main phone in the center contains a 32-number speed dial memory, facilitating easy access to other bookmakers and associates throughout the country. The five remaining phones are connected to a main number in a rollover system, where the next available individual takes the incoming call. The individuals seated take the bets, fill out a form in duplicate and place them on the other side of the table in front of them. Another time-stamps them. Orders are used for accounting purposes. Calls are taped. A monitor, following posted guidelines, ensures that too many bets are not being placed on any one side. (PCOC 1985, p. 58)

Bookmaking operations often use cordless phones and call forwarding or beepers to prevent their headquarters from being located and their calls from being traced. Wagers are generally recorded on flammable flash paper or water soluble paper, which is easily destroyed in case of a raid (PCOC 1985).

Chicago police sergeant Donald Herrion explained to PCOC how Cosa Nostra was able to control all illegal gambling in that city (PCOC 1985, p. 148). "The Outfit" (Chicago crime family) imposes a street tax (50 percent) on bookmakers who seek to operate in Chicago. Under a typical scenario, the bookmaker finds his own bettors and the Outfit supplies wire rooms, clerks, and telephones (p. 148). Often, Cosa Nostra will bypass the bookmaker intermediary by becoming friendly with the bookmaker's repeat bettors. When that bettor has a bad week, Cosa Nostra offers the following proposition: if phony bets are placed, the bettor will split profits with the clerk (from the Outfit) and the bookmaker will be cut out of the deal and eventually be drained of finances, enabling the Outfit to subsume the bookmaker's whole operation (p. 148).

A Milwaukee-based sports bookmaking operation, headed by Frank Balistrieri (boss), Steve DiSalvo (underboss), and Balistrieri's sons, was exposed by government interception of a large number of telephone calls related to gambling on college and professional football games (PCOC 1985, p. 165). Individuals called "writers" answered phones and dealt with customers directly, while an overseer (who totaled the accounts) decided which bets could still be taken. If the wagering action on a particular sporting contest was too heavy on one side, the operation would use a "beard" or front to place layoff wagers with other bookmakers to disguise their layoff and obtain a betting advantage (p. 165).

Naturally, Cosa Nostra gains an even greater advantage where games can be fixed through control of the athletes involved. The notorious Boston College basketball case began with a small time bookie, Tony Perla, who was familiar with Rick Kuhn, a member of the basketball team (PCOC 1985, p. 280). Perla convinced Kuhn to stay within the point spread by shaving points. Because bookmakers will not take large bets on college basketball games, Perla decided that he needed a multicity network to increase his profits. This necessity led him to the Lucchese family. Ultimately, Kuhn and team captain Sweeney were accepting $2,500 per game from Cosa Nostra, in addition to cars, women, and drugs (PCOC 1985). Similar schemes seem to be more common in horse racing and boxing because of the limited number of players who need to be corrupted.

The 1985 PCOC report also discussed efforts by New Jersey authorities to investigate the sale and use of illegal video gambling devices. These machines are designed to have both a permissible amusement mode (where a player inserts a quarter and accumulates points) and the capability (with the push of a hidden few buttons or the insertion of a secret code) of being used for illegal gambling (PCOC 1985). The patron/player would be paid at the end of the game by the store owner or bartender. A recent New Jersey case (*State v. Taccetta*, 301 NJ Super 227 [1997]) exposed Cosa Nostra's placement of "Joker Poker" video slot machines in taverns, restaurants, and other businesses. The Lucchese and Bruno-Scarfo crime families shared the revenue from the machines with the business owners and extorted money from SMS, the "Joker Poker" manufacturer. Bruno-Scarfo turncoat

Philip Leonetti explained that a conflict arose between the two families over who controlled SMS. Taccetta, the Lucchese family member who collected payments from SMS, was convicted on counts of gambling and extortion. Similar video poker machines have turned up in other cities, including Chicago (PCOC 1985).

Evidence suggests that control of the gambling industry has shifted significantly in recent years. While many of the major casinos were formerly run by Cosa Nostra, now they are controlled by Fortune 500 companies. However, the Italian organized crime families are still involved in a wide range of gambling operations (Trends in Organized Crime 1997, 3:28).

3. *Drugs.* Cosa Nostra bosses and families have had differences of opinion about illegal drug trafficking. Since Prohibition, some Cosa Nostra individuals, crews, and families have profited from illicit drug distribution. Lucky Luciano was arrested at one point for carrying heroin (Kenney and Finckenauer 1995). Vito Genovese, who achieved the title of "boss of bosses" in the late 1950s, was ultimately convicted for drug trafficking (Hanna 1974). However, many Cosa Nostra members have been opposed to drug trafficking, either because they feared the law enforcement attention or for moral reasons (*United States v. Tieri*; *United States v. Salerno*; Maas 1997). Frank Costello (Luciano family boss) laid down a no-drugs rule in his own family and later tried to extend it to other families (Peterson 1983). Costello is said to have feared a law enforcement crackdown and negative public opinion (Kenney and Finckenauer 1995 [citing Valachi testimony]). Chicago boss Tony Accardo reportedly paid his subordinates up to $250 a week to stay out of drug trafficking (Peterson 1983). In the 1980s, the Bonanno family was expelled from the New York City Commission for its involvement in narcotics distribution. Of course, the very fact of this expulsion demonstrates that some Italian organized crime families have been heavily involved in drug trafficking right up to the present day.

Bonanno family involvement in drug trafficking was unmasked in *United States v. Badalamenti* (known as the "pizza connection" case because several of the defendants used pizzerias as fronts for engaging in heroin distribution). The government exposed an international drug-trafficking network coordinated through the combined efforts of Cosa Nostra (primarily the Bonanno family) and a Sicilian Mafia group (See Jacobs, Panarella, and Worthington 1994). Over two hundred participants were involved in the trafficking network and, ultimately, twenty-two of the thirty-five indicted defendants were tried together in the largest and most complex megatrial of the decade. *Badalamenti* demonstrated what observers of organized crime long suspected: even if Cosa Nostra has stated rules prohibiting drug trafficking, these edicts are often honored in the breach (Jacobs, Panarella, and Worthington 1994).

Paul Castellano, Gambino family boss, prohibited members of his family from participating in drug trafficking, but at the same time accepted a cut of Sonny Black Napolitano's (Bonanno family) heroin business in exchange for supporting Napolitano in the Bonanno family feud (Bonavolonta and Duffy 1996). Moreover, Castellano's edict against drug trafficking did not stop capos and soldiers in his own family from drug trafficking. Angelo Ruggiero, John and Gene Gotti, and their entire Bergen Hunt and Fish Club crew were all profiting from drugs. When Castellano learned that Ruggiero's home had been bugged as part of the government's investigation of the Gambino family and the commission, he sought copies of the tapes. Ruggiero, well aware that the tapes clearly documented his heroin trafficking, resisted Castellano's request because he feared draconian repercussions (Bonavolonta and Duffy 1996). Castellano's ongoing conflict with his subordinates on their involvement in the narcotics business (he is alleged to have informed Gotti that he would break up Gotti's crew) was one of the factors that ultimately led to his assassination (Bonavolonta and Duffy 1996; *United States v. Gotti*).

Angelo Bruno, head of the Philadelphia crime family, is said to have adopted a similarly hypocritical approach (Fresolone and Wagman 1994). The Genovese family, also claiming to observe a drug-free rule, has also had many members involved in drug trafficking (Peterson 1983). Turncoat Alphonse D'Arco testified that while he acted as Lucchese family crime boss, he was not directly involved with the distribution of drugs, but that some of his subordinates were (*United States v. Avellino*, 136 F.3d 249 [2d Cir. 1998]).

D. Traditional Crimes

Cosa Nostra crews engage in all manner of traditional crimes for economic gain. Industrial racketeering, for example, created opportunities for other crimes. Because of its entrenched position on the waterfront (Jensen 1974) and in the construction industry (New York State Organized Crime Task Force 1990), and through its influence in cargo operations at Kennedy Airport (Kwitny 1979), Cosa Nostra was able to identify valuable materials and cargo and set up lucrative thefts, truck give-ups, and hijackings.

Cosa Nostra's ability to profit from air cargo operations at Kennedy Airport was grounded in the Lucchese family's control of two Teamsters locals. This control ensured that Cosa Nostra determined the assignment of personnel, including truck drivers and dispatchers. Selective assignment of drivers was critical to the orchestration of a give-up, in which the driver would leave his truck unattended in accordance with a prearranged plan. To set up a hijacking, the Cosa Nostra crew ascertained from the dispatcher the schedule and route of a particular truck, which would later be intercepted by a crew member (Jacobs 1999). The most ambitious of these thefts was the $5 million heist of the Lufthansa cargo hangar in 1978 (the basis for the movie, *Goodfellas*) (Jacobs and Panarella 1998).

On some construction projects, theft of equipment and materials was so predictable that contractors incorporated these costs into their estimates and bids and, in some cases, repurchased their own equipment from the thieves (New York State Organized Crime Task Force 1990). Where materials and equipment were not taken, they were in jeopardy of being destroyed. Cosa Nostra used sabotage as a punishment, threat, or means of generating more work (New York State Organized Crime Task Force 1990).

Cosa Nostra also has a record of perpetrating thefts and frauds in the securities industry, dating back at least to the early 1960s (Kwitny 1979). The mob profited from the theft of poorly protected stock certificates. When brokerage firms tightened security, Cosa Nostra members turned to fraud schemes; they began setting up sham corporations and luring unsuspecting investors, counterfeiting stock certificates, and taking control of smaller brokerage houses (Kwitny 1979). The bilking of Dean Witter by employee Joey Franzese (whose uncle was a member of the Colombo family) is a notorious example of this type of securities fraud. Franzese would create phony accounts and then sign checks to himself from the account before deleting all record of the transaction from the computer (Kwitny 1979).

In 1997, seventeen individuals (many of them high-ranking members of the Genovese and Bonnanno crime families) were indicted for securities fraud, bank fraud, and extortionate activity (Jacobs 1999; *United States v. Gangi*, Ind. 97 Crim. 1215 [SDNY 1997]). The indictment alleged that members of the Genovese and Bonanno families "shook down" employees of a small brokerage firm to obtain low-cost shares in a corrupt company called HealthTech. Then, with coopera-tion from the HealthTech CEO, Cosa Nostra members inflated the trading price of the securities and resold them through the brokerage firm to unsuspecting consumers (Weiser 1997). This "pump and dump" scheme ultimately cost investors three million dollars (Jacobs 1999).

The mob also has an extensive record in bankruptcy fraud ("bust out" schemes), taking over a legitimate company, looting its assets, and leaving its creditors high and dry. A variation on this scheme involved the creation of a company for the same purposes (Hanna 1974; Kwitny 1979). Tax evasion (*United States v. Ianniello,* 808 F.2d 184 [2d Cir. 1986]) and stolen credit cards are also routine conduct for organized crime figures.

Cosa Nostra is responsible for a good deal of personal violence, usu-ally used for internal discipline or as a means of furthering its eco-nomic crimes. Murder has also frequently appeared in the list of predi-cate offenses in several high-profile Cosa Nostra cases. In his testimony about the activities of his boss, John Gotti, Sammy "The Bull" Gravano explained that murder is employed as a tool for main-taining family order (*United States v. Gotti;* Jacobs, Panarella, and Wor-thington 1994). Gotti was ultimately convicted of the murder of Gam-bino crime boss Paul Castellano and several other Cosa Nostra members. The murder of Carmine Galante (Bonanno family boss) and two of his associates were predicate offenses in the commission case (*United States v. Salerno*). The discovery of two murdered mob mem-bers buried in the concrete below the Arista windows factory in Brook-lyn (which was owned by Pete Savino, the leader of the Cosa Nostra windows scam) enabled the government to turn Savino against his cor-rupt colleagues in the window replacement business (Bonavolonta and Duffy 1996).

IV. Cosa Nostra and Politics

Cosa Nostra bosses have functioned as "fixers" to whom businessmen, politicians, and criminals reached out in order to solve a variety of problems with other criminals, labor organizations, law enforcement agencies, and government regulators (Jacobs, Panarella, and Worthing-ton 1994). In their communities, mob members could be relied on to circumvent government regulation and market failure and even to bring stability when warring criminal gangs created instability (Bell 1964). At the same time, where it has been necessary to advance their own interests, mobsters have frequently relied on various forms of bribery and extortion.

The power that Cosa Nostra exerted over labor unions and cartels was skillfully parlayed into political clout, such that in many major cities, the mob was closely allied with the Democratic Party power structure (Peterson 1983). This was especially true during the heyday of the urban political machines. In some cities, Cosa Nostra infected the political process so thoroughly that mob bosses were essentially power brokers, anointing Democratic Party candidates and supporting their campaigns with funding and manpower drawn from the unions. In return, Cosa Nostra was protected from law enforcement. These symbiotic arrangements were the focus of the Kefauver hearings in the early 1950s and of occasional prosecutions in the years that followed.

One target of the Kefauver Commission investigations was New York City Mayor William O'Dwyer, who served from 1946 until his resignation in 1950 (Block 1983). Members of the Kefauver Commission suspected O'Dwyer of having protected the leaders of organized crime from prosecution during his tenure as Brooklyn district attorney. Later, O'Dwyer sought (and ultimately received) the support of Luciano family boss Frank Costello in the 1945 mayoral election (Block 1983; Peterson 1983). Costello, who was the top Cosa Nostra boss in New York City at the time, had extensive ties to Tammany Hall (Block 1983; Kenney and Finckenauer 1995). Among other things, he controlled judicial appointments. In a famous wiretap-recorded conversation between New York Supreme Court Judge Thomas Aurelio and Costello, in 1943, Aurelio credited and thanked Costello for his judicial nomination (Bell 1964, p. 145; Abadinsky, 1994). O'Dwyer's resignation did not cut off Cosa Nostra's influence in city hall; his successor Vincent Impellitteri (1950–54) allegedly had ties to the Lucchese family and was later linked to Costello as well (Peterson 1983).

In 1967, Antonio Corallo and Daniel Motto (high-ranking Cosa Nostra members) were indicted with James Marcus, commissioner of the water department in the Lindsay administration, for criminal offenses stemming from the award of a million-dollar water rehabilitation contract to a mobbed-up company. Marcus admitted that he had accepted cash bribes from the mob figures for his assigning the contracts to the firm they designated (Jacobs 1999; *United States v. Corallo*, 413 F.2d 1306 [1969]).

Their position as labor officials gave some Cosa Nostra officials high status in legitimate society. For four decades, Harry Davidoff, president of IBT Local 295, that operated at Kennedy Airport, moved in high political circles in New York City. Governor Hugh Carey testified as a character witness in the successful prosecution of Anthony Scotto, a capo in the Gambino crime family and boss of the New York Longshoremen's Union. In the 1970s, John Cody, president of Teamsters Local 282, was one of the most powerful labor officials in New York City. It is reported that he asked Carlo Gambino (the boss of bosses at the time) to be a greeter at his son's wedding reception in 1973 (Kwitny 1979). Likewise, Ralph Scopo, president of a Laborer's local and an official of the Concrete Workers District Council (Colombo crime family) (New York State Organized Crime Task Force 1990), wielded power in the upperworld and the underworld.

Examples of Cosa Nostra's political influence are by no means limited to New York City. In Kansas City, Cosa Nostra was, for years, connected to the Pendergast political machine, which provided police protection for the mob's gambling enterprises (Abadinsky 1994). In 1983, Teamsters president Roy L. Williams, Teamsters central states pension fund broker Allen Dorfman, and Chicago mobster Joseph "The Clown" Lombardo were convicted of conspiring to bribe U.S. Senator Howard S. Cannon (Democrat, Nevada) (PCOC 1983). The defendants wanted the senator (who was not charged) to work to shelve a trucking deregulation bill in exchange for low-cost property in Las Vegas (*United States v. Williams*, 737 F.2d 594 [7th Cir. 1984]). Under Carlos Marcello's leadership, the New Orleans crime family exerted enormous influence throughout Louisiana politics. For decades, the Outfit controlled Chicago's downtown first ward. At the national level, President Nixon was criticized for attending Teamsters parties at Conta Costa country club and for entertaining Cosa Nostra figures at the White House.

Links between Cosa Nostra and public officials still come to light from time to time. A recent Pennsylvania case exposed Cosa Nostra corruption of a Philadelphia city councilman (*United States v. DiSalvo*). Testimony from turncoats Philip Leonetti (former Bruno-Scarfo underboss) and Nicholas Caramandi led to the convictions for attempted extortion of several Bruno-Scarfo family members, Leland Beloff, Philadelphia city councilman, and his legislative aide Robert Rego. Beloff and Rego, because they were in the powerful position of moving a multimillion dollar construction project funding bill through the council, conspired with several members of the Bruno-Scarfo crime family (including Nicodemo Scarfo [boss]) to share a cut of the

$100,000 fee that they requested from Rouse and Associates (the developer chosen to construct the project), in order to ensure the safe passage of the bill. After Rego approached Peter Balitsaris, the Rouse employee in charge of the project, Balitsaris contacted federal authorities and cooperated in the investigation (*United States v. DiSalvo*).

Behind these high-profile cases of sociopolitical influence is the day-to-day reality of Cosa Nostra presence in local communities. In New York City, for decades, the presence and influence of Cosa Nostra figures was obvious and well known to all who worked in New York City's construction industry, the Fulton Fish Market, the garment center, the waste hauling industry, and several other industries and economic sectors (Gambetta and Peltzman 1995; Jacobs and Panarella 1998, p. 3). Some Cosa Nostra figures were popular with the rank-and-file union members, who viewed them as powerful and effective advocates (New York State Organized Crime Task Force 1990, p. xxv). As community residents, Cosa Nostra bosses kept their neighborhoods safe from street crime, fixed problems for local residents, mounted colorful street fairs, and strutted around like heroes (Bell 1964). In many respects, Cosa Nostra was a known and predictable aspect of informal local government and community life.

V. The Evolution of Effective Organized Crime Control

Government success over the past twenty years in eroding Cosa Nostra's power base can be attributed to a change in the perception and understanding of the problem, the FBI's commitment to destroying Cosa Nostra, political support at the highest governmental level, the use of extensive electronic surveillance, the ability to protect government witnesses, the criminal and civil provisions of the powerful RICO statute, and recent innovative administrative strategies pioneered by the Giuliani administration in New York City. Beginning in the late 1970s and continuing to date (1998), the U.S. Department of Justice and the FBI (with the assistance and many independent contributions of other federal, state, and local law enforcement agencies) have maintained an unprecedented assault that threatens Cosa Nostra's survival into the twenty-first century.

A. Early Days of Organized Crime Control

Serious congressional attention to the problem of organized crime dates to 1950, when the U.S. Senate created a Special Committee to Investigate Organized Crime chaired by Tennessee Democrat Estes

Kefauver (Kefauver 1951). The Kefauver Committee, as it would come to be known, investigated the ties between organized crime and local government in a number of U.S. cities. In 1956, Senator John McClellan began a fifteen-year series of hearings for the Senate Select Committee on Improper Activities in the Labor or Management Field (McClellan 1962). During Robert F. Kennedy's tenure as chief counsel to that committee, he focused attention on corruption and racketeering in the IBT and engaged in acrimonious exchanges with Jimmy Hoffa that touched off a feud that continued until Kennedy's death (Kennedy 1960).

The U.S. Department of Justice essentially made no efforts to attack Cosa Nostra until Robert Kennedy became attorney general in 1961 and revitalized the Organized Crime and Racketeering Section (OCRS) of the U.S. Department of Justice. While the unit achieved some early successes (e.g., investigating and convicting Jimmy Hoffa) it became quiescent after Kennedy left the U.S. Department of Justice (see U.S. Department of Justice 1987). However, it was not until the death of long-time FBI director J. Edgar Hoover in 1972 that the FBI and the U.S. Justice Department made Cosa Nostra an important law enforcement priority (see Nash 1972; Schlesinger 1978; and Powers 1987 for a discussion of Hoover's denial of the existence of the Mafia). From that point forward there was increased effort and achievement.

In the early 1970s, the OCRS launched its gambling initiative on the theory that gambling proceeds were the main source of revenue for Cosa Nostra. But the gambling program was not a success, largely because courts and trial juries were not sympathetic, indeed they were often hostile to gambling prosecutions. It was the wrong approach to take if the goal was to convince the courts and the public that organized crime posed a serious threat to American society (U.S. General Accounting Office 1976).

Toward the late 1970s, the FBI changed its focus from gambling to labor racketeering. The disappearance of Jimmy Hoffa provided the impetus for a major investigation of the relationship between the Teamsters and organized crime. The FBI made labor racketeering its top organized crime priority. For example, UNIRAC (the investigation of racketeering in the Longshoremen's Association) started as a Miami Strike Force project and widened to include New York City and ultimately the whole East Coast. Operation BRILAB, directed by the New Orleans Strike Force, involved strike force attorneys in New Orleans, Los Angeles, and Washington, D.C., and resulted in the conviction of

New Orleans Cosa Nostra boss Carlos Marcello and numerous other organized crime members and associates. The PENDORF investigation focused on Cosa Nostra corruption of the Teamsters Central States Pension fund and resulted in convictions of Teamsters President Roy Williams and organized crime figures in Chicago, Milwaukee, Cleveland, Las Vegas, and Kansas City (Jacobs, Panarella, and Worthington 1994).

B. Department of Justice Organized Crime Strike Forces

In 1967, the U.S. Justice Department formed the Organized Crime Strike Forces, comprised of prosecutors and representatives of the federal investigative agencies in fourteen cities (Ryan 1994). The strike forces were autonomous from the U.S. attorneys; they reported to the head of the OCRS of the central Justice Department. According to supporters, the strike force lawyers stayed in their jobs longer than typical U.S. attorneys and assistant U.S. attorneys, developed more specialized expertise in organized crime control, and were more successful in gaining the confidence of the FBI and other law enforcement agencies (Jacobs, Panarella, and Worthington 1994).

Nevertheless, up to the late 1970s, the strike forces were criticized for their inability to define organized crime, for pursuing low-priority targets (i.e., gambling), and for lacking the authority to control the activities of the investigative agencies on which they depended (U.S. General Accounting Office 1976, 1981). Eventually, however, the strike forces began functioning more effectively, and the FBI significantly elevated its commitment to organized crime control. The payoff soon became evident as success followed success.

From the outset, the strike forces were anathema to many of the U.S. attorneys in whose jurisdictions they operated. Historically, the U.S. attorneys decided how to deploy prosecutorial resources and who would prosecute what cases. Many U.S. attorneys, therefore, objected to the strike forces' independence. When Richard Thornburgh, a former U.S. attorney in Pittsburgh and a strike force opponent, became attorney general in 1988, he moved to disband the strike forces and transfer their mission and personnel back to the U.S. attorneys. Although there was some opposition in Congress, which held hearings on the matter, the strike forces as independent entities were disbanded in 1989 and merged into the U.S. attorneys' offices (Jacobs, Panarella, and Worthington 1994). Many experienced strike force prosecutors resigned from the U.S. Justice Department.

C. Federal, State, and Local Law Enforcement Cooperation

Historically, effective organized crime control was severely hampered by bitter rivalry among federal, state, and local law enforcement agencies. Each agency distrusted the others, even to the point of charging that rival agencies were neither secure nor trustworthy; frequently, each felt that the others were trying to take unfair credit for successes. The history of American law enforcement, especially in combating organized crime, is replete with lost opportunities due to inability or unwillingness to reach interagency agreements. The emergence of joint federal, state, and local task forces in the 1970s made significant headway in overcoming agency parochialism (Jacobs, Panarella, and Worthington 1994).

In 1970, the National Council on Organized Crime was established to formulate a strategy to eliminate organized crime. While the council failed to formulate a national strategy, it began to address the bitter rivalries that had long prevented interagency cooperation. The Department of Justice strike forces played an important role in bringing federal, state, and local agencies together in concerted investigations. In 1976, the National Organized Crime Planning Council was formed to facilitate planning and coordination between the strike forces and the federal law enforcement agencies. In 1980, the Executive Working Group for Federal-State-Local Prosecutorial Relations was established.

Many informal multiagency agreements supplemented and reinforced these formal mechanisms (Jacobs, Panarella, and Worthington 1994). The arrangement that was developed in New York City is illustrative. The FBI and the New York Police Department (NYPD) shared information and cooperated in numerous investigations. Former FBI organized crime supervisor Jules Bonavolonta estimates that by the mid-1980s, the New York City FBI offices had 350 agents assigned to the organized crime division, assisted by more than one hundred NYPD officers (Bonavolonta and Duffy 1996, p. 270). This cooperation was necessary to staff the round-the-clock investigations of each of the families, especially the labor-intensive monitoring of electronic surveillance equipment (Jacobs, Panarella, and Worthington 1994).

D. Political Support from Washington

President Ronald Reagan strongly supported the attack on organized crime. At the Department of Justice, Attorney General William

French Smith and Deputy Associate Attorney General Rudy Giuliani were more committed to fighting organized crime than any administration since Robert Kennedy (Jacobs, Panarella, and Worthington 1994). Reagan established a presidential commission that was charged with undertaking a comprehensive analysis of organized crime, including Cosa Nostra's organization, membership, and activities (PCOC 1983). From 1983 to 1987, the PCOC held public hearings and issued twelve reports; among other things, these reports laid out the structure of the organized crime families, documented their extensive involvement in drug trafficking, gambling, and labor racketeering, and recommended that the Department of Justice bring a civil RICO suit against the International Brotherhood of Teamsters in order to have that union placed under a court-appointed trusteeship.

The executive branch attack on Cosa Nostra was complemented by high-visibility congressional hearings and inquiries which, in the tradition of Kefauver and McClellan, kept the spotlight on organized crime. The U.S. Senate's Permanent Subcommittee on Investigations, under the leadership of Georgia Democrat Senator Sam Nunn, held dramatic hearings on the role of Cosa Nostra in legitimate industry and illicit rackets (U.S. Senate 1988). The committee held hearings and called numerous witnesses (including many of the Cosa Nostra defectors) who provided testimony on the history, customs, and operations of Cosa Nostra. All the pieces were coming together. Support and resources from Washington marked a crucial change from the past.

E. The FBI Strategy

In the post-Hoover period, the FBI's strong commitment to putting Cosa Nostra out of business heralded the modern era in organized crime control. The FBI adopted a "major cases" approach which sought to identify the structure, hierarchy, and vulnerabilities of each of the Italian organized crime families as a method of developing significant prosecutions. Investigative teams concentrated on collecting intelligence on each Cosa Nostra crime family. The FBI's most significant new tool was electronic surveillance, which yielded massive evidence. FBI agent Joe Pistone's six-year undercover operation provided the government with invaluable information on the organization and activities of the Bonanno crime family. Moreover, for the first time in history, mobsters turned on their confederates and agreed to serve the government as cooperating witnesses in exchange for leniency and placement in the Witness Security Program.

1. *The Family Teams.* Under operation GENUS, teams of FBI agents were assigned to gather intelligence on each of New York City's five Cosa Nostra families. Each team was responsible for detailing a family's "table of organization," identifying all the members and their status in the organization, and determining which rackets and industries the family was involved in. From there, the prosecutions would fall into place (Bonavolonta and Duffy 1996). The FBI also organized squads for Cosa Nostra crime families in other cities. After documenting the family's command structure and criminal activities, the squads obtained eavesdropping orders. Eavesdropping provided inculpatory evidence that convinced some mobsters that conviction was certain and that making a cooperation deal with prosecutors was the only way to avoid a long prison term. Federal prosecutors used the evidence in a continuous stream of criminal and civil suits.

2. *Electronic Surveillance.* Electronic eavesdropping figured prominently in almost every organized crime prosecution of the modern period; some prosecutions were based almost entirely on intercepted conversations. The FBI and state and local agencies used both telephone intercepts and hidden microphones in cars, homes, restaurants, and social clubs. In some cases, the FBI used sophisticated microphones to pick up conversations on the streets.

One of the most productive bugs was one the FBI placed in Gambino family boss Paul Castellano's kitchen. For months it picked up conversations that ultimately led to the indictment of Castellano and others in the commission case. (Castellano was murdered before the trial.) The bug that the FBI placed in East Harlem's Palma Boys Social Club recorded conversations in which Genovese family boss Anthony "Fat Tony" Salerno discussed commission business and Teamsters politics (Bonavolonta and Duffy 1996). These conversations provided critical evidence for the commission case and for the government's complaint in the civil RICO suit against the General Executive Board of the Teamsters (*United States v. International Brotherhood of Teamsters*). The FBI's bugs in the Ravenite Social Club and in the apartment above it recorded inculpatory conversations between Gambino boss John Gotti and his subordinates and eventually led to the successful prosecution of Gotti, the most flamboyant mob figure of modern times.

The FBI was able to place listening devices in the home of acting Colombo family boss Tommy DiBella after one of DiBella's underlings, Frankie Falanga, noticed a video camera "security" system in the home of a Colombo associate who was surreptitiously cooperating with the government. Falanga requested that a similar system be installed for the Colombo family boss. The FBI was pleased to oblige (Bonavolonta and Duffy 1996). Even more productive bugs were placed in the Colombo Family's Maniac Club (frequented by Dominick "Donnie Shacks" Montemarano) and in Brooklyn's Casa Storta Restaurant (where Donnie Shacks and Colombo family underboss Gennaro "Gerry Lang" Langella regularly held meetings) (Bonavolonta and Duffy 1996).

Philadelphia's Bruno crime family boss John Stanfa (who succeeded Nicky Scarfo after Scarfo's incarceration) attempted to protect himself from eavesdropping by using his lawyer's office to hold meetings, on the assumption that attorney-client privilege would prohibit the government from bugging the office. Unfortunately for Stanfa (and for his attorney), the government obtained judicial permission to place an eavesdropping device in the office on a showing that the attorney had played a participatory role in the organized crime family. (This was in addition to the car and home bugs on Stanfa.) (See *United States v. Stanfa*, 1996 WL 417168 [EDPA]; Fresolone and Wagman 1994; see also Goldstock and Chananie 1988 for a related discussion.) By the end of the decade, there was no place where Cosa Nostra members could converse without having to worry about government eavesdroppers.

3. *Donnie Brasco—Infiltration of the Mafia.* FBI agent Joseph Pistone's penetration of the Bonanno family in New York City from 1976 to 1982, recounted in Pistone's autobiography (Pistone and Woodley 1987) and later dramatized in the 1997 film *Donnie Brasco*, is the most extraordinary undercover operation in U.S. law enforcement history (Pistone and Woodley 1987; Bonavolonta and Duffy 1996). No law enforcement agent had ever before infiltrated a Cosa Nostra family. Indeed, that the FBI would even attempt to place a secret agent in the ranks of organized crime reveals how committed, confident, and creative the agency had become. J. Edgar Hoover had never permitted FBI agents to work undercover (Nash 1972; Schlesinger 1978).

Pistone, posing as a jewel thief and burglar, hung out at the bars and restaurants frequented by organized crime members and associates. Eventually, he was noticed by an organized crime figure, whom he cut in on a number of phony schemes (Pistone and Woodley 1987). In the course of some of these "crimes," he was able to bring other agents into contact with members of Cosa Nostra (Bonavolonta and Duffy 1996). Pistone's undercover operation lasted six years; just before he had to surface and break his cover (he had been ordered to carry out a murder and was himself in danger of a preemptive strike), he was promised induction into the Bonanno crime family (Bonavolonta and Duffy 1996). Pistone provided the FBI a mountain of intelligence material. His pivotal role in the investigation of the Bonannos led to indictments in Milwaukee, Tampa, and New York (Bonavolonta and Duffy 1996). He served as a witness at a number of major Cosa Nostra trials, including the commission case, *United States v. Salerno.* No doubt, this infiltration was a blow to Cosa Nostra morale, raising doubts about how many of its secrets had been revealed and whether any other associates or even members were government agents or informers.

F. State and Local Law Enforcement

State and local efforts, in conjunction with increasingly successful federal investigations and prosecutions, have been an integral part of the successful law enforcement attack. The New York State Organized Crime Task Force (NYSOCTF), led by Ronald Goldstock, was particularly creative in the 1980s. In 1983, NYSOCTF placed a "car bug" in Salvatore Avellino's Jaguar after noticing that Avellino frequently chauffeured Lucchese family boss Anthony "Tony Ducks" Corallo. The bug, which ran for six months, intercepted incriminating conversations that ultimately led to the successful prosecution of Corallo, Avellino, and underboss Salvatore Santoro (Bonavolonta and Duffy 1996). It also provided evidence for the civil RICO suit that put an end to the Long Island carting cartel (Abadinsky 1994). In addition to seeking successful criminal prosecutions, Goldstock encouraged law enforcement agents to build civil cases to remove Cosa Nostra from infected industries (Jacobs 1999). Goldstock and chief assistant Martin Marcus also deserve the credit for drafting and lobbying the state RICO law through the state legislature (Jacobs 1999).

New York City Mayor Rudy Giuliani continued the campaign against organized crime that he had begun as U.S. Attorney. Mayor Giuliani successfully attacked mob control of the Fulton Fish Market, the Feast of San Gennaro, and the waste hauling industry, and has recently turned his attention to the mob-dominated construction industry (Jacobs 1999). Removal of the Gambino brothers from the garment district should be attributed to the Manhattan district attorney, as should achievements in the carting and painting industries (Jacobs 1999).

VI. The Mobilization of Legal Resources

The development and creative application of new legal tools has been an important factor in the government's success. While technological advances in electronic surveillance made possible FBI goals of comprehensive intelligence on Cosa Nostra, legislative authorization (via Title III) made such strategies permissible. The Witness Security Program, another legislative device, enabled (and arguably encouraged) individuals from within Cosa Nostra families to defect safely. Finally, Cosa Nostra prosecutions were facilitated by use of the RICO statute that enabled law enforcement agents and prosecutors to target entire crime families and to confront defendants with draconian potential punishments.

A. Title III

In 1968, following publication of *Challenge of Crime in a Free Society*, the report of the President's Commission on Law Enforcement and Administration of Justice, Congress passed new legislation authorizing electronic eavesdropping (wiretaps and bugs) with a warrant and according to other guidelines (Title III of the Omnibus Crime Control and Safe Streets Act of 1968). The two main justifications for Title III of the Omnibus Crime Control and Safe Streets Act of 1968 (United States Code, vol. 18, secs. 2510–20 [1982]), according to its proponents, were the necessity for electronic surveillance in national security and in organized crime investigations (Goldsmith 1983). Title III brought federal, state, and local wiretapping within the framework of a comprehensive statute. The statute permits electronic eavesdropping only with a judicial warrant issued on a showing of probable cause and of necessity due to the absence of alternative means. The interception is limited to thirty days, although extensions can be obtained. The law requires "minimization"; the eavesdropping device must be turned off if, after a brief period of listening, it is apparent that the intercepted conversation is not relevant to the subject matter of the warrant. Amendments in 1986 strengthened the law and, for the first time, authorized "roving surveillance" to cover sophisticated criminals who use a number of different phones or sites to conduct business (Goldsmith 1987; Jacobs, Panarella, and Worthington 1994). In *United States v. Bianco*, the court upheld the provision of a "roving bug" Title III order that authorized electronic surveillance in a case where the government (investigating the New England Patriarca crime family) specified only the names of the parties expected to be at a Cosa Nostra induction ceremony, but could not identify where or when the initiation would occur.

Cosa Nostra defectors were practically unheard of when Title III was passed, and victims rarely wished to testify against Cosa Nostra, so surreptitiously recorded conversations between mobsters were the most likely source of evidence for organized crime investigators. In a few years, organized crime bosses were blanketed with eavesdropping devices, to the point that they could never assume, no matter where they were, that law enforcement agents were not listening in.

The sheer number of federal electronic eavesdropping orders increased over the course of the 1980s (in 1980, the number was 564), peaking in 1984 (801), and then jumping to a new plateau in the 1990s (by 1992, the number had reached 991) (Jacobs, Panarella, and Worthington 1994, p. 26). The absolute number of authorizations, however, is only a rough indicator of surveillance activity, because some of the interceptions lasted many months, covered multiple phones and locations, and resulted in the surveillance of thousands of conversations.

B. Witness Security Program

Historically, the unwillingness of victims, witnesses, and mob members themselves to testify for the government represented a major impediment to successful organized crime prosecutions. With many examples of potential witnesses having been murdered or beaten, fear of retribution was well-founded. The Witness Security Program, authorized in the Organized Crime Control Act of 1970, sought to guarantee the safety of witnesses who agreed to testify in organized crime cases. Run by the U.S. Marshalls Service, the program covers witnesses before, during, and after trial. Those with prison sentences are protected while incarcerated and, on release, relocated with new identities, jobs, and homes. This protection has made it possible to testify against Cosa Nostra and survive.

The Witness Security Program has facilitated a number of major Cosa Nostra defections. Until the trials of the 1980s, no member of organized crime, with the single exception of Valachi in 1963, had ever broken the code of *omerta* and gone public, much less testified at a criminal trial against fellow Cosa Nostra members. In the late 1980s and early 1990s, facing the prospect of long prison terms, a number of mob figures "flipped," agreeing to testify for the government in exchange for concessions in the charges against them and admission into the Witness Security Program (Pileggi and Hill 1985).

Shortly after Jimmy "the Weasel" Fratiano (acting boss of the Los Angeles crime family) flipped and testified against Genovese boss Funzi Tieri and later in the commission case, Angelo Lonardo, underboss of the Cleveland crime family, became a government witness. For the government's civil racketeering suit against the General Executive Board of the Teamsters Union, Lonardo provided an extraordinary deposition detailing Cosa Nostra's role in choosing the presidents of the Teamsters Union. He also provided important testimony in the commission case. The prosecution in the famous "pizza connection" case (*United States v. Badalamenti*) was assisted by the testimony of Tomasso Buscetta, a former high-ranking member of the Sicilian mafia who agreed to testify for the Italian and American governments after his two sons and son-in-law were murdered by a rival Sicilian mafia faction. Vincent "Fish" Cafaro (Genovese family) likewise was extensively debriefed and used in many prosecutions. Bruno-Scarfo crime underboss Philip Leonetti (Scarfo's nephew) and family member Nicholas "Crow" Caramandi became government witnesses after being implicated in a construction industry sting (*United States v. DiSalvo*). Their testimony was critical to the successful prosecutions of the ranking members of the Bruno-Scarfo family (Abadinsky 1994). Other defectors include Dominick Lofaro (Gambino family associate), Big Peter Chiodo (Lucchese family capo), Peter Savino (Genovese family associate), John Pate (Colombo family capo), Carmine Sessa (Colombo family consigliere), Anthony Accetturo (New Jersey Lucchese family), Anthony "Gaspipe" Casso (Lucchese family underboss), and William Raymond Marshall (Gambino family associate). Probably the most notorious Cosa Nostra member turned government witness is Sammy "The Bull" Gravano, Gambino crime family underboss and John Gotti's long-time comrade. A mob defector of his stature would have seemed unimaginable only a decade earlier. Gravano admitted to having carried out nineteen gangland murders on orders from Gotti and his other superiors (Maas 1997). Recently, the convictions of eight members and associates of the Lucchese crime family for racketeering, conspiracy, extortion, and murder turned on the testimony of government witness and former acting boss of the Lucchese crime family, Alphonse D'Arco, who subsequently entered the Witness Security Program (*United States v. Avellino*).

C. Racketeer Influenced and Corrupt Organizations Act (RICO)

In 1970, Congress passed the most important substantive antiorganized crime statute in history. The RICO Act makes it a crime to acquire an interest in, to participate in the affairs of, or to invest the profits acquired from, an enterprise through a pattern of racketeering activity (for comprehensive discussion of RICO, see Lynch 1987). Criminal RICO penalties are severe: a defendant is subject to a twenty-year maximum for a RICO violation and to twenty additional years if a RICO conspiracy count is proved. In addition, a defendant may be sentenced for each predicate offense. RICO also provides for massive fines and for mandatory forfeiture of the portion of the defendant's property that can be traced to the proceeds of racketeering activity.

The RICO Act contains two civil remedial provisions. The provision that gives private victims the right to sue racketeers for treble damages has not been used against organized crime, although it has become very popular (and controversial) in commercial litigation. However, the second provision, which allows the government to sue racketeers for injunctions, restraining orders, and other equitable remedies to prevent the defendants further racketeering, has been used a great deal and has proven to be a very powerful and effective tool for purging organized crime from labor unions and industries (Jacobs, Panarella, and Worthington 1994). Civil RICO cases are governed by civil discovery rules and preponderance of the evidence proof standards, both of which are more favorable to the government than corresponding criminal procedures. A successful civil RICO suit can result in a court-appointed trustee being assigned the task of reforming a union, business, or employer association.

1. *Criminal RICO.* To the frustration of RICO drafter and law professor, G. Robert Blakey, it took a decade for federal prosecutors to begin using RICO. In the late 1970s, Blakey persistently attempted to persuade law enforcement officials to use RICO, but to no avail (Wallance 1994; Bonavolonta and Duffy 1996). Finally, in the summer of 1979, Blakey invited FBI agents, assistant U.S. attorneys, and state prosecutors to Cornell University for a summer law enforcement training institute at the Cornell Institute on Organized Crime. Blakey criticized traditional methods for resulting in a "merry-go-round effect" and urged law enforcement officials to pursue evidence of crimes and of associations connected to a RICO enterprise. His careful presentation of the purpose of RICO and his explanation of the necessary

investigative and prosecutorial adjustments required by the statute ultimately produced a profound change in the FBI's approach to organized crime investigations (Wallance 1994; Bonavolonta and Duffy 1996). The FBI began focusing on the entire crime family (enterprise) rather than on individuals. Conceptualizing their investigations in this way facilitated the construction of probable cause necessary for successful Title III (electronic surveillance) applications.

Since 1980, practically every significant organized crime prosecution has been brought under RICO (Jacobs, Panarella, and Worthington 1994). The U.S. Attorney for the Southern District of New York, Rudolph Giuliani, obtained indictments against the bosses of four of the families alleging that they were participating in the affairs of an organized crime commission through a pattern of racketeering activity; the predicate acts included loan-sharking, directing the assassination of Carmine Galante (Bonanno family boss) and two of his associates (*United States v. Salerno*), and running the New York City concrete industry through a cartel of concrete contractors. The government's success in the commission case demonstrates the advantages of RICO, which allowed prosecutors to bring to a single trial the elite of New York City Cosa Nostra. The requirement that the government prove the existence of an enterprise provided prosecutors the opportunity to introduce devastating evidence on the history, structure, and operations of the Cosa Nostra crime families (for a full examination of *United States v. Salerno*, see Jacobs, Panarella, and Worthington 1994).

In *United States v. Badalamenti*, investigation of an international heroin-trafficking operation, including a Sicilian mafia faction and New York City's Bonanno crime family and involving over two hundred participants, resulted in a successful prosecution of two dozen defendants. Twenty-two of the thirty-five indicted individuals were tried together as codefendants. Louis Freeh (later appointed federal judge and then FBI Director) was the lead prosecutor. This trial, generating over forty thousand pages of transcript from indictment to verdict, lasted three years. Ultimately, fifteen of the nineteen remaining defendants were found guilty on all charges; one defendant was acquitted on all charges (for a full examination of *United States v. Badalamenti*, see Jacobs, Panarella, and Worthington 1994).

In 1997, federal prosecutors obtained the conviction of Genovese crime family boss Vincent "the Chin" Gigante (*United States v. Gigante*, 982 F.Supp 140 [EDNY 1997]). After his highly publicized efforts (for years Gigante wandered his neighborhood in a bathrobe) to be treated as incompetent to stand trial failed, a jury found Gigante guilty of the following offenses: RICO conspiracy, extortion conspiracy, labor payoff conspiracy, and two counts of conspiring to murder in aid of racketeering (*United States v. Gigante*). Gigante's conviction was grounded in his role as Genovese family boss and as the leader of the New York City commission. Gigante and his subordinates were found to have illicit interests in such business sectors as window replacement, concrete, trucking, waste hauling, painting, and the convention center. According to the court, Gigante "earned millions of dollars from these activities as well as from loan-sharking, hijacking, gambling, and other criminal conduct" (*United States v. Gigante*).

Still pending in 1999 are charges against John Gotti, Jr., who, along with twenty-two other alleged Gambino family members, is charged with participating in the affairs of the Gambino crime family through such racketeering activity as extortion, fraud, loan-sharking, money laundering, obstruction of justice, and illegal gambling (*United States v. John Gotti, Jr.*, 1998 WL 568974 [2d Cir. 1998]). It is alleged that the defendants earned twenty million dollars annually from these activities (see also appendix for list of federal Cosa Nostra investigations).

2. *Civil RICO.*   Cosa Nostra's labor and business racketeering enterprises have been seriously disrupted by successful civil RICO suits against Cosa Nostra members, associates, and mobbed-up unions and business enterprises. In many cases, the civil RICO litigation has been resolved by negotiated consent decrees involving court-appointed trustees to oversee reform of corrupted unions, businesses, and industries.

As a result of civil RICO suits, court-appointed trustees and monitors have been assigned to a number of historically mobbed-up union locals affiliated with the Carpenters, Hotel and Restaurant Workers, Longshoremen, and Teamsters (Jacobs and Panarella 1998). Some monitorships have been imposed directly by the judge; some pursuant to negotiated settlements. The monitors are usually former prosecutors (in some cases, former federal judges as well). They have brought a day-to-day government presence into the heart of corrupt organizations and have followed up on the original government suits with disciplinary actions to expel mobsters and mob-tainted associates from the union, company, or association (Jacobs, Worthington, and Panarella 1994).

a. *Labor Racketeering Cases.*   In 1982, the U.S. Department of Justice's Newark Strike Force made history by filing the first civil RICO suit against a labor union, IBT Local 560 in New Jersey (*United States v. Local 560 [IBT]*, 581 F.Supp. 279 [DNJ 1984], aff'd 780 F.2d 267 [3d Cir. 1985]). Local 560 had, since the 1950s, been dominated by Cosa Nostra, through the influence of Anthony "Tony Pro" Provenzano (a soldier of the Genovese crime family) and his brothers (Goldberg 1989). The RICO litigation, which lasted into the 1990s, resulted in a court-imposed trusteeship, which gave the trustee extensive powers to run the union until the organized crime element could be purged and fair elections held. The monitorship lasted for ten years. Among other things, the monitor set in motion a long-term program of investigations and purges of union officials and members with mob connections (for a full treatment of the Local 560 litigation, see Jacobs, Panarella, and Worthington 1994).

In 1988, the U.S. Attorney's Office for the Southern District of New York filed a civil RICO suit against the International Brotherhood of Teamsters, its general executive board, and a number of Cosa Nostra members. It charged the defendants with conspiring to participate in the affairs of the union (the enterprise) through such predicate offenses as conspiracy to defraud union members of union funds and of union control (see Jacobs, Panarella, and Worthington 1994 for an extensive discussion of *United States v. International Brotherhood of Teamsters*). Under the consent decree that settled the case, the whole general executive board resigned. The Teamsters agreed to a court-appointed three-person trusteeship whose goals were to purge corruption and racketeering and to supervise a direct election (which had never before been held) of the president and general executive board. As a consequence of the investigation officer's disciplinary actions in the years that followed, hundreds of Teamster officials and members with organized crime ties were removed from locals. In the first general election in which the rank and file could vote, an insurgent reformer, Ron Carey, won the presidency (Crowe 1993). He, along with the trustees, continued to purge racketeers from various locals around the country (Jacobs and Panarella 1998). (In 1997, Carey was found to have illegally diverted Teamster funds to his election campaign, was forced to step down as president, and was barred from running in the next IBT presidential election.)

Federal prosecutors have subsequently brought civil RICO suits against two of the three other national unions that the PCOC had cited as thoroughly dominated by organized crime. The Laborers International Union of North America (LIUNA) was the next union targeted. In November 1994, the LIUNA general counsel was warned by the Department of Justice that, because of credible evidence of Cosa Nostra influence over LIUNA, a civil RICO action against the union was imminent (*Serpico v. Laborers' International Union of North America,* 97 F.3d 995 [7th Cir. 1996]). This prompted negotiations between the union and the Department of Jusice and ultimately resulted in serious internal reform in the union, including the removal from office of several individuals who were believed to have Cosa Nostra ties and the establishment of new positions in the union (filled by unaffiliated individuals) that were responsible for investigating and prosecuting allegations of wrongdoing (*Serpico v. Laborers' International Union of North America*). The government appears to be satisfied with these internal reforms and has not filed its civil RICO suit.

In 1995, the Hotel Employees and Restaurant Employees International Union entered into a consent decree to resolve a civil RICO suit (alleging over twenty-five years of Cosa Nostra corruption) brought by the United States (*United States v. Hotel Employees and Restaurant Employees Int'l Union,* 974 F.Supp 411 [D.NJ 1997]). According to the consent decree, Kurt Muellenberg was appointed as monitor and given the power to investigate the national union, to review various union actions, and to prevent certain individuals from seeking office (*United States v. Hotel Employees and Restaurant Employees Int'l Union*). In May 1998, Muellenberg asked Edward T. Hanley to retire as union president, a position he had held for twenty-five years (Crowe 1998).

Numerous civil RICO suits have been brought against union locals. (For a more extensive list of trustee appointments in civil RICO cases, see Jacobs 1999, chap. 15.) For example, the government initiated a civil RICO suit against the implicated union in the New York City concrete cartel, exposed during the commission case (*United States v. Local 6A, Cement and Concrete Workers,* 663 F.Supp 192 [SDNY 1986]). Union activities had long been under the direct control of the Colombo family. The consent judgment required the removal of sixteen of the union's twenty-five officers and appointment of a trustee to oversee union operations (Goldberg 1989).

In 1985, the Bonanno family's twenty-five year corruption of Teamsters Local 14 was the basis for labor racketeering and conspiracy convictions of Bonanno family leaders, union officials, and others (*United States v. Rastelli*). Shortly thereafter, the government initiated a civil RICO action against the Bonanno family and Local 14 (*United States v. The Bonanno Organized Crime Family*, 683 F.Supp. 1411 EDNY 1988). Almost immediately, the defendants entered into a consent judgment. The trustee's powers were less than those granted to the Local 560 trustee. The judgment established an interim executive board to control daily union operations (Goldberg 1989).

The labor racketeering suits have not been limited to New York City. In Philadelphia, criminal investigations of the Bruno-Scarfo crime family provided the grist for a civil RICO suit against the local roofers union (*United States v. Local 30, United Slate, Tile and Composition Roofers*, 686 F.Supp. 1139 [EDPA 1988]). Cosa Nostra domination of the union had, over the course of two decades, resulted in extortion of Philadelphia roofing contractors, embezzlement of Local 30's pension and benefit funds, and bribery of public officials (Goldberg 1989). Opting to satisfy neither the government (seeking a trusteeship) nor the defendants (pressing for maintenance of the status quo), the court imposed a "decreeship" that removed convicted union leaders from their positions, but otherwise left the union bureaucracy untouched. In an attempt to improve on what it saw as the invasive nature of court-imposed union trusteeships, the court appointed a "principal enforcement officer" to chaperon meetings between the union and employers and to certify any resulting agreements (Goldberg 1989; *United States v. Local 30, United Slate, Tile and Composition Roofers*).

b. *Court-Appointed Trustees as a Remedial Model.*   State and local law enforcement agencies have begun to seek trusteeships in their criminal and civil litigation. For example, in 1992, the Manhattan District Attorney's Office brought a major criminal prosecution against Thomas and Joseph Gambino and several other defendants alleging extortion and racketeering in the New York City garment district, which had been dominated by organized crime since the 1920s. The case ended mid-trial with an unprecedented plea bargain in which the defendants pled guilty to a single felony count of restraint of trade and agreed to the appointment of a monitor to oversee their total withdrawal from the garment industry, to sell all their garment center-related trucking interests, and to pay a $12 million fine (Jacobs 1999).

A 1994 settlement in the civil RICO suit brought against 112 defendants (including sixty-four Gambino and Lucchese crime family members and numerous carting companies) established a monitorship over

Cosa Nostra's Long Island waste hauling cartel (*United States v. Private Sanitation Indus. Assoc. of Nassau/Suffolk, Inc.*, 793 F.Supp. 1114 [EDNY 1994]). Michael Cherkasky, a former prosecutor (who led the Manhattan district attorney's successful prosecution of the Gambino brothers) was selected to be the industry's compliance officer (Kessler 1990; Jacobs 1999). The consent decree, which prohibits the defendants from having any contact with Cosa Nostra, has been successful (in part because the inefficient Cosa Nostra firms are unable to survive in a competitive market); many national waste hauling corporations have entered the Long Island market since the settlement was negotiated (Jacobs 1999).

D. New York City's Regulatory Initiatives

Regulatory policies intended to strip Cosa Nostra from its economic bases are on the cutting edge of organized crime control initiatives. When Rudolph Giuliani, formerly the U.S. attorney (SDNY) who brought numerous criminal and civil organized crime cases, became mayor of New York City (1993), he embarked on an administrative strategy to continue the purge of organized crime from the city's economy. The first initiative was directed at the Fulton Fish Market which had been dominated by organized crime since the 1930s (see Jacobs and Hortis 1998). The city used its regulatory and licensing power to get rid of corrupt unloading companies and to recruit a new outside company.

The Giulani administration similarly used its regulatory authority and licensing powers to liberate the colorful Feast of San Gennaro, one of the city's most famous annual street fairs, from the control of organized crime (Jacobs 1999). The Cosa Nostra-dominated organization that ran and profited from the street fair for decades was replaced by an untainted organization and the Roman Catholic Archdiocese.

In June 1996, the New York City Council created the Trade Waste Commission (TWC) with the explicit goal of eliminating Cosa Nostra control of the waste hauling industry and restoring competition (Jacobs and Hortis 1998). While the TWC is structured as a regulatory agency, its composition and agenda are those of a quasi-law enforcement agency. Its executive officers, attorneys, monitors, and police detectives were recruited for their experience in organized crime investigations and prosecutions (Jacobs and Hortis 1998).

The powers granted to the TWC were designed to affect both the supply and demand elements of the carting industry. The law establishing the TWC authorized the agency to license carting companies. Individuals with a criminal record or known associations with the mob or the mob-dominated cartel are denied licenses (Jacobs and Hortis 1998). The TWC was granted broad powers to conduct background investigations related to its license decisions. The TWC also sought to strengthen the customer's position by setting maximum rates, regulating contract duration, and keeping customers informed of their rights.

The TWC has been remarkably successful. By driving corrupt firms from the industry and simultaneously protecting customers from exploitation, new companies (with no ties to organized crime) have entered the industry (Jacobs and Hortis 1998). For the first time in history, national waste-hauling companies have entered the New York City market. In addition, waste-hauling rates have fallen dramatically (recent estimates claim decreases of 30–40 percent in the past two years [Raab 1998c]). Thus New York's Cosa Nostra crime families have to contend with the loss of a significant revenue source and power base.

The TWC provides a very promising model for using government regulatory powers to battle organized crime. Indeed, the Giuliani administration has proposed an ambitious plan to set up a New York City construction commission that would attempt, through licensing, to purge the mob from the sprawling multibillion dollar construction industry. The TWC is already serving as a model for other municipalities, for example, Westchester County is holding hearings on the possibility of creating a trade waste commission to combat a local hauling cartel (Jacobs and Hortis 1998).

VII. Cosa Nostra at the End of the Twentieth Century

By the early 1990s, the accumulated prosecutions had been so extensive and the internal deterioration of the families so severe that some law enforcement experts began to predict the end of Cosa Nostra, at least in anything like its historical form. While there is no definitive way to determine whether Cosa Nostra will survive this onslaught, a scorecard of prosecutorial success, promising data from formerly mob-dominated unions and businesses, and observations about the internal health of the crime families all point to serious decline.

A. Criminal Prosecutions

There is no exact figure on how many criminal and civil cases have been brought by the federal government (much less state and local prosecutors) against organized crime in the 1980s and 1990s, but it is certainly a large number. In 1988, FBI Director William Sessions reported to the Senate Subcommittee on Investigations that, since 1981, nineteen bosses, thirteen underbosses, and forty-three capos (crew chiefs) had been convicted (Jacobs, Panarella, and Worthington 1994). Another witness, David Williams, director of the U.S. Government Accounting Office's Office of Special Investigations, stated that between 1983 and 1986 there had been twenty-five hundred indictments of Cosa Nostra members and associates (this does not mean that twenty-five hundred separate individuals had been indicted). There were major prosecutions in every city where organized crime families have been identified. The following list of Cosa Nostra bosses who were convicted between 1981 and 1998 (Jacobs, Panarella, and Worthington 1994) shows that several Cosa Nostra families have had more than one boss convicted during this period:

Funzi Tieri—Genovese family, New York City
Anthony Salerno—Genovese family, New York City
Anthony Corallo—Lucchese family, New York City
Carmine Persico—Colombo family, New York City
Philip Rastelli—Bonanno family, New York City
Carlos Marcello, New Orleans family
Eugene Smaldone, Denver family
Joseph Aiuppa, Chicago family
Nick Civella, Kansas City family
Carl Civella, Kansas City family
Dominci Brookleir, Los Angeles family
Frank Balistrieri, Boston family
Gennaro Anguilo, Boston family
Russel Buffalino, Pittston, Pennsylvania family
Nicodemo Scarfo, Philadelphia family
James Licavoli, Cleveland family
Michael Trupiano, St. Louis family
Sam Russoti, Buffalo family
John Gotti—Gambino family, New York City
Raymond Patriarca—Patriarca family, Providence, Rhode Island
Vittorio Amuso—Lucchese family, New York City
Vicorio Orena—Colombo family, New York City
John Riggi—DeCavalcante family, New Jersey
John Stanfa, Philadelphia family
Vincent Gigante—Genovese family, New York City

The appendix includes a recent (but incomplete) list of more recent investigations and prosecutions of Cosa Nostra members and associates. These federal cases, supplemented by some state and local prosecutions, systematically decimated whole organized crime families. The New York City commission reportedly has ceased to function and Cosa Nostra families in Cleveland and Philadelphia appear to have been eliminated.

B. Internal Disintegration

The internal deterioration of Cosa Nostra is most strongly evidenced by the number of organized crime figures who have served as cooperating witnesses for the government in exchange for leniency and protection. Several Cosa Nostra members have also written books and autobiographies that expose aspects of an organization that were previously kept secret. Bonanno's description, in his autobiography (Bonanno and Lalli 1983), of the commission helped to inspire Giuliani's prosecution of the commission in *United States v. Salerno* (Bonavolonta and Duffy 1996). The numerous defections that occurred in the 1980s represent an unprecedented breakdown of *omerta* that may be attributed to several factors: much more powerful and effective law enforcement than ever before (including both increased risk of prosecution and draconian RICO sentences), the possibility of survival after defection (due to the Witness Security Program), and a different attitude among Cosa Nostra members about the value of loyalty to their organization (see Goldstock).

The defections compounded the internal chaos resulting from the government's successful efforts to decimate the leadership of all of the families. Leadership succession conflicts, in the past, had often been resolved with assistance or direction from other families. The government's simultaneous attack on all of the families has significantly undermined this mechanism. In New York City, the heads of the Bonanno and Genovese families are described as "wary" of interfamily meetings because of the increased dangers of informant leaks or government surveillance (Raab 1998*a*, p. 1). In some cases, intrafamily assassinations (or attempts) ensued. The recent violent conflict between the Persico and Orena factions of the Colombo crime family, described in *United States v. Orena* (145 F.3d 551 [2d Cir. 1998]), is an example. Following Nicodemo Scarfo's incarceration, Philadelphia's Bruno-Scarfo family was wracked by similar violence (*United States v. Stanfa*). The court's justification for denial of bail to six members of the Scarfo family in *United States v. Leonetti* was grounded in a fear of the group's "collective danger": "The release of all six would enable the organization to rejuvenate itself from its semi-dormancy caused by the incarceration of its members and inflict retribution against witnesses and their families" (1988 WL 61738 [E.D.Pa. 1988] *3). Recent vacancies in the leadership ranks have, by necessity, been filled by young leaders like John Gotti Jr., or by old-timers who have been called out of retirement.

C. Purging the Mob from the Legitimate Economy

There are very encouraging signs that the efforts to purge the mob from its base in unions and industries has been successful. Cosa Nostra businesses, from concrete batching plants to restaurants, have been seized by the government by means of powerful criminal and civil forfeiture laws. The New York City concrete cartel is gone. Economic data from the fish market and the carting industry indicate that the Cosa Nostra cartels that were dominant for half a century are no longer operative. Informed sources at the Javits Exhibition Center believe that the mob presence has been completely eliminated. On the union front, the Teamsters Union is much more democratic than it has ever been. While the cancellation of Ron Carey's election is a great blow to reformers, the winds of change are strong.

D. Looking Ahead

This analysis of the law enforcement strategies and legal resources that have incapacitated Cosa Nostra provides lessons for the future of organized crime fighting. While this legacy of domestic success is clearly applicable to the fate of organized crime in the United States, it may also be transferable to law enforcement agencies in other countries that currently face major organized crime problems.

1. *The Future of Cosa Nostra: A Caution.*   It is important to recall that despite (perhaps because of) all of the mob's economic and political power, there was no constituency pressing for its elimination. Local police forces did not have the resources, strategies, or tools to engage in long-term investigations of secret societies that carefully covered their tracks and insulated their leaders from scrutiny through hierarchical organization and a code of silence. Sometimes local law enforcement personnel, as well as prosecutors and judges, were dissuaded from organized crime control by potentially adverse political or even professional consequences; sometimes they were just bribed (Jacobs, Pana-

rella, and Worthington 1994). The only antiorganized crime constituency was an invigorated law enforcement establishment that eventually mounted a campaign against organized crime, sometimes in spite of politicians' efforts to stop it. Many of the economic and social forces that allowed organized crime to achieve such immense power are still operative. The citizenry's demand for illicit goods and services remains strong. Unions remain vulnerable to labor racketeering, and those that have been "liberated" from organized crime have been very slow to repudiate their mob ties, if they have done so at all. The danger is that the government's attention will be drawn away from organized crime control to other pressing law enforcement priorities and that, while the law enforcement machinery sleeps, Cosa Nostra will reconstitute itself. Finally, even if Cosa Nostra is permanently weakened, society would not be better off if other organized crime groups took over Cosa Nostra's activities.

2. *Successors to Cosa Nostra.*   There are, of course, other significant ethnically based organized crime groups in the United States—Jamaican, Russian, Colombian, African-American, among others—but they all focus on illicit goods and services, especially drugs. None of these groups has the economic or political power base that Cosa Nostra enjoyed for so long. Such groups could accumulate more power, but their development is more likely to follow the historical pattern of underworld syndicates than to recreate the Cosa Nostra model of an organization that functions equally well below and above ground.

3. *Organized Crime in Other Countries.*   Organized crime has become an increasingly serious threat in Europe, and other parts of the world.[4] There has been a great deal of popular and scholarly writing about the power and omnipresence of the Russian mafia, which seems to have a foothold in every facet of the Russian economy. The European Union is concerned about the growth of organized crime groups in Eastern European countries and their movement into Western Europe. Japanese law enforcement officials are seeking new powers to deal with the Boryokudan. How relevant is the U.S. experience with Cosa Nostra to these countries?

The answer remains to be seen, but it is likely to be different for different countries. The legal and organizational tools that have

[4] The scholarly journal *Trends in Organized Crime* is a useful resource for scholars and policy makers interested in learning about organized crime trends, government crime control initiatives, and scholarly studies on organized crime around the world. See also Adamoli et al. (1998) and Fijnaut and Jacobs (1991).

proven so effective against Cosa Nostra in the past twenty years are predicated on the existence of a strong state, an incorruptible FBI and Department of Justice, and a civil liberties tradition that can accommodate undercover policing and electronic surveillance. Countries like the Netherlands, Germany, and Japan are also, of course, strong states with honest and highly professional law enforcement agencies and courts, but they have only reluctantly begun to accept the idea that undercover policing and electronic surveillance may be necessary to thwart organized crime groups.

The post-Soviet Eastern European countries have been fertile ground for organized crime (Voronin 1997; Williams 1997). With ineffectual governments that are, to varying degrees, still plagued by the corruption of the Soviet system, a general lack of resources, and unstable legal systems, they face very severe organized crime problems that are compounded by the existence of law enforcement agencies and courts that are vulnerable to corruption. Moreover, they suffer from the stigma of having been the steel fists of the previous dictatorial regimes. Given recent history and the fragility of the civil liberties tradition, undercover policing and electronic surveillance may well not be viable options, and perhaps they should not be. Russia is an extreme case. It appears that members of the old KGB and of police agencies are now directing the Russian mafia. The state is weak; there is not yet an efficient system of tax collection. Law enforcement agencies and courts do not inspire confidence or enjoy much legitimacy. Undercover policing and electronic surveillance smack of the old totalitarian regime. Thus it would be foolhardy to suggest that all Russia needs to do is to adopt the organized crime control program that seems to have worked so well in the United States. However, Russian policy makers continue to seek U.S. assistance and value collaboration on the organized crime problem (Shelley 1997).

Recognizing that the U.S. experience will be of more relevance to some countries rather than others, we suggest that the following conclusions can be drawn from the U.S. experience of the past two decades:

1. Don't wait until organized crime syndicates become entrenched before responding to them. In the United States there was no concerted effort for decades. By that time, organized crime was a political and economic force capable of insulating itself from attack.

2. Electronic surveillance is crucial—the attack on Cosa Nostra could not have been successful without electronic surveillance, both

wiretaps and bugs. The organized crime families were blanketed by electronic surveillance so that it became very difficult for them to conduct business anywhere.

3. There has to be long-term political and organizational commitment. Crime syndicates are quite capable of retreating and waiting for bursts of moral fervor to dissipate. Therefore, it is important to institutionalize the organized crime control program.

4. Law enforcement is not enough. Law enforcement is a necessary but not sufficient force for purging a full-blown syndicate from the economy. The use of long-term trustees to oversee the remediation of businesses and unions has been a great innovation in organized crime control. Likewise, the mobilization of government's regulatory powers on behalf of the organize crime control effort has proven remarkably successful.

APPENDIX
Organized Crime Investigations and Prosecutions
The following list of successful investigations and prosecutions (from 1986 to 1999, beginning with the most recent) was supplied by the U.S. Department of Justice. Apparently, the Department of Justice maintains no systematic record of Cosa Nostra cases, so this list may be both overinclusive and underinclusive. This enumeration is intended to provide a starting point for further research and includes jurisdictional information (in parentheses) and some details of the outcome for the named defendants.

United States v.:

Alphonse Persico et al. (EDNY) 92 CR 351: Acting head of Colombo crime family, arrested February 1999.
Andrew Russo and Dennis Hickey et al. (EDNY): Colombo family boss and associate, pleaded guilty February 1999.
Lenine Strollo et al. (NDOH): Youngstown, OH/Mahoning Valley boss, cooperated February 1999.
Gregory Scarpa, Jr., et al. (EDNY) 94 CR 1119, 95 CR 1155: Colombo family soldier, convicted October 1998.
Jack William Tocco et al. (EDMI): Detroit family boss, convicted April 1998.
Louis Malpeso, Jr., et al. (EDNY): Colombo family associate, pleaded guilty February 1998.
James Tartaglione et al. (EDNY) 97 CR 1068: Bonanno family acting consigliere, arrested January 1998.
Vito Giacalone et al. (EDMI): High-ranking Detroit family member, pleaded guilty January 1998; also pleaded guilty 1986.
Nicholas Corozzo et al. (EDNY/SDFL) 97 CR 80: Gambino capo, alleged successor to Gotti, pleaded guilty August 1997.
Vincent Gigante (EDNY) 93 CR 368: Genovese boss, convicted July 1997.

Frank Calabrese et al. (NDIL): High-ranking Chicago Outfit loanshark, pleaded guilty March 1997.

Liborio Bellomo et al. (SDNY): Acting Genovese boss, entered guilty plea February 1997.

Carmine Avellino et al. (EDNY) 95 CR 31: Lucchese family associate, convicted June 1996.

Natale Richichi (DNV): Gambino family capo: convicted June 1996.

Francesco Scibelli et al. (DMA): Genovese family captain, pleaded guilty June 1996.

Thomas Petrizzo et al. (EDNY) 95 CR 141: Colombo family capo, pleaded guilty May 1996; acquitted on other charges June 1995.

John Palazzolo et al. (EDNY) 96 CR 386: Bonanno family soldier, pleaded guilty January 1996.

John Stanfa et al. (EDPA): Philadelphia family boss, convicted November 1995.

Thomas DePhillips et al. (DNJ): New Jersey Genovese family boss (Gerardo-DePhillips faction), entered plea November 1995.

Marco D'Amico et al. (NDIL): Chicago sports-betting boss, pleaded guilty October 1995.

Anthony S. Carollo and Frank J. Gagliani, Sr., et al. (EDLA): New Orleans Marcello crime family boss and underboss, pleaded guilty September 1995.

Joseph Iacobacci et al. (NDOH): Cleveland crime family, pleaded guilty September 1995.

Robert P. Deluca, Sr., et al. (DRI): Patriarca family associate, convicted Fall 1995.

Frances P. Salemme et al. (DMA): Patriarca family boss, indicted 1995, case pending.

Joseph Giampa et al. (DNJ): Lucchese crime family captain, convicted August 1995.

Louis Malpeso, Sr., et al. (EDNY): Colombo family capo, convicted August 1995.

Joseph Amato et al. (EDNY): Colombo family capo, convicted August 1995.

Joseph Legrano et al. (EDNY) 93 CR 1231: Colombo family lieutenant, convicted August 1995.

Anthony Morelli et al. (EDNY) 93 CR 239: Gambino family capo, convicted May 1995.

Charles Quintina et al. (DMA): Patriarca family consigliere, pleaded guilty April 1995.

James Ida et al. (EDNY): Genovese family consigliere, convicted April 1995.

Anthony Spero et al. (EDNY): Bonanno family consigliere, convicted April 1995.

Laborers International Union Of North America (LIUNA) (NDIL): consent decree, November 1994.

Leonard Falzone et al. (WDNY): Buffalo crime family member, convicted July 1994.

Pasquale Conte et al. (EDNY) 93 CR 85: Gambino family capo, pleaded guilty June 1994.

Frank Sciortino (EDNY): Colombo family soldier, pleaded guilty May 1994.

James Failla et al. (EDNY) 93 CR 294: Gambino family capo, pleaded guilty April 1994.

Robert Sasso et al. (EDNY): Teamsters Local 282 president, with alleged Gambino ties, pleaded guilty March 1994.

Anthony Accetturo et al. (MDFL): Lucchese family boss, cooperated February 1994 after New Jersey conviction.

John Gambino et al. (EDNY): Gambino family capo, pleaded guilty January 1994.

Anthony Casso et al. (EDNY) 90 CR 446: Lucchese underboss/acting boss, pleaded guilty and cooperated in 1994.

Samuel Carlisi et al. (NDIL): High-ranking Chicago Outfit member, convicted December 1993.

Anthony Liberatore et al. (NDOH): Cleveland crime family, convicted June 1993.

Gregory Scarpa, Sr. (EDNY) 93 CR 124: Colombo family capo, pleaded guilty April 1993.

Chester Liberatore et al. (NDOH): Cleveland crime family, pleaded guilty March 1993.

Joseph Corrao et al. (EDNY) 91 CR 1343: Gambino family capo, pleaded guilty 1993.

Salvatore Lombardi et al. (DNJ): Genovese family captain, indicted July 1993.

Steven Crea et al. (EDNY) 93 CR 506: Lucchese family capo/acting underboss, case pending.

Victor Orena et al. (EDNY) 92 CR 351, 93 CR 596: Colombo family acting boss, convicted December 1992.

Edward Capaldo et al. (EDNY) 92 CR 1112: Lucchese family associate and officer of painters union, pleaded guilty to state charges, indicted on federal charges November 1992.

Vittorio Amuso et al. (EDNY): Lucchese family acting boss, convicted June 1992.

John Riggi et al. (DNJ): New Jersey De Cavalcante family boss, pleaded guilty May 1992; also convicted June 1990.

John Gotti et al. (EDNY): Gambino boss, convicted April 1992.

Ernest Rocco Infelice et al. (NDIL): Chicago/Cicero family, convicted March 1992.

Thomas Gambino (EDNY) 90 CR 1051: Gambino family member, pleaded guilty February 1992.

Robert F. Carrozza et al. (DMA): Patriarca crime family member, pleaded guilty January 1992.

Peter J. Simone et al. (WDMO): Kansas City underboss, pleaded guilty January 1992.

Anthony Civella et al. (WDMO): Kansas City Civella family boss, convicted 1992.

James Messera et al. (EDNY): Genovese family capo, pleaded guilty 1992; also pleaded in November 1990 Mason Tenders case.

Raymond J. Patriarca et al. (DMA): Patriarca family boss, pleaded guilty December 1991.

Nicholas Bianco et al. (DCT): Patriarca boss, convicted August 1991.

Anthony Calagna et al. (EDNY): Lucchese family associate, convicted January 1991; also convicted May 1989.

Peter Marcello et al. (EDLA): New Orleans Marcello family, convicted July 1990.

Peter Vario et al. (EDNY): Lucchese family capo, convicted March 1990.

Mario Renda (EDNY): Stockbroker with Lucchese family ties, pleaded guilty May 1988.

Joseph Aiuppa et al. (NDIL): Chicago Outfit boss, convicted in 1986.

Gennaro Angiulo et al. (DMA): Patriarca family underboss, convicted 1986.

REFERENCES

Abadinsky, Howard. 1994. *Organized Crime*. 4th ed. Chicago: Nelson Hall.

Adamoli, Sabrina, Andrea Di Nicola, Ernesto U. Savona, and Paola Zoffi. 1998. *Organised Crime around the World*. Helsinki: European Institute for Crime Prevention and Control (HEUNI).

Bell, Daniel. 1964. *The End of Ideology*. Glencoe, Ill.: Free Press.

Block, Alan A. 1983. *East Side, West Side: Organized Crime in New York*. New Brunswick, N.J.: Transaction.

———. 1994. "Organized Crime: History and Historiography." In *Handbook of Organized Crime in the United States*, edited by Robert Kelly, Ko-Lin Chin, and Rufus Schatzberg. Westport, Conn.: Greenwood.

Bonanno, Joseph, with Sergio Lalli. 1983. *A Man of Honor: The Autobiography of Joseph Bonanno*. New York: Simon & Schuster.

Bonavolonta, Jules, and Brian Duffy. 1996. *The Good Guys: How We Turned the FBI 'Round—and Finally Broke the Mob*. New York: Simon & Schuster.

Brill, Steven. 1978. *The Teamsters*. New York: Simon & Schuster.

Chin, Ko-Lin. 1990. *Chinese Subculture and Criminality: Non-traditional Crime Groups in America*. New York: Greenwood.

———. 1994. "Chinese Organized Crime in America." In *Handbook of Organized Crime in the United States*, edited by Robert Kelly, Ko-Lin Chin, and Rufus Schatzberg. Westport, Conn.: Greenwood.

Cressey, Donald. 1969. *Theft of a Nation: The Structure and Operation of Organized Crime in America*. New York: Harper & Row.

Crowe, Kenneth. 1993. *Collision: How the Rank and File Took Back the Teamsters*. New York: Scribner's.

———. 1998. "Sealed Deal: Hotel Union Head Pushed to Retire." *Newsday* (May 21), p. A71.

Demaris, Ovid. 1980. *The Last Mafioso: The Treacherous World of Jimmy Frattiano*. New York: Times Books.

English, T. J. 1990. *The Westies: Inside Hell's Kitchen Irish Mob*. New York: G. P. Putnam's Sons.

Fijnaut, Cyrille, and James B. Jacobs, eds. 1991. *Organized Crime and Its Containment: A Transatlantic Initiative.* Deventer and Boston: Kluwer.

Finckenauer, James. 1994. "Russian Organized Crime in America." In *Handbook of Organized Crime in the United States,* edited by Robert Kelly, Ko-Lin Chin, and Rufus Schatzberg. Westport, Conn.: Greenwood.

Florentini G., and S. Peltzman, eds. 1995. *The Economics of Organized Crime.* New York: Cambridge University Press.

Fox, Stephen. 1989. *Blood and Power: A History of Organized Crime in the Twentieth Century.* New York: Morrow.

Fresolone, George, and Robert J. Wagman. 1994. *Blood Oath.* New York: Simon & Schuster.

Gambetta, Gianluca, and Sam Peltzman. 1995. "Conspiracy among Many: The Mafia in Legitimate Industries." In *The Economics of Organized Crime,* edited by G. Florentini and S. Peltzman. New York: Cambridge University Press.

Goldberg, Michael J. 1989. "Cleaning Labor's House: Institutional Reform Litigation in the Labor Movement." *Duke Law Journal,* pp. 903–1011.

Goldsmith, Michael. 1983. "The Supreme Court and Title III: Rewriting the Law of Electronic Surveillance." *Journal of Law and Criminology* 74:1–17.

———. 1987. "Eavesdropping Reform: The Legality of Roving Surveillance." *University of Illinois Law Review,* pp. 401–30.

Goldstock, Ronald. n.d. "Some Ruminations on the Current and Future Status of Organized Crime in the United States and on Efforts to Control Illicit Syndicates and Enterprises." Unpublished report for the New York State Organized Crime Task Force.

Goldstock, Ronald, and Steven Chananie. 1988. " 'Criminal' Lawyers: The Use of Electronic Surveillance and Search Warrants in the Investigation and Prosecution of Attorneys Suspected of Criminal Wrongdoing." *University of Pennsylvania Law Review* 136:1855–77.

Goldstock, Ronald, and Dan T. Coenen. 1978. "Extortionate and Usurious Credit Transactions: Background Materials." Ithaca, N.Y.: Cornell Institute on Organized Crime.

Haller, Mark H. 1990. "Illegal Enterprise: A Theoretical and Historical Interpretation." *Criminology* 28:207–35.

Handelman, Stephen. 1995. *Comrade Criminal: Russia's New Mafia.* New Haven, Conn.: Yale University Press.

Hanna, David. 1974. *Frank Costello: The Gangster with a Thousand Faces.* New York: Tower Books.

Hutchinson, John. 1969. "The Anatomy of Corruption in Trade Unions." *Industrial Relations* 8(2):135–50.

Ianni, Francis, and Elizabeth Reuss-Ianni. 1972. *A Family Business: Kinship and Social Control in Organized Crime.* New York: Russell Sage Foundation.

Jacobs, James B. 1999. *Gotham Unbound: How New York City Was Liberated from the Clutches of Cosa Nostra.* New York: New York University Press.

Jacobs, James B., and Alex Hortis. 1998. "NYC as Organized Crime Fighter." *New York Law School Law Review* 42(3/4):1073–96.

Jacobs, James B., and Christopher Panarella. 1998. "Organized Crime." In *The*

Handbook of Crime and Punishment, edited by Michael Tonry. New York: Oxford University Press.

Jacobs, James B., Christopher Panarella, and Jay Worthington. 1994. *Busting the Mob*. New York: New York University Press.

Jensen, Vernon. 1974. *Strife on the Waterfront*. Ithaca, N.Y.: Cornell University Press.

Kefauver, Estes. 1951. *Crime in America*. New York: Doubleday.

Kennedy, Robert F. 1960. *The Enemy Within*. New York: Popular Library.

Kenney, Dennis J., and James O. Finckenauer. 1995. *Organized Crime in America*. New York: Wadsworth.

Kessler, Steven L. 1990. "And a Little Child Shall Lead Them: New York's Organized Crime Control Act of 1986." *St. Johns Law Review* 64:797–823.

Kleinknecht, William G. 1996. *New Ethnic Mobs: Changing Face of Organized Crime in America*. New York: Free Press.

Kwitny, Jonathan. 1979. *Vicious Circles: The Mafia in the Marketplace*. New York: Norton.

Landesco, John. 1968. *Organized Crime in Chicago*. Chicago: University of Chicago Press. (Originally published 1929.)

Lynch, Gerald E. 1987. "Rico: The Crime of Being a Criminal." *Columbia Law Review* 87:661–764, 920–84.

Maas, Peter. 1968. *The Valachi Papers*. New York: G. P. Putnam's Sons.

———. 1997. *Underboss: Sammy the Bull Gravano's Story of Life in the Mafia*. New York: Harper Collins.

McClellan, John. 1962. *Crime without Punishment*. New York: Duell, Sloane, & Pearce.

Moldea, Dan E. 1978. *The Hoffa Wars*. New York: Charter Books.

Moore, William H. 1974. *The Kefauver Committee and the Politics of Crime*. Columbia: University of Missouri Press.

Nash, J. R. 1972. *Citizen Hoover: A Critical Study of the Life and Times of J. Edgar Hoover and His FBI*. Chicago: Nelson-Hall.

New York State Organized Crime Task Force. 1990. *Corruption and Racketeering in the NYC Construction Industry*. New York: New York University Press.

O'Brien, Robert, and Andris Kurins. 1991. *Boss of Bosses: The FBI and Paul Castellano*. New York: Dell.

Pennsylvania Crime Commission. 1990. *Organized Crime in Pennsylvania: A Decade of Change*. Conshohucken: Pennsylvania Crime Commission.

Peterson, Virgil. 1983. *The Mob: 200 Years of Organized Crime in New York*. Ottawa, Ill.: Green Hill.

Pileggi, Nick, and Henry Hill. 1985. *Wiseguy: Life in a Mafia Family*. New York: Simon & Schuster.

Pistone, Joseph D., and Richard Woodley. 1987. *Donnie Brasco: My Undercover Life in the Mafia*. New York: New American Library.

Power, Richard Gid. 1987. *Secrecy and Power: The Life of J. Edgar Hoover*. New York: Macmillan Free Press.

President's Commission on Law Enforcement and the Administration of Justice. 1967. *Task Force Report: Organized Crime*. Washington, D.C.: U.S. Government Printing Office.

President's Commission on Organized Crime (PCOC). 1983. *Organized Crime: Federal Law Enforcement Perspective.* November 29, Record of Hearing I. Washington D.C.: U.S. Government Printing Office.

————. 1985. *Organized Crime and Gambling.* Record of Hearing VII, New York. Washington, D.C.: U.S. Government Printing Office.

————. 1986*a. The Impact: Organized Crime Today.* Washington, D.C.: U.S. Government Printing Office.

————. 1986*b. The Edge: Organized Crime, Business, and Labor Unions.* Washington, D.C.: U.S. Government Printing Office.

Raab, Selwyn. 1998*a.* "Mob's 'Commission' No Longer Meeting, as Families Weaken." *New York Times* (May 11), sec. B, p. 1, col. 2.

————. 1998*b.* "A Who's Who, and Who's Where, of Mafia Families." *New York Times* (April 27), sec. B, p. 4, col. 1.

————. 1998*c.* "Costs Plummet as City Breaks Trash Cartel." *New York Times* (May 11), sec. B, p. 1, col. 5.

Reuter, Peter. 1983. *Disorganized Crime.* Cambridge, Mass.: MIT Press.

————. 1985. "Racketeers as Cartel Organizers." In *The Politics and Economics of Organized Crime,* edited by H. Alexander and G. Caiden. Lexington, Mass.: Heath.

————. 1987. *Racketeering in Legitimate Industries: A Study in the Economics of Intimidation.* Prepared for the National Institute of Justice, U.S. Department of Justice. Santa Monica, Calif.: Rand.

————. 1993. "The Cartage Industry in New York." In *Beyond the Law: Crime in Complex Organizations,* edited by Michael Tonry and Albert J. Reiss, Jr. Vol. 18 of *Crime and Justice: A Review of Research,* edited by Michael Tonry. Chicago: University of Chicago Press.

————. 1994. "Research on American Organized Crime." In *Handbook of Organized Crime in the United States,* edited by Robert Kelly, Ko-Lin Chin, and Rufus Schatzberg. Westport, Conn.: Greenwood.

Rubinstein, Jonathan, and Peter Reuter. 1994. "Bookmaking in New York." Unpublished manuscript. New York: Policy Sciences Center. Cited in Howard Abadinsky, *Organized Crime,* 4th ed. Chicago: Nelson Hall.

Ryan, Patrick J. 1994. "A History of Organized Crime Control: Federal Strike Forces." In *Handbook of Organized Crime in the United States,* edited by Robert Kelly, Ko-Lin Chin, and Rufus Schatzberg. Westport, Conn.: Greenwood.

Schatzberg, Rufus. 1993. *Black Organized Crime in Harlem: 1920–1930.* New York: Garland.

Schlesinger, Arthur M., Jr. 1978. *Robert Kennedy and His Times.* New York: Ballantine.

Seidman, Harold. 1938. *Labor Czars: A History of Labor Racketeering.* New York: Liveright.

Shelley, Louise. 1997. "The Criminal–Political Nexus: Russian Case Study." Paper presented at the Institute for Contemporary Studies and NSIC Con ference, "Confronting the Challenge of the Political–Criminal Nexus," Mexico, March, pp. 1–12. Also in *Trends in Organized Crime* 3(1):28.

Sifakis, Carl. 1987. *The Mafia Encyclopedia.* New York: Facts on File.

Skolnick, Jerome. 1978. *House of Cards: Legalization and Control of Casino Gambling.* Boston: Little, Brown.

Smith, Dwight. 1975. *The Mafia Mystique.* New York: Basic Books.

Taft, Philip. 1970. *Corruption and Racketeering in the Labor Movement.* Ithaca: Cornell University, New York School of Industrial and Labor Relations.

Teresa, Vincent, and Thomas Renner. 1973. *My Life in the Mafia.* Garden City, N.Y.: Doubleday.

Trends in Organized Crime. 1997. Interview with Frederick T. Martens, former executive director, Pennsylvania Crime Commission.

U.S. Department of Justice, Criminal Investigation Division, Organized Crime Section. 1987. *Chronological History of La Cosa Nostra in the United States: January 1920–August 1987.* Washington, D.C.: U.S. Department of Justice.

U.S. General Accounting Office. 1976. *War on Organized Crime Faltering: Federal Strike Forces Not Getting the Job Done.* Washington, D.C.: U.S. General Accounting Office.

———. 1981. *Stronger Federal Effort Needed in Fight against Organized Crime.* Washington, D.C.: U.S. General Accounting Office.

U.S. Senate Permanent Subcommittee on Investigations. 1981. *Waterfront Corruption.* Washington, D.C.: U.S. Government Printing Office.

———. 1983. *Organized Crime in Chicago.* Washington, D.C.: U.S. Government Printing Office.

U.S. Senate Permanent Subcommittee on Investigations of the Committee on Governmental Affairs. 1988. *Twenty–Five Years after Valachi.* 100th Congress, 2d Sess. Washington, D.C.: U.S. Government Printing Office.

Voronin, Yuriy A. 1997. "The Emerging Criminal State: Economic and Political Aspects of Organized Crime in Russia." In *Russian Organized Crime: The New Threat?* edited by Phil Williams. Portland, Oreg.: Frank Cass.

Wallance, Gregory J. 1994. "Outgunning the Mob." *ABA Journal* 80:60–68, 109–15.

Weiser, Benjamin. 1997. "Brokers and Mob Linked in Swindle." *New York Times* (November 26), p. 1.

Williams, Phil. 1997. "Introduction: How Serious a Threat Is Russian Organized Crime?" In *Russian Organized Crime: The New Threat?* edited by Phil Williams. Portland, Oreg.: Frank Cass.

Zeiger, Henry. 1973. *Sam the Plumber.* Bergenfield, N.J.: New American Library.

———. 1975. *The Jersey Mob.* Bergenfield, N.J.: New American Library.

Roger Lane

Murder in America:
A Historian's Perspective

ABSTRACT

As of 1933, the U.S. murder rate stood at 9.3 per 100,000 annually; in 1993 it was 9.5. But the figures dropped sharply in between, to 4.5 in the 1950s, at the height of the urban industrial revolution. Despite the lack of reliable national figures before the 1930s, it is clear that a peak was reached shortly before the Civil War, and then dropped for generations. Rural areas, especially in the South and West, were more deadly than urban areas until the 1960s. The downturn after 1993 will likely be short-lived, depending on a number of conditions and policies that will either end soon or are reaching their effective limits. In any case, the public is less frightened by the numbers than by the nature of homicides, and several scary kinds, including mass, ideological, and felony murder, have been on the increase. Absolute poverty and the judicial system have been less important than have industrial or postindustrial growth, "relative deprivation," family stability, the drug trade, and, in recent decades, color television. High American rates, finally, owe much but not all to our gun culture; our violence is rooted not in the frontier but in the brutality of Southern slavery and its "culture of honor."

We all know about murder in America; it's been in all the papers. And we all have strong opinions about it. Different opinions, of course—some liberal, some conservative, others harder to classify. While we agree that our homicide rates are too high, higher than in any other nation in the developed world, we disagree about what makes them go up and down and almost everything in between.

The one constant in virtually all public and most academic debate about these questions is an almost utter ignorance of history, even

Roger Lane is professor of history at Haverford College in Pennsylvania.

191

short term, and certainly long term. Perhaps there is some excuse in the fact that the relevant history is quite new. Evidence in ancient bones tells us that we have been committing murder ever since we have been human—indeed, before we became *Homo sapiens*—and the literary evidence is quite clear that we have always been fascinated by it: the central themes in the stories of Cain and Abel, Oedipus, Hamlet, and Macbeth are matched in the creation stories and epics of peoples and cultures around the globe. But while written history has been dominated by sanctioned homicide, or war, social historians have only recently discovered how much criminal homicide has to tell us about the attitudes and practices of the societies in which it occurs, their fears and sore spots, or the value they place on human life or on different kinds of human life.

Professional historians ask essentially the same questions of homicide as everyone else. But we often get answers that are different, sometimes very different, in ways that provide useful perspective on the United States and the problem of murder as we approach the millennium. This essay uses the historical record to help illuminate just four related issues of contemporary concern.

Section I deals with the question of how contemporary murder rates compare with those of the past. While the records are often hard to establish, the answer, in brief, is that historic rates have been both higher and lower than those of this millennial era. Section II inquires into the significance of the recent downturn in these rates and concludes not only that zigs are always followed by zags but that quite apart from the raw numbers there are several unprecedented trends in contemporary homicide that are a legitimate cause for concern. Section III, on the conditions that have historically pushed rates up and down, clears a number of the usual suspects while indicting others. Section IV, which deals with why the United States has been so much more murderous than its national peers and rivals, also challenges the conventional wisdom: the culprit is not the frontier heritage, not even guns and the gun culture in themselves, so much as the heritage of slavery and its long-term effect on American attitudes toward personal honor and violent behavior.[1]

---

[1] This article is largely taken from the fuller and richer treatment provided in Lane (1997). References to specific figures, incidents, and significant studies are also provided below.

I. On Homicide Rates Then and Now

The one question most often asked of a professional historian of criminal violence is, How do today's murder rates compare with those of earlier times? The question is best divided into two parts. One, covering the last sixty-odd years, is relatively easy to answer. The other, stretching back to the Middle Ages, is much harder, although not impossible.

What makes the last several decades relatively easy is that truly national mortality statistics and the FBI's Uniform Crime Reports both date from the early 1930s.[2] And the answer to the question of how much has changed since then is superficially easy: not much. That is, the national "murder rate," defined as the number of homicides committed per 100,000 of population each year, stood at 9.7 in 1933, according to the Vital Statistics and, according to the FBI, at 9.5 in 1993.

This is not, of course, the whole story. In general, if graphed, the rates from the 1930s to the early 1970s would appear as a kind of U-curve, dropping down fairly sharply in the late 1940s and 1950s to under 5 per 100,000 and then rising steeply from very late in the 1950s through the 1970s to a peak of 10.4 in 1974. From that time on the rates have fluctuated between the low eights to the low tens, with no really clear direction until the recent and widely publicized drop—the subject of the next section—from 9.5 in 1993 down to 7.4 in 1996.

Before the 1930s, in the absence of reliable national figures based on body counts, the question is harder to answer with certainty. Professional historians work much like homicide detectives in that we work with whatever clues past events have left us in the attempt to reconstruct as accurate a version of those events as possible.[3] Sometimes

---

[2] The United States has been publishing homicide rates since the year 1906, but these are not reliable until 1933 simply because they were based on death certificates taken from a "registration area" that did not until then cover the whole nation. This fact has caused much confusion; the period from 1906 to 1933 shows an apparent rise that is simply an artifact of the way the figures were collected. In the early years the registration area was confined to those states that already had good public health records and then gradually extended to others as they improved them. By no coincidence, the states with good records, in New England, e.g., were those with low homicide rates, while those slow to join were those with high rates, as in the South. The apparent rise results entirely from the addition, over the years, of places like Louisiana and Texas to New Hampshire and Vermont. In general, the homicide figures taken from the Vital Statistics of the United States are slightly higher than those from the FBI's Uniform Crime Reports for the same years. Those given here are from the Vital Statistics unless otherwise noted.

[3] It is no accident that historians, in recognition of these parallels, tend to be great fans of murder mysteries and police procedurals.

the clues, the records, are relatively complete and trustworthy and can be used with a combination of logic and imagination to establish a case beyond all reasonable doubt. But too often the records are incomplete; in trying to establish annual "murder rates," for example, we may lack not only accurate body counts, the numerator in establishing such rates in any given jurisdiction, but we may have no firm population estimates, either, as a denominator. There are often problems, too, with just what, or whose, bodies are being counted. The legal definition of "homicide" has not much changed since the Middle Ages: nothing more complex than the (in varying degree) unjustified killing of one human being by another. But its practical definition has varied greatly over time. For rather different reasons the authorities have often overlooked the murders of infants, for example, or of slaves, blacks, and Indians. And in some places, too, certainly in the Middle Ages, they have also ignored killings done by persons too powerful to antagonize. (All of these omissions, of course, are themselves important clues to life in the societies that commit them.) And finally, we too often have no "body counts"—as supplied by coroner's inquests, for example— but only such indirect clues to the number of homicides officially dealt with (itself a lower figure than the number actually committed) as arrests, indictments, or convictions.

But still, with all these caveats, it is possible to reconstruct at least rough comparative estimates of past rates, beginning in the thirteenth and fourteenth centuries with those from medieval England.

The case of medieval England is instructive for many reasons. This is the time and place from which we inherit most of the legal mechanisms and institutions we still use for dealing with homicide: inquest by the coroner, arrest by the sheriff, arraignment by a magistrate, indictment by a grand jury, trial before a petit jury, sentence by a judge, perhaps pardon by the head of state. And, not coincidentally, it is also the time and place that yields the oldest reasonably reliable set of what might be called "criminal statistics" on the planet. That is, although population estimates are only educated guesses, the officers who administered the king's "common law" left records of several thousand inquests, trials, and executions that enable historians to establish the number of murders, and the official reaction to them, with relative certainty for several counties over many decades (for key studies for this period, see Given [1977] and Hanawalt [1979]).

Many of the patterns they reveal have been with us, with some variations, ever since. Most homicides involved males, who accounted for more than 90 percent of the killers and 80 percent of the victims. The majority of those involved knew each other. The event was most likely to occur in the warm months, in the twilight or evening hours of the traditional day off, which in those days was Sunday, when there was time, among other things, to drink. Medieval attitudes or prejudices, too, may be deduced from conviction rates. Given that hanging was the punishment for all felonies, without distinction as to degrees of moral guilt or heinousness, jurors excused those whom they did not want executed simply by committing the "pious perjury" of finding them innocent, whatever the evidence. Routine homicides, typically involving fights among groups of village neighbors, brought few guilty verdicts. Women, whatever the evidence, were more likely to get off than men. Those most likely to be convicted were robber-murderers, strangers to the victim, rapists, or others whose crimes were felt unusually frightening or repugnant.

Two classes of legal homicide, both of them quite common, were in practice exempt from prosecution: infanticide, usually committed by poor people in desperately hard times, and killings committed by the feudal nobility, their bullying retainers, or outlaw protégés. Even without counting these, it appears that the medieval murder rate was quite high, averaging something well over 20 per 100,000, that is, two to three times the rate of the modern United States and twenty to thirty times that of contemporary England.[4]

The records for early seventeenth-century England, from which the first American settlers emigrated, are not as good as those for the thirteenth and fourteenth centuries. But it is clear that lawless homicides had declined markedly, despite the fact that, by then, fewer escaped the justice system. The growing power of the state insured that the nobility no longer had private armies, or were able to protect outlaw bands, without having to answer in court. Infanticide, too, typically a crime of abandoned servant girls who had strangled or drowned their newborns, was no longer exempt; the religious fervor abetted by the new Protestant Reformation assured that these poor women, guilty of transgressing at least two of the Ten Commandments, were prosecuted severely and in considerable number. Even so, estimates for the three counties that may be measured over the last decades of the sixteenth century—Essex, Sussex, and Hertfordshire—suggest annual homicide

---

[4] This figure is a composite, taken from the studies by Given (1977) and Hanawalt (1979): see Lane (1997), chap. 1.

rates of 7, 14, and 16 per 100,000, respectively, or collectively perhaps a little over half those for the earlier centuries, but still far higher than those of the modern United States (Cockburn 1977).

The first colonies of British North America were founded in the following generation. And both the first settlers and their descendants were thoroughly familiar with violent behavior. As a reflection of quarrels usually originating across the Atlantic, all of the colonies were officially at war with one or another European power for one-third of the time between 1607 and 1776 and were subject to raids at sea or along their wilder frontiers. Each of them also separately carried on less formal hostilities with fiercely resistant native warriors, often armed by the French in Canada or the Spanish in Florida. As a result, virtually all freemen were required to carry arms, a privilege restricted back in England to a small elite. Large and resentful ethnic minorities, notably the Dutch and Scots-Irish, helped keep internal politics turbulent. Meanwhile, much of the white labor force, when not composed of indentured servants, who were mostly unmarried young males—always the most violent portion of the population—was made up of actual convicts, transported across the Atlantic as an alternative to hanging. Added to these unruly young men were kidnapped Africans or their enslaved descendants, at best sullen when not mutinous and always a source of tension. It was thought to be the civic, and indeed Christian, duty of male householders not only to fight external enemies but to "correct" their slaves, servants, wives, and children directly and physically. And yet despite all of these potentially violent ingredients, white-on-white aggression very rarely erupted into homicide.

The dearth of white murder cases was not the result of official neglect: colonial magistrates were generally vigilant about investigating and prosecuting suspicious deaths, even on the rare occasions when masters killed servants. But trials, certainly convictions, for homicide were quite rare; in all of the Chesapeake region there were just ten such trials before 1660. In the entire history of colonial Pennsylvania, only about forty-five killers were hanged. And in populous Massachusetts, partly because it eased up on infanticide as it moved away from its strict Puritan origins, homicide convictions during the last generation before the American Revolution averaged far fewer than one per 100,000 a year (Teeters 1963, pp. 62–63; Chapin 1983, p. 58; Hull 1987, p. 66).

But much of this apparently benign colonial record resulted simply from the displacement of violence down and out, onto slaves within colonial boundaries and Indians on their fringes.

If the continual process of white expansion onto Indian land was the underlying reason for war with the natives, in the great majority of cases the precipitating incident, then and always, was homicide. The natives, on their part, did not subscribe to newly evolving European conventions of war and usually announced hostilities with raids on out-lying cabins and the slaughter and sometimes mutilation of men, women, and children, rather than with formal proclamations ahead of time. The whites, who on their part did not apply these same Euro-pean conventions to the natives, defined this as murder rather than warfare, although the warriors responsible could rarely be captured and tried and so counted. The natives themselves, in the absence of any formal "state" in the European sense, generally treated homicide much like the Anglo-Saxon ancestors of the English: that is, a killing within the tribe was a matter to be settled by the families involved, ideally through compensation, if not through blood feud. But Indians who killed whites or other Indians in areas of effective white jurisdic-tion were subject to the usual criminal proceedings, in a strange lan-guage, under strange rules, before hostile juries. This procedure, and a cultural horror of hangings as ignominious, was, among other things, one of the major resentments behind King Phillip's War in 1676, the biggest conflict of its century. However, the colonists did not easily understand that a chief or council had no real power to punish or sur-render a warrior who had killed a white. This incomprehension, in turn, might lead to a new round of fighting.

And if colonial homicides involving Indians are past counting, the situation with respect to blacks is even murkier. Much of the justice system in the South was devoted to keeping slaves "affrighted" and in line, but it does not lend itself to quantification. It was not generally a crime to kill a recalcitrant slave, say by whipping her to death, so long as this was done as part of the process of "correction." Slaves who killed slaves were still, of course, valuable property, so a master would rather sell than hang them, effectively keeping them out of the justice system where the crime might be counted. And while in theory a white killing of a black might qualify as manslaughter, it was virtually impos-sible to bring such a case into the system. Under the special laws or "black codes" that obtained almost everywhere, no black could testify against a white, so that a murderous master, overseer, or other white man could not be prosecuted unless he had done the deed in the presence of peers willing to bring him to court.

But it is clear both that killings involving blacks were quite common and that white jitters, even paranoia, about murderous rebellion ran high. The Romans had noted that "as many slaves, so many enemies," and that was millennia before the special hatreds generated by the American system of bondage compounded by caste. Fear and hatred marked colonial race relations everywhere, and rumors fed on each other. And when rumor had some real basis in fact, retribution could be savage in the extreme. In 1712, following an incident in New York City in which a number of black men fired on a building and shot some whites, several of the perpetrators were killed during pursuit or committed suicide. The nineteen who survived were all swiftly convicted of murder. Of these, thirteen were simply hanged, but while Americans by that time had largely abandoned more grisly forms of execution, one was left to die of thirst, in chains; four were burnt to death, one of them under a slow daylong fire; and one more was broken on a wheel. The story of this famous incident is well told in Jordan (1968, pp. 115–16).

The era of the American Revolution and the early Republic continued earlier patterns in many respects. Homicides involving slaves and Indians, although still hard to count, probably dropped off proportionally. The natives, although still fearsome, were essentially doomed once the land-hungry Americans were no longer counterbalanced by French, British, or Spanish authorities with more complex diplomatic or commercial agendas. Hostilities, as a result, were increasingly one-sided and quick. At the same time, the institution of slavery, while still harsh, was eased at least somewhat both by the fact that both races came to share Christianity and language together and by white defensiveness. Slavery, by the early nineteenth century, had been abandoned everywhere in Europe and in most European colonies. As a result, white Southerners, aware that they were on trial before the Western world, moved to make their slave codes more just, defined murder as murder, or at least manslaughter, and in a few cases actually tried and convicted whites for killing blacks. As always, however, the great majority of such incidents were ignored by the justice system, and so their numbers evade historians.

White-on-white killings, meanwhile, remained relatively few for some decades after the Revolution, at least in the settled areas of the northern and middle states. Edgar Allen Poe's invention of the detective story and the first reforming attacks on the death penalty were both reflections of the fact that, among the literate public, murder was less a subject of fear than of social concern, mystery, and romance. The one ominous note was sounded in the South, and along the southwestern frontier, where justice systems were primitive and a man was generally expected to settle his own quarrels directly and was excused for doing it violently. As the habits of formal dueling at the one end of the white social spectrum and informal brawling at the other were generally ignored by the law and applauded by the bystanders, a violent reputation became something like a qualification for public office. The trend is best symbolized by General Andrew Jackson, who, even apart from the souvenirs of his days as an Indian fighter, had at least one notch in his pistol and a number of scars and bits of lead in his body when raised to the presidency of the United States in 1829.

And in the following decades, although the quantitative evidence is still scattered, it is clear that the white murder rate soared to new heights, probably the highest in our history, throughout the growing nation.

To the West, as the United States stretched to the Pacific, the verb "to lynch" lost its original meaning of "to whip," and came to mean "to kill," as vigilantes battled alleged outlaws in disorderly new settlements from Tennessee to San Francisco, sometimes sparking small civil wars. In the East, great waves of hard-drinking Irish Catholic immigrants, fleeing famine and resenting authority, arrived in Boston, New York, Philadelphia, and Baltimore. As the early industrial revolution was still confined to water mills upriver, such commercial port cities had far too little unskilled work to absorb these newcomers, whose desperation was a form of social dynamite. In the South, meanwhile, the growing tradition of interpersonal aggression gathered strength under the looming threat of the Civil War. During the summer of 1831 the charismatic slave preacher Nat Turner, of Southampton County, Virginia, led a group of blacks who slaughtered about sixty whites before they were overpowered. While this is the only slave rebellion that actually reached the stage of collective action, fear and rumor sometimes pushed the always nervous region over the verge and into hysteria. At the same time, the lethal potential in violent confrontation everywhere was multiplied by the presence of the little handguns invented by Samuel Colt in 1832.

In the cities, this was a period of epic homicidal riots, beginning in the 1830s, over the three big, closely related issues of religion, race,

and politics. Anti-Catholic mobs burned a nunnery in Boston and can-
nonaded a church in Philadelphia; an election riot in Baltimore cost
more lives, an observer claimed, than the crucial Battle of Palo Alto in
the Mexican War (Sharf 1971). These affrays inspired local authorities
to introduce urban police for the first time, but the cops were often
overmatched and sometimes even joined the mobs, leaving the state
militia, or even federal troops, to put them down. Any group might be
targeted, but northern free blacks, as a largely helpless and still small
minority, were the most regular victims. Everywhere, they were held
vaguely to blame for rising sectional tensions over slavery. And in actions resembling medieval pogroms, Irish Democrats, in particular,
their economic competitors, invaded and burnt out their small neighborhoods, sometimes killing the inhabitants, with little fear of resistance or judicial consequences.

During this period, for the first time, the historical record allows a
long continuous run of official statistics in a big city, Philadelphia, beginning in 1839. Taken from indictments only, these are far lower than
actual body counts would allow: they omit many riot deaths, which the
authorities feared to prosecute for political reasons, and of course mur-
der-suicides. At a time when neither the police nor any other officials
accepted any real responsibility for "solving" homicide in the modern
sense, they also tend to undercount many dubious deaths; it was point-
less, even embarrassing, for the coroner to find that nonresidents or
friendless citizens had been murdered.[5]

Above all, like any urban count of criminal deaths in the nineteenth
century, it omits all but a handful of infanticides, which were then very
numerous. There had been few single women in the colonial era, and
were still only a few in rural areas, but their numbers had multiplied in
the city. The complementary labor of both sexes was needed to work a
farm and farm household, and young children were extra hands. But
wage-earning men had no economic need for marriage, and kids in the
city were not hands but mouths. Unmarried women found it hard
enough to support themselves and utterly impossible with a little one
in tow. Although in midcentury Philadelphia an unburied dead infant
was found in public every other day, guilt was hard to prove. Public
sympathy for accused young women ran high; everyone was aware that
their alternatives were few in an era when adoption was rare and when,

---

[5] The study from which the following material was taken was done for Lane (1997),
chaps. 4 and 5. See also Lane (1997), pp. 112–30.

before modern sanitation and knowledge of the germ theory, the poor-house was near-certain death for a newborn. As a result, the men who ran the justice system struggled hard and usually successfully to keep infanticides out of court.

But even with all these omissions, the city's homicide figures are significant. In addition to the totals, the indictment series when used with newspaper stories about each incident provides a statistical profile for the first time of the who, what, and where of urban homicide. The black rate was high but not markedly so; young white men were the most dangerous people in Philadelphia, as in other urban centers. In an era before the industrial revolution had moved into the city, as noted, underemployment was the norm for large numbers of these young men, especially after the Irish arrived. Such men, transients in many cases, were often foreign born and married late in life, if ever. And in their "bachelor subculture," for want of alternatives almost all recreation centered on drinking and fighting. They watched fighting cocks and fighting dogs and fighters in the ring; they fought fires and fire-fighters, formed gangs to fight political rivals and other ethnic groups, fought over hot words and cross glances. And as a result, even with all the omissions and undercounting, the indictment rate of 4.0 per 100,000 in 1853–59, the years just before the Civil War, was the highest for the whole of the nineteenth century.

The Civil War itself marked a major turn in the history of American homicide. In the South, the years between 1861 and 1868 witnessed the most significant nonmurders in our history, as the paranoia of generations proved wholly groundless. That is, as the slaves were freed across the region they reacted in dozens of ways, many of them unexpected, but there was simply none of the long-feared outbreak of vengeful homicide and rape. Elsewhere, as in big wars generally, the "murder rate" in most places dipped down during the fighting as young men were siphoned off to do their killing with official sanction, followed by a brief surge as they returned. But in the generations that followed, the direction was unmistakably down.

The pace and timing of the drop was uneven across the nation, as rates themselves had always been, with decline in the rural South and West trailing the more peaceful urban East.

In the South, the white majority nullified much of its wartime defeat through a successful terrorist campaign to rid the region of black or Republican voters and to push the freed ex-slaves back down both economically and socially. The period of Reconstruction to 1877 was marked by much organized violence. The lynchings that peaked in the 1890s were more episodic. The number of these lynchings declined thereafter, through the early twentieth century, largely because they had made their point; black voters had been largely eliminated from the rolls, public facilities had been segregated, and black farmers and laborers were securely locked into a variety of dependent arrangements.

Otherwise, as earlier, southern law enforcement was weak and tolerance of homicide high. The lawyer for the survivor of any fatal encounter that could be passed off as a fight could call it a duel and win acquittal as a matter of honor. (Jurors generally heard only from the survivors of these alleged fights, the loser being silent as the grave.) Hatfields, McCoys, and other feuding families in the hill country continued to settle their own murderous quarrels. Blacks, who could be sold by state or county authorities to private chain-gang contractors if convicted of any crime, had their own reasons to distrust the law, contributing to the fact that black-on-black murders were often ignored nearly as systematically as white-on-black, again making them hard for a historian to count. But even white-on-white homicides, according to one contemporary, were "proportionately greater than in any country on earth the population of which is numbered as civilized" (Redfield 1880). His figures, unsystematically taken from newspaper reports in South Carolina, Kentucky, and Texas, suggested for the year 1878 a "murder rate" roughly eighteen times that of New England.

In the West, these years began with the era of "Cowboys and Indians." Homicide, as before, continued to spark interracial conflict until the last Sioux and Apache were herded onto reservations, and, by the 1880s, in theory, all residents of the United States were subject to the traditional institutions of white law. The great postwar drives from Texas to Kansas had long ended by then, and it is in any case the duty of a professional historian to tell readers that no two cowboys, or anyone else, ever challenged each other to a fatal quick draw contest on a dusty western street. And while they were as aggressive as other poor and single young men, the hands who herded other men's steers were not nearly the gunslingers of Hollywood legend.

It is true that some parts of the West were dangerous, and as individuals and then corporations battled over its land, water, and minerals, there were many casualties. It is also true that gunmen like the Earp brothers sometimes worked as official sheriffs and marshals, sometimes as hired Pinkertons or other rented retainers, sometimes on their own as robbers and rustlers. But while we have tended to make mythical figures of murderous individuals, like New Mexico's Billy the Kid, we have overlooked the less glamorized but more common labor and ethnic violence that marked western settlement, the unrecorded killings of Mexicans across the Southwest, the unpunished slaughter, as one example, of perhaps fifty Chinese railroad workers in Rock Springs, Wyoming, in 1885 (Hollon 1974, pp. 95–101). The highest documented homicide rates—sometimes soaring over 100 per 100,000 a year—tended to occur in mining towns, where the inhabitants were "young, single, intemperate, and armed" (McGrath 1989, pp. 122–46). Especially high rates were recorded in places like Las Animas County, New Mexico, where the giant mining companies, in an effort to keep out union organization, deliberately mixed white immigrants with native Apaches and Hispanics, people whose only recreational outlet was drink and whose only common meeting place was the company saloon.

Labor troubles also contributed to the homicide totals back East. In the great Railway Strike of 1877 alone, ten men were killed in Baltimore, twenty-five in Pittsburgh, and fifty more in Chicago (Taft and Ross 1978, pp. 218–51). In addition to the major incidents like these, the toll routinely taken on picket lines added up each year, often compounded by ethnic hostilities as blacks, Hungarians, or Italians were brought in to take the jobs of striking Irish or German workingmen. But beneath all this, a profound transformation was taking place that helped push down murder rates all over the world.

Everywhere they have been studied, rates dropped from sometime in the mid-nineteenth century to the mid-twentieth century, in cities from Stockholm to Sydney as well as across the United States (for the international study, see Gurr [1989], chap. 1; for the United States study, see Lane [1989], chap. 2). In the United States, shortly after the Civil War, the newly created city police were able to win the battle for the streets and to put down murderous riots. In Philadelphia, after the war as well as before it, the range of those involved in homicide included husbands and wives, single mothers and infants when the justice system could not ignore them, landladies and tenants, robbers and victims. As always and everywhere, however, the great majority of killers and victims remained single young men: it is simply that fewer of them committed homicide.

One helpful difference after the war was that in rapidly growing and prosperous industrial cities there were now a host of distractions to engage young men other than drinking and fighting: bicycles and ball clubs, amusement parks, and, later, movies. In an important symbolic move, ethnic prize fighters, surrogates for direct battles between hostile groups, finally put on the gloves.

Beneath all this, an even more fundamental pacifying force was the urban industrial revolution itself. Once the steam engine allowed industry to move out of the countryside into the city, a truly golden age of urban development was born, an era of high-rise buildings, stadiums, museums, universities, department stores, and subway systems. The growth of factory and bureaucracy soaked up the underemployed, providing higher and more regular wages than before, and the ability to marry and, in many cases, own a home. Beyond that, the work itself, together with such ancillary institutions as the new public schools and the temperance movement, demanded regular orderly behavior and sobriety on the job in ways that tempered the free-swinging, hard-drinking, potentially lethal habits of earlier generations. That very fact, together with prosperity and such new technologies as photographs and fingerprints, for the first time allowed police and prosecutors, beginning around the turn of the century, to move the solution of routine homicides higher on their list of official priorities.

The steady downward pressure on murder rates was felt by successive waves of those who participated in this economic revolution. Only blacks, significantly, experienced growing rates between the 1890s and the 1920s. This was the very height of racist sentiment and discrimination, when African Americans were systematically excluded from the new urban economy and not only denied a foothold on the American "ladder of opportunity" but often kicked directly off its rungs. By the end of the nineteenth century, the once unruly Philadelphia Irish, in contrast, had lower rates than those of the city at large. Their place as the most feared ethnic group was then taken by Italians, emigrants from the region with the highest murder rates in Europe, their dispositions unimproved by the sea voyage and their arsenals upgraded by the American gun culture. Around the turn of the century their young men killed each other and occasional bystanders at record rates, far higher than those of urban blacks. But by the 1920s, within a single generation, as they were integrated into the new economy, the rates of those of Italian birth or descent fell dramatically, by a factor of five (Lane 1986, pp. 163–64).

Specific events, such as World War I and then Prohibition, affected American murder rates everywhere. And during the "Roaring Twenties" the popularity of the automobile—the most important technological aid to felonious homicide since the revolver—helped push up the total of robbery-murders and organized gang killings. In general, however, the long-term trend here, as elsewhere in the world, including, more slowly, the increasingly civilized American South and West, was down from the mid-nineteenth century into the 1930s, when the first reliable national statistics were compiled as given at the top of this section.

In sum then, to compare contemporary rates with those of earlier times is a matter often of educated guesswork, although some trends and patterns are clear. English homicide rates in the Middle Ages were far higher than ours today and, despite a drop, remained higher in the sixteenth and early seventeenth centuries. In America during the colonial period, white-on-white rates were remarkably low, although killings involving Indians and blacks were numerous and largely uncountable. Those patterns continued after the American Revolution and into the early national period, but between the 1830s and 1850s white homicides soared upward, and overall rates were almost certainly higher than modern totals, especially if hard-to-count urban infanticides could be added to the murder of blacks and those along the unsettled frontier. The rural West and especially the South continued to lead the nation in homicides in the generations after the Civil War, but by about 1870 the effect of the urban industrial revolution and other developments in the cities led the way to a gradual but marked and long-term shift. In the United States, as everywhere in the developed world, from then on, rates of homicide and other violent crimes, if graphed, would form a kind of long, ragged, reverse J-curve. That is, while short-term events might create zigs and zags, the basic line dropped from the mid-nineteenth century down to the mid-twentieth, bottoming out with the 4.5 per 100,000 reached in 1955. Thereafter it rose, quite rapidly during the 1960s, to reach a peak of 10.4 per 100,000 in 1974, to form the right-hand portion of the reverse J-curve. Since then it has wavered within a relatively narrow range, between somewhere over ten and somewhere over eight, until the current fairly sharp downturn that began in 1994.

II. Interpreting the Recent Drop in Homicide Rates

The U.S. homicide rate, according to the FBI's Uniform Crime Reports, stood at 9.5 per 100,000 in 1993, fell to 9.0 in 1994, and again to 8.2 in 1995, together with parallel drops in other violent crimes. As early as the following January 15, the cover of *Time* magazine declared that "Finally, We Are Winning the War against Crime," long before the official homicide figure came in at 7.4 for 1996, and 1997 and 1998 showed every sign of following the trend. The statistics are real and reflect truly good news. The obvious questions are, How good is it? Will it all last?

Alert readers will sense, of course, that a professional historian is going to tell them to hold the champagne, that short-term rates have zigged and zagged before, that not so long ago a high of 10.3 was recorded in 1981, falling over the next three years to 8.4 in 1984 before shooting up again to 10.5 in 1985. But the evidence for caution, while in part based on the cyclical—and sometimes inexplicable—nature of the relevant statistics, goes deeper than this. Historically, it is not so much the number as the nature of homicide that has disturbed or scared us, and on this score there are dark shadows over the good news.

As we all try to understand the recent declines in the rates, liberals, conservatives, and others may justly point to, and argue about, their own favorite explanations. Liberals may identify surging prosperity under a Democratic administration (conservatives claiming credit for reduced government spending), with employment as full as Alan Greenspan will allow. Conservatives can point to a judicial crackdown on crime of all kinds, begun years before, and argue with President Clinton about who best deserves credit for more recent moves toward tougher and more efficient policing. Demographers, of whatever persuasion, will note that there have been proportionately fewer teenage males in the population than there were just a few years ago. Criminologists will add that changes in drug use and the drug trade account for at least some recent declines in homicide. All of them are at least partially right, and even a historian must admit that some of the factors they identify are without real precedent in the past. At the same time, we cannot count on any of them to continue for long.

There is little question, first, that since the 1980s the drug trade, and especially the rise and fall in the use of crack cocaine, has accounted for many ups and downs in crime rates of all kinds. Alcohol use has fluctuated greatly over time. Contemporary Americans drink far less than those of the colonial or early national periods, but the fluctuations have moved slowly over time. Fashions in drug use and methods of drug distribution have, in contrast, changed with great speed. The fact that, having witnessed its ugly effects, young people, including young dealers, have moved away from crack in recent years is good news and does help explain in multiple ways some of the recent decline in homicide rates. But it takes no academic credentials to know that it is risky to rely on the continued good sense of teenagers and that, given the ingenuity of modern chemists, the next fad may be for something with more explosive effects than heroin or marijuana.

The effect of a relatively low percentage of teenagers in the population is even more surely doomed. Young males have always accounted for far more than their share of violent crime. And the young males of the millennial era are already with us, little kids now, getting ready inexorably to end the current (and welcome) dip in the number of teens. And as they turn pubescent they will, just as inexorably, bring troubles bigger than pimples for all of us.

For some time now, the courts have been reacting strongly to those who do make trouble, and with real effect. Ever since the mid-1980s, longer sentences have swelled the prison population each year. This trend may not deter reckless young men from committing crimes, and it may be argued, at least, that for various reasons it is bad, and certainly expensive, public policy. It is still true that those locked up for violent offenses are unable to kill civilians for at least a few years and that they emerge if not wiser at least older, their hormones less turbulent, and so less inclined to aggressive behavior. From this perspective, the only trouble is that for homicide this trend is close to a dead end, with conviction rates and sentences at historic highs and little room left to go up any further.

It is less clear how far the current trend toward better and tougher policing will take us. Ex–Police Commissioner William Bratton's policy of "zero tolerance" for disorderly behavior has certainly had its effect in New York and elsewhere. Among street thugs, there is no real fear of arrest for pissing on the sidewalk or doing drugs on the street, per se, but the fact that any arrest means a search has had a sobering effect on the habit of carrying illegal guns. In the absence of such guns, a man pissing on the street is less likely to get into a lethal argument with neighboring homeowners or with passersby whose shoes are in peril, while a man stoned or high but without a weapon is less likely to attempt a reckless robbery. Much of the fall in street crimes owes at least something to this policy, and as more cities adopt it there may be further improvement in rates until it reaches its limit.

The effect of prosperity and (relatively) full employment on crime rates is harder to measure. But whatever it is, it is even surer not only to reach its limit but to fall back. It takes no Ph.D. in history for anyone but a stockbroker to foresee that the current run of prosperity will crash and for anyone not a politician to see that stringent new changes in the welfare laws will produce more crimes of desperation, at least in the short run.

But from a historical perspective, the problem with the celebration over recent FBI reports is not merely that zigs in homicide rates are generally followed by zags but that the overall numbers are not the whole story and do not by themselves reveal the several disturbing trends that have developed over the past generation.

Twenty-five years ago, and certainly fifty, the vast majority of homicides resulted from fights among family, friends, or at least drinking acquaintances.[6] Some of these murders were savage, the savagery often directly related to the closeness of killer and victim, and many were severely condemned; modern feminists are no more indignant about husbands killing wives than were the all-male jurors of history, stretching back to the Middle Ages. But neither domestic nor barroom murders have ever much scared those not immediately involved, the rest of us, the general public. The kinds that really frighten us are felony murders, those committed in the course of other crimes, such as robbery or rape, especially those that strike apparently at random, the victim taken unaware. Those that are unsolved, the relationship between the parties remaining a mystery, are also, obviously, a source of deep concern. And it is precisely these kinds of murders that have gone up since the good old days of the 1950s, when the homicide rate reached an all-time low, and even since the bad old days of the early 1970s, when the rapid upturn of the 1960s reached its peak at levels higher than today's. And some, although not all, of these disturbing trends in murder have continued over the past few years, despite the overall drop in annual rates.

The FBI announced the drop in the number of homicides for 1996 in early June of 1997. In the month after that, as if to remind us that murder does not die, the front pages of the *New York Times* as well as the tabloids featured stories about a series of infanticides, the trial of Jesse Timmendequas for the rape-murderer of little Megan Kanka, the robbery-murder of Jonathan Levin, son of the chief executive officer of Time-Warner, the apparently motiveless killing of middle-aged Michael McMorrow by two teenagers in Central Park, and above all the conviction of Timothy McVeigh for the bombing of the Alfred P. Murrah Federal Building in Oklahoma City.

---

[6] The classic account of murder in midcentury America, and one whose questions and approach have inspired many others, is Wolfgang (1958).

And while it is hard to correlate rape-murder with any other social trend, and infanticide is repellent without being personally frightening, the other stories all represent, but do not exhaust, the kinds that scare us.

Robbery-murders, although down over the past few years as part of the general drop in street crimes, are still proportionately more numerous than they were in 1974, when the "murder rate" as reported by the Bureau of Vital Statistics hit 10.3 per 100. Serial killings have become more common and frighten us out of all proportion to their numbers, as do mass killings, in which five, ten, or more office workers, school children, or fast-food customers are gunned down in minutes. So, of course, have terrorist murders, dramatically but not uniquely exemplified by the bombings in Oklahoma City in 1995 and of Manhattan's World Trade Center in 1993.

Mass killings are always committed by men, usually middle-aged, whose psychological profiles more nearly resemble the suicidal than the homicidal, and if they do not kill themselves, they are killed or captured almost immediately. But all of the other deadly categories of crime on the rise are not only scarier but harder to solve than the older categories in which the principals generally knew each other. A domestic murder or tavern brawl was and is a "slam dunk" for an experienced detective, and as a result the rate of police "clearance by arrest" for murder averaged nationally over 90 percent during the 1950s. But it dropped under 80 percent in the 1970s and has fallen well under 70 percent during the 1990s. The FBI noted for the first time in 1991 that the number of killings by strangers or those with an "unknown" relationship to the victim had reached a majority of the total; the clearance rate that year was 67 percent. In 1994, the first year of the drop in homicide rates, the clearance rate also dropped, to 64 percent; in 1995 it had recovered only a single percentage point, to 65 percent.

Moreover, declining homicides among family, friends, and acquaintances, whether measured since either the mid-1970s or the mid-1990s, is at best a kind of good news/bad news story. Few categories have fallen as steeply as spousal murders, which accounted for 12 percent of the total in 1974 but just 5 percent in 1995. But while we would like to credit the police and justice system for better handling of cases of domestic abuse, the major reason fewer married folks are killing each other is just that fewer folks are getting married, especially in the categories most at risk: the young, the poor, and the black, a trend with obviously disturbing implications for the future. The long-term drop in barroom brawling, too, has its bad news side: if the neighborhood taproom these days is less likely than in 1955 to fill up with potentially quarrelsome males after the shift gets off, this is too often the result of the fact that those good old factory jobs have simply dried up and blown away.

In sum then, the recent drop in murder rates is likely to be short-lived, but the rise in some of the "scary" categories is not. There is no clear explanation of why serial killings have become more common, and at least some of the apparent rise in such cases may be because of better police work. But the stubborn rise in killings by strangers or "unknowns" is a long and strong trend. Assault weapons have made mass killings far easier, with new records set continually. And while the accused terrorists in both the Manhattan and Oklahoma City bomb-ings survived and denied all guilt, the arrest in July 1997 of two young Palestinians allegedly bent on a suicide-bomb attack on the New York City subway system reminds us that there may be worse to come. The arrest itself was a bit of last minute luck; suicide-bombers are virtually impossible to stop. And as in the post–Cold War era the world's innu-merable grievances tend to attach to Uncle Sam and are joined now by new kinds of rage among our own citizens, short-term declines in mur-der rates should inspire no more than modest applause.

III. On What Makes Homicide Rates Rise and Fall

The third of the questions for this essay is, What makes homicide rates go up and down? This is not quite the same as "Why murder?" an issue that requires a theologian more than a social scientist; a historian, in particular, is handicapped by the fact that the usual records, trial and newspaper accounts, rarely allow much profound plumbing into individual motivation. Individual motivation, too, is more complex for homicide than for any other major crime and spans a wider social as well as psychological range: women rarely rape, rich folks do not rob gas stations, poor folks do not commit stock fraud, but anyone may commit murder. History can supply only statistical generalizations about the social conditions or phenomena that have tended over time to push the rates. Still, some of these generalizations do not fit the con-ventional wisdom and may be useful both in correcting current mis-conceptions and placing current concerns in perspective.

But before approaching this question through American history it will be useful to do a kind of warm-up exercise. For this purpose a historian will insist on returning again to the beginning, in this case to the Middle Ages. The exercise is this: readers should test their liberal or conservative opinions about what causes homicide against conditions in the thirteenth and fourteenth centuries among, as Shakespeare had it, "This happy breed of men" who then occupied "this precious stone. . . . This blessed plot, this earth, this realm, this England."

There were then, of course, in that "sceptered isle," no guns, which had yet to be invented. There were no blacks or other racial minorities. There were by our standards no cities: the residents of London numbered perhaps 35,000–50,000, or about as many as in modern Kokomo, Indiana, and in any case they committed fewer homicides than their country cousins. The great majority of Englishmen lived, and killed, in homogeneous village communities of the sort that we moderns tend to idealize from a distance. There was no equivalent, in a society overwhelmingly illiterate, of any artificial or commercial "media"; only the songs and stories human beings have always told each other around the fire. Respect for religion, tradition, and family governed most lives to a degree rarely found in our world today. Capital punishment was the penalty prescribed for homicide of any degree, indeed for any felony, with hanging normally within minutes after conviction. And in this Bloody Olde England, it will be recalled, official "murder rates," although they substantially undercounted the real number committed, averaged something over 20 per 100,000 annually, or two to three times those of the contemporary United States (see Given 1977; Hanawalt 1979).

The hope is that this exercise will get the reader's attention, as in the story of the farmer, the mule, and the two-by-four between the eyes, and clear the head of potentially misleading preconceptions. This done, we may approach the issue of what "causes" homicide rates by examining some of the usual suspects in the light of the historical evidence, underlining each of them in turn, with special emphasis on the difference between the contemporary world and past times.

The role of drugs, first, in the zig-zagging of recent rates, has already been suggested. There are two issues here: one is the pharmacological effect of a given substance, the other the effect of illegal market competition. Alcohol, of course, stimulates reckless behavior, and historically all observers agree that it played a role in the majority, often the great majority, of those adult male fights that in most times and places account for most homicides. Much of the long drop in the reverse J-curve in murder rates described earlier resulted in fact from a drop in alcohol consumption, as it was effectively banned from the workplace and confined to off-hours. The behavioral effects of the more varied contemporary pharmacopoeia run a greater gamut. But one thing they all share is the problem of illicit distribution, a problem inherently greater than faced by those who ran booze during national prohibition in the 1920s.

Despite the well-publicized 400-plus gangland killings in Al Capone's Chicago, the size of bulky beer trucks and the permanent location of saloons made territorial monopoly and cooperation the norm. The result in most American cities during Prohibition was that competition was usually eliminated quickly and permanently, and a relative peace then normally reigned. But drugs, in contrast, are marketed in expensive little packets that may be sold individually on any street corner, a simple fact that continually tempts small-scale enterprisers to break existing rules. So long as drugs remain illegal—and in this country no end to their prohibition is in sight—then lethal arguments about individual transactions and territory will tend to push up murder rates.

Observers have been complaining about the effect of the media on criminal violence for nearly two centuries. Outside of word-of-mouth, the principal medium for disseminating crime news in the early colonial era was the official sermon delivered on the occasion of a public hanging, later reprinted as a pamphlet. (Puritan ministers loved public hangings as opportunities to warn bystanders about original sin and the seventeenth-century equivalents of sex, drugs, and rock 'n' roll.) But by the late eighteenth century, free enterprise pushed these reprints aside, together with their pious message, in favor of saltier fare in which the exploits of criminals were romanticized or "the system" blamed for mistakenly condemning or even framing them. Any homicide involving middle-class folks and the hint of romance—Dedham, Massachusetts's Jason Fairbanks and Betsy Fales in 1801, New York's Richard Robinson and "Helen Jewett" in 1835, Boston's Albert Tirrell and Maria Bickford in 1845—inspired a small flood of pamphlets and poems taking one "side" or the other on the issue of guilt.[7] Sex and violence were the mainstays, too, of the first mass-produced "penny papers," beginning in the late 1830s, and of the *Police Gazette* and "dime novels" that first appeared about a decade later. Moralists de-

---

[7] Accounts of these cases, and their treatment in the media, are provided in Cohen (1993).

cried all of them and their effect on leading impressionable youth to commit violent crimes.

The problem with this outcry against the media is, however, that during most of the nineteenth century, while literacy and the mass market expanded, murder rates were declining. The same held early in the twentieth century, when the new "movies," featuring Tom Mix and shoot-'em-up westerns, were also subjects of pious disapproval.

But we are now unquestionably in a new and historically unprecedented era. In the old movies, the heroes wore white hats and the villains black, there was no ambiguity about who represented good and evil, and justice always triumphed in the end. But these rules are at best blurred today. And there is no blurring the effect of color television: the average kid now views several thousand homicides, it is claimed, in the preteen years alone, many of them in vividly graphic detail. And although the study of this phenomenon may be viewed with the kind of skepticism that any major academic industry deserves, the findings are too powerful to dispute: television surely contributes to the high rate of homicide committed by those modern juveniles who seem to lack any sense of what death is really about but can make it happen with an easy pull on the trigger.

The effect of family instability is another contribution, one long noted by students of crime. In this country, the amateur ancestors of modern criminologists first appeared not long after the American Revolution and began to suggest that crime was less a matter of an evil will or original sin than of external, environmental causes, among them broken or absent families. It has always been true that homicide has been a matter principally of unmarried young men, both as killers and victims, while marriage seems a kind of cure for their reckless aggression. It is equally true, and has been demonstrated with increasing sophistication over the decades, that boys without fathers have trouble grasping the full range of masculine behavior, including tenderness and responsibility, and tend instead to focus on the kind of sexually predatory tough-guy roles most obvious on the street or maybe on the tube. During the early 1930s, H. C. Brearly, the first systematic student of American homicide rates, was concerned about the effect of divorce, then affecting about one marriage in eight; the issue of out-of-wedlock children did not apparently occur to him (Brearly 1932). Now that one marriage in two gets broken, and one out of three children are born to single mothers—a figure that rises to three out of four among big-city blacks—we have good reason to worry.

Sociology, ever since its nineteenth-century origins, has tended to idealize life in small village communities and given us reasons for associating urban growth with crime: just at the top of the alphabet we have been warned ad nauseam about the ill effects of *alienation, anomie,* and *anonymity.* And metropolitan areas in the United States do in fact have higher murder rates than rural ones. Now. But it must be recognized that this is historically a new development. Some specific kinds of homicide have been associated, sometimes, with urban growth: certainly infanticide, possibly spousal murder, as the family bond was weakened by the move out of the farm household. But cities for most of their history have usually helped in various ways literally to "civilize" their inhabitants. It has already been noted that medieval London was more peaceful than the English countryside, and nineteenth-century Philadelphia less murderous than the contemporary South and West. But only old folks, and historians, remember that as late as the 1950s the Big Apple itself, New York City, had lower homicide rates than the national average.

The issue, obviously, is not the city, or even growth, per se, but rather the kind of city, the kind of growth. The urban industrial revolution, as shown earlier, had a clearly positive effect. The problem of crime, just as clearly, is instead associated with postindustrial cities like those in the contemporary United States: those that no longer provide regular jobs and other opportunities to soak up the time and use the energies of potentially aggressive young men.

Many complaints about homicide rates in the modern United States center on the justice system. And it is true that trials, for example, take far longer than they once did, not to mention appeals, and that, for reasons outlined earlier, "clearance by arrest" rates have fallen rapidly over the past two generations. But homicide detection is far more efficient than it used to be; it was only in the early twentieth century that police departments generally accepted responsibility for the "solution" of ordinary murder cases, let alone gave them high priority, and not until the 1960s did black homicides, for example, get taken seriously in many jurisdictions. The modern conviction rate, in which 70 percent of those indicted for homicide are found guilty in some degree, is at a historic high. Even apart from the 12 percent averaged in the Middle Ages, only in highly authoritarian times and places, such as Puritan New England or in the antebellum "slave courts" of South Carolina, have rates much exceeded 50 percent. Sentences, too, in the modern era are comparatively quite high.

The issue of capital punishment is in this context a red herring. For most of our history, murder was only one of the crimes subject to the death penalty, and very often it was not the most feared. During the colonial period, and for some time afterward, probably half of all women hanged were guilty of infanticide, hardly a threat to the adult community, and perhaps half the men had committed property crimes. It was for treason—then a broad category that included such crimes as counterfeiting—that nervous Tudor monarchs invented new forms of execution, including cutting off the genitals and pulling out and burning the living bowels. Puritan New Englanders hanged not only a couple of adulterers, a handful of Quakers, and a bunch of witches but also an occasional youth caught in buggery with one or another form of livestock. (The full sentence in the latter case required, in accordance with the Book of Leviticus, that the complaisant heifer, ewe, or sow be slaughtered before the eyes of the offending human [Oakes 1978, pp. 268–81].) The rationale in all these cases was at best deterrence—there was little talk of revenge and certainly none of psychological "closure."

But with respect to deterrence, the opponents, historically, have made a better case than the proponents. In general, those times and places that have had high rates of execution in proportion to the number of homicides committed have been times and places that have had high murder rates as well, while those jurisdictions that have eliminated the death penalty have had low murder rates. It may be argued that the process is in effect circular, that high homicide states like Texas have simply felt the need to execute killers more sharply than low homicide states like, say, North Dakota, which in 1915 abolished capital punishment for all offenses except treason and first-degree murder by a prisoner already serving a life sentence for first-degree murder. But in any case, these days the arguments on neither side turn on deterrence but instead on moral and psychological questions that no appeal to social science can answer. Whatever the effect of the death penalty, in short, it simply cannot be shown that it has much effect on homicide rates.

As early as the first decade of the 1800s, reformers, using social statistics for the first time, noted that most of those who committed homicide tended to suffer from lack of education, broken families, excessive drinking, and other ills associated with poverty. The association still holds, but it is not a simple one now, nor was it simple in the past.

Logically, poverty is neither a necessary nor sufficient cause of murder: some of the most notorious killers have been rich, while the great majority of poor Americans of course never commit any kind of violent felony. Demographically, it is not those who feel the bite of want most fiercely—the old, the sick, family heads—who are most likely to kill. Historically, some of the poorest places in America, such as early nineteenth-century Vermont, have also been its least murderous.

Attempts to correlate murder rates with the business cycle over time have yielded very different results. Some, in nineteenth-century England, appear to show falling rates in bad times, perhaps because alcohol was harder to afford. And American history is full of occasions when booming prosperity was accompanied by rising homicide rates—perhaps the 1920s and certainly the 1960s in the twentieth century, which witnessed both a record reduction in poverty and record rises in violent crime. A few crimes, like infanticide, have historically been products of economic desperation, but many well-publicized incidents over the past few years, involving middle-class teenagers, show that the link is not essential. There are some signs that rising bread prices in the English Middle Ages sparked an increase in violent deaths, and in the United States there was an obvious economic edge to lethal battles over jobs, picket lines, and labor organization well into the 1930s. But hunger and cold have not usually or directly contributed much to murder rates in this richest nation on the planet.

Still the constellation of other, long-term, factors associated with poverty—ignorance, lack of regular work, and family instability—have now and always stoked the tendency to aggressive behavior. And if not poverty directly, then the sense of "relative deprivation," of being left out of a world of affluence has. Such a sense has clearly played a part in contributing to robbery-murder, the resort to dangerous illicit activities from drug dealing through prostitution, and to boiling frustration in general. If early nineteenth-century Vermonters were poor but peaceful, early nineteenth-century Vermonters did not have the lifestyles of the rich and famous beamed daily into their kitchens, in living color. South Central Los Angelenos do.

Much of the contemporary violence of our inner cities is inspired by the deadly combination of a kind of social rage coupled with the rage to possess. Urban armed robbery, as distinct from the relatively harmless rolling of drunks, say, is essentially a twentieth-century phenomenon; when a New York bar was held up in the fall of 1895 it was headline news in Philadelphia for a week, and the city's cops, in despair, figured finally that the gunman must have come to town with Buffalo Bill's Wild West Show (Lane 1986). But urban armed robbery has been scaring city folks for a long time now, in many cases scaring them all the way out to the suburbs. And it really began to take off, together with robbery-murder, during the 1960s. The 1960s were prosperous, but they were also a time when the good factory jobs were beginning to leave the city, when color TV came even to the poorest, and when a heavy emphasis on instant gratification through consumption was being pitched to large numbers of young men who were no longer involved in production.

That volatile combination has been with us ever since. The fact that the upward climb in murder rates turned flat and sputtered by the mid-1970s is a sign that most of the population by then was learning to adjust to the new postindustrial, high-tech, high-education, high-consumption economy. But a large fraction was left behind, still bombarded with messages to get, take, and have, more, here, and now. Those without the skills to satisfy these artificially created wants legitimately, filled with frustration, are tempted to obey the advertising command to "Just Do It," and so make trouble for themselves and others. So long as the American economy continues to widen the gap between rich and poor, these economic losers are not going to go away, and they will commit more than their share of violent crimes.

IV. On Why American Homicide Rates Are So High

The final question posed by American homicide rates is, Why are they so high in comparison to other developed nations? Many places, full of poverty and desperation, are markedly more murderous than we are—post-Communist Russia, Colombia, South Africa, and the Philippines are examples. But the most nearly "comparable" group should include England, Germany, France, and Japan, all of which have rates around 1.0 per 100,000 or less.[8] Of the major social conditions and historical experiences that set us apart from these peers and rivals, the ones most often discussed in this context are guns and the frontier. I would add race and slavery to this short list, and deal with each in turn.

The widespread availability of guns in this country goes a long way toward explaining our homicide rates, but not nearly far enough.

The gun culture in America is as old as the first settlements in Brit-

---

[8] International homicide statistics are published annually in World Health Organization (1997) and earlier editions.

ish North America. Early arrivals found muskets essential in fighting hostile natives, useful in shooting game and fending off predators. In time, outside of Quaker Pennsylvania, all of the colonies required their able-bodied male residents to carry them for use in the militia. And while full compliance was never achieved, ownership was always far wider than in Europe, where class fears and poverty kept firearms legally and practically out of the hands of all but an elite or members of small professional armies. The right of ownership was of course enshrined in the Second Amendment to the Constitution of the United States, adopted in 1791. And yet, as noted earlier, white-on-white homicide rates remained quite low in the colonies and for several decades after independence.

Not only were such killings relatively rare, but firearms did not figure very heavily in them. The simple fact is that neither the muzzle-loading muskets nor the cumbersome single-shot dragoon nor the dueling pistols of the era were well suited as murder weapons. However valuable as military or hunting weapons, they were expensive, hard to use, and rarely as close to hand as ax, knife, brick, or hoe when sudden anger flared. The revolution in civilian use of firearms began only with Samuel Colt's 1832 invention of the revolver: small, cheap, and easily hidden. By no coincidence, it was only when these deadly little weapons became widely available, beginning in the 1840s, that white-on-white homicide rates really rose and when rates in places like New York began to soar above those for Liverpool and stayed there (Monkkonen 1989). The effect of revolvers on urban riots has already been noted; even more important was, and is, their effect on abrasive everyday human interactions; a man on a barstool or in a traffic jam with a hidden gun is a kind of booby trap, liable to explode without warning if bumped the wrong way.

Attempts to limit the use of handguns are almost as old as the guns themselves are. The most famous, and generally successful, was the 1911 "Sullivan Law" in New York State, which forbade the carrying of concealed firearms of any kind. But in recent years, most states have followed Florida and Texas in making it not harder but easier to own and carry handguns. And despite new federal laws, assault weapons, which added a whole new dimension to legal and illegal arsenals beginning in the 1980s, are still widely available.

Of course, the American gun culture, in particular our fondness for hidden handguns, makes a difference in homicide rates. A little over two-thirds of the annual murders in this country are now committed with guns, the great majority of them handguns. And a great number of these in turn are committed in brief fits of anger. Men and women who argue in bedrooms and kitchens, motorists in the grip of "road rage," street kids dissed by peers and rivals would, in the absence of guns, perhaps indulge in drunken pushing matches, regretted or forgotten the next morning. But the presence of guns may transform the situation and turn an instant's adrenaline rush into a bloody event that will forever change a life—or end it.

Yet there is some truth to the famous argument of the National Rifle Association that "Guns Don't Kill People: People Do." Even if all of the gun killings were subtracted from our national totals, while those of our peer nations were left in, we would still have murder rates close to three times theirs. There is something in the American people that makes us more homicidal than the English or the French, even if we must resort to knives, fists, feet, teeth, and bricks.

Historically, our own favorite explanation for this difference has been the unique experience of the frontier. For years American historians tended to explain everything different about us in terms of this frontier experience, a thesis that remained popular for generations because we wanted to believe it. We made heroes of our Daniel Boones and Davy Crocketts, rugged explorers and Indian fighters, and of Jesse James, Wild Bill Hickock, and Billy the Kid, seen simply as tough guys who refused to be pushed around. And we have liked to think that there is a little of them in all of us, that if a certain touchiness and tendency toward violence marks the American character, these are only venial sins and are the inevitable price of centuries of carving a nation out of a hostile wilderness.

The only problem with this argument is that it simply does not fit the historical evidence. Some of our many frontiers were, indeed, violent places, such as parts of Texas, where aggressive young men fanned out ahead of courts and sheriffs, or parts of Colorado, where they were imported to work the mines. But most of these western territories calmed down as soon as women arrived, followed as inevitably by children. And many of them, from Ohio to North Dakota, were settled peacefully from the first by family groups, even religious communities who moved in en masse.

Above all, a look at the map of American homicide shows little correspondence with the date when a given state or territory was founded, the nature of its experience with the Indians, or its later history of lethal violence. Minnesota was the site of the biggest Indian massacres in our history, South Dakota of the last encampments of Colonel George Armstrong Custer, and later of Sitting Bull; neither state has been much noted afterward for murderous behavior. New Orleans, in contrast, one of the oldest cities in the nation, and in some ways the most civilized, is now the most violent.

What the map does show is not the western but the southern wellsprings of American homicide. Through most of our history the South has led all sections in violent behavior, sometimes joined by western jurisdictions, such as post–Civil War Wyoming, which were settled, often via Texas, by refugees from the Confederacy. The principal contribution of the West was only indirect, a legacy of the seventeenth century, when the outlying regions of the Chesapeake were the frontier. In the English common law that then in theory governed the use of unpaid labor, there was no such category as racial or lifelong slavery, only indentured servitude for a finite term of years. But out along the creeks of Virginia and Maryland, beyond the reach of legal authority, armed planters were able to defy the law and to transform their African indentured servants into slaves for life, and then their descendants into slaves forever, a movement that was eventually validated by colonial legislatures.

Slavery, based as it was on physical force, contributed in obvious ways to a southern tolerance for violent behavior. The rural, spread-out character of the plantation economy, and the fact that a master on his own place was in effect his own law, also helped to weaken other institutions of law enforcement. But there was another and somewhat less obvious way in which slavery fostered the famous southern "tetchiness" about questions of honor.

What slavery meant for both races was fear, fear on one side of murderous rebellion, fear on the other of whip, gun, and gallows. And in terms of the master's daily work of grinding labor out of the unwilling, fear of violence was far more efficient than violence itself. Among masters, a reputation for zero tolerance of shirking or disrespectful behavior was prized. Among all white men, a zero tolerance for breaking the rules of racial caste was encouraged. If it was nearly impossible to win genuine internalized respect, or cooperation, it was possible to insist at least on the external signs of deference. What applied most especially to dealings with slaves came to be applied to dealings with all others. And the value placed on reputation helped to foster what social anthropologists have called a "culture of honor," in which a man's worth is measured by what others think of him, and how others behave toward him.

In a naturally violent society, the insistence on male "honor" comes easily to mean that what seems a trivial slight to outsiders must be answered immediately, physically if necessary. Such a "code of honor" is easily recognized: it is in many ways the code of the schoolyard, the code of the "bachelor subculture," whether of antebellum Philadelphia, Tennessee, or Texas or of Irish or Italian newcomers to the city. It may be contrasted with the more difficult "culture of dignity" that was slowly cultivated to the North, in which worth is an internal matter of conscience, a matter between a man and his God. And it may be contrasted, too, with the simple lesson that our mothers tried to teach us in order to keep us safe from schoolyard bullies: "Sticks and stones may break my bones, but names can never hurt me."

Most of us eventually listen to our mothers, grow up and get married, or otherwise learn somehow to avoid dangerous confrontations over trifles. What distinguished the South was that the "code of honor" was not primarily a matter for kids, or street toughs, or bottom rungs on the social ladder. Instead, as embodied in the "code duello," it was endorsed and exemplified by community leaders, settled men, statesmen. And it spread not only into the upper echelons of the white social structure and across it, but to the lower echelons—the slaves and their descendants.

African Americans currently commit homicide at eight to ten times the Caucasian rate. The gap is not recent; during most of the past times and places when it has been possible to measure it, a roughly similar disparity has appeared. There are many reasons for this, some of which have already been sketched in this essay, but "southernness" and slavery are at its root. While certainly familiar with warfare, the African villages from which North American slaves were originally kidnapped were not given to incessant interpersonal aggression among their inhabitants. Their descendants learned this over here. Without recourse to a justice system—even a hostile one—with no other means of settling disputes, and with the master class setting an example, a premium on fighting in reaction to slights and insults became part of black culture as well as white.

In May 1994, the social anthropologist Elijah Anderson wrote an article about the "Code of the Streets" in an effort to explain the appalling murder rate among inner-city black teenagers (Anderson 1994, pp. 80–94). And while adherence to the code is exaggerated by ghetto conditions—the frustrations of poverty shorten the fuse—its basic values are easily identified by a historian. They are precisely those of the antebellum southern aristocracy: "The heart of the code is the issue of respect, loosely defined as being . . . granted the deference one deserves" (Anderson 1994, p. 82).

Southerners of both races have lived in this country longer on average than any other racial, ethnic, or cultural groups, apart from the original natives. And in good ways and bad they have forcefully stamped their manners and mores on its culture, so that all of us, whether raised in Oregon, New England, or Vietnam, have been affected by them. And it makes us ambivalent about homicide. An appreciation for violent behavior pervades the pop culture that we export to the world, and we are proud of it. We condemn the monsters—the Charles Mansons, Jeffrey Dahmers, and Richard Specks—as all people do. But most killers are not obvious psychopaths, only rather ordinary men who have reacted violently to some kind of frustration. And even if we would not ourselves react the same way, we have tended to admire those who do. President Andrew Jackson—slave owner, Indian fighter, and lethal brawler—actually walked the walk, but even so naturally gentle a soul as President Ronald Reagan talked the talk.

An admiration for "toughness" has long been institutionalized in American law. In Great Britain, before a man may claim he has killed in "self-defense," he has a "duty to retreat" in the face of another's aggression until his back is literally to the wall. In many jurisdictions in the United States there is no such legal duty, and in the popular imagination such retreat is easily confused with cowardice (Brown 1991). And where the line is not clear, we find it hard to distinguish between those who manfully stand up for their rights and outright thugs, and so John Wayne somehow morphs into Billy the Kid, and Clint Eastwood into Al Capone.

The historic line of descent is clear. Homicide anywhere may perhaps result from an original sin inherited from our universal ancestors and is first manifested in Cain's slaying of his brother Abel. It is easier to show that high rates of homicide in America result from our own version of original sin, the racial slavery that followed shortly after the arrival of the first permanent white settlers on this Edenic continent. And the continual round of killings on the streets, across kitchen tables, and in bedrooms, barrooms, and schoolyards is part of the price we have paid for it.

Historians are in the business of understanding, not the business of problem solving. And a historical perspective does not necessarily yield a scenic view. With respect to murder in America, we have more bad news than good; the social, cultural, and institutional factors that encourage it run deep in our history. None of them will easily or quickly go away. But unlike early nineteenth-century economics, history is not a "dismal science." Its only law is that things will change, and sometimes they change in healthy directions.

We have had high murder rates in the past, higher than today's, that then moved down in time. The violent "bachelor subculture" of the nineteenth century is largely a thing of the past. Their contemporary descendants are no longer trapped by the conditions and attitudes that once led to murderous behavior among mid-nineteenth-century Irish immigrants or early twentieth-century Italians, to say nothing of four-teenth-century Anglo-Saxons. And it may be that if we can understand the past we will all be better able, with time and patience, to transcend it.

REFERENCES

Anderson, Elijah. 1994. "The Code of the Streets." *Atlantic Monthly* 273(5): 80–94.

Brearly, H. C. 1932. *Homicide in the United States*. Chapel Hill: University of North Carolina Press.

Brown, Richard Maxwell. 1991. *No Duty to Retreat: Violence and Values in American History and Society*. New York: Oxford University Press.

Chapin, Bradley. 1983. *Criminal Justice in Colonial America, 1606–1660*. Athens: University of Georgia Press.

Cockburn, J. S. 1977. "The Nature and Incidence of Crime in England, 1559–1625: A Preliminary Survey." In his *Crime in England, 1550–1800*. Princeton, N.J.: Princeton University Press.

Cohen, Daniel A. 1993. *Pillars of Salt, Monuments of Grace: New England Crime Literature and the Origins of American Popular Culture, 1674–1860*. New York: Oxford University Press.

Given, James Buchanan. 1977. *Society and Homicide in Thirteenth-Century England*. Palo Alto, Calif.: Stanford University Press.

Gurr, Ted Robert. 1989. "Historical Trends in Homicide: Europe and the United States." In *The History of Crime*, vol. 1 of *Violence in America*, edited by Ted Robert Gurr. Newbury Park, Calif.: Sage.

Hanawalt, Barbara. 1979. *Crime and Conflict in English Communities, 1300–1348.* Cambridge, Mass.: Harvard University Press.

Hollon, W. Eugene. 1974. *Frontier Violence: Another Look.* New York: Oxford University Press.

Hull, N. E. H. 1987. *Female Felons: Women and Serious Crime in Colonial Massachusetts.* Urbana: University of Illinois Press.

Jordan, Winthrop D. 1968. *White over Black: American Attitudes towards the Negro, 1550–1812.* Williamsburg: University of North Carolina Press.

Lane, Roger. 1986. *Roots of Violence in Black Philadelphia, 1860–1900.* Cambridge, Mass.: Harvard University Press.

———. 1989. "On the Social Meaning of Homicide Trends in America." In *The History of Crime,* vol. 1 of *Violence in America,* edited by Ted Robert Gurr. Newbury Park, Calif.: Sage.

———. 1997. *Murder in America: A History.* Columbus: Ohio State University Press.

———. 1999. *Violent Death in the City: Suicide, Murder, and Accident in 19th Century Philadelphia.* Columbus: Ohio State University Press. (Forthcoming. Originally published 1979.)

McGrath, Roger D. 1989. "Violence and Lawlessness on the Western Frontier." In *The History of Crime,* vol. 1 of *Violence in America,* edited by Ted Robert Gurr. Newbury Park, Calif.: Sage.

Monkkonon, Eric. 1989. "Diverging Homicide Rates: England and the United States, 1850–1875." In *The History of Crime,* vol. 1 of *Violence in America,* edited by Ted Robert Gurr. Newbury Park, Calif.: Sage.

Oakes, Robert. 1978. "Things Fearful to Name: Sodomy and Buggery in Seventeenth Century New England." *Journal of Social History* 12(2):268–81.

Redfield, Horace V. 1880. *Homicide North and South: Being a Comparative View of Crime against the Person in Several Parts of the United States.* Philadelphia: Lippincott.

Sharf, J. Thomas. 1971. *History of Baltimore City and County.* Baltimore: Regional Publishing Co. (Originally published 1881.)

Taft, Philip, and Philip Ross. 1978. "American Labor Violence: Its Cause, Character, and Outcome." In *Riot, Rout, and Tumult: Readings in American Political and Social History,* edited by Roger Lane and John J. Turner. Westport, Conn.: Greenwood.

Teeters, Negley K. 1963. *Scaffold and Chair: A History of Their Use in Pennsylvania, 1682–1962.* Philadelphia: Temple University Press.

Wolfgang, Marvin E. 1958. *Patterns in Criminal Homicide.* Philadelphia: University of Pennsylvania Press.

World Health Organization. 1997. *World Health Statistics Annual.* Geneva: United Nations Press.

Jeffrey Fagan and Richard B. Freeman

Crime and Work

ABSTRACT

Crime and legal work are not mutually exclusive choices but represent a
continuum of legal and illegal income-generating activities. The links
between crime and legal work involve trade-offs among crime returns,
punishment costs, legal work opportunity costs, and tastes and preferences
regarding both types of work. Rising crime rates in the 1980s in the face
of rising incarceration rates suggest that the threat of punishment is not
the dominant cost of crime. Crime rates are inversely related to expected
legal wages, particularly among young males with limited job skills or
prospects. Recent ethnographic research shows that involvement in illegal
work often is motivated by low wages and harsh conditions in legal work.
Many criminal offenders "double up" in both legal work and crime, either
concurrently or sequentially. This overlap suggests a fluid and dynamic
interaction between legal and illegal work. Market wages and job
opportunities interact with social and legal pressures to influence decisions
to abandon crime for legal work. Explanations of the patterns of legal and
illegal work should be informed by econometric, social structural, and
labeling theories. The continuity of legal and illegal work suggests the
importance of illegal wages in research and theory on criminal decision
making.

Beginning in the 1980s and continuing today, the number of persons
incarcerated in the United States increased massively, incapacitating

Jeffrey Fagan is professor of public health and director of the Center for Violence
and Prevention, Columbia University School of Public Health and visiting professor,
Columbia Law School. Richard Freeman is professor of economics at Harvard University and program director for Labor Studies at the National Bureau of Economic Research. An earlier version of this essay was presented at the Workshop on the Metropolitan Assembly on "Dealing with Urban Crisis," Northwestern University, October 1994.
We are grateful to Phil Cook, John Hagan, Michael Tonry, and an anonymous reviewer
for helpful comments.

many criminals and increasing the risks of punishment for those still active (Cohen and Canela-Cacho 1994; Mauer and Huling 1995; Levitt 1996; Blumstein and Beck 1999). These factors should have greatly reduced the crime rate. Yet through the early 1990s, officially recorded crime failed to decline and self-reports of victimization declined less rapidly than expected as the incarceration rate increased (Freeman 1995; Tonry 1995; Zimring and Hawkins 1995). Although crime rates have recently declined from their peak in the early 1990s, they remain at high levels in the face of increasing costs of crime (Nagin 1998).

An economic explanation would turn first to the labor market determinants of the supply of young men to crime. Young men, usually out-of-school people with limited job skills and employment or earnings prospects, commit a disproportionate number of crimes (Freeman 1996a; Short 1997). For crime to persist at high levels during periods of massive increases in incarceration and punishment risk, there must be offsetting increases in the returns to crime, or a highly elastic supply curve of youths to crime because of shifts in the social and economic factors that produce criminality.

Neither the economic nor the criminological literatures offer clarity on this question. Much of the literature before 1980 was based on fairly simplistic concepts of criminality and also about how people divide their time between legal and illegal economic activities. For example, economists emphasized labor market participation and income returns as measures of employment but paid little or no attention to the returns from illegal activities. But the economic lives of unemployed people were sideshows in this literature, and the extent to which their incomes included returns from either crime or licit informal economic activities was poorly understood.

Criminologists also ignored crime as illegal work, or illegal income as a motivation for criminal activity. Instead, they focused on the underlying causes of crime and unemployment and attempted to model the two behaviors, establish their causal order, and determine their relationship to proximate individual-level causes such as family background and peer networks. Accordingly, efforts to explain the relationships between crime and legal work, or the effects of unemployment on criminal involvement, resulted in limited tests of theory and a generally unsatisfactory literature.

These questions have been revisited more closely in the past decade with the growing involvement of young men and women in expanded street-level drug markets, the intensification of poverty and racial segregation, and the economic restructuring of U.S. cities (Massey and Denton 1993; Hagan 1994; Wilson 1996). In the past, analyses of crime and the labor market usually addressed the effects of unemployment or other labor market conditions on crime, and results typically went in the expected direction (Freeman 1983, 1995; Witte and Tauchen 1994; Crutchfield and Pitchford 1997). The growth of illegal income opportunities in the 1980s, in a context of declining wages and job losses in inner cities, increased the potential returns from crime and perhaps altered the basic economic calculus for many young people. Thus labor market conditions and crime opportunities may influence employment in ways not considered before (Fagan 1992*b;* Freeman 1992; Hagedorn 1994*b*).

Until recently, researchers often viewed legal and illegal economic activities as mutually exclusive. One view suggests that through processes of self or social selection, a formidable social and economic wall separates many young men and women from the world of legal work. This separation is the product of several forces that are concentrated in inner-city areas and may account for their persistently higher unemployment rates. Excluded from legal work, their earnings are likely to be heavily skewed toward informal economic activity and also toward crime incomes.[1] For some, juvenile and criminal court records create a cumulative disadvantage that may lead to being labeled as poor risks for hiring, resulting in their exclusion from licit work (Sampson and Laub 1993). Others may be excluded from legal work by poor job skills or low education, a weak labor market, the racial hiring preferences of employers, or spatial mismatches that make jobs inaccessible for urban youths. Also, chronic unemployment and low incomes among adults in poor neighborhoods have shaped social norms that devalue legal work (Sullivan 1989; Anderson 1990). These dynamics leave few income options open other than public assistance, the licit informal economy, or illegal work in crime or drug selling. Still other young men may forgo legal work for what they perceive to be more lucrative careers in crime or drug selling. Others shift back and forth over time, while some juggle legal and illegal economic activities at the same time (Hagedorn 1994*b;* Venkatesh 1997).

At the core of this view is a presumed divide between legal and illegal economic activity that leads many to choose the latter and forgo

[1] Illegal activities are distinguished from the myriad activities of the informal economy, activities that generally involve no criminal law violations. See, e.g., Bourgois (1989); Taylor (1990); Fagan (1992*a*); Freeman (1992).

the former. Economic theory suggests that the person considering crime compares the present value of earnings from crime, net the loss of earnings because of being apprehended and imprisoned, with the present value of earnings from legal work. This person also weighs the riskiness of the crime and then makes a decision. Thus three factors enter the calculus: legal earnings, risks and extents of penalties, and illegal earnings.

Given the alternatives of low-wage payoffs from legal work and the expectation of relatively high returns from income-generating criminal activities, coupled with high incarceration risks that may appear to be independent from crime commission, illegal activity may seem a rational choice not unlike choices made among legitimate occupational pursuits (Becker 1968; Viscusi 1986*b*; Freeman 1991). Whatever the origins of the decision to engage in illegal work, the onset of an illegal career is often viewed as narrowing later economic and social options for engaging in legal work, foretelling a lengthy career of illegal pursuits outside the social world of legal enterprise (Hagan and Palloni 1990; Freeman 1992; Sampson and Laub 1993). Nevertheless, as we illustrate in this essay, these decisions, and the supply of young men to crime, are far more elastic than they appear.

A. Types of Illegal Work

Any discussion of the general link between crime and work requires a careful elaboration of the different types of crimes and their potential relationship to legal work.[2] Consider the following examples: (1) employee theft and embezzlement, white-collar crime; (2) fencing, selling stolen goods, running a chop shop or other criminal distribution system; (3) tax evasion; (4) drug dealing, prostitution; (5) vehicle theft, burglary, robbery; (6) kidnapping; (7) domestic violence, child abuse, barroom brawling, driving while intoxicated. The first category requires that the criminal hold a licit job, while the second and third ordinarily are committed by people who are legally working and whose work provides access if not motivation for their criminal activities. People in the fourth category often are not working legally, but they may work legally as a cover or to provide an economic backup if their illegal work is disrupted by police activities. These jobs have the characteristics of work: they require a significant time commitment as well as skill and commitment (Letkemann 1973). The fifth type of crime involves small trade-offs of time between legal and illegal work. That

[2] We are indebted to Phil Cook for helping shape these distinctions and their meaning for this essay.

is, for people in this category, time most likely is not an important issue in deciding whether to participate. However, the returns from crime in categories 5 and 6 may reduce monetary incentives to work legally. The last category requires no competition for time with legal work, and work will be unrelated to these types of crime.

This essay is primarily concerned with offenders in categories 4 and 5. Here, the choice to engage in these crimes involves both monetary returns and time allocation. Although these considerations may not be totally independent, neither are they closely linked. For example, drug dealing more closely fits Isaac Ehrlich's (1973) time allocation model of participation in illegitimate activities. The individual divides his or her time according to the anticipated monetary returns and the risks of punishment. The fifth category, however, may not involve any decisions regarding time allocation and reflects the model of rationality described by Gary Becker (1968): these activities are more like gambles (where the concerns are risks and payoffs) rather than time allocation dilemmas. Time may still be an indirect factor in the form of time-consuming prison terms or wage-reducing social stigma (Cook 1980).

These varying relationships between crime and work suggest different types of links, based on the two streams of criminal choice: time allocation and risk preference. The latter ignores time allocation (Becker 1968) and is the stronger of the two streams of thought in this literature. We follow that logic in this essay, and we analyze the evidence in a framework that integrates punishment risk and cost, comparative monetary returns, and the social returns and costs of criminal involvement. We also use the term "unemployment" to refer to the condition in which an individual is not working, or jobless, regardless of whether the person is actively seeking legal work. Whether in the formal labor force or not, we assume that individuals are always seeking streams of income. It is the choice of the licit or illicit stream that we examine here.

B. Continuity between Legal and Illegal Work

Both empirical research and theory challenge a deterministic view of an exclusive relationship between crime and legal work. Rather than dichotomous choice, economic activity for some people seems to vary over a continuum of legal and illegal "work." This is especially true in U.S. inner cities, where a split or "dual" labor market has distanced adolescents and young adults from work that offers the potential for wage growth, skill acquisition, and job stability (see, e.g., Crutchfield [1989, 1995], and Crutchfield and Pitchford [1997], on labor stratification, legal work, and crime). In the absence of such opportunities, the connection between legal and illegal markets is closer than in more advantaged communities with broader labor markets. Several studies show a fluid, dynamic, and complex interaction between legal and illegal work. Legal and illegal work often overlap both within time periods and over developmental stages. Among young drug sellers, more than one in four is also employed in legal work (Reuter, MacCoun, and Murphy 1990), and legal wages do not necessarily decline as illegal wages increase (Fagan 1992a, 1994).[3] Many drug sellers are only sporadically involved in drug sales, ducking in and out of conventional labor markets at regular intervals (Hagedorn 1994a, 1994b).

Ethnographic studies (Sullivan 1989; Williams 1989; Taylor 1990; Padilla 1992; Adler 1993) suggest a blurring of distinctions between legal and illegal work, and a broader conceptualization of work that neutralizes the legal distinctions among licit and illicit income-generating activities. Individuals involved in illegal work may change their evaluations over time of the costs and returns of such work compared to legal pursuits, leading to career "shifts" from illegal to legal sources of income (Shover 1985, 1995; Biernacki 1986; Tunnell 1992; Decker and Wright 1995; Wright and Decker 1997).

Recent theoretical developments also challenge deterministic conceptions of illegal work. In part, economists and criminologists have viewed crime and work as exclusive choices because most study designs are single-period individual choice models that ignore within-individual changes over time (Good, Pirog-Good, and Sickles 1986; Witte and Tauchen 1994). Beginning with Becker (1968) and Ehrlich (1973), crime and legal work have been viewed by economists as the result of rational choices among options that carry both costs and returns. In their simplest form, crime and work are substitutes: each takes time and each produces income. Making decisions to engage in one or both behaviors is a process akin to an optimization model that reflects the distribution of opportunities and the costs and returns of alternative pursuits (Clarke and Cornish 1985; Stephens and Krebs 1986; Grogger 1994). Nothing in this framework argues against a vector of income-generating activities that involves simultaneous activities across legal

[3] The "doubling up" of legal work and cocaine sales in the Fagan (1992a, 1994) and Reuter, MacCoun, and Murphy (1990) studies indicates that, for many young men, illegal work may be temporary or transitional work that supplements difficult low-wage or otherwise unsatisfactory work. For others, legal work provides options to riskier illegal work or perhaps broadens markets for sellers of illegal goods or services.

boundaries, constrained by time and the distribution of opportunities, and varying over time.

Life-course models present another challenge. In this view, individuals move in and out of activities (roles) that reflect specific developmental stages and the social and economic contingencies attached to each stage (Sampson and Laub 1993). Behavioral trajectories of crime or legal work change as individuals progress through predictable life stages that expose them to changing contingencies and opportunities. These perspectives stand in stark contrast to theories of deviance that attempt to explain involvement in illegal behavior as the product of criminal "traits" that are stable and enduring over the life course (see, e.g., Gottfredson and Hirschi 1990). Instead, the active and fluid movement of individuals in and out of illegal work suggests active management of their income-producing activities and a great deal of human perception and agency in their choices.

In this essay, we view crime and legal work as a continuum of income-generating behaviors over the life course. This leads to several conclusions that challenge conventional views. First, the tradeoff in wages between legal and illegal work suggests that decisions to earn money through crimes or drug selling are rational ones. For younger people leaving school, their entry into legal and illegal work is influenced by processes of adolescent development in the complex developmental stage of school-to-work transitions. These transitions are further complicated in inner cities with narrow and highly segmented labor markets, recent unskilled labor surpluses, and expanded illegal markets. This is especially salient for adolescents entering the workforce with limited employment and earnings prospects. For workers already in the work force, decisions to enter illegal work reflect their experiences in the legal work force, both economic and social, and a rational economic assessment of the risks and returns from illegal work.

Second, despite rising incarceration rates, the threat of punishment does not seem to be a meaningful cost of crime. In earlier historical periods, the threat of incarceration would discount the monetary returns from crime. But low wages for unskilled workers reduce the legal opportunity costs of punishment. And, in periods of high incarceration, punishment appears to no longer be a low probability event but a near certainty from involvement in crime. This reduces the salience of social stigma associated with punishment, and the contingent value of punishment costs. In addition, a criminal conviction record has an adverse effect on future employment and earnings. The disadvantage of early criminal justice participation compounds over time, making entry to legal work often difficult and limited to low-wage, low-skill jobs.

Third, the relationship between illegal and legal work appears to be fluid and dynamic rather than deterministic. Many legal workers are involved concurrently in illegal economic activity. This "doubling up" suggests an active management of income-producing activity that capitalizes on opportunities in illegal markets while maintaining the social, legal, and economic benefits of legal work. Others move back and forth between legal and illegal work, carefully managing the benefits and risks of each economic sector and activity. These decisions are based in part on wages and in part on punishment risk, and they also reflect developmental stages in which crime and legal work have changing social value.

Fourth, although crime wages seem to be a strong factor influencing the choice of illegal over legal work, "market" wages in legal work compete well with illegal wages and can tip work choices toward legal activities. The choice of illegal work seems to be contingent on the alternative of low legal wages tied to unskilled or entry-level jobs. However, the young males who are most prone to crime will choose legal work over illegal work when legal wages approach a rate or "market" value for skilled labor, wages that are comparable with skilled labor. A corollary lesson is that tight labor markets may drive up wages and create wage incentives that compete with illegal markets.

Fifth, the decision to abandon crime is influenced by legal work opportunities. Desistance is a natural process for many offenders, hastened by a combination of intrapsychic, social, and legal pressures. Work is a central part of the process of desistance (Sampson and Laub 1993). To the extent that these exits from crime are accessible, desistance from crime can begin earlier in the life course and can proceed with fewer setbacks and stumbles. Finally, the increasing but poorly understood participation of women in illegal work raises additional issues about gender and the dual nature of work.[4] We explore these themes in depth in the sections that follow.

[4] Like their male counterparts, many women drug sellers "double up" in drug selling while working legally (Fagan 1994). Some have had long careers of petty hustles and paper frauds or prostitution work. But many others have not been involved in illegal work until the expansion of the drug economy created new opportunities. Their pathways into illegal work are little understood and likely reflect gender issues in both the licit and illicit economies.

The interaction of legal and illegal work raises several questions that are the focus of this essay. We begin Section I with a review of quantitative studies of crime, unemployment, and legal work. This review compares macro-structural with individual studies and finds some conflicting evidence between them. We turn then to analyses of longitudinal data to illustrate the effects of criminal justice involvement on future employment and earnings. Next we examine the effects of both legal and illegal wages on work choices. Estimates of illegal wages are reviewed, including a close examination of income from drug dealing. We then examine empirical studies that estimate models of econometric choices of legal and illegal work. We review several studies that integrate deterrence and econometric perspectives by including punishment costs with perceptions of monetary gains in both legal and illegal sectors.

In this section, we address issues related to both theory and policy. First, does illegal work draw workers away from legal work? Few studies have examined the extent to which illegal work (especially in drug selling) draws young workers from the legal economy or whether people doing illegal work are nonparticipants in legal work. To what extent do human capital issues, as well as work opportunities, mediate work-crime relationships? How do regional variables, including the spatial distribution of legal employment and the redistributive functions of illegal markets, influence crime-work relationships?

This first section concludes with an analysis of the extent to which individuals "double up" by combining legal and illegal work in an overall strategy of income production. If workers are active decision makers, how often do they "double up" in the legal and illegal economies? To what extent are work and crime mutually exclusive in short periods or across years?

Section II reviews qualitative evidence on the social meaning of legal and illegal work and on decision making with respect to choices for generating income. In this section, we construct a social framework for explaining decisions to shift between legal and illegal work. Recent ethnographic research suggests several factors that influence shifts by workers from legal to illegal work and back again. For those who have abandoned the formal labor force for illegal work, what experiences shaped and influenced their decisions? How have those transitions occurred? How do nonworkers view work in an era of declining legal work opportunities? For some, the transition from legal to illegal work may be temporary, raising questions about their experiences in illegal work and the factors that influence their return to legal work. How and why do they decide to return to legal work? Still others may shift back and forth over time. This raises a corollary question about how "dual" careers are managed and the factors that trigger shifts into or out of illegal work.

Section III examines empirical evidence on the abandonment of crime for legal work. We rely primarily but not exclusively on qualitative studies of decision making by active offenders. Implications from both life course and econometric research are discussed. Section IV concludes the essay. First, we identify the methodological issues in studying income-producing careers and the prospects for using incomes as a dependent variable. Then we apply perspectives from contemporary criminological theories to interpret the empirical evidence on the crime-work relationship and conclude by offering an agenda for both basic and policy research on crime and work.

I. Crime, Work, and Unemployment

Two often disparate literatures inform our understanding of crime and unemployment. Economists view work, whether legal or not, as a rational decision on how to allocate one's time for income production. It suggests that economic costs and incentives have explicit effects on decisions to engage in legal or illegal work. Becker (1968) proposed a risk preference model in which consumers choose legal work or crime as a function of risk, legal wages, and criminal returns. Several variables are thought to influence this relationship. First, the expected returns from crime and the expected income from legal work establish the economic prospects of competing alternatives. Second, the returns from illegal work are discounted by the potential costs of criminal sanctions from illegal work. Third, labor market variables influence the perception of the likelihood of legal income, where loose job markets (and high unemployment) drive down wages from legal work. Fourth, the discount from criminal sanctions depends on whether prison is a price worth avoiding. When crime incomes are potentially high, the costs of incarceration may be relatively low compared to forgone illegal wages.[5]

---

[5] Predictions in this framework depend critically on attitudes toward risk and on moral views. Higher criminal incomes relative to legal incomes are needed to induce people to commit crimes when they are risk averse or are morally principled. We return to this question later in discussing the nonmonetary returns from "lifestyle" and taste variables.

Criminologists tend to divide in their views of crime and work in several ways. While many agree that crime and unemployment are negatively associated, there is strong disagreement on both causal order and the underlying causal mechanisms. Several studies attribute crime to unemployment (e.g., Good, Pirog-Good, and Sickles 1986), while some economists suggest that crime causes unemployment (e.g., Freeman 1992). Some view the negative association between crime and unemployment as spuriously attributable to a common underlying personality trait, such as lapses in self-control (Gottfredson and Hirschi 1990).

Some view the choice of crime as a reflection of strain resulting from the gap between expectations and opportunities for legal work (Agnew and White 1992). This perspective is part of an older tradition in which unemployment and joblessness are markers of the degree of deprivation or social inequality afflicting persons or groups (see, for a review, Short [1997]). Other perspectives suggest that crime and work are reciprocally related. Early involvement in crime may attenuate occupational attainment, in turn increasing the likelihood of subsequent crime, a sequence that repeats several times over developmental stages (Thornberry and Christenson 1984).

Still others claim that the association is conditional: avoidance of crime is contingent on some quality of employment beyond simple entry into any occupational status. This perspective reflects the traditions of economists who are concerned about the characteristics of work or joblessness that promote or limit involvement in crime. These models effectively translate structural concepts about crime causation into models centered on individual change over the life course. For example, Sampson and Laub (1993, p. 304) claim that "employment by itself" does not increase social control but that work leads to internalized social controls through commitment and stability. Legal work also exposes workers to the social controls of the workplace. Uggen (1996) argues that exposure to high-quality jobs reduces criminal activity and that stratification in job opportunities affects decisions to pursue criminal activity (see also Rosenfeld and Messner 1989).[6]

However, stratification of illegitimate work may also influence the work-crime relationship. Higher positions in illegitimate occupations may constrain mobility toward legal work, as well as reducing its ap-

---

[6] Occupations themselves represent a stratification of opportunities, a manifestation of Merton's concept of "legitimate means" (1938).

peal (Matsueda et al. 1992). Thus, for both economists and criminologists, the comparative advantage of legal versus illegal work involves both status returns and economic returns. How the two are weighed in decisions about income has rarely been studied.

Conceptual approaches to the crime-work relationship also have differed in how work is operationalized and measured. Measures of labor market attachments have included work participation (job participation, time spent in work, job stability), occupational status, and returns from work. Despite the importance of the net returns of legal versus illegal activities, illegal wages have rarely been studied, nor has status in deviant networks been studied closely (see, for an exception, Matsueda et al. 1992). Also, because crime and legal work are often viewed as trade-offs or time substitutes, little consideration has been given to the simultaneity of crime and work. Accordingly, to analyze trends in the empirical literature, we conceptualize crime and legal work from three perspectives: crime and the legal labor market; crime, legal work, and illegal wages; and the joint distribution of crime and legal work.

A. Crime and Unemployment

While studies at the aggregate level show some connection between labor market variables and crime, they "fail to show a well-defined, quantifiable linkage" (Freeman 1983, p. 106; see also Freeman 1995). These studies take several forms: comparison of crime rates with labor market variables (such as unemployment or wages) over time, cross-area studies that compare crime and economic characteristics across states or countries, and individual studies that compare crime and work variables across people, sometimes over time. For example, time-series data allow us to examine the effects of the business cycle on crime and to estimate what might happen to crime if overall job prospects or wages improved or worsened.[7] Freeman (1983) reviewed ten time-series studies and found crime-labor market linkages in nine. That is, changes in labor market characteristics—employment and unemployment rates, wages for various groups in the workforce, the distribution of jobs by skill level—influenced changes in the crime rate. Improving work prospects were associated with declining crime rates.

However, in the three studies that also included deterrence vari-

[7] Time-series data suffer from a number of problems that make social scientists leery of their results. For example, variables tend to move together over time, providing little independent variation from which to infer relations. Also, the unexplained part of the dependent variable is correlated from one year to the next.

ables, the net effects of labor market variables were weaker than the legal sanction variables. These studies showed a positive association between the certainty of arrest and crime rates. When labor market variables were added to these models, the effects of the legal sanction variables were greater than the effects of the labor market characteristics. Freeman (1983) also reviewed fifteen cross-sectional studies and again found weak links using income variables but more positive effects when deterrence variables were included. However, the deterrence studies focused more intensively on legal sanctions and the expected costs of crime and rarely analyzed the anticipated net returns from crime. This imbalance in models may have produced (artifactually) stronger deterrence effects compared to market incentives (Viscusi 1986b).

Analyses with data from the 1980s suggest a clearer positive association between crime and unemployment at the aggregate level. One reason for this may be the declining economic (wage) position of unskilled men (and increasingly, women) throughout the 1980s (Blackburn, Bloom, and Freeman 1990; Moss and Tilly 1991; Corcoran and Parrott 1992). These recent macro-level studies tend to locate unemployment as a cause of crime in a specific causal sequence. Reviewing sixty-three studies, Chiricos (1987) reported a positive relationship between unemployment and property crime. Using time-series models in which unemployment is lagged and therefore presumably antecedent in the causal sequence leading to crime, both Cantor and Land (1985) in the United States and Reilly and Witt (1996) in the United Kingdom reported a positive effect of unemployment on crime. Land, McCall, and Cohen (1990) extended this finding by showing that this relationship is stronger at the intracity level compared to intercity or national comparisons. The Land et al. (1990) study also reduced the persistent and extreme collinearity in aggregate measures of crime and unemployment.

Individual-level studies suggest that relationships between crime and unemployment differ when viewed concurrently at specific times or in sequence over time. Both the contemporaneous and longitudinal behaviors also may be spuriously related to disadvantages in social and developmental contexts. In several studies, adult crime and unemployment are linked (in a nonspurious relationship) from parental behavior problems through childhood behavior problems to diminished adult employment prospects and involvement in crime (see, e.g., Hagan 1993a). Unlike the macro-level studies, in which changes in aggregate unemployment rates precede increases in crime rates, these individual level studies posit a causal sequence in which crime precedes unemployment in a sequence of developmental stages. However, when the time units are smaller, it is unclear whether crime or unemployment is the dominant social role and what are the (nonspurious) proximal causes of each behavior. These studies generally lack information on the closely timed sequences of unemployment and crime. Also, as with most literatures, there are potentially confounding artifacts of measurement and study design that must be sorted out.

Research in the United States suggests that there are both contemporaneous and reciprocal effects between unemployment and crime. Good, Pirog-Good, and Sickles (1986) observed employment and arrest records monthly for 300 youths aged thirteen to eighteen in a crime prevention program in inner-city Philadelphia. They reported a contemporaneous relationship between crime and employment in the expected (negative) direction, where "employability" had a substantial deterrent effect on crime. But the contemporaneous effects of crime on employment were weaker. Put another way, prior criminal record reduced employability, leading in turn to higher rates of crime.

Using four-wave panel data and a 1945 Philadelphia birth cohort, Thornberry and Christenson (1984) obtained much the same result. Unemployment had significant instantaneous effects on crime, and crime had significant and primarily lagged effects on unemployment. They also found that social class mediated these effects both longitudinally and cross-sectionally: the relationships were strongest for African American youths and youths from blue-collar backgrounds. Witte and Tauchen (1994) also used this birth cohort to estimate the effects of wages and employment on crime using deterrence variables that are dependent on the individual's level of criminal activity and neighborhood.[8] Employment (but not wages), school attendance (but not educational attainment), and increased arrest probabilities exert significant negative effects on crime.

Sampson and Laub (1993) reanalyzed data from Glueck and Glueck's *Unraveling Juvenile Delinquency* (1950), a longitudinal study of 500 delinquents and 500 carefully matched controls, and later follow-ups (1968). The delinquent sample was constructed in 1939 and

---

[8] According to Witte and Tauchen (1994), individuals face a deterrence "schedule" or function that relates levels of criminal activity to a probability of arrest. They assume that there are exogenous shifts in the schedule because of differences in police policies or budgets, or changes in the legal code. They also assume that crime and work are not independent and frequently overlap (i.e., they are not substitute uses of time).

consisted of white males ages ten to seventeen from several Boston neighborhoods and who had been committed to one of two state juvenile correctional institutions. The controls were recruited from the Boston public schools. Sampson and Laub (1993) found consistent (negative) effects of job stability during early adult years (seventeen to twenty-five) on annual adult arrest rates for several crime types, after controlling for juvenile crime rates. Like several other studies, Sampson and Laub claim that "job stability is central in explaining adult desistance from crime" (1993, p. 162). Juvenile incarceration time not only had no significant effect on crime rates as an adult, but its stigmatizing effects may "mortgage" (p. 165) opportunities for and prospects for stable employment in adult life (p. 168). During middle adult years, job stability during ages twenty-five to thirty-two had a significant negative effect on crime participation during later (thirty-two to forty-five) adult years, and no other variable had a larger coefficient.

The effects of employment stigmatization from arrest differ for young persons in the "spot" versus career labor markets. Bushway (1996) analyzed National Youth Survey data, a longitudinal study with a representative sample of 1,725 adolescents who were eleven to seventeen years of age in 1976 (Elliott, Huizinga, and Menard 1989). Eight subsequent waves provided detailed histories of work and both self-reported and official crime. Within three years of an arrest, respondents who were arrested worked seven weeks less and earned $92 per week less than would otherwise be expected without an arrest (Bushway 1996, p. 35). Arrest, regardless how minor the offense, had adverse impacts on job stability and earnings, after controlling for individual differences in criminality, even while criminality by itself had no effect on earnings (Bushway 1996, p. 59). But there also is an interaction with age producing a paradoxical effect: persons below twenty-two years of age earn more if arrested. These results are consistent with other analyses based on data with samples of British youths (Nagin and Waldfogel 1995). Evidently, the short-term effects of arrest redirect youths from long-term or career tracks to spot or secondary labor markets where earnings are higher in the short run but have limited wage growth over subsequent life stages. One important limitation of this analysis is the exclusion of African Americans from the sample, citing concerns by Weis (1986) "about the consistency of self-reported arrest data for African Americans" (Bushway 1996, p. 72).

For this essay, we reanalyzed the National Longitudinal Survey of Youth (NLSY) to assess the effects of crime and legal work in late adolescence on later work experience and incarceration. The NLSY is a panel study of (n = 5,332) randomly selected youths beginning in 1979, with oversamples of minority and poor youths. Comparisons by Bushway (1996) of the NLSY and NYS samples showed nearly identical annual earnings from legal work in 1980 ($7,300) and work participation (1,480 hours) during the survey year. Unlike the NYS, the NLSY affords estimates of illegal income. We found the predicted positive association between crime and unemployment in the 1980 waves. Work and incarceration outcomes in 1983, 1986, and 1989 were then estimated from the cumulative effects of incarceration, crime, and work in the preceding intervals. Controls for demographic and human capital variables at 1979 were included in each model. Crime measures were available only for the 1979 wave, and the proportion of income from illegal sources was computed. In each wave, incarceration was a dichotomous measure based on whether the interview took place in a jail (or prison). Human capital variables included school participation, grade, weeks worked, and test scores from the Armed Forces Qualifications Test (AFQT) (O'Neill 1990).

Table 1 shows that the effects of involvement in crime, detachment from legal work, and human capital in 1979 on future incarceration were stable and consistent over the successive waves. The percentage of income from illegal sources significantly contributes to the probability of incarceration in later years. The higher the pay from crime (relative to legal sources) in 1980, the greater the likelihood of being incarcerated in later years. Analyzing data only for those respondents with any illegal income in 1980, Freeman (1994, fig. 4) obtained much the same result. The increase in the coefficient for illegal income in both these analyses suggests an elasticity of relative rewards from crime, a function of the decline of legitimate wages for youths over this period (see also Grogger 1994, 1998).

Next, we estimated models for two employment outcomes in each of the three time periods: weeks worked during the year and legal income.[9] The effects of incarceration were estimated using measures of the number of years of incarceration from 1980 to 1982. Adolescent involvement in crime and illegal wages in 1980 also were included. Table 2 shows the t-values for each parameter for each outcome by period. Over the three waves, incarceration produced a significant negative effect on each work outcome, even after adjusting for the

---

[9] We also estimated a model for occupational status. The results were nearly identical with those of the wage model and are not shown. Results are available from the authors.

TABLE 1

Linear Probability Estimates of Effects of Illegal Income in 1979 on Later Incarceration (Unstandardized Coefficient, t)

	Jail in 1980		Jail in 1983		Jail in 1986		Jail in 1989	
	b	t	b	t	b	t	b	t
% income from crime 1979	.154	4.96***	.046	2.63**	.074	3.86***	.087	4.27***
Total crimes 1979	.001	7.53***	.0002	3.61***	.0002	3.91***	.001	8.31***
Weeks worked 1979	-.0004	-2.26*	-.0001	-1.54	-.0003	-2.80**	-.0002	-2.05*
Age 1979	-.002	-1.21	-.002	-1.36	-.002	1.05	.001	.87
Grade 1979	-.006	-3.47***	-.001	-0.67	.001	1.11	-.001	-.54
AFQT	-.001	-5.16***	-.0002	-2.31*	-.0004	-3.35***	-.0003	-2.73**
Race (nonwhite)	.067	7.52***	-.028	5.64***	.012	2.18*	.025	4.18***
In school 1980[a]			-.013	-2.49*	-.020	-3.34***	-.012	-1.86
Constant	.190	4.73***	.065	2.71**	.052	1.95	.014	.49
N	4,124		4,031		3,336		3,302	
F	63.22		18.55		17.46		31.19	
$p(F)$	.000		.000		.000		.07	
Adjusted R^2	.096		.034		.038		.068	

[a] Excluded from the 1980 model: respondents were in either school or jail in 1980.

* $p < .05$.

** $p < .01$.

*** $p < .001$.

TABLE 2
OLS Regression of Effects of Incarceration in 1980–82 on Work Outcomes (t-Values)

	1983		1986		1989	
	Legal Income	Weeks Worked	Legal Income	Weeks Worked	Legal Income	Weeks Worked
Years in jail (1980–82)	−4.60***	−7.16***	−4.62***	−8.99***	−2.43***	−12.99***
% income from crime 1979	−.15	−0.08	−.45	−.34	1.66	−.87
Total crimes 1980	.08	−.06	−.69	−.80	.08	−1.25
Weeks worked 1980	19.12***	23.27***	10.87***	12.28***	3.55***	10.47***
Age 1979	11.33***	6.45***	8.98***	4.77***	3.36***	.33
Grade 1979	−3.74***	−4.19***	−.45	−.83	2.75***	.81
AFQT 1980	5.42***	2.43*	8.30***	.96	4.50***	1.80
Race (nonwhite)	−5.24***	−6.58***	−4.04***	−5.89***	−2.28*	−4.20***
Constant	−6.39***	2.07*	−5.47***	−5.38***	−3.61***	10.79***
N	4,031		3,336		3,302	
F	93.35		50.62		54.85	
p(F)	.000		.000		.000	
Adjusted R^2	.171		.118		.128	

* $p < .05$.
** $p < .01$.
*** $p < .001$.

simultaneous effects of race, human capital, and intelligence. Moreover, early incarceration negatively affected later work outcomes independent of the effects of the level of crime activity in 1980. Work is a stable behavior over a ten-year period, with weeks worked in 1980 predicting weeks worked in 1989. Labor force participation and AFQT scores in 1980 were positively associated with work outcomes in the later waves. However, school participation in 1980 was not a consistent predictor of work outcomes in any subsequent period.

These trends suggest that the adverse consequences of incarceration and exclusion from work during adolescence, compounded by human capital advantages or deficits, endured over a ten-year period through middle adult years for both incarceration and employment. Others report similar results. For example, Grogger (1995) also used NLSY data to show that arrests early in adulthood reduced future legal wages in the short term net of either "criminal capital" or human capital variables. However, any disadvantage from arrests in future legal earnings was overtaken by other human capital deficits over a ten-year interval.

Studies with ex-offenders also show the significant effects of unemployment on crime. For example, the TARP (Transitional Aid Research Project) was a randomized experiment that tested the effects of income supports for ex-offenders from Texas and Georgia released from prison in 1976–77 (Berk, Rossi, and Lenihan 1980; Rossi, Berk, and Lenihan 1980). There were no significant effects of income supports on short- or long-term returns to prison in either the Texas (Needels 1993) or Georgia (Needels 1994) samples. However, analyses of the pooled experimental and control samples show that both employment and (legal) earnings have strong significant effects on subsequent crimes following release from prison, even when those wages are sporadic and well below the poverty level. For example, among the Georgia releasees, legal earnings over a ten-year follow-up period have a large and significant effect on criminal desistance but not on the timing (hazard) of return to prison among those who are reincarcerated (Needels 1994). Perhaps most important is the negative effect of crime on earnings: individuals who were not criminally active over the follow-up period earned about 40 percent more than their criminally active counterparts (34 percent). These effects are likely to be conservative estimates, since this population has relatively low human capital, their employment is sporadic and not well paying, and their crime rates were quite high both before and after incarceration.[10]

[10] Witte (1980) obtained similar findings with a cohort of North Carolina prison releasees, even with limited information on employment activities and no data on educa-

European studies complement research in the United States. For example, Albrecht (1984) used aggregate data from (the former West) Germany to show that the offender rate within the unemployed youth population actually declined from 1977–82 while overall unemployment was rising dramatically. Albrecht further disaggregated the phenomenon between short- and long-term unemployed and between short- and long-term juvenile delinquents. While crime rates among the long-term unemployed were unchanged, the crime rates among the short-term unemployed actually fell during this period. Albrecht's findings show the importance of the length of unemployment and the effects of longer-term unemployment on crime motivation and propensity. It may be that as unemployment lengthens, expectations of a return to work diminish, and a decay of prosocial norms ensues without the reinforcing interactions of the workplace.

Farrington et al. (1986) used interview data from the Cambridge Study of Delinquent Development, a longitudinal study of 411 adolescent males, to show that crime rates were higher when subjects were unemployed. However, this relationship was conditional on a number of factors. Crime was more likely only among unemployed youths who held attitudes more favorable to offending; those who generally were law-abiding did not commit crimes during periods of unemployment. The crime-unemployment relationship was stronger among youths with histories of low status jobs. Moreover, only income-generating crimes were more likely during periods of unemployment, but violent crime rates did not change.

Using the concepts of embeddedness and social capital in analyses of the Cambridge data, Hagan (1993a) argues that adult unemployment and criminality are developmental outcomes of adolescent embeddedness among delinquent peers and parental criminality. Hagan states that "parental criminal conviction interacts with early adolescent conviction to produce later adolescent delinquency and adult unemployment above and apart from other factors" (Hagan 1993a, pp. 486–87). Accordingly, youths who are socially embedded during early childhood in social contexts of peer and parent criminality are likely to be isolated in their adult years from legitimate employment opportunities. Like Sampson and Laub (1993), Hagan's analysis is "deracialized" (Lemann 1991) and shows that the processes of social embeddedness

---

tion. Using length of time for releasees to find a job and the wage of the first job, Witte found that employment and earnings suppressed crime rates.

are generic and occur even in the absence of the aggravating effects of concentrated poverty in the contemporary U.S. context.

In a sample of young males from the Netherlands, Huurne (1988) showed that human capital variables further mediated the effects of unemployment: having a high school degree or coming from a higher social class background mitigated the social consequences of unemployment. Ploeg (1991) obtained similar findings among 300 long-term unemployed Dutch men twenty to fifty years of age. Unemployed men who avoided crime prior to unemployment were unlikely to engage in law violations, but former delinquents continued their crimes. Like the Farrington et al. (1986) study, Ploeg concluded that unemployment is iatrogenic with respect to crime by engendering feelings of deprivation and injustice that precede crime.

B. Crime, Work, and Illegal Wages: Market Incentives for Crime

An econometric, rational choice perspective on crime and work suggests that individuals will allocate time to criminal behavior when its returns are higher than from other activities, net of perceived punishment costs and estimates of forgone illegal wages. That is, decisions to engage in crime suggest that offenders find the current net benefits of crime to be positive. Not only do labor market variables account for an individual's assessment, but factors including tastes and tolerances for risk, preferences for work, and time allocation also are part of the decision processes (see, e.g., Katz 1988; Taylor 1990).

One side of this calculus is returns of legal work, both personal (internal) and material. The legitimate earnings opportunities of low-skilled males deteriorated substantially from the mid-1970s through the 1990s (Topel 1993). Real earnings fell sharply for the least educated and for those in the bottom rungs of the earnings distribution. The exact magnitude of the decline in earnings depends on the specific measure of earnings chosen, the deflator, years picked, the age and skill group chosen, and so on, but drops on the order of 20 to 30 percent that accelerated in the 1990s are a reasonable estimate (Mishel and Bernstein 1994). Despite the putative job-creating effects of reduced pay, there was no offsetting improvement in hours worked or employment/population rates for the less skilled (see, e.g., table 2 above). To the contrary, hours worked over the year fell among those in the bottom rungs of the wage distribution (Juhn, Murphy, and Topel 1991); and employment-population rates for this group worsened in the 1970s (though not in the 1980s [Blackburn, Bloom, and Freeman 1990]). The implication is that demand for less skilled male labor plummeted, as did its attractiveness for putative workers. Indeed, consigned to a secondary labor market, workers find these jobs readily available, but they generally pay low wages and have no permanence or career opportunities associated with them.

On the other side of the incentive equation are criminal earnings. However, few studies have measured illegal wages either cross-sectionally or examined changes in criminal earnings over time, and fewer have studied the intangible "tastes" and preferences that contribute to decisions to commit crime or work legally. There are significant obstacles to collecting accurate illegal wage data, such as valuations of non-cash exchanges, including discounts in fencing stolen goods. Moreover, since reliable official data (e.g., social security records) on illegal wages obviously are unavailable, the few efforts in this area rely on self-reports of crime frequencies and crime incomes. We summarize them in table 3 and review them below.

1. *Income from All Crimes.*   Wilson and Abrahamse (1992) estimated illegal wages as the returns from an "average" offense among prison inmates. They used National Crime Victimization Survey (NCVS) data on average losses by victims to estimate the earnings from crime among prison inmates in three states (see Chaiken and Chaiken [1982] for details on the samples).[11] To compute a daily wage from crime, they estimated days free on the street per year after subtracting incarceration time and extrapolated to a full "work" year. Legal earnings were estimated at $5.78 per hour, after discounting by 20 percent to reflect taxation. Summing across eight crime categories, they reported annualized crime incomes of $2,368 (in 1988 dollars) for burglars and thieves with mid-level offending rates. Drug selling generated the highest returns ($1,014 per year), and business robberies the lowest ($29). For high-rate burglars and thieves, crime incomes were $5,711. Wilson and Abrahamse claim that legal work would actually have paid more than crime for all but one type of offender: auto thieves. For high-rate offenders, crime incomes exceeded work incomes for all crime types. For reasons not stated by the authors, drug incomes (the most lucrative crime category) were omitted in the crime-work wage comparisons. Overall, the analyses by Wilson and Abrahamse (1992) show that self-reported crime incomes are consistently

---

[11] Finding no published estimates of losses from forgery and theft, Wilson and Abrahamse "guessed" (1992, p. 364).

TABLE 3
Illegal Wage Estimates

Study	Data	Year	Annualized Crime Income ($)	
Wilson and Abrahamse (1992)	NCVS	1988	2,368	(mid-rate burglars)
			5,711	(high-rate burglars)
Freeman (1991)	Three cities	1980	1,807	(active offenders)
Freeman (1992)	Boston	1989	3,008	(active offenders)
			752	(infrequent offenders)
			5,376	(high-rate offenders)
Freeman (1991)	Three State Prison Inmate Survey	1986	24,775	(prison inmates)
Viscusi (1986)	Three cities	1989 (adjusted)	2,423	(underreported by .33)
Reuter, MacCoun, and Murphy (1990)	Washington, D.C.	1988	25,000	($30 per hour)
Fagan (1992b)	Two New York City areas	1987–89	6,000	(infrequent drug sellers)
			27,000	(frequent drug sellers)
Hagedorn (1994a)[a]	Milwaukee	1987–91	12,000	(29%)
			20,000	(20%)
			36,000	(25%)
Huff (1996)	Five cities	1990–91	30/hour	(reservation wage)
Grogger (1995)	NLSY	1979	11,476	(crime income as % of total income)

[a] Drug sellers only.

low compared to estimated legal work incomes across all crime types and for both mid- and high-rate offenders.

Estimates of crime incomes in general adolescent populations were developed by Freeman (1992). A 1989 survey of Boston youths showed self-reported annual earnings that ranged from $752 for infrequent offenders to $5,376 for youths committing crime at least once a week. Hourly rates varied from $9.75 for frequent offenders to $88 for infrequent offenders in the Boston Youth Survey, suggesting a diminishing return from criminal activity. Average hourly wages from crime were $19, and estimated hourly drug wages ranged from $13 to $21. All these estimates, including the lowest rate of $9.75 from crime, exceed the average legal wage of $7.50 that these young men reported and substantially exceeded their after-tax take-home pay of $5.60 per hour. Freeman summarizes by stating that the lowest hourly pay rate from crime of $9.75 "is seventy-three percent greater than take-home pay from a legitimate job, whereas the $19/hour average from crime is over three times the take-home pay" (Freeman 1992, p. 230).

In a survey of adolescents in three cities (Freeman and Holzer 1986; Viscusi 1986b), crime incomes were $1,607 in 1980 dollars or $2,423 in 1989 dollars. However, Viscusi (1986a) adjusted these figures by a factor of three for likely underreporting. Using this revised income estimate, crime incomes accounted for one-fourth of the total income earned by the young men in the sample. Viscusi's model using the three-city sample also included a crime-versus-legal income variable. He compared illegal incomes among those who expected to earn such incomes, with incomes of respondents with low expected illegal income. He found significant upward positive effects of expected illegal wages on crime incomes, and the effects of these variables in regression equations on crime incomes were roughly twice as large as the influences on the actual crime participation rate. Viscusi (1986b) also compared the differences in legal and illegal incomes as a function of whether the respondent was working or in school. About one in five employed youths and one in eight students committed crimes, but their illegal incomes on average were only a fraction of their total incomes. Because of the skew in crime incomes, crime income was a substantial income supplement for many working youths. Among the NOJOBSCHOOL group, incomes were evenly divided between legal and illegal sources, but only one-half of this group participated in crime in the study year.

Once again, those participating in crime earned substantially more from crime than from other sources. The results suggest that being in school or holding a job exerted significant downward pressure on crime participation, but only for crimes that had relatively low payoffs. Higher-income crimes such as drug dealing provided stronger economic incentives than the labor market could bear. Yet the mixing of crime and work appears to be a powerful trend. Legal incomes would have to sharply exceed illegal incomes to influence work decisions: Viscusi claims that equalizing legal and illegal wages would deter only one in six youths who participated in crime (1986a, p. 343).

Two studies measured illegal incomes using the NLSY. Although an illegal income amount was not reported, each study developed an estimate of illegal wages by multiplying respondents' reports of what fraction of their 1979 income came from crime by their total income estimate for that year.[12] According to Grogger (1994, 1995, 1998), crime income in 1979 was reported by 274 of the 1,134 respondents in the analysis (24.1 percent); mean income for this group was $1,187, an estimate comparable to Freeman's (1991) estimate of $1,607 for inner-city youths in Boston. Grogger also analyzed the NLSY data to determine the effects of legal wages on crime participation among males.[13] Criminal participants worked fewer hours legally than nonparticipants and earned a lower wage. Hourly market (legal) wages were about 8 percent higher for respondents with no crime income ($4.60) compared to those with criminal income ($4.26).

Grogger (1998) also estimated a model of legal income using four predictors: market human capital, criminal human capital,[14] nonlabor income, and abilities (the AFQT). Wages increase predictably with skill, experience, and ability and decline for those with probation sentences within one year of interview (about 15 percent lower in the following year but returning to prearrest trajectories after two years). Models estimated for crime income show that criminal human capital had predictably strong, positive effects. Crime incomes increased with

[12] Response categories for the percentage of income from crime were set in fourths, ranging from "none," to "about one-fourth," "about one-half," "about three-fourths," to "almost all."

[13] Women were excluded from the analyses because of their lower crime participation rates. Males in school or the military were excluded to limit the sample to males for whom the primary alternative uses of time would be market work or crime. Males in jail from 1979 to 1981 (the first three years of the panel) were excluded since they were censored from legal work opportunities.

[14] Criminal human capital was an index of criminal productivity and included prior criminal arrests, prior criminal convictions, family members with criminal records or convictions, and jail sentences during the ten-year analysis interval.

lower market (legal) wages, suggesting a rational allocation of time toward the higher income-producing activity. This finding is confirmed
in Grogger's third model, an equation for market labor participation.
The effect of legal wages on market hours is large: a 10 percent increase in wages leads to an increase in labor supply of sixty-seven
hours, the equivalent of nearly two full work weeks (seventy-five
hours). And, arrests and convictions had significant negative effects on
market participation, as did criminal human capital. Finally, for each
hour of crime, market labor supply appears to decline by about 1.4
hours.

We also analyzed illegal income using the NLSY 1979 and 1980
waves and detailed measures of the frequency of eleven income-producing crimes. In linear probability (regression) models of gross illegal
income, little specialization was evident. Coefficients were significant
for five crime categories: drug sales (two types), robbery, fraud, fencing, and running numbers (gambling assistance). Incomes from marijuana and "hard drug" sales had the highest coefficients by a factor of
two compared to the next strongest predictors. But legal labor force
participation also had a significant positive association with illegal income. Consistent with Fagan's (1992a, 1992b) study of drug sellers,
involvement in multiple social networks from both work and deviant
activities seems to expand opportunities for sale of illegal goods and
services.

These studies suggest that young persons, especially males, appear
to be particularly sensitive in their time allocation decisions to market
incentives: legal work and criminal participation both are responsive to
legal wages and criminal returns in the preceding year. That is, young
males respond quite rationally to the economic returns to crime.
Moreover, illegal wages appear to be quite elastic. Grogger (1998) concludes that a 10 percent increase in wages would reduce total criminal
hours in the population by about 1.4 percent, with most of the change
due to the overall participation rate but some also to the number of
hours allocated by legally working men to crime.

While Grogger's analysis focused on individuals, Gould, Weinberg,
and Mustard (1998) have obtained strong results using aggregate data
from 352 counties over a seventeen-year period (1979–95). Using
crime data from the Uniform Crime Reports and the Current Population Survey, they used retail wages to estimate the returns of legal
work. The results showed the inverse relationship of wages with both
property and violent crime rates. The effect is stronger for property

crimes: wage declines over the period contributed to a 13.5 percent increase in burglary, a 7.1 percent increase in larceny, a 9.2 percent increase in aggravated assault, and an 18 percent increase in robbery. Three other findings in the Gould, Weinberg, and Mustard analysis are noteworthy. First, the results are specific to young, unskilled men, the population group most likely to commit these offenses. Second, their analysis showed that several measures of unemployment were small contributors to crime increases, with predicted increases ranging from 1 to 2 percent, far lower than the predicted increases based on market wages. Third, wage and unemployment rates had larger effects on property crimes than on murder and rape. If market wages are the opportunity costs of crime, then raising these costs may predict declines in the crime rate over relatively short periods of time.

2. *Income from Drug Dealing.*   Estimates of drug dealing income deserve special attention for two reasons. First, drug incomes usually are among the highest income-producing criminal occupations and show more pronounced effects of the returns from illegal work. Second, the expansion of street-level drug markets in the past decade has provided broader opportunities for illegal work during a time of declining legal wages and work opportunities (Johnson et al. 1990).

A survey of 186 convicted drug dealers in Washington, D.C., showed that "drug dealing is much more profitable on an hourly basis than are legitimate jobs available to the same persons" (Reuter, Mac-Coun, and Murphy 1990, p. viii). The dealers reported net (mean) monthly income of $1,799 from drugs and $215 from other crimes, which projects to an annual crime income of $25,000, and an implied hourly rate of $30 (see also MacCoun and Reuter 1992).[15] Freeman (1992) points out that even if these men had worked full-time for a full year, their illegal pay exceeded $19 per hour. These figures compare poorly with mean legal wages of $1,046 per month or median legal monthly earnings of $715 for the 75 percent who reported such income. Drug income rates were higher and more skewed for younger respondents aged eighteen to twenty-four. Moreover, drug incomes were far greater than other crime income sources and, unlike the general crime incomes reported by the Boston general adolescent population, did not diminish with frequency.

Drug incomes also exceeded legal (work) incomes by a wide margin

---

[15] Because the income distributions were highly skewed, Reuter, MacCoun, and Murphy also report median net earnings of $721 per month from drug sales, but $2,000 per month among the 37 percent who reported selling drugs on a daily basis.

in a recent study of 1,003 drug users and dealers in two northern Manhattan neighborhoods in New York City (Fagan 1992a, 1994). Fagan divided the sample into nonsellers (fewer than two days per month selling), independent sellers, and sellers who worked in organizations or crews. More than half the males and one-third of the females were involved in either independent or organized drug selling during the three-year period from 1986 to 1988. Monthly drug incomes ranged from $2,000 for nonsellers to $4,800 for group sellers. (Nonsellers were able to produce drug incomes through barter or informal exchanges of goods and services or through incidental or infrequent sales.) After adjusting for average drug expenses of $1,500 per month, net annual drug incomes ranged from $6,000 to $27,600. Over one-fourth of the sellers also had legal incomes, ranging from $150 to $750 per month. These estimates included off-book work and income from a variety of transfer payments and income supports. The percent of total income from legal, taxed wages ranged from 7 to 33 percent. Accordingly, like the Washington, D.C., sample of male dealers, legal work and crime were combined by many drug sellers in these two neighborhoods. Fagan (1992a, p. 121, n. 18) notes that there remain logical incentives for joint participation in legal work even while earning far higher incomes from drug sales: expanding networks of contacts, expectations of drug selling as a temporary occupation, and an escape route should legal or social pressures push sellers out of the business.

Fagan (1992a) also tested whether illegal incomes were substitutes for legal work and whether "tastes," especially drug consumption, accounted for illegal work. The effects varied by neighborhood. Legal work exerted a significant downward effect on total income in Washington Heights, a vigorous drug market, suggesting that legal work may actually pose an opportunity cost relative to crime incomes. He found no significant effect for human capital on illegal wages and concluded that the drug sellers and users were unlikely to hold legal jobs at unskilled labor wages. But models of legal work suggested that drug consumption (a proxy for taste/preference variables) did exert significant downward pressures on labor market participation. Nevertheless, legal workers did have higher education levels, and the two models together indicate that drug selling was a vocation for those who were detached from legal work and unlikely to do well in that context.

Gang members in Milwaukee reported a wide range of drug incomes (Hagedorn 1994a). Three in four of the 236 "founding members" of fourteen male gangs (72 percent) had sold cocaine between 1987 and 1991. Of the ninety gang members interviewed, seventy-three were active drug sellers between 1987 and 1991. About one in four (28.7 percent) claimed they made no more money from drug selling than they could have made from legal work at the going rates for unskilled labor (about $6 per hour). One in five (20.7 percent) earned the equivalent of $7–$12 per hour, and one in four (28.7 percent) reported drug incomes in the range of $13–$25 per hour, or $2,000–$4,000 per month. Few (three of the seventy-three sellers) reported "crazy money" (more than $10,000 per month) at any time in their drug-selling careers (Hagedorn 1994a, p. 202). Mean monthly drug sale income was $2,400, or about $15 per hour, compared to legal monthly incomes of $677.[16]

The fungibility of legal and illegal sources of income was examined by Huff (1996) in surveys of matched samples of gang and nongang youths in four cities. Respondents were asked about their "reservation wage," the net income at which they would forgo illegal wages "to go to work legally." Nearly all illegal income, for both gang members and neighborhood case controls, came from drug selling. Gang members reported reservation wages comparable to the wage thresholds reported by case controls, who were "at risk" youths from the same neighborhoods and demographic groups: $30 per hour, the same wage levels earned by drug sellers in Washington, D.C., in the Reuter, Mac-Coun, and Murphy (1990) study.

Most of these studies depend on self-reports of illegal incomes. Accordingly, the validity and reliability of self-reports are crucial factors in estimating returns from crime. While Wilson and Abrahamse (1992) claim strong validity for self-reported crime incomes, both Viscusi and Freeman claim that crime rates and crime incomes are conservative estimates[17] since criminal behavior is seriously underreported, especially for African American inner-city youths (Hindelang, Hirschi, and Weis 1981). Thompson and Cataldo (1986) directly question the veridicality of self-reports in their criticism of Viscusi's (1986a) analysis. What is important for purposes of this essay is the consistency observed in the

---

[16] To better illustrate the higher expected returns from drug selling, Hagedorn (1994a, pp. 202–3, table 2) reports: "The *maximum* amount of money earned monthly by any gang member for legal income was $2,400, the *mean* for gang drug sales" (emphasis in original).

[17] Wilson and Abrahamse (1992) draw on Chaiken and Chaiken's (1982) analyses to suggest that self-reports and official records are stable within a factor of 1.5 (Wilson and Abrahamse 1992, p. 361).

effects of incarceration and early criminal involvement on later crime, work, and incarceration, regardless of whether crime and income are measured through official records or self-reports.

Research on returns from illegal work suggests the importance of net returns and illegal market incentives in explaining the relationship between crime and unemployment. Crime, especially drug selling, provides economic incentives for young inner-city males that raise income prospects in ways that legal markets cannot. Freeman, Fagan, and Viscusi found that those with higher illegal incomes did not possess characteristics conducive to success in legal labor markets. They either were detached from legal work or had been excluded as a result of the accumulation of legal sanctions. Moreover, as Hagan (1993*a*) also found, their greater involvement with gangs, organized drug selling, and other illegal activities suggests their social embeddedness in contexts that close them off from conventional opportunities. In samples of both drug dealers and general adolescent populations, illegal and total incomes were highest among those who were most active criminally, and these differed systematically from others with far lower criminal involvement.

C. Risk and Discounted Returns from Crime

The risk and extent of penalties is the third dimension of an economic calculus of crime. The returns from crime are in part a function of the likelihood of crime success or avoidance of punishment. Not only are crime returns forgone if one is incarcerated, but opportunities for legal earnings—however inferior they may be—also are lost. Moreover, if one is incarcerated, earnings on release will be reduced (Freeman 1992). Depending on the community, there also may be social costs from punishment through stigma and expulsion from socially rewarding networks. Overall, then, assuming that marginal offenders are risk averse, punishment creates a compensating differential premium for crime. In other words, punishment risk discounts the returns from crime.

How real is this discount? Consider the following example. Since the probability of incarceration increased in the 1980s, it is possible that the real rewards of crime actually fell, despite the fall in legitimate earnings for young men during the decade.[18] The magnitude of the

---

[18] The earnings of African American young males, who make up the majority of the prison population in the most urbanized states, fell far more through the 1980s compared with other demographic groups (Moss and Tilly 1991; Wilson 1996). Throughout

worsened job market opportunities for less skilled young men was sufficiently large—drops in real earnings of 20–30 percent, accelerating in the 1990s (Mishel and Bernstein 1994)—to have at least potentially raised their propensity to choose crime.[19] We then weigh the reduced income probabilities against punishment risk. Using estimates from Langan (1994), we assume that the probability of imprisonment for robbery rose from 1974 to 1986 by 9.1 percent, and median time served was fifteen months. This increase in incarceration would cut an offender's legitimate earnings by about 11 percent (1.25 years $\times$ .091) during this time. This falls well short of the 30 percent lower return from legitimate work compared to crime.[20] The increased rate of incarceration should, net of other factors, discount the returns from crime (Freeman 1996b). But the decline in legitimate earnings neutralized the costs of punishment. In the short run, there is no comparative economic advantage from avoiding punishment, even in the face of increasing punishment risk.[21]

But what about the nonmonetary costs of punishment, such as harsh conditions, physical and sexual victimization, and social stigma on release? If incarceration carries with it substantial nonpecuniary costs, these increased costs might still have deterred many marginal offenders away from income-producing crimes. As we show below, the social stigma from incarceration has weakened greatly as the proportion of the population incarcerated increases. Nagin (1998) suggests that fear of stigmatization, which is the foundation of the deterrent effect, may be eroded by the escalating, very high incarceration rates of the past twenty years. The increase in the prison population will increase the percentage of the population with a prison record, making prison records commonplace and socially unexceptional (Nagin 1998, p. 73). This saturation is even greater when we consider the social and spatial concentration of prison records among nonwhite young males in cities.

Moreover, the heavy traffic between street and prison in high-crime

---

the 1980s, the position of these young men in the earnings distribution also fell as overall income inequality skyrocketed (Freeman 1996a).

[19] The exact magnitude of the decline in real/relative earnings depends on the specific measure of earnings chosen, the deflator, years picked, the age and skill group chosen, etc., but it is invariably large.

[20] Langan (1994) calculated increases of 5.8 percent for burglary, 10.0 percent for larceny, and by over 20 percent for drugs. These are conservative estimates given punishment trends in the second half of the decade (Cohen and Canela-Cacho 1994; Tonry 1995; Blumstein and Beck 1999). Cohen and Canela-Cacho report that between 1975 and 1989, expected prison time for a violent crime nearly tripled.

[21] A more detailed analysis would examine these tradeoffs over a work career.

neighborhoods spreads and popularizes prison culture, even making it perhaps a passage into adulthood, as well as an expected event of adolescence or early adulthood. The "prisonization of the streets" also discounts or mythologizes the harsh physical conditions of prison, further discounting punishment costs for young men in the population groups most likely to be incarcerated (see, e.g., Anderson 1997; Wilkinson and Fagan 1996).

There also is a contagious effect of involvement in illegal work that reduces social stigma. Crime activity has external effects on the level of crime activity of people in the same (peer) social networks: the crime activity of one person influences the preferences toward crime of others in the same age stratum in the same community (Glaeser, Sacerdote, and Scheinkman 1996). Also, increases in overall crime rates in a community can affect decisions to engage in crime by reducing the likelihood of apprehension for each individual (Sah 1991). Accordingly, if the psychic costs of crime are lower when others are committing more crimes, the crime decision of one person can affect crime involvement among others (Gould, Weinberg, and Mustard 1998).

Perceptions of illegal and legal earning potentials also weaken evaluations of the costs of punishment. Freeman (1996b) reported results from surveys with inner-city youths in Boston on perceived criminal and legitimate earnings and employment opportunities at the outset of the 1980s and at the end of the decade. In 1980, the NBER Inner-City Youth Survey asked youths in Boston, Chicago, and Philadelphia whether they thought they could make more "on the street" than in a legitimate job. It also asked them about their perceptions of the availability of criminal opportunities. The 1989 Boston Youth Survey, conducted at the peak of the booming "Massachusetts Miracle" job market, asked the same questions. Between these dates, the proportion of youths who reported that they could earn more on the street went up, from 31 percent in the three cities and 41 percent in Boston in 1980 to 63 percent in Boston in 1989. Similarly, the proportion who said they had "chances to make illegal income several times a day" roughly doubled over the period, to reach nearly 50 percent in 1989 (Freeman 1992). Huff (1996) reports a reservation wage of $30 per hour to abandon illegal work, an unrealistically high rate but indicative of the perceived disparity among inner-city adolescents between legal and illegal incomes.

In sum, even when incarceration costs are factored in, the hourly rewards from crime seem to exceed legal wages for unskilled young men subject to many of the risk factors for crime and incarceration. And the hourly returns from crime rose at a faster rate through the 1980s—while incarceration rates spiked—than did legal wages. Wages count heavily in the decision to commit crimes or work legally. And, as we show later on, the disparity between legal and illegal wages is widened even more by increasing social rewards from crime.

D. "Doubling Up" in Crime and Work

Whether individuals "double up" in legal and illegal work addresses several important issues. First, social embedment perspectives (Hagan 1993a) suggest that many youths are excluded from legal work as a result of their earlier involvement in crime and deviant social networks. But active shifting between work and crime occupations suggests greater human agency and job mobility that prior research on crime and work had assumed. Second, the decisions to maximize incomes by crossing legal boundaries suggest opportunities for interventions focused on investments in job skills and wages that could increase legal occupational status if suitable jobs were available. Investments in both skills development and job creation may bear on decisions to straddle the two worlds of work. Third, a high rate of doubling up suggests that an optimizing rather than satisficing model of decision making may be operating. Satisficing models (see, e.g., Cornish and Clarke 1986, pp. 181–82) suggest that individuals will select from among the first few alternatives rather than consider a longer set, one of which might provide greater returns. Satisficing may also entail nonmaterial returns, such as excitement or status (Katz 1988). But optimization suggests that their returns are maximized by carefully juggling and analyzing among alternatives. Unfortunately, doubling up has been a relatively neglected question in research on crime and unemployment. We briefly review some of the findings.

Doubling up appears to be quite common among active offenders, including drug sellers earning relatively high illegal incomes. Both studies of drug dealers discussed earlier suggest doubling up. More than one-fourth of the dealers in the Fagan (1992a) and Reuter, Mac-Coun, and Murphy (1990) studies were involved in work and crime. Illegal incomes were the same regardless of whether these people were also working legally. Among the general population studies, Viscusi (1986b) reported that about one in five employed youths committed crimes, one in eight students reported crime in the past year, and one-half of the NOJOBSCHOOL group committed crimes. Hagedorn

(1994*a*) reported that 75 percent of active gang drug sellers working in 1992 at the time of interview had sold drugs within the previous five years. Work was sporadic, however: respondents said they had worked only fourteen months in the past thirty-six in legal jobs, and only 25 percent worked in legal jobs more than twenty-four of the thirty-six months before the interview. Hagedorn (1994*b*) suggested that movement between legal and illegal work was common, a decision reflecting a combination of market (legal and illegal) conditions and other legal and social pressures.[22]

Using the NLSY, we determined overlaps between crime and work. In 1980, the year when detailed crime information was available in the NLSY, 56.6 percent of those working reported any crime, and 20.5 percent participated in at least one income-producing crime.[23] Conversely, 74.4 percent of those involved in crime also worked, but only 33.8 percent of people reporting income-producing crimes also worked.[24] In fact, the percent working in 1980 in the NLSY did not vary significantly for those involved in any crime or in income-producing crimes (Freeman 1996*b*). The relatively high returns from drug selling would predict lower rates of doubling up, since drug sellers might be unwilling to allocate their time to legal work with its lower returns. But when drug selling is examined separately, there is little difference in employment rates between those who did and did not sell drugs: about 4 percent of those working sold drugs, and 4.8 percent of those not working sold drugs. Looking in reverse, more than two in three (69.2 percent) of the drug sellers reported also working legally in the survey year. This is a far higher figure than the rates reported by Reuter, MacCoun, and Murphy (1990) and Fagan (1992*a*, 1994). Only for those who ended up the following year in jail was there a substantial difference in employment rates (Freeman 1996*b*). Without detailed information on drug incomes, the motivations for working while selling drugs are hard to explain.

Doubling up and job switching contradict the perspective of the "formidable wall" that underlies much of the literature on crime and unemployment. It suggests an active process of optimization, in which

[22] As pointed out by Hagedorn (1994*a*, p. 205), doubling up reflects the confusion of streetcorner lives depicted by Liebow (1967) in an earlier era in Talley's Corner: "Traffic is heavy in all directions" (p. 219).
[23] Robbery, sale of cocaine or heroin, sale of marijuana, grand theft, petty theft, shoplifting, frauds and "cons," aid to gambling activities, fencing, burglaries, auto theft.
[24] Using self-reports of any income from crime in the NLSY, Grogger (1995) estimated the "doubling up" rate at 25.6 percent.

offenders take advantage of economic opportunities that present themselves. Doubling up also reflects the coexistence of conventional and deviant values within individuals, a contradiction noted in delinquency research for decades (see, e.g., Cohen 1955; Matza 1964; Sullivan 1989; and Fagan 1990) and articulated in detail by Anderson (1998) as an adaptive strategy necessary for status and survival. Hagedorn (1994*a*) notes that gang members involved in drug selling had long-term attachments to women and most were "unhappily" (p. 215) enduring low-status, low-wage jobs that brought daily slights and personal humiliations. While offenders with criminal histories may face barriers to legal work, those without such barriers face fewer obstacles in "doubling up." Taking a second job is quite common in the United States today, in work as diverse as skilled labor or door-to-door franchise sales. Highly decentralized drug markets offer the chance to earn income through occasional work at hourly rates that are widely perceived to be higher than conventional second jobs. There are few commitments of time and capital, although the risks of injury and incarceration are not trivial.

Doubling up may represent not so much a problem of the rejection of normative codes and behaviors, but of the closeness of the legal and illegal markets in many communities. Both historical and contemporary studies of immigrant and minority communities suggest that at both the normative and behavioral levels, the distinction between legal and illegal activities is more of a continuum than a sharp, distinct separation (see, e.g., Chin [1995] on Chinese gangs, and Sassen-Koob [1989] on the informal economy; see also Crutchfield [1995]). This trend can be seen in the fine line that exists between legal and illegal conduct in white-collar crimes and the extensive involvement of many ethnic groups in illegal gambling and liquor distribution schemes during the era of Prohibition and beyond (see, e.g., O'Kane 1992). The involvement of young males in these same neighborhoods today in drug selling and other income-generating crimes may be a continuation of the interplay of crime and work that is symptomatic of their peripheral attachment to the larger work force.

II. Crime as Work

There is a long, rich, and recently revived tradition of study of people who think about crime as their work. Many of the early studies on crime took an occupational perspective, emphasizing the "work" of crime and its similarities to conventional careers. Early descriptive studies included Sutherland's *The Professional Thief* (1937), Shaw's *The Jackroller* (1930), Maurer's *The Big Con* (1940) and *Whiz Mob* (1964), Jerome Hall's *Theft, Law and Society* (1952), Donald Cressey's *Other Peoples Money* (1953), Ned Polsky's *Hustlers, Beats and Others* (1967), Bruce Jackson's *A Thief's Primer* (1969), W. J. Eistadter's (1969) study on armed robbery, Dan Waldorf's *Careers in Dope* (1973), and Peter Letkemann's *Crime as Work* (1973). These studies showed that, as in conventional careers, access is restricted to those with requisite background and skills and that these skills are taught and transferred in a manner not dissimilar to apprenticeships (Letkemann 1973, p. 8). They also show how conventional career concepts such as specialization, professionalism, apprenticeship, and work satisfaction are applicable to crime as work. More important, these early studies show the continuities between the socialization patterns of noncriminals and those criminals for whom crime is occupational.

Recent ethnographic research on inner-city youth has revived and updated these early studies on crime as work. These studies show the importance of illegal work in developmental sequences leading to adult joblessness and criminality and the contextual influences on these developmental outcomes. This literature describes how structural changes in neighborhoods and cities have influenced not only the income options and decisions of adolescents but also normative attitudes toward work and the sources of status available through social networks and social roles. The decline of manufacturing work has limited legal employment opportunities for inner-city youths[25] and has occurred in contexts of concentrated poverty and narrowing job opportunities (Wilson 1987, 1996) and racial and residential segregation (Massey and Denton 1993). The attractions of illegal work are reflected in variables often unmeasured in quantitative studies on crime and work, especially tastes and preferences.

In turn, structural changes have reshaped the composition of social networks, the salience of informal social controls, and access to nonmaterial sources of social status (Sullivan 1989; Fagan 1992*b*). Fueled by economic restructuring (Kasarda 1989), the spatial concentration of poverty (Jargowsky and Bane 1990), and increasing residential segregation (Massey and Denton 1993), these neighborhood processes are difficult to capture in individual-level quantitative studies but are of

[25] In the past, manufacturing jobs have provided stable if not spectacular wages for people living in inner cities, and especially for African Americans (Farley 1987).

obvious importance as mediating processes that explain differences over time and across ecological units. The continuous effects of these changes across recent generations have contributed to new definitions of work that effectively blur legal boundaries and choices about income.

Recent ethnographic work illustrates how the abandonment of legal work has been accompanied by shifts in conceptions of work among young men and women in poor areas. Anderson (1990, 1994) describes how young males in inner-city Philadelphia regard the drug economy as a primary source of employment and how their delinquent street networks are their primary sources of status and social control. Similar accounts were offered by Hagedorn (1988, 1994a, 1994b), Taylor (1990), Moore (1992a, 1992b), and Padilla (1992, 1993). Participants in the illegal economies in inner cities were engaged in a variety of income-producing crimes, including drug selling, fencing, auto theft, petty theft and fraud, commercial extortion, and residential and commercial burglary. In diverse ethnic communities in cities far apart, young men use the language of work ("getting paid," "going to work") to describe their crimes.[26] The confounding of the language of illegal and legal worlds of making money seems to signal a basic shift in the social definition of work. For the young men using this language, money from crime is a means to commodities that offer instrumental value as symbols of wealth and status.

Much of this illegal work is organized within ethnic enterprises combining shared economic and cultural interests. For gangs in these cities, there is less concern than in the past with the neighborhood or the traditional "family" nature of gang life. Moore (1992a) shows how gang members with limited exits from gang life remained longer in the gang, assuming leadership roles and manipulating the gang for their own economic advantage through perpetuation of gang culture and ideology. Chin and Fagan (1994) and Chin (1995) describe the complex economic relationship between street gangs and adult social and economic institutions in three Chinatown neighborhoods in New York City. The adult groups, descendants of the tongs that were the shadow governments in Chinatowns a century ago, are involved in both legal, well-respected social and business activities and a variety of illegal

---

[26] See Sullivan (1989); Williams (1989); Taylor (1990); Padilla (1992); Bourgois (1995). For example, Felix Padilla describes how gang members in a Puerto Rican Chicago neighborhood regarded low-level drug sellers in their gang as "working stiffs" who were being exploited by other gang members.

businesses that employ street gangs. The gangs guard territories and act as surrogates in violently resolving conflicts and rivalries between the adult groups. Chin (1995) concludes that the gangs prosper economically while functionally maintaining the cultural and economic hegemony of these ambiguous adult leadership groups. Moreover, the gangs are involved in a variety of income-producing activities, especially commercial extortion, that are shielded from legal pressures by cultural processes that tolerate and integrate their activities into the social fabric of everyday life in Chinatown (Chin and Fagan 1994).

Padilla (1992) describes how the new pattern of exploitation of lower-level workers (street drug sellers) in the gang was obscured by appeals by older gang members to gang ideology (honor, loyalty to the gang and the neighborhood, discipline, and ethnic solidarity) combined with the lure of income. Taylor (1990), describing drug gangs in Detroit, and Padilla (1992) also write about the use of money rather than violence as social control within African American and Latino drug selling gangs—if a worker steps out of line, he simply is cut off from the business, a punishment far more salient than threats to physical safety. Drug-selling groups in these two studies superficially are ethnic enterprises but function more substantively as economic units with management structures oriented toward the maintenance of profitability and efficiency. The institutionalization of these sources of illegal work, and their competitiveness with the low-status and low-income legal jobs left behind after deindustrialization, combine to maintain illegal work careers long after they would have been abandoned in earlier generations.

Patterns of illegal work vary in this literature. Some abandon legal work after a period of employment, others drift in and out of legal work, and a few seem from the outset to choose exclusive "careers" in illegal work. Sanchez-Jankowski (1991, p. 101), for example, claims to have found an "entrepreneurial spirit" as the "driving force in the work view and behavior of gang members" that pushes them to make rational decisions to engage in the profitable worlds of drug sales or auto theft. Hagedorn (1994b) describes how gang members drift in and out of legal work over time, with decisions closely bundled and often reciprocal. Hagedorn shows that among Milwaukee gang members income from drug selling far exceeded incomes from legal work. However, many in the drug economy "appeared to be on an economic merry-go-round" (Hagedorn, 1994b, p. 205), continuing to look for legal work, despite its lower wages, low status, danger, and part-time nature. But for others, the hazards and indignity of low-wage and low-status legal jobs discount the returns from legal work and ultimately lead to its rejection. For example, Bourgois (1989, p. 641) claims that drug dealers who leave legal jobs to embrace the risks and rewards of drug selling are evidence of a "culture of resistance," preferring the "more dignified workplace" of drug selling than the low wages and "subtle humiliations" of secondary labor markets where racism dominates work conditions and social interactions.

Structural changes, especially the decline of manufacturing and unskilled labor, have contributed to the continuity of these views into adulthood. Manufacturing jobs traditionally provided "exits" from gang life and eased the transition from adolescence to adult social roles. Millions of these jobs have disappeared since the 1960s. Hagedorn (1988), Sullivan (1989), and Taylor (1990) showed how neighborhoods in the past reproduced their employment patterns in succeeding generations through networks of job referrals. Today, what is reproduced is joblessness (Tienda 1991; Wilson 1991).

The changes in the structure of employment shaped not only job outcomes for young adults but the outcomes of early legal problems as well. Sullivan (1989) tells how early involvement in crimes was normative in three ethnically diverse neighborhoods, but the outcomes of arrest varied by neighborhoods. White families helped resolve disputes informally, using family support and job networks to soften the potential stigma of arrest. With high rates of joblessness, nonwhite families had few social buffers or job networks between them and the legal system. Not only did they lack access to job networks, but also their families were of little help when their income-producing crimes (robberies) evoked official responses. Their disrupted job networks were unable to mitigate legal problems or ease the school-to-work transition, contributing to the continuity of criminality and adverse legal responses. In contrast, youths in predominantly white neighborhoods were able to make sometimes difficult but successful escapes from adolescent crime networks. Hagan (1993b) links this to processes of social embeddedness that truncate future options and amplify the adverse effects of adolescent entanglements in the legal system.

These processes were institutionalized in many inner-city neighborhoods by the twin processes of deindustrialization and expansion of drug economies. Fagan (1992b) describes the sequence of changes in eight neighborhoods in six cities, from the decline of manufacturing through the disruption of intergenerational job networks and social controls, through the institutionalization of illegal work, especially in drug selling. The growing social isolation, resulting from concentrated poverty and segregation, gave rise to a skewed emphasis on exaggerated displays of material wealth as a source of status (see also Anderson 1990, 1994). Motivations for the perceived higher returns from illegal work were influenced by such tastes for quick "crazy" money (Anderson 1990) and were important components of decisions to engage in illegal work.

The ethnographic literature is consistent with longitudinal and other quantitative studies in several respects. Both literatures reverse the conventional assumptions of macro-level research about the temporal ordering of crime and unemployment: most adolescents were involved in income-generating crimes well before they sought (or considered) the legal labor force. Both in the ethnographic and longitudinal quantitative literatures, the effects of incarceration in early adolescence carried over to adult employment and crime outcomes. The protective influence of human capital variables was evident as well (see, e.g., Padilla's description of avoiding gang involvement).

III. Abandoning Crime for Legal Work

Many offenders drift back and forth over time between legal and illegal work. Hagedorn (1994*b*), for example, shows how drug dealers move back and forth between legal and illegal work, at times doubling up and at other times specializing. There has been little research on how these changes come about, how often they occur, individual differences in shifts, or the decision processes that result in changes. However, there has been research, much of it based on qualitative life history analyses (Frazier 1981), on desistance from criminality. Many of these studies describe a gradual shift over time from crime careers to relatively mundane conventional careers. Many of these studies describe desistance from criminal careers for people who were deeply embedded in deviant social networks and who had accumulated many of the social and human capital deficits that seem to predict adverse employment outcomes. What is instructive are the lessons regarding how the decision heuristic changes with advancing age.

Research on "career" robbers and burglars, drug users and sellers, and juvenile offenders describes factors and processes that influence persistent offenders to abandon illegal work.[27] In most cases, desistance

[27] See, e.g., Mulvey and LaRosa (1986) on juvenile offenders; Shover (1985, 1995) and Tunnell (1992) on burglars; Cusson and Pinsonneault (1986) and Irwin (1970) on rob-

centers around a process ascribed to "aging out," in which there is a shift in the calculus of rewards and costs of criminality. An accumulation of aversive experiences, changes in personal circumstances, and contingencies in neighborhoods or crime opportunities all may lead to the decision to desist from crime. Greenberg (1977) and Biernacki (1986) concluded that "occupational" criminality may be incompatible with family demands or with holding down a steady (legal) job. Biernacki (1986) also showed that desistance from heroin use and attendant crime was contingent on reversing the addict's immersion in the subcultures and social worlds of addiction and, conversely, isolation from more conventional roles and norms. Reestablishing ties with legitimate activities and social networks was far less difficult for those who had not drifted very far, but more difficult for others. Having decided to quit, successful desisters relied on social networks of nonaddicts for support and maintenance of their new roles as well as for access to job contacts and networks.

Fagan (1989) analyzed the desistance literature and identified the sequence of stages leading to decisions to quit and stay away from crime. The decision to quit was often preceded by a series of adverse consequences or social sanctions from illegal work. A combination of pressures—family, legal, health, and a changing view of their former social world—preceded the decision to quit. Some were motivated by the threat of loss of loved ones or children, others by the threats of social sanctions from peers or neighbors, and still others by a desire not to face incarceration (again). Many described how their social supports for illegal work were weaker or disappeared. Some mentioned the physical costs: crime was more difficult to complete successfully, and the anxieties it aroused took an increasing emotional toll (see, e.g., Shover 1985; Cusson and Pinsonneault 1986). For some, decisions were "spontaneous" or were described as instant conversions to another way of life (see, e.g., Biernacki 1986; Mulvey and LaRosa 1986).

Adler's (1985, 1993) portrait of drug dealers shows the difficulty of detaching from illicit work that extends beyond the net of legal and illegal returns. Many drug dealers resolved and attempted to leave illegal work but found the conventional world boring. Their return to dealing was motivated less by income than by their "withdrawal" from the excitement of their illegal work. Biernacki also described the bore-

---

bers; Adler (1985, 1993) on drug dealers; Biernacki (1986) on opiate addicts who also were involved in a variety of income-producing crimes. See also Fagan (1989) on a conceptual model for spousal assailants.

dom of the "straight" world for many former addicts. Transition from illegal work became episodic, with periods of cessation increasing in length and frequency until becoming final. But the longing for excitement (or psychological and physiological cravings, as described by Biernacki) persisted well after the illegal behavior was abandoned. Other voices in this literature discuss the intrinsic rewards of the "life," while diminishing the salience of its costs. There are important roles of tastes, intrinsic rewards, status rewards, and even emotional thrills (Katz 1988) from illegal work and its social context in the decision to persist in crime. These factors are difficult to control or defeat in the process of desisting from crime and may play a central role in heuristic processes to persist in illegal work.

These rewards often provide powerful reinforcements. Fagan (1989, p. 408) notes that "With social embedment comes the gratification of social acceptance and social identity. The decision to end a behavior . . . implies withdrawal from the social reinforcement it brings" and fear of social rejection in new networks. Maintaining the decision to quit illegal work required the construction of new social networks, changes in physical locales, changes in self- and social identity, changes in the functional definitions of crime, substitution of new social roles and behaviors for the old ones (including legal work), new sources of social reinforcement for legal work and a conventional lifestyle, and the development of a strong belief system in the soundness of these changes (Fagan 1989, p. 403).

However, desisters rarely mentioned economic logic in their decision making. Although desistance has been characterized as a predictable process associated with advancing age (Hirschi and Gottfredson 1983; Farrington 1986), no theoretical meaning has been attached to the age curve. Desistance studies suggest that with age, there are changes in the heuristic processes that offenders use to assess the costs and benefits of crime commission (Clarke and Cornish 1985). Their decisions were unrelated to access to legal work and were based more on changing perceptions and evaluations of nonlegal social sanctions from illegal work. While they perceived little change in the returns of illegal work, desisters seemed to increase their evaluations of the potential sanction costs of their crimes: loss of loved ones, rejection by social peers, and self-rejection. This changing evaluation of external costs was preceded by internal changes in their self-perceptions.

Accordingly, one consequence of advancing age is a substantive shift in the utility function underlying decisions to engage in illegal work.

Evaluation of the costs of illegal work seems to change with age, although perceived returns from illegal work seem undiminished. Because youth participation in crime is highly responsive to legal wages (Grogger 1995), an alternative explanation suggests that declining crime participation with age may reflect expectations of higher earning potential from legal work. In addition, factors born out of new social roles (marriage, adult friend, father) and informal social control appear to receive increasing weight with age. Perhaps also the weight accorded to tastes and "thrills" diminishes with age or is defeated by other emotional states such as anxiety and fear. The revised calculus of illegal work also seems to be shaped by the social contexts of everyday life that offer new social roles, perceptions and conceptions of work, and by changing self-identity and emotional states.

IV. Directions for Theory and Research

Research on the interactions among crime, work, and unemployment has been limited in several ways. For example, most efforts reflect theory and methods of specific disciplines; conceptual and methodological integration is rare. Measures are inconsistent and often indirect. Single samples are more common than multiple samples to address period and cohort effects. In this section, we start the summary of directions for future research with the bad news on the limitations of current knowledge. But even with these gaps, we identify important areas where the literatures converge, leading to more optimistic views and promising directions for theory and research. We conclude with an agenda for research.

A. Methodological Dilemmas

Specifying the crime-unemployment relationship is complicated by a bifurcation in the empirical literature. It is difficult to compare single-period, cross-sectional models of individual choices with longitudinal studies. In the single-period studies, crime and work are presented as alternative choices only because of the limited time period measured, overlooking variation over time. Several studies have used data that have at least two time points (e.g., Gottfredson 1985; Good, Pirog-Good, and Sickles 1986), while only a few others (Thornberry and Christenson 1984; Farrington 1986; Viscusi 1986a, 1986b; Freeman 1992; Nagin and Waldfogel 1995; Bushway 1996) used panel data extending over several years. Crime and work are events that are likely to occur close in time. The use of annual observations data over lengthy time periods makes it difficult to determine whether crimes occurred during periods of unemployment, underemployment, active employment, or exile from the labor force.

Second, studies of crime and unemployment often omit (legal) deterrence variables that are necessary to compute how individuals discount the returns from legal work based on the potential punishment costs. This is especially important considering that deterrence variables are significant in macro-level studies, often outweighing the importance of labor market variables in the explanation of crime. When included, deterrence usually is measured indirectly using aggregate city-wide arrest rates or probabilities (see, e.g., Good, Pirog-Good, and Sickles [1986]; but see Witte and Tauchen [1994] for an exception), but rarely is it measured as the individual's perceived likelihood of sanctions. This is particularly problematic since crime rates at the neighborhood level and arrest probabilities are not independent (Smith 1986). Accordingly, we are likely to observe both intracity and intercity effects when multi-city samples are used, similar to the fluctuations in labor market variables. This suggests the need for careful specification and disaggregation of deterrence variables at the level of neighborhood and city, and the use of hierarchical models to estimate the simultaneous effects of macro-level forces with more proximate neighborhood effects.

Third, estimates of the work-crime association have been confounded with sampling strategies. Comparisons of general population samples that span broad ecological areas create risks of correlation-causation confounding due to the concentration of crime and unemployment in subareas. Research with prison releasees (e.g., Berk, Rossi, and Lenihan 1980; Witte 1980) or intervention program participants (Good, Pirog-Good, and Sickles 1986) may have samples with truncated distributions of human capital variables and concentrations or "ceiling rates" of other risk factors. Similarly, studies that use "street" samples of offenders may effectively control for neighborhood factors but also risk truncated or unmeasured human capital variables (e.g., limited work experiences) (see, e.g., Fagan 1992a). Studies with adult samples may overlook the important events during adolescence that shape later work outcomes.

Fourth, despite the central role of expected returns in economic models of crime and unemployment, measures of illegal wages have been weak, if measured at all. Returns from legal work have been measured in dollars, occupational status, and in labor market participation.

But measurement of returns from illegal work is quite rare (see, for exceptions, Viscusi 1986*a;* Reuter, MacCoun, and Murphy 1990; Fagan 1992*a,* 1994; Hagedorn 1994*a*). Other studies use proxies or estimates (e.g., Wilson and Abrahamse 1992; Grogger 1994, 1995; Freeman 1996*b*). Just as labor markets vary across neighborhoods within cities and across cities themselves, so too do illegal markets, especially drug markets (Fagan 1992*b*). Measurement of illegal wages and illegal labor market participation is critical to both sociological and econometric specification of crime decisions and the effects of unemployment. Thus there are intrinsic weaknesses in estimates of the net utility of legal versus illegal work.

A corollary problem is evident in the measurement of crime. Not only are the economic returns from crime not measured, but the measures of criminal activity themselves vary extensively as well. The published commentary of Thompson and Cataldo (1986) on the Viscusi articles reflects the split among analysts on whether self-reports or official records provide more reliable measurement of crime. Like many criminologists, the economists Thompson and Cataldo questioned the validity of Viscusi's results based on offender self-reports of criminality. These weaknesses lead many researchers to hold their noses and use official records of police contacts or arrests, despite their validity problems at the individual level (Elliott and Huizinga 1986).[28] Moreover, the analytic aggregations of crime measures also are quite limited. Many studies use gross, dichotomous measures of any police contact, while others use arrests. This distinction is particularly problematic in studies of adolescents since many police contacts are resolved informally. Many studies avoid measures of crime frequency since their distributions often are skewed. Others fail to distinguish types of crime, collapsing instrumental (income-producing) and "expressive" (often violent) crimes into single scales. Yet the distinction between income-producing and other crimes is particularly critical to models specifying actions based on estimates of returns from crime. Official records also seem particularly ill suited to measuring returns

[28] Others are more cautious about using self-reports. Thompson and Cataldo (1986) criticize Viscusi (1986*b*) for exclusively using self-reports. Viscusi failed to detect the absence of muggings, burglaries, and robberies in the self-reports in his sample and fails to note the typical age-crime relationships found in a wide range of criminological studies (see, e.g., Hirschi and Gottfredson 1983; Gottfredson and Hirschi 1990). Yet Elliott and Huizinga (1986), using a general population sample, claim that the extent of underreporting in arrest statistics is overwhelming for nearly all crime types, and the underreporting factor increases with the frequency of self-reported crime.

from illegal work. Using estimators from other datasets for the value of stolen goods or drug income ignores the importance of individual differences in skills on the total income from crime or drug sales.

Fifth, as we discuss in more detail later on, there have been significant changes in legal and illegal labor markets over the 1980s and in the social processes in inner-city neighborhoods that may affect decisions about crime and work (Wilson 1991, 1996). The percentage of "unskilled" young males in inner cities grew throughout the 1980s (Mangold 1994). The returns from both legal and illegal work changed significantly throughout the decade, creating the possibility of shifts in the decisions of inner-city youths toward illegal work. So too did tastes and preferences (Fagan 1992b). These changes introduce period effects that complicate comparisons of earlier studies with more recent efforts. For example, manufacturing and unskilled labor jobs, the types of jobs typically available to youths in economically distressed inner-city neighborhoods, declined throughout this period (Kasarda 1992). Wages for minority youths remained flat, even in a tight labor market in the mid-1980s (Blackburn, Bloom, and Freeman 1990; Bound and Freeman 1992; Freeman 1992).

A variety of factors complicated access of young African American males to legal work (Kirschenman and Neckerman 1991; Moss and Tilly 1991), increasing search costs and devaluing the returns from legal work. These factors also influenced the supply of young men to crime (Freeman 1996b). Arrests and incarceration of young African American males increased throughout the 1980s (Irwin and Austin 1994; Tonry 1995), again posing barriers to legal employment and, according to the crime-causes-unemployment view, decreasing labor force participation. Finally, illegal markets (especially drug markets) expanded contemporaneously with the decline of legal work in inner cities (Fagan 1993), while informal social controls and social capital declined precipitously throughout the preceding decade (Sampson 1987; Wilson 1987; Sampson and Wilson 1994). Accordingly, we may assume that the outcomes of work decisions reflected the growing imbalance between legal and perceived illegal returns in drug markets and other illegal work for inner-city youths. These period-specific effects also suggest that past research may not be applicable in the future. The aggregate effects of high rates of joblessness may create problems of scale that affect individual probabilities of successful outcomes.[29]

[29] If, e.g., crime rates increase beyond some threshold, employers may flee cities or regions for safer environments for their workers. A perception of an unskilled labor force

B. Theoretical Domains

Despite these gaps, there are several consistent themes for building a foundation for theory and research. First, early involvement in crime and incarceration as an adolescent have negative effects on employment and positive effects on crime in later adult years. Both longitudinal and ethnographic studies place delinquency before unemployment in the sequence of developmental events over the life course. Studies based on data from the United States, England, and other European countries consistently identify the legacy of adolescent experiences for future work outcomes. Sampson and Laub (1993) suggest that adolescents "mortgage" their future job stability and work outcomes through adolescent involvement in crime but that incarceration intensifies these effects over the life course. The importance of family context, especially parental criminality rather than parental unemployment, suggests important leverage points for intervention. The effects of high rates of incarceration for today's adolescents, especially African Americans, may be compounded in the labor market outcomes of their children in another generation.

Second, crime does in fact appear to pay for many offenders. In the few studies that have measured returns from crime, there are calculable market incentives from illegal work. Perhaps more than other types of crime, drug dealing seems to provide substantial earnings above what legal work pays. Careers in illegal work also accord relief from the mundane and often abusive conditions encountered by nonwhites in white-owned businesses. The returns from what Bourgois (1989) terms the "Horatio Alger" benefits of illegal work are difficult to calculate but carry value even in the face of the absence of a net increase in monetary returns.[30] However, the data on illegal wages are extremely limited, and extensive research is needed to analyze the role of market incentives in decisions about legal and illegal work.

Third, human capital and early work experiences are protective factors that help avoid poor job outcomes and illegal work in early adult years. Even in models of work outcomes showing the effects of early crime and incarceration, there are consistent positive effects from human capital variables on legal work outcomes in early adulthood. The

---

may also motivate employers to relocate their businesses to places with higher productivity, lower wages, more skilled workers, or less troublesome employees.

[30] Bourgois writes of how drug workers are willing to work under difficult working conditions, with no benefits and substantial health and safety risks, to escape the humiliations they encounter daily in low-wage service and manufacturing jobs.

measurement of human capital varies widely in crime and unemployment studies, and further research is needed using measures of human capital that are truly independent from work outcomes. The use of AFQT scores provides one such independent measure. The importance of social capital also has been shown but has received far less research attention (cf. Sampson and Laub 1993). Human and social capital overlap through job networks and referrals and through the social embedment of work experiences in social networks where both skills and personal relationships are exchanged.

Fourth, the effects of legal deterrence variables, or the punishment costs of crime, are inconsistent and remain unknown pending further study. In macro-level studies, deterrence variables appear significantly to depress crime rates. In individual-level studies, analyses of deterrence strategies are marked by inconsistencies in conceptualization and measurement. Deterrence rarely is disaggregated by neighborhood or area, even though arrest probabilities vary within and across cities. Measurement usually is limited to the threat of arrest, not of incarceration. Occupational risk also is not included, even in drug selling where injury rates are quite substantial (Fagan and Chin 1990). There are several dimensions of deterrence, but usually only perceived sanction threat, or actual sanction, is included (Nagin 1998). However, incarceration risks may be tolerable or even expected and may be only a minor discount on the net returns from illegal work. A fully specified deterrence model should include also how important these risks are perceived to be and whether a high risk would actually influence illegal work decisions. It also should address the discount on informal sanctions in neighborhoods where work is infrequent and its rewards are limited.

Finally, there are threshold effects in the structure of opportunity that can launch social processes undermining both monetary and non-monetary incentives to work and that support definitions of crime that are conflated with work. In Wilson's (1996) comparison of Mexican and African American neighborhoods in Chicago, he describes the effects of social and spatially concentrated joblessness on work and crime. He notes a process in which the disappearance of jobs in one generation disrupts attachments to work that are reinforced through within- and between-generation interactions around work and income. Under these circumstances, (legal) work is no longer a regulating social process. The cultural isolation that develops in this vacuum shapes definitions and conceptions of work that erode its social value. This "cultural disorganization" accompanies social disorganization to establish conditions in which crime can flourish. The process is reinforced by the expansion of illegal opportunities, including both drug dealing and everyday hustling. Cultural adaptations that develop in these circumstances support the conflation of crime and work. These adaptations to the systematic blockage of legal opportunities for income production are intensified when they are spatially and socially concentrated in closed social networks (see, e.g., Hannerz 1969; Rainwater 1970). In this context, access to illegal opportunities furnishes material returns and social status that is unavailable through legal work and that compromises whatever vestiges of legal work norms that remain.

Together with recent ethnographic literature, Wilson's view helps explain the growing isolation of inner-city adolescents from the worlds of conventional work. With limited access to legal work, and in segregated neighborhoods with high concentrations of joblessness, alienated views of legal work and diminished expectations for conventional success spread through social contagion and become normative (Tienda 1989). Tastes and preferences are driven by definitions of status dominated by material consumption. Violence substitutes for social control as a means to resolve disputes and attain status (Katz 1988; Sullivan 1989; Anderson 1994), increasing the likelihood either of mortality or incarceration. Legal work at low pay is defined poorly and carries a negative social stigma (Bourgois 1989; Taylor 1990). With intergenerational job networks disrupted, the ability of young people to gain access to increasingly complex labor markets with limited human capital or personal contacts foretells poor work outcomes. What starts as a growing class of unskilled workers in isolated neighborhoods quickly becomes a means for social contagion and rapid detachment from legal work.

We apply the framework of Uggen (1996) and Uggen, Piliavin, and Matsueda (1992) to discuss the theoretical implications of the work-unemployment literature. Support for four broad theoretical frameworks is evident in the empirical literature, and the causal mechanisms they specify suggest opportunities for convergence and integration.[31] Choice, opportunity, and labeling perspectives have dynamic properties that include both structural elements and the processual elements

[31] These perspectives may reflect the special conditions of disadvantaged communities with job markets that are structurally distinct from the job markets in more advantaged areas. There are important contextual influences on the link between legal and illegal work at both the individual and aggregate levels.

necessary for a theory of individual development and work outcomes. We add to these theories borrowed from ethology to formalize observed behaviors in the search for income. We briefly review these perspectives and the prospects for theoretical synthesis.

1. *Econometric Choice Models.* Economic and choice theories have been the most common basis for empirical research. They portray crime as the result of a decision to seek the (perceived) higher rewards of the illegal labor market compared to the legal market, adjusted for the potential punishment costs of illegal behavior (Becker 1968; Ehrlich 1973). Rational choice theorists (Clarke and Cornish 1985; Cornish and Clarke 1986) extended this model by assuming that offenders in fact do proceed according to a heuristic process, but this heuristic model includes elements of income satisficing as well as income optimization. Others (Block and Heineke 1975) claimed that a process of neutralization is necessary to permit ethical decisions to engage in crime and that psychic rewards also figure in the decision to engage in illegal work (see, e.g., Katz 1988; Grasmick and Bursik 1990). Choice theorists also have used economic choice models to explain deterrence (Miller and Anderson 1986).

There is some support for the economic position in this empirical literature, and choice models have obvious importance in a theoretical model of work decisions. The role of market incentives suggests that crime indeed pays compared to the types of work available to criminal offenders, particularly for drug sales. There are important roles for status and psychic payoffs from illegal work, particularly in social contexts where crime participation is high, labor force participation is low, and crime provides a skewed form of "occupational status." That is, the status and personal costs of legal work motivate selection of illegal work. Participation in illegal work also may reflect the proximity of illegal work compared to low-wage legal work and a choice to minimize search time or circumvent lengthy job queues.

Accordingly, the decision to select illegal work may indeed reflect its net benefits and structural features of labor markets for urban youths and young adults. If the distribution of opportunities is uneven and skewed away from inner-city urban areas, decisions to seek illegal work may reflect the income-satisficing model of decision making (Cornish and Clarke 1986). Moreover, the role of deterrence in economic choice seems clear, yet it has been studied inconsistently. Sociological tests of deterrence often focus on the risks of deviance, discounting the rewards of offending. Even so, there is only weak support for the deterrence components of this model compared to criminal rewards (e.g., Piliavin et al. 1986).

2. *Opportunity Structures.* According to opportunity theories, difficulty in attaining conventional goals—affluence, social status—creates conditions of anomie or strain, leading to criminal pursuits (Cloward and Ohlin 1960; Agnew and White 1992; Paternoster and Mazerolle 1994). These themes are evident in the ethnographic literature. Young males and females have turned to a wide variety of informal economic activities, some of them illegal, as stable and well-paying legal jobs became more scarce. Uggen (1996) calls them innovators who reject low-wage legal work and embrace illegal work in pursuit of the twin goals of affluence and social status, while Sanchez-Jankowski (1991) notes their independent spirit of entrepreneurship. Throughout the ethnographic literature, young males in different neighborhoods and ethnic groups report the coexistence of conventional and nonconventional goals, signs that their frustrations with the legal labor market in part motivate their decisions to seek illegal work.

Barriers to conventional success may result from job scarcity or access to work that provides status and monetary reward. In some neighborhoods, the distribution of opportunities is such that unemployment is as common as employment among nonwhite adolescents, and there are more illegal than legal opportunities. Wages reflect these persistent trends (Bound and Freeman 1992). Wages for unskilled workers in the United States are far lower than in other industrialized Western countries, and this disparity has grown steadily for nearly three decades (Freeman 1994). Legal opportunities appear to be low-status, low-paying, and generally exploited labor (Padilla 1992; Hagedorn 1994*a*), and expansions in the workforce appear to be in "contingent" jobs rather than "permanent" ones (Freeman 1994). The effects of declining wages and opportunities are strongest for unskilled workers, the group of working-age men with the highest crime rates.

In these conditions, detachment from legal work has become normative; illegal activities are defined as "work," and the returns from crime as "getting paid" (Sullivan 1989). Pursuing "conventional" goals through illegal work has become dangerously close to becoming institutionalized in an oppositional culture, just as legal work may become the exception for a "growing underclass of the unskilled" (Wacquant and Wilson 1989; Mangold 1994). Recent studies in Canada suggest similar dynamics (Baron and Hartnagel 1997; Hagan and McCarthy 1997). Accordingly, the importance of the balance of opportunities for the decision to seek illegal work is another central feature of the crime and unemployment relationship.

3. *Labeling.* The exclusion of incarcerated young offenders from legal work is evident in the longitudinal studies of Sampson and Laub (1993) and Freeman (1992). In the labeling perspective, early involvement in the criminal justice system has sustaining negative effects on future behavior. The mechanisms are compounding. Excluded from legal work by criminal records, young offenders in turn may come to define themselves through that label. This may lead to further embedment in deviant networks and a deepening self-concept as an outsider to legal work. Accordingly, the label has both exogenous effects for employers and psychological effects for the individual seeking work. Such labels may attach and persist even before individuals seek access to legal work. Through parental criminality, adolescents may be embedded in social networks that are outside conventional job networks (Hagan 1993*a*), leading to early criminal involvement and the attachment of a legal sanction that in turn may exclude young people from future legal work.

4. *Work and Crime: A Foraging Model.* Treating the decision to engage in crime as a dichotomous choice between legal and illegal work misses an important aspect of criminal activity. Because most offenders work outside of criminal organizations, and because the U.S. job market is characterized by considerable mobility and flexibility, it is easy to combine work with crime at one time or to move between the two activities over time. These decisions are simplified and facilitated not only by labor mobility but also by the distribution of criminal opportunities and restraints in neighborhoods where crime often is concentrated (Sampson 1987; Massey and Eggers 1990; Bursik and Grasmick 1993). The structure of wages, and the comparative advantage of illegal wages relative to limited legal wages, also motivates such switching and short-term decision making.[32]

Ecological models of foraging behavior (Stephens and Krebs 1986) offer an insightful way to analyze the tendency for youths to engage in both illegal and legal work activities, either simultaneously or by moving back and forth between them. These models apply economic opti-

[32] The "doubling up" of legal work and cocaine sales in the Fagan (1994) and Reuter, MacCoun, and Murphy (1990) studies indicates that for many young men illegal work may be temporary or transitional work that supplements difficult low-wage or otherwise unsatisfactory work. For others, legal work provides options to riskier illegal work or perhaps broadens markets for sellers of illegal goods or services.

mizing analysis to the problems faced by animals that forage for food. The animal must make several decisions in a short period of time: whether it should "prey" on a particular food source it encounters or turn that prey down to search for better prey; exploit opportunities in a given patch or search for new opportunities, and so forth. The parallels with youths "foraging" for earnings, legal or illegal, are striking. The youth must decide whether to engage in robbery, take a short-term (and perhaps low-paying) job when he encounters an offer; steal in the local community or try some adjoining area; sell drugs to employees, if working, or to customers in a street market. Empirical evidence of such short-term switching and career juggling is evident in recent studies with prison inmates (Horney, Osgood, and Marshall 1995), drug sellers (Reuter, MacCoun, and Murphy 1990; Fagan 1994), career property offenders (Decker and Wright 1995; Shover 1995), and robbers (Decker and Wright 1995).

The foraging models direct attention to differing "reservation wages" of various money-making activities and their determinants. When returns fall below the reservation wage, the youth will reject an opportunity and go on to something different. Freeman (1992) showed that young men in inner-city poverty areas encounter both illegal and legal opportunities in a relevant (and short) time period: McDonald's may be hiring this week; Jones Construction may need a laborer; robbers may need someone to fence stolen goods; an elderly woman may wander along the wrong street; a car with an expensive stereo system may be parked in an alley, etc. In a world where short-run legal and illegal earnings opportunities arrive more or less randomly, it is natural for individuals to move between them, commit crimes while working, or take a legitimate job if one happens to be available even when engaged in criminal activities. If this hypothesis is correct, and the behavior of crime-prone youths is similar to that of foraging animals as opposed to that of adults with permanent careers, the supply of youths to crime will be quite elastic, consistent with the observed failure of incapacitation to reduce crime.

C. Research on Crime, Work, and Development

In addition to basic research, research in the contexts of policy experiments and interventions can provide data to understand problems of crime and unemployment. Several topics deserve research attention.

1. *Basic Research: Illegal Wages and Illegal Markets.* There is little consistent information on the diversity of illegal labor markets and ille-

gal wages. There has been extensive research on drug selling, but drug sellers are involved in a variety of illegal income-generating activities. Research is needed that focuses on the economic lives of people active in illegal markets. Studies are needed that examine market incentives for illegal work and the economic and social dimensions of illegal work that compete with the legal labor market. Similarly, research on illegal markets is needed to explain demand for illegal work, especially the social organization of illegal work and its opportunity structures. Basic social processes including recruitment and the flow of capital also will inform knowledge about the competing economic structures of crime.

a. Models of Decision Making. A fully specified model of economic decision making will provide necessary information on the cognitive processes leading to decisions to engage in illegal work. Similar models have been developed by economists for addictions (Becker and Murphy 1988) and to specify deterrence of illegal behavior (Miller and Anderson 1986). Cognitive models of decision making also have been developed to explain involvement in violence (Dodge and Crick 1990), but these focus less on economic variables than on strategic decision making.

Perspectives from economic choice, opportunity, control, and labeling theories can be integrated in a conceptual framework of decision making about work preferences and choices. Prior work experiences should be included to measure conceptions of work and changes over time in response to experiences in the workplace. Transitions from legal to illegal and back to legal work should be closely analyzed, as should the difficult transitions from school to work and incarceration to work. Samples should include several neighborhoods to assess the mediating influences of peer networks and local economies. A range of informal and formal economic activities should be specified, and data collection points should occur with sufficient frequency to address the close timing of work and crime decisions. Age cohorts should vary as well, recognizing the varying places in the natural histories of crime and work of people at different stages in the life course.

b. Employer-Employee Relationships. Conflicts in the workplace are one barrier to employment for unskilled or semi-skilled young males at the end of the job queues. These conflicts are the source of frequent absenteeism and the discount on job quality that may influence decisions to turn to illegal work. Studies on the sources and outcomes of conflicts in the workplace for inner-city youths are needed to help fashion interventions to maintain job stability. This effort may be part of a larger qualitative research effort to understand the work experiences of young males who are at the cusp of decisions regarding legal and illegal work. If conflicts are a source of attrition from the labor force, the origins of and solutions to these conflicts have important implications for maintaining labor force attachments.

2. *Policy Experiments.*   Research in applied settings provides laboratories for testing economic theories of crime and legal and illegal work. There is the obvious intuitive appeal of jobs programs as an intervention to reduce criminality.[33] When offenders can be put to work at sufficient wages to compete with illegal income, logic suggests that they will desist from crime. Research is needed on the effects of increasing market incentives for legal work (see Fagan 1992*a*, 1994; Freeman 1992, 1994; Grogger 1994, 1995, 1998). Pay scales would have to be set to meet individual needs and to reflect market wages. The type of work and occupational status are additional considerations (Matsueda et al. 1992). Work outcomes are contingent on job quality, wages, and the status accorded to particular types of work. Placement in unskilled labor or work for work's sake may not attend to theoretically important dimensions that the illegal market sometimes fulfills. Setting also is an important dimension of work that merits additional research (Uggen, Piliavin, and Matsueda 1992). Hostile work environments confront many nonwhite males entering the workforce (see, e.g., Bourgois 1989, 1995; Kirschenman and Neckerman 1991), discounting the returns from legal work by raising social and personal costs. Disputes in the workplace between young minority males and white employers are all too common (Ferguson and Filer 1986; Sullivan 1989; Anderson 1990), adding additional downward pressures on the returns from legal work.

Age also will be an important variable in the relationship of work, wages, and crime. For younger people, especially those who have

---

[33] Of course, an alternative policy would focus on reducing the returns from illegal work to match wages for legal work. Current illegal work involves a diverse set of activities, but drug selling appears to be the most lucrative and widespread. Reducing the returns from drug selling would require either a decline in demand (an unlikely prospect given the past two decades of drug crises in American cities), or the deregulation of drugs and the substitution of market rules for legal controls. This has proven to be a politically unpopular option and is not feasible in the short run. Experiments with increasing punishment costs over the past decade also have not stemmed participation in violent crime but have been associated with declines in burglary rates. The connection between incarceration rates and property or drug crime rates is tenuous at best, since the bulk of those imprisoned have not been property crime offenders (Reiss and Roth 1993).

avoided legal sanctions but who face uncertain futures in the labor market, work experiences take place in the developmental context of emerging human capital and school-to-work transitions. Older individuals have different motivations, shaped by the changing conceptions of work and needs at later developmental stages. Having experienced prison, perhaps they are more willing to discount the returns from illegal work in light of higher punishment costs and (if married) higher commitment costs. Especially for those returning from prison, job placements may be more important than skill development. Yet these individuals face a scary list of obstacles: criminal labels, skill and human capital deficits, and limited access to job networks. They are no doubt at the end of the job queue for a shrinking demand for unskilled labor.

Racial preferences of employers also present an important contextual factor in measuring work outcomes. This involves both initial hiring decisions and termination decisions. Employers are quite open in their racial hiring preferences (Wilson 1996). Their biases are based on perceptions of African American males as making "trouble" through higher wage demands, poor productivity, frequent absenteeism, and conflicts with coworkers and supervisors. However, discrimination in hiring poses a formidable barrier to the development of initial job contacts and the human capital that accrues through employment. Firing decisions also may reflect racial imbalance and bias.

The supported work experiments of the 1970s provided several lessons for moving offenders from crime to legal work. The analyses of the TARP experiments suggest limited effects of supported work programs for ex-offenders but promising effects in the samples overall for offenders whose human capital "protected" them from failure (Needels 1994). Rethinking TARP to incorporate lessons from basic research suggests the possibility of further experiments that include ancillary services as well as financial support and disaggregated interventions for older versus younger offenders.

The cessation of crime with age, and the return of many offenders to legal work at the end of crime careers, suggests a final research context to understand the transition from crime to work. The processes of reintegration from illegal work (Biernacki 1986; Adler 1993) require social psychological adjustments to new roles and circumstances. Research on the natural history of desistance should focus on the economic contingencies and strategies that support that transition. This would involve micro-study of the cognitive decisions and processes beginning with cohorts of offenders returning from prison or currently on parole or probation supervision. Measures would look closely at assessments of illegal and legal work in terms of both pecuniary and social "costs" and "payoffs," and the changes in self- and social identity that accompany the shift away from deviant networks to the more predictable "straight" world.

REFERENCES

Adler, Patricia. 1985. *Wheeling and Dealing: An Ethnography of an Upper-Level Dealing and Smuggling Community.* New York: Columbia University Press.

———. 1993. "The Post-phase of Deviant Careers: Reintegrating Drug Traffickers." *Deviant Behavior* 13:103–26.

Agnew, Robert, and Helene Raskin White. 1992. "An Empirical Test of General Strain Theory." *Criminology* 30:475–99.

Albrecht, Hans-Jörg. 1984. "Youth Unemployment and Youth Crime." *Kriminologisch Journal* 101:218–29.

Anderson, Elijah. 1990. *Streetwise: Race, Class and Change in an Urban Community.* Chicago: University of Chicago Press.

———. 1994. "Code of the Street." *Atlantic Monthly* (May), pp. 81–94.

———. 1997. "Violence and the Inner City Code of the Streets." In *Violence and the Inner City,* edited by Joan McCord. New York: Cambridge University Press.

———. 1998. "The Social Ecology of Youth Violence." In *Youth Violence,* edited by Michael Tonry and Mark H. Moore. Vol. 24 of *Crime and Justice: A Review of Research,* edited by Michael Tonry. Chicago: University of Chicago Press.

Baron, Stephen W., and Timothy F. Hartnagel. 1997. "Attributions, Affect and Crime: Street Youths Reactions to Unemployment." *Criminology* 35:409–34.

Becker, Gary. 1968. "Crime and Punishment: An Economic Approach." *Journal of Political Economy* 76:169–217.

Becker, Gary, and Kevin M. Murphy. 1988. "A Theory of Rational Addiction." *Journal of Political Economy* 96:675–700.

Berk, Richard A., Peter Rossi, and Kenneth Lenihan. 1980. "Crime and Poverty: Some Experimental Evidence from Ex-Offenders." *American Sociological Review* 45:766–86.

Biernacki, Patrick. 1986. *Pathways from Addiction: Recovery without Treatment.* Philadelphia: Temple University Press.

Blackburn, McKinley, David E. Bloom, and Richard B. Freeman. 1990. "The Declining Economic Position of Less Skilled American Men." In *A Future of Lousy Jobs? The Changing Structure of U.S. Wages,* edited by Gary Burtless. Washington, D.C.: Brookings Institution.

Block, Michael K., and J. M. Heineke. 1975. "A Labor Theoretic Analysis of the Criminal Choice." *American Economic Review* 65:314–25.
Blumstein, Alfred, and Allen Beck. 1999. "Population Growth in U.S. Prisons." In *Prisons*, edited by Michael Tonry and Joan Petersilia. Vol. 26 of *Crime and Justice: A Review of Research*, edited by Michael Tonry. Chicago: University of Chicago Press.
Bound, John, and Richard B. Freeman. 1992. "What Went Wrong? The Erosion of Relative Earnings and Employment among Young Black Men in the 1980s." *Quarterly Journal of Economics* 107:201–32.
Bourgois, Phillipe. 1989. "In Search of Horatio Alger: Culture and Ideology in the Crack Economy." *Contemporary Drug Problems* 16:619–50.
———. 1995. *In Search of Respect.* New York: Cambridge University Press.
Bursik, Robert J., Jr., and Harold Grasmick. 1993. *Neighborhoods and Delinquency.* Lexington, Mass.: Lexington.
Bushway, Shawn D. 1996. "The Impact of a Criminal History Record on Access to Legitimate Employment." Doctoral dissertation, Carnegie Mellon University, Heinz School of Public Policy and Management.
Cantor, David, and Kenneth C. Land. 1985. "Unemployment and Crime Rates in the Post–World War II United States: A Theoretical and Empirical Analysis." *American Sociological Review* 50:317–23.
Chaiken, Jan M., and Marcia R. Chaiken. 1982. *Varieties of Criminal Behavior.* Santa Monica, Calif.: RAND.
Chin, Ko-lin. 1995. *Chinatown Gangs.* New York: Oxford University Press.
Chin, Ko-lin, and Jeffrey Fagan. 1994. "Social Order and Gang Formation among Chinese Gangs." *Advances in Criminological Theory* 6:149–62.
Chiricos, Ted. 1987. "Rates of Crime and Unemployment: An Analysis of Aggregate Research." *Social Problems* 334:187–212.
Clarke, Ronald V., and Derek B. Cornish. 1985. "Modeling Offenders' Decisions: A Framework for Research and Policy." In *Crime and Justice: An Annual Review of Research*, vol. 6, edited by Michael Tonry and Norval Morris. Chicago: University of Chicago Press.
Cloward, Richard, and Lloyd Ohlin. 1960. *Delinquency and Opportunity.* New York: Free Press.
Cohen, Albert. 1955. *Delinquent Boys.* Glencoe, Ill.: Free Press.
Cohen, Jacqueline, and José Canela-Cacho. 1994. "Incarceration and Violent Crime." In *Understanding and Preventing Violence*, edited by Albert J. Reiss, Jr., and Jeffrey A. Roth. Washington, D.C.: National Academy Press.
Cook, Philip J. 1980. "Research in Criminal Deterrence: Laying the Groundwork for the Second Decade." In *Crime and Justice: An Annual Review of Research*, vol. 2, edited by Michael Tonry and Norval Morris. Chicago: University of Chicago Press.
Corcoran, Mary, and Susan Parrott. 1992. "Black Women's Economic Progress." Paper presented at the research conference on "The Urban Underclass: Perspectives from the Social Sciences." Ann Arbor, Mich., June.
Cornish, Derek B., and Ronald V. Clarke, eds. 1986. *The Reasoning Criminal.* New York: Springer-Verlag.

Cressey, Donald R. 1953. *Other Peoples' Money: A Study of the Social Psychology of Embezzlement*. Glencoe, Ill.: Free Press.

Crutchfield, Robert D. 1989. "Labor Stratification and Violent Crime." *Social Forces* 68:489–512.

———. 1995. "Ethnicity, Labor Markets, and Crime." In *Ethnicity, Race, and Crime: Perspectives across Time and Place*, edited by Darnell F. Hawkins. Albany: State University of New York Press.

Crutchfield, Robert D., and Susan R. Pitchford. 1997. "Work and Crime: The Effects of Labor Stratification." *Social Forces* 76:93–118.

Cusson, Maurice, and Pierre Pinsonneault. 1986. "The Decision to Give Up Crime." In *The Reasoning Criminal*, edited by Derek B. Cornish and Ronald V. Clarke. New York: Springer-Verlag.

Decker, Scott, and Richard Wright. 1995. *Burglars on the Job*. New York: Cambridge University Press.

Dodge, Kenneth E., and Nicki R. Crick. 1990. "Social Information Processing Bases of Aggressive Behavior in Children." *Personality and Social Psychology Bulletin* 16:8–22.

Ehrlich, Isaac. 1973. "Participation in Illegitimate Activities: A Theoretical and Empirical Investigation." *Journal of Political Economy* 81:521–65.

Eistadter, W. J. 1969. "The Social Organization of Armed Robbery." *Social Problems* 17:64–83.

Elliott, Delbert S., and David Huizinga. 1986. "The Validity and Reliability of Self Reports of Juvenile Delinquency." *Journal of Quantitative Criminology* 2:327–46.

Elliott, Delbert S., David Huizinga, and Scott Menard. 1989. *Multiple Problem Youth*. New York: Springer-Verlag.

Fagan, Jeffrey. 1989. "Cessation of Family Violence: Deterrence and Dissuasion." In *Family Violence*, edited by Lloyd Ohlin and Michael Tonry. Vol. 11 of *Crime and Justice: A Review of Research*, edited by Michael Tonry and Norval Morris. Chicago: University of Chicago Press.

———. 1990. "Social Processes of Delinquency and Drug Use among Urban Gangs." In *Gangs in America*, edited by C. Ronald Huff. Thousand Oaks, Calif.: Sage.

———. 1992a. "Drug Selling and Licit Income in Distressed Neighborhoods: The Economic Lives of Street-Level Drug Users and Dealers." In *Drugs, Crime and Social Isolation: Barriers to Urban Opportunity*, edited by George E. Peterson and Adelle V. Harrell. Washington, D.C.: Urban Institute Press.

———. 1992b. "The Dynamics of Crime and Neighborhood Change." In *The Ecology of Crime and Drug Use in Inner Cities*. New York: Social Science Research Council.

———. 1993. "The Political Economy of Drug Dealing among Urban Gangs." In *Drugs and Community*, edited by Robert Davis, Arthur Lurigio, and Dennis P. Rosenbaum. Springfield, Ill.: Charles Thomas.

———. 1994. "Women and Drugs Revisited: Female Participation in the Cocaine Economy." *Journal of Drug Issues* 24:179–226.

Fagan, J. A., and Ko-lin Chin. 1990. "Violence as Regulation and Social Control in the Distribution of Crack." In *Drugs and Violence*, edited by Mario de la Rosa, Bernard Gropper, and Elizabeth Lambert. NIDA Research Monograph no. 103. Rockville, Md.: U.S. Public Health Administration, National Institute of Drug Abuse.

Farley, Reynolds. 1987. "Disproportionate Black and Hispanic Unemployment in U.S. Metropolitan Areas." *American Journal of Economics and Sociology* 46:129–50.

Farrington, David P. 1986. "Age and Crime." In *Crime and Justice: An Annual Review of Research*, vol. 7, edited by Michael Tonry and Norval Morris. Chicago: University of Chicago Press.

Farrington, David P., Bernard Gallagher, Lynda Morley, Raymond J. St. Ledger, and Donald J. West. 1986. "Unemployment, School Leaving and Crime." *British Journal of Criminology* 26:335–56.

Ferguson, Ronald, and Randall Filer. 1986 "Do Better Jobs Make Better Workers? Absenteeism from Work among Inner-City Black Youths." In *The Black Youth Unemployment Crisis*, edited by Richard B. Freeman and Harry J. Holzer. Chicago: University of Chicago Press and the National Bureau of Economic Research.

Frazier, Charles E. 1981. "The Use of Life Histories in Testing Theories of Criminal Behavior: Toward Reviving a Method." *Qualitative Sociology* 2:122–42.

Freeman, Richard B. 1983. "Crime and Unemployment." In *Crime and Public Policy*, edited by James Q. Wilson. San Francisco, Calif.: Institute for Contemporary Studies Press.

———. 1991. "Employment and Earnings of Disadvantaged Young Men in a Labor Shortage Economy." In *The Urban Underclass*, edited by Christopher Jencks and Paul E. Peterson. Washington, D.C.: Brookings Institution.

———. 1992. "Crime and the Economic Status of Disadvantaged Young Men." In *Urban Labor Markets and Job Opportunities*, edited by George E. Peterson and Wayne Vroman. Washington, D.C.: Urban Institute.

———. 1994. *Working under Different Rules*. New York: Russell Sage Foundation.

———. 1995. "The Labor Market." In *Crime and Public Policy*, 2d ed., edited by James Q. Wilson and Joan Petersilia. San Francisco, Calif.: Institute for Contemporary Studies.

———. 1996a. "The Supply of Youths to Crime." In *Exploring the Underground Economy*, edited by Susan Pozo. Kalamazoo, Mich.: W. E. Upjohn Institute for Employment Research.

———. 1996b. "Why Do So Many Young American Men Commit Crimes and What Might We Do about It?" *Journal of Economic Perspectives* 10(1):25–42.

Freeman, Richard B., and Harry J. Holzer, eds. 1986. *The Black Youth Unemployment Crisis*. Chicago: University of Chicago Press and the National Bureau of Economic Research.

Glaeser, Edward, Bruce Sacerdote, and Jose Scheinkman. 1996. "Crime and Social Interactions." *Quarterly Journal of Economics* 111:507–48.

Glueck, Sheldon, and Eleanor Glueck. 1950. *Unravelling Juvenile Delinquency*. Cambridge Mass.: Harvard University Press.

Good, David H., Maureen A. Pirog-Good, and Robin C. Sickles. 1986. "An Analysis of Youth Crime and Employment Patterns." *Journal of Quantitative Criminology* 2:219–36.

Gottfredson, Denise. 1985. "Youth Employment, Crime and Schooling." *Developmental Psychology* 21:419–32.

Gottfredson, Michael R., and Travis Hirschi. 1990. *A General Theory of Crime.* Palo Alto, Calif.: Stanford University Press.

Gould, Eric D., Bruce A. Weinberg, and David B. Mustard. 1998. "Crime Rates and Local Labor Market Opportunities in the United States, 1979–95." Paper presented at the annual meeting of the American Economics Association, Chicago.

Grasmick, Harold G., and Robert J. Bursik, Jr. 1990. "Conscience, Significant Others, and Rational Choice: Extending the Deterrence Model." *Law and Society Review* 24:837–61.

Greenberg, David F. 1977. "Delinquency and the Age Structure of Society." *Contemporary Crises* 1:189–223.

Grogger, Jeffrey. 1994. "Criminal Opportunities, Youth Crime, and Young Men's Labor Supply." Unpublished manuscript. Santa Barbara, Calif.: University of California, Department of Economics.

———. 1995. "The Effect of Arrests on the Employment and Earnings of Young Men." *Quarterly Journal of Economics* 110:51–72.

———. 1998. "Market Wages and Youth Crime." *Journal of Labor Economics* 16:756–91.

Hagan, John. 1993a. "The Social Embeddedness of Crime and Unemployment." *Criminology* 31:465–92.

———. 1993b. "Structural and Cultural Disinvestment and the New Ethnographies of Poverty and Crime." *Contemporary Sociology* 22:327–32.

———. 1994. "The New Sociology of Crime and Inequality in America." *Journal of Studies on Crime and Crime Prevention* 4:7–23.

Hagan, John, and Bill McCarthy. 1997. *Mean Streets.* New York: Cambridge University Press.

Hagan, John, and Alberto Palloni. 1990. "The Social Reproduction of a Criminal Class in Working Class London, circa 1950–80." *American Journal of Sociology* 96:265–99.

Hagedorn, John M. 1994a. "Homeboys, Dope Fiends, Legits, and New Jacks." *Criminology* 32:197–219.

———. 1994b. "Neighborhoods, Markets and Gang Drug Organization." *Journal of Research in Crime and Delinquency* 31:264–94.

Hagedorn, John, with Perry Macon. 1988. *People and Folks: Gangs, Crime and the Underclass in a Rustbelt City.* Chicago: Lake View Press.

Hall, Jerome, 1952. *Theft, Law and Society.* Indianapolis: Bobbs-Merrill.

Hannerz, Ulf. 1969. *Soulside: Inquiries into Ghetto Culture and Community.* New York: Columbia University Press.

Hindelang, Michael, Travis Hirschi, and Joseph Weis. 1981. *Measuring Delinquency.* Beverly Hills, Calif.: Sage.

Hirschi, Travis, and Michael Gottfredson. 1983. "Age and the Explanation of Crime." *American Journal of Sociology* 89:552–84.

Horney, Julie, D. Wayne Osgood, and Ineke H. Marshall. 1995. "Criminal Careers in the Short-Term: Intra-individual Variability in Crime and Its Relation to Local Life Circumstances." *American Sociological Review* 60:655–73.

Huff, C. Ronald. 1996. "The Criminal Behavior of Gang Members and Non-gang At-Risk Youth." In *Gangs in America*, edited by C. Ronald Huff. Thousand Oaks, Calif.: Sage.

Huurne, A. ter. 1988. *Unemployed Youths, Three Years Later.* The Hague: Staats-drukkesrij.

Irwin, John. 1970. *The Felon.* Englewood Cliffs, N.J.: Prentice-Hall.

Irwin, John, and James A. Austin. 1994. *It's about Time: America's Imprisonment Binge.* New York: Wadsworth.

Jackson, Bruce. 1969. *A Thief's Primer.* New York: Macmillan.

Jargowsky, Paul, and Mary Jo Bane. 1990. "Ghetto Poverty: Basic Questions." In *Inner City Poverty in the United States*, edited by Lawrence J. Lynn, Jr., and Michael G. H. McGeary. Washington, D.C.: National Academy Press.

Johnson, Bruce D., Terry Williams, Kojo Dei, and Harry Sanabria. 1990. "Drug Abuse and the Inner City: Impacts of Hard Drug Use and Sales on Low Income Communities." In *Drugs and Crime*, edited by Michael Tonry and James Q. Wilson. Vol. 13 of *Crime and Justice: A Review of Research*, edited by Michael Tonry and Norval Morris. Chicago: University of Chicago Press.

Juhn, Chinui, Kevin Murphy, and Robert Topel. 1991. "Why Has the Natural Rate of Unemployment Increased over Time?" *Brookings Papers on Economic Activity* 2:75–142.

Kasarda, John D. 1989. "Urban Industrial Transition and the Underclass." *Annals of the American Academy of Political and Social Science* 501:26–47.

———. 1992. "The Severely Distressed in Economically Transforming Cities." In *Drugs, Crime and Social Isolation*, edited by Adele V. Harrell and George Peterson. Washington, D.C.: Urban Institute Press.

Katz, Jack. 1988. *Seductions of Crime.* New York: Basic Books.

Kirschenman, Joleen, and Kathryn M. Neckerman. 1991. "'We'd Love to Hire Them, But . . .': The Meaning of Race for Employers." In *The Urban Underclass*, edited by Christopher Jencks and Paul E. Peterson. Washington, D.C.: Brookings Institution.

Land, Kenneth C., Patricia L. McCall, and Lawrence E. Cohen. 1990. "Structural Covariates of Homicide Rates: Are There Any Invariances across Time and Space?" *American Journal of Sociology* 95:922–63.

Langan, Patrick. 1994. "America's Soaring Prison Population." *Science* 251:1568–73.

Lemann, Nicholas. 1991. "The Other Underclass." *Atlantic Monthly* 268(April):96–110.

Letkemann, Peter. 1973. *Crime as Work.* Englewood Cliffs, N.J.: Prentice-Hall.

Levitt, Steven D. 1996. "The Effect of Prison Population Size on Crime Rates: Evidence from Prison Overcrowding Litigation." *Quarterly Journal of Economics* 111:319–51.

Liebow, Elliot. 1967. *Talley's Corner.* Boston: Little, Brown.

MacCoun, Robert, and Peter Reuter. 1992. "Are the Wages of Sin $30 an Hour? Economic Aspects of Street-Level Drug Dealing." *Crime and Delinquency* 38:477–91.

Mangold, Catherine. 1994. "Study Warns of Growing Underclass of the Unskilled." *New York Times* (June 2), p. A10.

Massey, D. S., and N. Denton. 1993. *American Apartheid: Segregation and the Making of the American Underclass.* Cambridge, Mass.: Harvard University Press.

Massey, Douglas S., and Mitchell L. Eggers. 1990. "The Ecology of Inequality: Minorities and the Concentration of Poverty, 1970–80." *American Journal of Sociology* 95:1153–88.

Matsueda, Ross, Rosemary Gartner, Irving Piliavin, and Michael Polakowski. 1992. "The Prestige of Criminal and Conventional Occupations." *American Sociological Review* 57:1156–72.

Matza, David. 1964. *Delinquency and Drift.* New York: Wiley.

Mauer, Marc, and Tracy Huling. 1995. *Young Black Americans and the Criminal Justice System—Five Years Later.* Washington, D.C.: The Sentencing Project.

Maurer, David. 1940. *The Big Con.* Indianapolis: Bobbs-Merrill.

———. 1964. *Whiz Mob.* New Haven, Conn.: College and University Press.

Merton, Robert. K. 1938. "Social Structure and Anomie." *American Sociological Review* 3:672–82.

Miller, J. L., and A. B. Anderson. 1986. "Updating the Deterrence Doctrine." *Journal of Criminal Law and Criminology* 77:418–38.

Mishel, Lawrence, and Aaron Bernstein. 1994. *The State of Working America, 1994–95.* Armonk, N.Y.: Sharpe.

Moore, Joan W. 1992a. *Going Down to the Barrio: Homeboys and Homegirls in Change.* Philadelphia: Temple University Press.

———. 1992b. "Institutionalized Youth Gangs: Why White Fence and El Hoyo Maravilla Change So Slowly." In *The Ecology of Crime and Drug Use in Inner Cities*, edited by J. Fagan. New York: Social Science Research Council.

Moss, P., and C. Tilly. 1991. "Why Black Men Are Doing Worse in the Labor Market: A Review of Supply-Side and Demand-Side Explanations." Paper prepared for the Social Science Research Council, Committee on Research on the Urban Underclass, Subcommittee on Joblessness and the Underclass. New York: Social Science Research Council.

Mulvey, Edward P, and John F. LaRosa. 1986. "Delinquency Cessation and Adolescent Development: Preliminary Data." *American Journal of Orthopsychiatry* 56:212–24.

Nagin, Daniel. 1998. "Criminal Deterrence Research at the Outset of the Twenty-First Century." In *Crime and Justice: A Review of Research*, vol. 23, edited by Michael Tonry. Chicago: University of Chicago Press.

Nagin, Daniel, and Joel Waldfogel. 1995. "The Effects of Criminality and Conviction on the Labor Market Status of Young British Offenders." *International Review of Law and Economics* 15:107–26.

Needels, Karen. 1993. "The Long-Term Effects of the Transitional Aid Research Project in Texas: Recidivism and Employment Results." Unpublished manuscript. Princeton, N.J.: Princeton University, Department of Economics.

———. 1994. "Go Directly to Jail and Do Not Collect? A Long-Term Study of Recidivism and Employment Patterns among Prison Releasees." Unpublished manuscript. Princeton, N.J.: Princeton University, Department of Economics.

O'Kane, James. 1992. *The Crooked Ladder.* New Brunswick, N.J.: Transaction.

O'Neill, June. 1990. "The Role of Human Capital in Earnings Differences between Black and White Men." *Journal of Economic Perspectives* 4:25–45.

Padilla, F. 1992. *The Gang as an American Enterprise.* New Brunswick, N.J.: Rutgers University Press.

———. 1993. "The Working Gang." In *Gangs,* edited by Scott Cummings and Daniel J. Monti. Albany: State University of New York Press.

Paternoster, Raymond, and Paul Mazerolle. 1994. "General Strain Theory and Delinquency: A Replication and Extension." *Journal of Research in Crime and Delinquency* 31:235–63.

Piliavin, Irving, Rosemary Gartner, Craig Thornton, and Ross Matsueda. 1986. "Crime Deterrence and Rational Choice." *American Sociological Review* 51:101–19.

Ploeg, G. J. 1991. *Maatschappelijke Positie en Criminaliteit.* Groningen: Wolters-Noordhoff.

Polsky, Ned. 1967. *Hustlers, Beats and Others.* Chicago: Aldine.

Rainwater, Lee. 1970. *Behind Ghetto Walls: Black Family Life in a Federal Slum.* Chicago: Aldine.

Reilly, Brian, and Robert Witt. 1996. "Crime, Deterrence, and Unemployment in England and Wales: An Empirical Analysis." *Bulletin of Economic Research* 48(2):137–59.

Reiss, Albert J., Jr., and Jeffrey A. Roth. 1993. *Understanding and Preventing Violence,* vol. 1. Washington, D.C.: National Academy Press.

Reuter, Peter, Robert MacCoun, and Patrick Murphy. 1990. "Money from Crime." Report R-3894. Santa Monica, Calif.: RAND Corporation.

Rosenfeld, Richard, and Steven Messner. 1989. *Crime and the American Dream.* Albany: State University of New York Press.

Rossi, Peter H., Richard A. Berk, and Kenneth J. Lenihan. 1980. *Money, Work and Crime: Experimental Evidence.* New York: Academic Press.

Sah, Raaj. 1991. "Social Osmosis and Patterns of Crime." *Journal of Political Economy* 99:1272–95.

Sampson, Robert J. 1987. "Urban Black Violence: The Effect of Male Joblessness and Family Disruption." *American Journal of Sociology* 93:348–82.

Sampson, Robert J., and John H. Laub. 1993. *Crime in the Making.* Cambridge, Mass.: Harvard University Press.

Sampson, Robert J., and William Julius Wilson. 1994. "Race, Crime and Urban Inequality." In *Crime and Inequality,* edited by John Hagan and Ruth E. Peterson. Palo Alto, Calif.: Stanford University Press.

Sanchez-Jankowski, M. 1991. *Islands in the Street.* Berkeley: University of California Press.

Sassen-Koob, Saskia. 1989. "New York's Informal Economy." In *The Informal Economy*, edited by Alejandro Portes, Manuel Castells, and Lauren A. Benton. Baltimore: Johns Hopkins University Press.

Shaw, Clifford. 1930. *The Jack-Roller.* Chicago: University of Chicago Press.

Short, James F., Jr. 1997. *Poverty, Ethnicity and Violent Crime.* Boulder, Colo.: Westview.

Shover, Neal. 1985. *Aging Criminals.* Beverly Hills, Calif.: Sage.

———. 1995. *Great Pretenders: Pursuits and Careers of Persistent Thieves.* Boulder, Colo.: Westview.

Smith, Douglas A. 1986. "The Neighborhood Context of Police Behavior." In *Communities and Crime*, edited by Albert J. Reiss, Jr., and Michael Tonry. Vol. 8 of *Crime and Justice: A Review of Research*, edited by Michael Tonry and Norval Morris. Chicago: University of Chicago Press.

Stephens, David W., and John R. Krebs. 1986. *Foraging Theory.* Princeton, N.J.: Princeton University Press.

Sullivan, M. 1989. *Getting Paid: Youth Crime and Unemployment in Three Urban Neighborhoods.* New York: Cornell University Press.

Sutherland, Edward. 1937. *The Professional Thief.* Chicago: University of Chicago Press.

Taylor, C. 1990. "Gang Imperialism." In *Gangs in America*, edited by C. Ronald Huff. Newbury Park, Calif.: Sage.

Thompson, James W., and James Cataldo. 1986. "Comment on Market Incentives for Criminal Behavior." In *The Black Youth Unemployment Crisis*, edited by Richard B. Freeman and Harry J. Holzer. Chicago: University of Chicago Press and the National Bureau of Economic Research.

Thornberry, Terence, and R. L. Christenson. 1984. "Unemployment and Criminal Involvement: An Investigation of Reciprocal Causal Structures." *American Sociological Review* 56:609–27.

Tienda, Marta. 1991. "Poor People and Poor Places: Neighborhood Effects and the Formation of the Underclass." In *Macro-Micro Linkages in Sociology*, edited by Joan Huber. Thousand Oaks, Calif.: Sage.

Tonry, Michael. 1995. *Malign Neglect: Race, Crime and Punishment in America.* New York: Oxford University Press.

Topel, Robert. 1993. "What Have We Learned from Empirical Studies of Unemployment and Turnover?" In *Papers and Proceedings of the American Economic Association.* Washington, D.C.: American Economic Association.

Tunnell, Kenneth D. 1992. *Choosing Crime: The Criminal Calculus of Property Offenders.* Chicago: Nelson-Hall.

Uggen, Christopher J. 1996. "Choice, Commitment, and Opportunity: An Event History Analysis of Supported Employment and Crime." Doctoral dissertation, University of Wisconsin—Madison.

Uggen, Christopher J., and Irving Piliavin. 1998. "Asymmetrical Causation and Criminal Desistance." *Journal of Criminal Law and Criminology* 88: 1399–1422.

Uggen, Christopher, Irving Piliavin, and Ross Matsueda. 1992. "Job Programs and Criminal Desistance." Washington, D.C.: Urban Institute.

Venkatesh, Sudhir Alli. 1997. "The Social Organization of Street Gang Activity in an Urban Ghetto." *American Journal of Sociology* 103:82–111.

Viscusi, W. Kip. 1986a. "Market Incentives for Criminal Behavior." In *The Black Youth Unemployment Crisis*, edited by Richard B. Freeman and Harry J. Holzer. Chicago: University of Chicago Press and the National Bureau of Economic Research.

———. 1986b. "The Risks and Rewards of Criminal Activity: A Comprehensive Test of Criminal Deterrence." *Journal of Labor Economics* 4:317–40.

Wacquant, Loic D., and William Julius Wilson. 1989. "The Costs of Racial and Class Exclusion in the Inner City." *Annals of the American Academy of Political and Social Science* 501:8–25.

Waldorf, Dan. 1973. *Careers in Dope*. Englewood Cliffs, N.J.: Prentice Hall.

Weis, Joseph G. 1986. "Issues in the Measurement of Criminal Careers." In *Criminal Careers and "Career Criminals,"* vol. 2, edited by Alfred Blumstein, Jacqueline Cohen, Jeffrey Roth, and Christy Visher. Washington, D.C.: National Academy Press.

Wilkinson, Deanna L., and Jeffrey Fagan. 1996. "The Role of Firearms in Violence 'Scripts': The Dynamics of Gun Events among Adolescent Males." *Law and Contemporary Problems* 59:55–90.

Williams, Terry. 1989. *The Cocaine Kids*. New York: Addison-Wesley.

Wilson, James Q., and Allan Abrahamse. 1992. "Does Crime Pay?" *Justice Quarterly* 9:359–77.

Wilson, William Julius. 1987. *The Truly Disadvantaged*. Chicago: University of Chicago Press.

———. 1991. "Studying Inner-City Social Dislocations: The Challenge of Public Agenda Research." *American Sociological Review* 56:1–14.

———. 1996. *When Work Disappears*. Chicago: University of Chicago Press.

Witte, Ann D. 1980. "Estimating the Economic Model of Crime with Individual Data." *Quarterly Journal of Economics* 94:57–87.

Witte, Ann D., and Helen Tauchen. 1994. "Work and Crime: An Exploration Using Panel Data." *Public Finance* 49:155–67.

Wright, Richard, and Scott Decker. 1997. *Armed Robbers in Action*. Boston: Northeastern University Press.

Zimring, F. E., and G. Hawkins. 1995. *Incapacitation: Penal Confinement and Restraint of Crime*. Chicago: University of Chicago Press.

Josine Junger-Tas and Ineke Haen Marshall

The Self-Report Methodology in Crime Research

ABSTRACT

Self-reports are often used in criminological research. Use of self-reports raises a number of important methodological issues including sampling options, participation and response rate concerns, and validity problems related to respondent characteristics, criminal involvement, and memory effects. Other central issues include instrument construction, conceptualization of the dependent variable, administration of the instrument, and reliability. The self-report method has improved greatly over the past fifty years. Many of its problems and limitations have been addressed. Although the self-report method does not replace other measures or methods, it has become a valuable tool for measuring criminal involvement and testing theory.

Self-report surveys are used in many social research domains, including public attitudes and opinions, health, education, family relationships, and leisure. The first self-report surveys were developed in the 1930s and 1940s and were essentially attitude measures. Later interest shifted toward measuring behavior (Sudman, Bradburn, and Schwarz 1996). Self-report research on delinquent or deviant behavior, however, differs from self-reports of other topics in several respects. It tries to measure behavior that is punishable by law, usually hidden, socially unacceptable, and morally condemned.

Dissatisfaction with official crime statistics is part of the background to development of self-report studies of offending. Official crime sta-

Josine Junger-Tas is visiting professor of criminology at the University of Lausanne and visiting research fellow at the University of Leyden. Ineke Haen Marshall is professor of criminal justice, Department of Criminal Justice, University of Nebraska at Omaha.

tistics are management tools devised by government agencies to assist them in solving policy questions. Crime definitions, data collection, and the publication of statistics are state activities. Researchers long ago came to realize that their findings would be limited to what official statistics allowed them to see (van Kerckvoorde 1995) as long as their studies were based on official statistical sources.

Police statistics have a number of important drawbacks. First, police activity is mainly reactive, depending on people's willingness to report offenses. Police detection of offenses is relatively rare. Many offenders such as shoplifters and burglars will never be arrested, and some types of crime, such as environmental or "white-collar" crimes, are extremely hard to discover. Second, there is much variation in victim reporting, depending on such variables as the nature and seriousness of the offense, insurance requirements, confidence in police effectiveness, and the hassle involved in going to the police station. In addition, crimes in which the victim is also the offender (such as drug dealing, or prostitution) will not be reported at all. Third, recording of crimes by the police is far from perfect and is influenced by offense seriousness, the probability of clearance by arrest, definitional problems of offense qualification, police priorities, and organizational requirements.

Self-reports have long been used, but most of the early studies were based on unstructured, in-depth interviews with a small number of people, such as, for example, Shaw's *Jack-Roller* (Shaw 1930). However, the movement toward use of more systematic self-report studies began in the 1950s with Short and Nye's study of an adolescent school population (Short and Nye 1957; Erickson and Empey 1963).

Use of self-reports spread rapidly, both in the United States and in Europe (Akers 1964; Christie, Andenaes, and Skirbekk 1965; Elmhorn 1965; Antilla and Jaakkola 1966; Gold 1966, 1970; Buikhuisen, Jongman, and Oving 1969; Hirschi 1969; Jongman 1971; Junger-Tas 1972; Elliott and Voss 1974). Its rapid spread is attributable in part to results that were interpreted as showing that police data were biased and that, although nearly everyone has committed crimes, only a few were picked up and officially processed. The self-report method is now the most commonly used method in criminology (Hagan 1993).

In the United States, the best known nationwide self-report study is the National Youth Survey (Elliott et al. 1985). In Sweden it is common practice to use self-report surveys together with other measures such as, for example, in Project Metropolitan, a longitudinal study of a Stockholm cohort, directed by Carl-Gunnar Janson (1982, 1984), or in school studies (Lindström 1993). Other recent large-scale self-report studies have taken place in Denmark (Balvig 1988), in Germany (Kreuzer et al. 1993), in England (Riley and Shaw 1985; Graham and Bowling 1995), Switzerland (Killias, Villetaz, and Rabasa 1994), Portugal (Gersao and Lisboa 1994), Spain (Barberet, Rechea-Alberola, and Montanes-Rodriguez 1994), and the Netherlands (Junger 1990; Terlouw and Bruinsma 1994; Rutenfrans and Terlouw 1994; Meeus and 't Hart 1993). The research center of the Dutch Ministry of Justice in 1986 started a biannual national self-report study among twelve- to seventeen-year-old juveniles (Junger-Tas and Kruissink 1987, 1990; Junger-Tas, Kruissink, and van der Laan 1992; Junger-Tas and van der Laan 1995).

Self-report studies have two main goals: to establish prevalence and incidence rates of crime and delinquency of specific populations that have higher validity than do official delinquency measures, and to search for correlates of offending and test etiological theories of crime. A subsidiary aim is to evaluate the effects of interventions, such as preventive measures or treatment programs. Most criticism of self-report studies has focused on the first goal, to provide an alternative, more valid measure of criminality. This aim may be somewhat overambitious. Victimization surveys sometimes do better, mainly because they are often based on very large samples, and also because self-report surveys tend to exclude or underrepresent chronic offenders and high-risk youths who are most likely to commit serious delinquent behaviors. However, studies using national random samples such as the National Youth Survey (Elliott, Huizinga, and Menard 1989) or the Monitoring the Future study (Bachman, Johnston, and O'Malley 1992), both in the United States, have included serious delinquency and have produced prevalence and incidence rates at least as valid as those from official or victimization data.

There is a growing recognition, however, that the complexity of offending behavior requires more than summary descriptions of prevalence and incidence. Indeed, self-report surveys have contributed significantly to our understanding of other dimensions of criminality, such as versatility, intermittency, escalation, and age of onset. Delbert Elliott (1994a), in his presidential address to the American Society of Criminology, criticized the National Research Council Panel on The Understanding and Prevention of Violence (Reiss and Roth 1993), because they had hardly taken self-report studies on violence into account. Elliott illustrated the contributions of self-reports by presenting information on the prevalence of aggravated assault, robbery, and rape, but also on age of onset, offending changes over time such as continuation or desistance, and gender, socioeconomic status, and race differences. In addition, Elliott, Huizinga, and Menard (1989) showed that the careers of serious violent offenders are characterized by diversification in offending and not by specialization.

I. Measures of Crime

Criminal career researchers have shown that self-reports may be used to estimate the prevalence and frequency of offending among incarcerated adults, and that self-report measures can provide more detailed data than do police and court records (Chaiken and Chaiken 1982; Mande and English 1987; Horney and Marshall 1991). Comparable studies in a variety of prison settings have consistently shown that the distribution of offending is highly skewed and that a small proportion of offenders is responsible for a large proportion of all crimes. Cross-validation of these self-reports with formal records indicates a reasonable degree of validity in the responses of adult inmates (Marquis with Ebener 1981).

The validity of self-report measures as a measure of crime may be judged at an aggregate level by their convergence with police statistics and victimization studies. O'Brien (1985) discusses convergence of absolute rates of offending, relative rates, demographic characteristics of offenders, and crime trends. With regard to absolute rates, it would be naive to expect that self-reports would produce estimates that are close to those found in police statistics. To the contrary, it should be expected that estimates of crime based on self-reports will be much higher than those based on police records or victimization surveys. It makes more sense to examine the convergence of relative rates (either between different self-report studies, or between self-reports and police statistics or victim surveys). Self-reports consistently show a comparable rank ordering of types of offenses among youth, within the United States (see Hindelang, Hirschi, and Weis 1981; Marshall and Webb 1994), the Netherlands (see Junger-Tas and Kruissink 1987, 1990; Junger-Tas, Kruissink, and van der Laan 1992), and among fourteen European countries and the United States (Junger-Tas, Terlouw, and Klein 1994). Self-report studies—although including more minor offenses—are consistent with police and victim studies in their heavy tilt toward property offenses.

Self-report studies, particularly those that include more serious delinquency items, show offender demographic characteristics consistent with arrest statistics and victim studies. Girls, middle- and upper-class youth, and majority populations tend to show less involvement in persistent, serious, and frequent misbehavior than do boys, lower-class youth, and minorities. The most convincing case for the relative validity of self-report measures is seen in its convergence with police and victim studies regarding crime trends. Jensen (1996) compared self-report panel data from high school seniors for armed robbery, serious assault, and group fights with police arrest data and National Crime Victimization Survey data. He argued that, even if base rates are low and the most violent youth drop out of self-report studies, self-report panel data may present valid trends in violent behavior over time. Jensen found that survey data on violence showed an upward trend before an increase in violence was shown in police data, suggesting that juvenile violence increases start before they are reflected in police arrests. Repeated self-report surveys of twelve- to eighteen-year-old juveniles in the Netherlands have also shown trends in delinquent and violent behavior that are consistent with trends in official police data (Junger-Tas 1996). Moreover, self-report data are vastly superior to police or victim data when data are sought on victimless deviant behavior, such as substance abuse.

Police, victim, and self-report data should all be used to discern trends in crime. When there is consistency, it is likely that some real underlying social reality has been measured. When the data conflict, research should be undertaken to find out why.

The case for self-reports is strong concerning the second objective—to search for correlates of crime and test etiological theories on crime. Self-report data provide data on sociodemographic and other background information and characteristics of offenders, which neither of the other two data sources can match. That makes self-report surveys appropriate for testing and developing criminological theories; one of the best-known theories—social control theory (Hirschi 1969)—was developed on the basis of a self-report survey. Self-reports from adult inmates have also been used to test the implications of developmental theories (Horney, Osgood, and Marshall 1995). That many self-report surveys use nonprobability samples in no way lessens the valuable etiological insights they can provide. Although official data and victim surveys can provide some sociodemographic information, these are of a limited nature. They cannot elucidate the processes by which people start offending, continue doing so, or change their behavior.

Questions of causality, motivation, change, and stability in criminal behavior can hardly be answered without self-reports of the persons concerned. A case in point is the Glueck study: it could not have been as important for theory development as it has turned out to be without the self-reports of the boys, their parents, and their teachers (Sampson and Laub 1993). Analyses of other longitudinal studies, such as the Pittsburgh study (Farrington et al. 1996) and the Rochester study (Smith and Thornberry 1995) have convincingly demonstrated that self-report data are a much-needed supplementary source of informa-- tion to police data.

Tremendous strides have been made in recent years in the use of self-report surveys (and victimization surveys) for international comparisons. Despite problems related to sampling and international data collection methods, the reliability and validity of data from these types of surveys are higher than for police data collected within each particular country; they are particularly suitable for theory testing. Self-reports are excellent sources of data for studies of the correlates of individual differences in delinquent participation or propensity.

A. Cross-National Research

Attempts are being made to use self-reports in international comparative research. Although cross-cultural research has long fascinated researchers (Clinard 1960; Friday 1974; Le Poole 1977), the globalization of the economy and growing interdependence of states in Europe and in the world at large has created the need for more comparative studies of crime and criminal justice. The United Nations initiated worldwide comparisons in this field (Vetere and Newman 1977; Pease and Hukkula 1990; Kangaspunta 1995). However, these comparisons were based on official measures, which present major problems. The limitations of official statistics when used for comparisons between cities, regions, or time periods within one country have been amply documented. It has also been convincingly argued that using national statistics for comparative purposes requires even greater caution (Bennett and Lynch 1990). Countries differ in what they define as criminal acts, in how police count units of crime, and in how they operate in collecting, processing, and recording data.

The Council of Europe is also undertaking efforts to achieve some comparability in police figures and court statistics (Council of Europe

1995). However, the lack of comparable legal definitions, crime categories, common measuring instruments, and common methodologies makes valid international comparisons of crime levels and crime very difficult.

Researchers have begun to collaborate on the development of cross-national self-report studies of offending and victimization (Klein 1989). Both the International Crime Victim Survey (ICVS) (van Dijk, Mayhew, and Killias 1990; van Dijk and Mayhew 1992; Alvazzi del Frate, Zvekic, and van Dijk 1993; Zvekic and Alvazzi del Fratte 1995) and the International Self-Report Delinquency Study (ISRD) (Junger-Tas, Terlouw, and Klein 1994) originated in the Netherlands. The ICVS was first carried out in 1989 with the Computer-Assisted Telephone Interview (CATI) technique in fourteen industrialized countries. Sample sizes ranged from one thousand respondents in Switzerland to 5,274 in Germany. A second sweep of the ICVS was conducted between 1992 and 1994 in industrialized, central and Eastern European, and developing countries (Zvekic 1996). The 1996 ICVS includes most of the countries that participated in the previous two sweeps and some new countries (Albania, Bolivia, Croatia, Kirgizistan, Latvia, Macedonia, Mongolia, Paraguay, Romania, Yugoslavia, and Zimbabwe; Zvekic 1996, p. 3).

The ISRD was started in 1990 with the construction of a common core self-report questionnaire. The Dutch Ministry of Justice's Research and Documentation Center took the initiative for the study, organizing meetings, and coordinating the work to be done. Because this was the first international comparative self-report study, the decision was made to limit the study to Western countries. Pilot studies were done and twelve countries carried out the self-report study of youthful misbehavior.

The ISRD had some clear limitations. Due to financial restrictions, only four country studies were able to draw a random national sample; other participants used city samples, most of them random, and some used school samples. Except for most school samples, where a self-administered questionnaire was used, data collection was usually based on face-to-face interviews. Some studies used a mixed approach in which the questions on delinquent behavior were self-completed.

One of the most interesting findings was the similarity in delinquency involvement in Western countries, despite significant methodological differences. The overall delinquency "ever" rates (excluding status offenses) were roughly similar for the four countries with national random samples (between 80 and 90 percent with the exception of England and Wales with a rate of 65.9 percent), and the seven countries with city samples (between 75.5 percent and 96.9 percent). Although international variations were more pronounced when focusing on particular offenses, typically the range was fairly narrow. For example, the "last twelve months" prevalence rate for carrying a weapon ranged between a low of 3.4 percent (Italy) and a high of 18 percent (United States; Junger-Tas 1994). Boys in all countries were two to four times more likely than girls to commit violent offenses and 1.5 to two times as likely to commit property offenses. Moreover, the peak ages for offending were also similar: fourteen to fifteen for vandalism, sixteen to seventeen for property offenses, and eighteen to twenty for violent offenses.

B. Purpose of This Essay

From its inception, students of the self-report method have complained about the limited knowledge available on the technique's validity and reliability. Yet, from the very earliest stages of development, methodological studies were carried out (see, e.g., Hardt and Bodine 1965). A 1965 report of a conference in which several of the pioneers participated (including Christie, Nye, Reiss, and Clark), attributed the limited knowledge about the validity and reliability of the self-report method to the recency of development of self-report instruments and a preference to apply the technique to substantive research rather than to methodological examination (Hardt and Bodine 1965, p. 15).

The self-report method is no longer novel and significant progress has been made in assessing its methodological strengths and weaknesses. Farrington and colleagues (1996, p. 495) claim that fewer methodological studies have been carried out since the landmark study by Hindelang and colleagues (1981) than before it. Be that as it may, it is clear that there have been remarkable advances in the self-report methodology over the past decades.

The self-report method has been used on a large variety of populations, samples, subgroups, and designs (longitudinal and cross-sectional), in a variety of contexts, in a number of different countries. Because of this wealth of experience, we have developed a much better understanding of the conditions under which the self-report method appears to "work" (and when it does not).

Victimization surveys have been invaluable in identifying major methodological issues in self-report research (including recall periods, telescoping, sampling bias, interviewer effects, coding unreliability and mechanical error, reverse validity checks, problems of under- and over-representation, credibility of respondents, and sampling questions; Hagan 1989, pp. 125, 134–37). They have contributed tremendously to our knowledge about the methodological limitations of survey research, and about issues related to sampling, questionnaire design, and administration. Another wealth of insights comes from methodological studies pertaining to survey research in general, with extensive consideration of issues related to reliability, validity, and sampling (Kish 1965; Sudman and Bradburn 1974, 1982; Dijkstra and van der Zouwen 1982; Bruinsma 1989, 1991, 1994; Elliott and Huizinga 1989; Morton-Williams 1993; Wentland and Smith 1993; Schwarz and Sudman 1994; Fowler 1995; Hessing and Elffers 1995; Lyberg et al. 1997). Needless to say, these general discussions have implications for use of self-reports in the study of crime and delinquency. Finally, recent theoretical developments in cognitive psychology as they apply to survey research have implications for the self-report method in delinquency (e.g., Tanur 1992; Sudman, Bradburn, and Schwarz 1996).

Our goal here is modest: to paint with broad strokes an overview of the self-report method in criminology. The amount of research and theorizing from which we can draw in the present essay is enormous. We cannot discuss all existing self-report studies of delinquency and crime or cover all methodological studies and issues, and we cannot provide a detailed historical account of the self-report method.

Drawing on a variety of European and American sources, we examine to what extent self-report studies have realized the goals identified earlier and assess the degree to which they have advanced criminological knowledge. Since the methodological problems associated with designing reliable and valid self-report studies for one country are magnified in a cross-cultural context, we discuss problems encountered in the ISRD study to illustrate particular points. The self-report method involves a set of interrelated decisions; decisions at earlier points influence options and alternatives at later points. This "total survey error" concept (Groves 1996, p. 389) is our organizing framework. The different sections—on sampling and differential participation rates, validity, and reliability—reflect the three main sources of error: coverage error, nonparticipation error, and measurement error (Schwarz and Sudman 1996).

Section II describes problems related to sampling and response rates. General population samples, disproportionate stratified samples,

and samples of known offenders are examined with respect to participation, retention, and nonresponse rates. Section III deals with the
conceptualization, definition, and operationalization of delinquency.
Section IV considers validity problems, such as respondent effects, effects related to the task at hand, and interviewer effects. Attention is
given to the impact of respondent characteristics, such as sex, age, ethnicity, nature and seriousness of the behavior, motivation and self-presentation, and also to the instrument's content, methods of administration, and memory effects. Section V examines testing of the reliability
of self-report scales. Section VI summarizes the main methodological
issues presented and offers suggestions for improving the self-report
method.

II. Sampling, Differential Participation, and Response Rates

Two different applications may be distinguished: surveys of offenders
and general population surveys (Maxfield and Babbie 1995, p. 213).
General population surveys employ samples that represent a broad
population, such as U.S. or Swedish households, adult males, or high
school seniors, and typically are descriptive and enumerative, with a
purpose to count; they count a representative sample and draw inferences about the population as a whole (Oppenheim 1992, p. 12). Studies of offenders, however, select samples of respondents known to have
committed crimes, such as prisoners or arrestees. These surveys often
deal with the question of "why"; they include enumeration, description, and analyses of causality (see ibid., p. 13). Surveys of prisoners
are useful to establish their rates of offending while free (e.g., to test
the effect of incapacitation). General population surveys present different types of difficulties with regard to internal and external validity and
reliability than do surveys of known offenders (Maxfield and Babbie
1995, p. 214).

A. General Population Surveys and Representative Samples

The number of self-report studies of delinquency using national
probability samples of adolescents is very limited. The National Survey
of Youth (NSY) was one of the first American national-level self-report
studies of delinquency using such a national probability sample of adolescents. Conducted by Martin Gold in 1967 (with Jay Williams) and
1972 (with David Reimer), the surveys evolved from Gold's original
Flint, Michigan study (Gold 1970). The 1967 NSY collected data from

a national probability sample of 847 adolescents ages thirteen to six-teen (Warr 1996, p. 20). More recently, the National Youth Survey (NYS), sponsored by the National Institute for Mental Health and the Office of Juvenile Justice and Delinquency Prevention, has collected nine waves of data on a national probability sample of 1,725 youth ages eleven to seventeen in 1976. This youth panel was composed of ages twenty-seven to thirty-three when last interviewed in 1993 (Elliot, Hu-izinga, and Menard 1989; Elliott 1994b).

European examples of self-report surveys in the framework of the ISRD study, involving nationwide probability samples of adolescents, were done in Switzerland (Killias, Villetaz, and Rabasa 1994), the United Kingdom (Bowling, Graham, and Ross 1994), Portugal (Ger-sao and Lisboa 1994), and the Netherlands (Terlouw and Bruinsma 1994). These examples illustrate the importance of an accurate sam-pling frame. For the British study, a national random sample was gen-erated by selecting households at random using the post office's post-code address file; this avoids the pitfalls of the main alternative sampling frame—the Electoral Register—which relies on individuals' voluntary registration and excludes those under age eighteen (Bowling, Graham, and Ross 1994, pp. 46–47). All too often, logistical con-straints influence the sampling frame employed in national probability samples of youth. Typically, the researcher will use some form of clus-ter sampling, such as regions, towns, or cities. For instance, in the Swiss study, a random sample of ninety-six towns (including twenty-eight in French-speaking and nineteen in Italian-speaking areas) was drawn from the total of some three thousand towns, according to a standard sampling procedure that takes the relative population of towns into account. Towns were sampled because, in Switzerland, population registers are kept only by towns, not by cantons or the fed-eral government. Nine towns refused to cooperate and six towns were found to substitute for the refusals, resulting in a total of ninety-three towns. From among these ninety-three towns, youth between fourteen and twenty-one were randomly selected on the basis of town registers (Killias, Villetaz, and Rabasa 1994, p. 189). In comparable fashion, the national probability sample of youth (fourteen to twenty-one) in the Netherlands also employed population registers. A stratified nation-wide random sample of seventeen cities was drawn, selected on the ba-sis of the degree of urbanization and geographical distribution. Both the Swiss and the Dutch surveys thus excluded rural respondents. This is also true for the Spanish ISRD survey (Barberet, Rechea-Alberola, and Montanes-Rodriguez 1994), which used a large stratified urban sample, excluding sampling sites from the rural areas.

Because of the serious logistical problems involved in drawing a representative national or local sample from the general (youth) population, many researchers have resorted to the alternative of using probability samples of high school students. These samples may be national or local, limited to public high schools or including all types of high schools. For example, since 1975 the Institute for Social Research of the University of Michigan has conducted an annual self-report study called "Monitoring the Future" designed to explore changes in values, behaviors, and attitudes of American youths. This study involves sampling some sixteen thousand high school seniors from approximately 125 schools in the United States. The sampling is done in such a way that the results are representative of the nation as a whole (Jensen and Rojek 1992, p. 135). Yet, it is important to remember that this study underrepresents delinquents, who may have dropped out, been sent to reform schools or juvenile jails, been sent to special schools for emotionally or cognitively disturbed youth, or be truant on the survey day.

Another American example of a nationally representative sample of public high school students is the Youth in Transition (YIT) survey, which employed a panel design and was based on a nationally representative sample of 2,213 male public high school students, who were interviewed for the first time in the fall of 1966, when they were beginning the tenth grade, and for the last time in the spring of 1969, when they were completing the twelfth grade (Brezina 1996, p. 46).

Although working with high schools is more manageable than using the entire youth population as the sampling frame, the obstacles encountered when drawing a representative nationwide sample of high school students are tremendous. Therefore, it is much more common to find self-report studies limited to high school students in one particular town or city, usually selected because of convenience. For example, the U.S. component of the ISRD used a random selection of students in the twelve public high schools in the Omaha, Nebraska metropolitan area, where the researchers happened to live (Marshall and Webb 1994). The Italian component of the ISRD study (Gatti et al. 1994) took place in three different cities: Genoa, Messina, and Siena; within these cities, the schools were randomly selected according to type (preparatory school, technical schools) and, within the schools, the subjects were selected at random. The Finnish sample of the ISRD study was restricted to one city (Helsinki), and included a nonrandom sample of ninth (fifteen- to sixteen-year-olds) and eleventh (seventeen- to eighteen-year-olds) classes from the register of schools in Helsinki (Aromaa 1994). Inevitably, the generalizability of these samples (often a combination of convenience/purposive/random) is very limited. Yet, they represent the bulk of the self-report studies and they provide a valuable contribution, even though they do not satisfy the stringent demands of probability sampling.

In the field of delinquency research, a third type of general population sample may be included: the birth (or primary school) cohort. Cohort samples are often confused with community samples, but they should not be because they do not share the problems of community samples. There are many cohort samples in criminology research, and they should probably not be included under either the community or secondary school samples. Examples include the Dunedin Multidisciplinary Study (birth register) (Bartusch et al. 1997), the youngest of the three panels of the Pittsburgh Youth Study (school register, taken at age six before any children left school; Farrington et al. 1996), and the Danish Adoption Study (adoption register; Mednick, Gabrielli, and Hutchings 1984). Because the original register is known, all original subjects can be contacted at each wave of longitudinal follow-up and as a result attrition does not necessarily result in a contracting sample size; in some cohort studies participation has improved as the children have grown older (the Dunedin study grew from 85 percent participation at age thirteen to 97 percent at age twenty-one). Such cohort samples are less likely than community or school samples to underrepresent serious offenders. If more serious offenders are needed for statistical power to study them, then high-risk stratification oversampling can be added to the cohort design.

B. Disproportionate Stratified Samples

Researchers often prefer probability sampling because it allows the estimation of sampling error. Indeed, if the primary purpose of a survey is to arrive at estimates of incidence and prevalence of delinquency in the population, it is crucial to be able to estimate the sampling error, and that the error is minimal. What complicates matters is that deviance (particularly serious deviance) is a rare event, which increases the likelihood of large sampling error. Experience with victimization surveys suggests that very large samples are needed to provide reliable estimates of rare events (e.g., rape). Low frequencies of events are associated with large confidence intervals (O'Brien 1985, p. 52), often making estimates unreliable. The sample size of the National Youth Survey, for example (roughly fifteen hundred respondents), is sufficient to generate reliable prevalence and incidence rates for the nation as a whole on most of the delinquent behaviors included in the interviews, but is not large enough to allow detailed breakdowns for geographic areas (e.g., rates for states, or cities; O'Brien 1985, p. 71), or for particular groupings of youth. If there are many different subgroups (based on gender, race, social class), a much larger sample is needed to reduce error and attain statistical significance (Oppenheim 1992, p. 44). Another important determinant of sample size is the nature of the dependent variable: if the dependent variable is nominal or categorical (e.g., sixteen different types of crime), then reaching statistical significance requires a much larger sample than an interval-level variable (where averages can be used; see ibid.).

In order to ensure that there are sufficient serious offenses and sufficient respondents in particular subgroups, disproportionate stratified sampling is used. "If we can find small strata that contain large portions of the rare trait, it is efficient to increase their sampling fractions" (Kish 1965, p. 406). The deliberate use of widely different sampling rates for various strata is routinely employed in crime victimization surveys, where one goal is to obtain some minimum number of crime victims in a sample. Persons living in large urban areas, where serious crime is more common, are disproportionately sampled (Maxfield and Babbie 1995, p. 199). With stratified, disproportionate random sampling, a major task is to assign weights in such a way as to permit unbiased estimates of population parameters (Hindelang 1981, p. 34). Because crime and delinquency research tends to focus on relatively rare events and "at risk" populations, examples of disproportionate stratified sampling abound among recent self-report surveys.

As a simple function of their relatively small numbers in the total population, members of ethnic and racial minority groups tend to be underrepresented in self-report studies (Natalino 1981, pp. 64–65). Because of their theoretical relevance for delinquency theory, oversampling of minorities is now a fairly common practice among delinquency researchers. The Dutch ISRD study, for instance, oversampled Turkish and Moroccan youth from Amsterdam and Rotterdam. The German ISRD study (Boers, Class, and Kurz 1994, p. 344), drew two oversamples to enhance the number of respondents from big cities. In the United Kingdom, the nationwide representative sample was complemented by a random sample in areas of high victimization, and a booster sample of ethnic minorities (Bowling, Graham, and Ross 1994, p. 46). Somewhat differently, in Switzerland, the Italian- and French-speaking parts were oversampled to allow conclusions not only for Switzerland as a whole, but also for the major language groups (Killias, Villetaz, and Rabasa 1994, p. 189).

An American example of oversampling is the Rochester Youth Development Study (RYDS), a multiwave panel study in which youth and their primary caretakers were interviewed every six months over four and a half years. The target population were students attending the seventh or eighth grades of the Rochester, New York, public schools in the spring of 1988. A stratified sample was selected from this population so that students at high risk for delinquency and drug use were proportionally over-represented and the findings could be weighted to represent the target population. The sample was stratified on two dimensions: males were oversampled (75 percent vs. 25 percent) because they are more likely than females to engage in delinquency, and students from high-crime areas were oversampled since living in a high-crime area increases the chance of offending (Smith and Thornberry 1995, p. 456).

Undersampling low crime-rate groups (females) magnifies the problem of having large confidence intervals for low-prevalence estimates. Indeed, if the primary purpose is to estimate the prevalence of (female) delinquency, one should oversample, not undersample low crime-rate groups. However, if the research question is focused on correlates of offending, for example, then oversampling (of high-risk groups) in order to ensure enough rare events for analysis is appropriate.

Sometimes the purpose of the study is exclusively to examine high-risk, high-crime youth, and there is no need to include the entire youth population (and thus to oversample). For instance, Fagan, Weis, and Cheng (1990) were interested in students in high-crime, innercity neighborhoods and they drew a general population sample from students in four such neighborhoods. Student samples were drawn from randomly selected classrooms in each school (grades 10–12; Fagan, Weis, and Cheng 1990). What this last example illustrates is that the distinction between general population surveys (with varying theoretical populations, varying from the national youth population to the high-risk population in a particular city) and surveys of known offenders best may be seen as representing two extreme poles of a continuum of possible sampling choices.

C. Samples of Known Offenders (Offender-Based Sampling Strategies)

Wells and Rankin (1991; cited in Weis, Crutchfield, and Bridges 1996, pp. 83–84) distinguish in their meta-analysis of self-report studies between general and local probability samples (possibly disproportionately stratified), convenience samples, and an "official/institutional 'contrived' sample, which is a delinquent group plus a nondelinquent control group." The last type (i.e., combination of delinquent/nondelinquent sample) is the typical manner in which delinquency researchers have tried to maximize variance on delinquency (Hindelang, Hirschi, and Weis 1981, p. 31), dating as far back as the Gluecks who collected life history data on five hundred delinquents and five hundred nondelinquents in the 1940s. The Gluecks' design was criticized for overestimating the strength of relationships with delinquency by omitting the middle category. This problem is avoided by Le Blanc and Fréchette's longitudinal study of male criminal activity in Canada (1989), one of the best current examples of comparing delinquency between a representative sample of the adolescent population, including also poorly behaved delinquents, and a sample of youngsters declared juvenile delinquents by the courts.

Samples of known offenders are often used in combination with general community-based samples (as in the examples above), or in lieu of general community-based population (youth) surveys. Sometimes oversampling simply is not possible, efficient, or even desirable. Weis (1986, p. 102), in his discussion of methodological issues in criminal career research, explains that—regardless of stratification—samples drawn from community-based sampling frames like schools and households are more likely to miss offenders than nonoffenders, and this problem is likely to be most severe for high-rate offenders, leading to their disproportionate underrepresentation in these samples. Also, those with highly transient living arrangements tend to be missed in household-based samples (ibid.). Thus, Weis suggests, researchers interested in serious offenders are best advised to concentrate on surveys of known offenders rather than on general population surveys.

A related point is the questionable general assumption—since general youth samples represent such a broad range of youth—that chronic offenders must also be included. That is not necessarily so. Cernkovich, Giordano, and Pugh (1985, p. 51) contend "that these offenders will not be included in very large numbers, if at all, as an automatic function of sound sampling techniques." Using comparisons between a general youth population survey and results from institutionalized samples, they document that "chronic offenders are involved in significantly more serious and more frequent delinquent activity than are adolescents typically identified in self-report surveys of the general youth population" (ibid.). That is, even when careful oversampling of high-risk groups has been accomplished, an institutionalized sample will provide basically different rates than rates generated from general population samples.

The undeniable advantage of working with samples of known offenders is that they possess—with virtual certainty—the characteristic of interest, that is, delinquent or offending behavior. A possible drawback is limited generalizability. The further the sample has penetrated into the criminal justice process, the greater the contrast or variance obtained (but also the greater the sample bias). Indeed, from the perspective of ensuring greater representativeness of the general population, samples of self-reported offenders are better than samples of arrestees, and samples of arrestees are better than inmate samples or even samples of convictees (Weis 1986, p. 103). Prison inmates are unlikely to be representative of all offenders: they are presumably the most serious (Canela-Cacho, Blumstein, and Cohen 1997), the oldest, and perhaps the most inept at avoiding detection (Visher 1986; Weis 1986, p. 102). Thus arrestees involved in the Arrestee Drug Abuse Monitoring program (ADAM)[1] in the United States represent a better cross section of the offending population—to the extent that refusing urinalysis is random—than do samples of those convicted and incarcerated.

Longshore, Turner, and Stein (1996) collected self-report data from a "criminal" sample of people extensively involved in serious crime: drug-using adult or juvenile offenders involved in Treatment Alternatives to Street Crime (TASC),[2] including 623 offenders (57 percent

[1] The Drug Use Forecasting (DUF) program was established in 1987 by the National Institute of Justice to test booked arrestees for illicit drug use. On a quarterly basis, data were collected through anonymous voluntary interviews and urinalysis from adult and juvenile booked arrestees in central lockups in twenty-three American cities (National Institute of Justice 1996). In 1998, the DUF program was replaced by ADAM (Arrestee Drug Abuse Monitoring), with another twelve sites added. ADAM expects to have seventy-five sites by the year 2000.
[2] Treatment Alternatives to Street Crime (TASC) programs identify drug-using adult and juvenile offenders in the criminal justice system, assess their treatment needs, place them in treatment, and monitor progress. Treatment may be in lieu of, or an adjunct to, a routine criminal justice disposition. Offenders sent to TASC programs may have been charged with a crime or may be sent to TASC by probation or parole officers who suspect a drug problem (Longshore, Turner, and Stein 1996).

African-American, 37 percent non-Hispanic whites, 6 percent others, mostly Hispanics); one-fourth women; one-fourth juveniles under eighteen; most with extensive criminal records; 86 percent having been incarcerated at least once. These researchers wanted "a heterogeneous sample of persons heavily involved in crime" (p. 215). Their TASC sample clearly serves their particular research objective better than a sample of male inmates, such as those used in a series of criminal careers studies (Chaiken and Chaiken 1982; Mande and English 1987; Horney and Marshall 1991, 1992). These criminal careers studies, with a primary focus on estimation of the prevalence, incidence, seriousness, and versatility of offending, have relied heavily on self-reports. They make a convincing case for the argument that the self-report method may also be used on particular adult populations.

The distinction between population-based sampling and samples of known offenders is particularly relevant with regard to the age of the target population. Most recent examples of self-reports of adults involve surveys of known offenders: adult arrestees (ADAM) or inmates. There are very few recent population-based self-report studies of adults. In the beginning of the self-report method, the interest was in adults (Reuband 1989, p. 89), but juveniles soon became the typical subjects. There are some examples, however, of community-based self-report surveys among adults. Surveys of self-reported noncompliance with income tax laws have been undertaken (Long and Swingen 1991). Reuband describes a German study, consisting of representative samples of the West German population age eighteen and older, one in 1982 ($n = 1,993$, response rate 68 percent), and one in 1987 ($n = 987$, response rate 70 percent). The questions dealt with nonserious deviance (hashish use, riding on public transportation without paying, shoplifting). The British Crime Survey also has included questions about offending.

D. Differential Participation and Response Rates

No matter how carefully and sophisticatedly the sample is planned, "the achieved sample will always be less accurate than the designed sample" (Oppenheim 1992, p. 45). The reality of sampling is bound to produce a sample that deviates from the original design. There may be many reasons why individuals who should (theoretically) be included in the study are not: inability to locate people, people not home, problems related to the sampling list (houses have been torn down, people have moved, population registers are inaccurate, individuals are not known at address, nonexisting address), unable to understand/speak the language, respondent is physically or mentally ill, refusals, parental refusal (Sutterer and Karger 1994, p. 160).

Some reasons for nonresponse are neutral and unlikely to affect the representative nature of the sample (e.g., nonexistent address, nobody living in the house), some may vary systematically with the criteria (e.g., absent for some time, poor command of the language, physically or mentally ill), some may be outright refusals (either by the respondent or his/her parents; Sutterer and Karger 1994, p. 160).

A crucial concern is that nonresponse may be selective. The likelihood of participation may differ depending on criteria related to the likelihood of being involved in delinquency and crime in the first place. The final sample may then be biased because it systematically overrepresents certain groups and underrepresents others. Those individuals for whom self-reports are not obtained may be more likely than average to engage in serious or frequent offending or to have characteristics associated with an increased risk of offending (Rutter and Giller 1983, p. 31). For example, high-rate offenders may be more likely than others to be uncooperative and to refuse to participate (Weis 1986, p. 102).

Although it is often argued that absence of response bias is more important than a high response rate (Maxfield and Babbie 1995, p. 227), such optimism may be unwarranted. True, depending on judicious presentation, the achieved sample may look like the target sample and, depending on sample size, the achieved sample may not be significantly different from the nonresponders. Yet, the literature suggests that, more often than not, missing cases are more elusive and uncooperative.

Nonparticipation is also problematic because it reduces the sample size. This difficulty is often solved by substituting, a procedure which may unwittingly further bias the final sample. In most instances, the researcher compares the characteristics of the final sample against the likelihood that the respondents look like a random sample of the population; this procedure can only partly solve the problem of sample bias, because of the limited nature of comparisons possible.

Any discussion of nonresponse in delinquency research must mention the extensive methodological study by Hindelang and colleagues (1981). In their systematic comparison between three types of (nonoverlapping) samples ("official nondelinquents," "police delinquents," and "court delinquents"), they found varying participation rates between different combinations of blacks and whites, males and females, nondelinquents, police delinquents, and court delinquents (Hindelang, Hirschi, and Weis 1981). The original samples were substantially reduced by a number of factors. First, 18 percent of the parents of the officially nondelinquent school sample indicated that they did not want their son's name to appear on the list from which study participants would be selected. The greatest attrition rates occurred after the initial sampling stage, however, when it was necessary to obtain positive consent from each participant (and from his guardian) who had been selected. As Hindelang et al. indicate, tracking down study participants "turned out to be an enormous—and often unsuccessful—task" (p. 33). The information provided by schools, police files, or courts was often incorrect or out-of-date. The most elusive target participants were—generally speaking—the female police and court delinquents: between one-third (white, low-SES female police delinquents) and about half (black female court delinquents) of these original subsamples could not be located. Of the total of 4,388 youth included in the three samples combined, about 24 percent could not be located (based on our calculations; see Hindelang, Hirschi, and Weis 1981, table 2.2, p. 34). Of those who could be located, significant numbers refused to participate. The highest refusal rate was among white female high-SES court delinquents: 58.9 percent of the ninety-seven females contacted refused; the lowest refusal rate was among the black female police delinquents: only 16.2 percent of the ninety-nine females contacted refused. Overall, about 32 percent of those located refused to participate, even though respondents were paid $10.00 and their choice of a popular record album. Thus for the three samples combined, less than half of the original sample participated. The Hindelang et al. study is a valuable exploration of the methodological problems of self-report research; however, the high nonresponse rates cast serious doubt on the value of their results for purposes other than its original research question: to determine experimentally the conditions under which self-report surveys appear to work best.

Self-report research based on known offenders reports widely varying participation rates. In the Second Rand Inmate Survey, 2,190 inmates selected to represent an incoming incarceration cohort of adult males in California, Michigan, and Texas, including both prison and jail inmates, participated in a self-report study of offending. The sample used was multistage, and it combined judgment, probability, and quota features. On the basis of judgment, state prisons in three states were selected. Prison inmates sentenced from specific counties were stratified on age, race, past prison record, and current conviction offense and selected with probability inversely proportional to sentence length. Substitutes were drawn from the relevant stratum if the selected inmate was unwilling or unable to participate (Marquis 1981, p. 25). The response rates were 50 percent in California and Michigan prisons, over 66 percent in California and Michigan jails, and 82 percent in Texas prisons (Chaiken and Chaiken 1982 p. 5).

Analysis of response patterns for sampled prisoners showed that after inclusion of replacement respondents in California and Michigan, there were no significant response biases by age group, prior record, race, or conviction offense, except that Hispanic inmates were underrepresented in the California sample. In all three states, inmates with reading difficulties were included in the sample but were underrepresented (Chaiken and Chaiken 1982, p. 5).

In a replication of the Rand study in Colorado, the overall participation rate was much higher at 91 percent, which is attributed by the researchers to the fact that their sample (inmates waiting further processing in the diagnostic unit) had nothing to do, there were no competing activities, and the inmates had only recently been sentenced (which may have minimized peer pressure); the inmates were also credited $5.00 to their accounts if they completed the interview (Mande and English 1987). A similar high participation rate occurred in the Nebraska Inmate Survey (Horney and Marshall 1991, 1992). Although the high nonresponse rate in the Rand Inmate Survey casts doubts on the value of its results, it is worth noting that roughly comparable observations were made in the Colorado and Nebraska replications with much higher participation rates (Horney and Marshall 1992; Mande and English 1987).

The Drug Use Forecasting (now ADAM) program reports high participation rates among arrestees: more than 90 percent agree to the voluntary interview and over 80 percent of these agree to provide a urine specimen (National Institute of Justice 1996). It is thus not correct to assume that samples of known offenders will be more reluctant to participate in self-report surveys than are community-based samples. Some problems encountered by self-report survey researchers sampling "captive" populations such as inmates are distinctive, and require particular guidelines in terms of ethical considerations, possible heightened social desirability effects, and problems related to conducting interviews in an institutional setting. These issues relate not only to obtaining cooperation of the offenders, but also to partial nonresponses, and possible limited validity and reliability of the responses.

Nonparticipation problems of a different nature are encountered by self-report research on youth populations in the "free world." Between 1967 and 1997 there has been a general decline in willingness to participate in surveys (Stouthamer-Loeber and van Kammen 1995; Meloen and Veenman 1990). Possible reasons include increased use of informed consent forms, greater difficulty contacting a household (with more women working), use of telephone answering machines, overinterviewing of people, and increasing reluctance to allow strangers in the home. It is, then, not realistic to expect 100 percent participation rates in population-based self-report surveys, in particular those involving questions about such socially sensitive subjects as offending. Stouthamer-Loeber and van Kammen (1995, p. 66) argue that "with good planning and care it is possible for [self-report] studies to reach participation rates of at least 80 percent."

In reality, community-based self-report surveys of crime and delinquency show widely differing participation levels. For instance, Terlouw and Bruinsma (1994) used a stratified sample of seventeen Dutch towns, with oversampling of ethnic minorities. Only 56 percent participated in the research; nonresponse for 48 percent was due to refusal; response rates were higher in the smaller and medium size cities, in comparison with the large cities. There was no significant difference in response rates between ethnic minorities and nonminorities. In the British ISRD study, there was an overall response rate of 69 percent (Bowling, Graham, and Ross 1994, p. 46); for the Helsinki school-based study it was 75 percent, varying between 38 percent and 92 percent (the low participation was explained by the beautiful spring weather! see Aaromaa 1994, p. 19). In the ISRD study conducted in Belfast, Northern Ireland, there was a very low refusal rate (8 percent), mostly from those of low- or lower-middle socioeconomic status (McQuoid 1994, p. 64). Perhaps the monetary remuneration of five pounds was instrumental in this. The Belgium ISRD surveys were conducted both inside the schools (for the fourteen- to eighteen-year-olds) and at home (for the nineteen- to twenty-one-year-olds). The response rate for the home interviews was about 70 percent, considerably lower than the very high response rate for the students in schools (about 98 percent; however, only sixteen of the twenty schools initially selected agreed to participate). Questionnaires were completed in small groups during school time with the researcher present; a factor which, the researchers argue, may explain the very high level of participation (Born and Gavrey 1994, pp. 134–35). Students who were attending alternative courses were contacted individually, sometimes several times, to avoid their exclusion from the sample. The Mannheim self-report study (Sutterer and Karger 1994, p. 161) reported a response rate of 51.3 percent. Overall, the lowest ISRD participation rate (31 percent) was reported by Killias and colleagues (1994, p. 189), partly because of problems with procedures involved for getting consent.

As the preceding examples show, researchers tend to provide a variety of speculations as to why they obtain high or low participation rates. There also exists an extensive body of systematic research on which factors influence participation rates, and how to improve participation rates. Stress of confidentiality, informed consent issues, remuneration, and willingness to invest large amounts of time and resources in reaching the last 10 or 20 percent of the sample are cited by Stouthamer-Loeber and van Kammen (1995, chap. 6).

Oppenheim (1992, pp. 104–6) lists many factors that have been found to increase the response rate: advance warning, explanation of selection, credible sponsorship, type of envelope, publicity, incentives, confidentiality, reminders, anonymity, appearance, length, topic, rapport, and return envelopes. The method of administration—face-to-face interview versus self-administered versus phone versus mail—is, of course, a main factor influencing willingness to participate. Response rates—defined as the proportion of approached people who actually complete the interview—tend to be higher with in-person than with phone interviews (Taylor 1994, p. 236).

It is not possible to develop a foolproof "how-to" recipe that guarantees high levels of response. More often than not, mere listings of factors fail to take into consideration that the salience of certain factors is contingent on the context, the type of study, the situation, characteristics of participants, and the characteristics of the researcher or interviewer. With the maturing of the self-report method, more scholars are beginning to develop comprehensive, integrated ways to look at issues of nonresponse, incorporating insights from cognitive and motivational psychology. "Perhaps the most important determinant both of response rate and the quality of the responses is the subject's motivation" (Oppenheim 1992, p. 82). Although motivation is a crucial factor in the quality of the respondent's responses, it is, of course, of utmost importance in the respondent's decision to participate in the survey in the first place.

Factors that influence motivation to participate may be divided into societal level factors, attributes of the study, characteristics of potential participants, and attributes of interviewers (cf. Groves, Cialdini, and Couper 1992, p. 71). Each of these clusters of factors may be viewed as increasing or decreasing a potential participant's motivation. First, societal factors comprise the social responsibility felt by the respondent, the number of surveys in which the participant has participated, and the perceived legitimacy of the study (who is the sponsor, who else is participating?).

Next, the attributes of the study may influence the likelihood to participate: the topic, the length of the interview, the interview location, intrusiveness of the questions, perceived benefits to the participant. Research focusing on delinquency or deviance may be unpopular, particularly if a study takes place among a population group (innercity blacks or Latinos in the United States or guestworkers in Germany) who are viewed by the public and the media as a major source of violent crime.

The likelihood of agreeing to participate varies by certain characteristics of the potential participant. Some studies have found differential participation rates for older versus younger subjects, between males and females, and for different socioeconomic status levels (Stouthamer-Loeber and van Kammen 1995). Other factors that may influence participation rates are inquisitiveness and the desire to be nice to the interviewer, and physical and mental health problems (Stouthamer-Loeber and van Kammen 1995, p. 71). People who are incarcerated will value a monetary reward of $5.00 more than college students; people who have just been arrested may be more inclined to cooperate with a (voluntary) survey in a police station than people who have just been convicted and sentenced.

And finally, the attributes of the interviewer or researcher who contacts the person may affect how potential respondents react to an invitation to participate. The sex, age, and race or ethnicity of the interviewers may interact with the participants' views, prejudices, and preferences (Stouthamer-Loeber and van Kammen 1995, p. 72). Potential respondents will be more likely to trust—and thus to cooperate with—members of their own group rather than with people perceived as outsiders. Members of socially marginal groups often have become cynical as a result of experiences with state bureaucracies and social control agencies; a survey researcher may be viewed as yet another representative of the out-group (cf. Lee 1993, p. 133; see also Morton-Williams 1993).

1. *Retention Rates: A Problem in Panel (Longitudinal) Studies.* Longitudinal self-report studies of delinquency present even greater challenges in terms of continued respondent participation than do cross-sectional studies. With the growing popularity of developmental theories of antisocial behavior (e.g., Bartusch et al. 1997), panel studies are becoming more common. These studies often involve repeated follow-up interviews, and more often than not they suffer from the problem of contracting sample size. As one interviewing wave follows another, it becomes more difficult to locate all panel members and to maintain their interest in the study; replacements are only a partial solution (Oppenheim 1992, p. 34). Attrition in follow-up waves creates the risk that the sample will become biased. Cordray and Polk (1983) conducted a secondary analysis of data from seven panel studies on deviant behavior to assess the potential bias and error resulting from respondent attrition over time. They conclude that the problem attrition poses for panel research depends in part on the purpose of the investigation (p. 234). If the objective is the development of univariate estimates of the level of deviant behavior, there will be slight but systematic biases. The attrition problem is less pressing in causal analysis (i.e., bivariate and multivariate relationships). Generally, studies have found that participants from disorganized families, those who move often, those who are more frequently involved in the use of alcohol and drugs, and those engaged in criminal activities are less likely to be re-captured in follow-ups (Stouthamer-Loeber and van Kammen 1995, p. 63). For the NYS, a sample of 2,360 eligible youth was selected. Of these, 73 percent agreed to participate in 1976. By 1980, the sample size was down to 1,494, or 63 percent of the original sample (O'Brien 1985, p. 72). A Swedish study by Sarnecki (1989) on drugs and crime reports that about one-third of the original group dropped out, including more of those with a long criminal record. In the Swedish study, the attrition was higher among the modestly to poorly socially adjusted. Stouthamer-Loeber and van Kammen report, however, that participants in the Pittsburgh Youth Study become more difficult to locate over time, but not more likely to refuse. They did not find over six waves "any disproportionate loss with regard to delinquency status, socioeconomic status, race, single parent status, and educational level of the mother" (1995, pp. 64–65). Unfortunately, even if participation

loss is randomly distributed, the cumulative effect of nonparticipation still can cause problems, in terms of escalating numbers of cases with missing data (1995, p. 64; see also Meloen and Veenman 1990).

The major forms and effects of nonresponse bias may occur prior to the initial data collection rather than in panel loss (Cordray and Polk 1983, p. 240). Extremely low response rates are not uncommon in cross-sectional self-report studies. It is conceivable that longitudinal researchers are more concerned about attrition, and thus put more effort into maximizing response rates, because they have to plan for repeated contacts. Whether this is indeed the case is an empirical question.

2. *The Problem of Partial Nonresponse (or Missing Data).* Even after people agree to (continue to) participate in the self-report study, parts and questions of the interview or self-administered questionnaire often are not completed. This partial nonresponse or item nonresponse creates problems for the researcher, some comparable to those resulting from sample nonresponse (or nonparticipation; see Meloen and Veenman 1990, p. 28). If partial nonresponse is random, there is not much of a problem; simple procedures like substituting means may be used. There is good reason to believe, however, that missing data are probably not randomly distributed; some types of respondents are more likely to skip answers (and some types of questions are more likely to be skipped).

Item nonresponse may occur because of lack of comprehension of the question, embarrassment, or lack of patience. Generally speaking, personal interviews, compared with self-administered questionnaires, have proven more effective in avoiding missing answers. (Whether the answers elicited in interviews are more truthful is another issue.) The Seattle study (Hindelang, Hirschi, and Weis 1981, p. 126) reported for the entire self-report instrument that 9 percent of males and 7 percent of females failed to answer all of the sixty-nine delinquency items. Twenty-six percent of the males and 21 percent of the females failed to provide at least one usable last-year frequency estimate when they indicated that they had committed the offense in question at some time in the past. The nonresponse rate was not randomly distributed across respondents: "Under all relevant method conditions, court delinquents, blacks, and males had higher rates of nonresponse on the last-year frequency items than did their counterparts" (ibid., p. 126). Other studies also report that the responses of black respondents are more likely to be missing and that chronic, serious offenders are more likely to fail to provide complete responses (Natalino 1981).

In the Second Rand Inmate Survey, a lengthy self-report instrument was used with complicated skip patterns and questions repeated with varying formats, resulting in a large amount of missing data. The questionnaire was self-administered, with instructions given to groups of fifteen to thirty-two inmates at a time. Some respondents left some questions blank (Visher 1986, p. 190). In particular the variable "juvenile drug use" suffered from a lack of response: 14 percent of the respondents failed to answer the questions on this topic (ibid., p. 170). Chaiken and Chaiken (1982) calculated fifteen indicators of omission, based on whether the respondent failed to provide answers to questions (p. 239). Unfortunately, in their analysis they present only aggregate data (including also confused and inconsistent answers together referred to as "bad internal quality indicators"), thus not allowing estimates of the number of missing answers. According to Chaiken and Chaiken (p. 9), "over 83 percent of respondents filled out the questionnaire very accurately, completely, and consistently"—leaving about 17 percent of the participating inmates who apparently did not perform adequately as respondents.

Hindelang and colleagues note that the impact of differential response rates is largely a function of how missing data are handled (Hindelang, Hirschi, and Weis 1981, pp. 126–27). That point is well illustrated by severe criticisms of the Second Rand Inmate Survey. Since Rand researchers had to deal with the problem of many missing or ambiguous responses, they made adjustments that may have resulted in exaggerated estimates of crime incidence (Chaiken and Chaiken 1982). Visher (1986), using more conservative strategies for handling the missing and ambiguous responses, reanalyzed the data for inmates who reported committing robbery and burglary and obtained single estimates of lambda (average annual offending frequency) that were very close to the Rand minimum estimates, but quite different from the Rand maximum estimates (Horney and Marshall 1992, pp. 104–5). In a replication of the Second Rand Inmate Survey on a sample of Nebraska convicted felons, Horney and Marshall (1992) reported virtually no missing data, most likely because of the use of face-to-face interviews.

There is no way around it: studies in the social and behavioral sciences frequently suffer from missing data, either because some individuals refuse to participate or do not supply answers to certain questions, and panel studies often have incomplete data due to attrition (Little and Schenker 1995, p. 39). Fortunately, statistical procedures are available for alleviating the three major problems—biased analyses, less efficient estimates, and more complicated analyses—created by missing data (ibid.). Since the early 1970s, quantitative sociologists and econometricians have made advances in techniques for modeling biases arising from missing data and for replacing missing values via regression prediction (Little and Rubin 1987; Little and Schenker 1995).

III. Conceptualization and Content of the Instrument

Because the self-report method depends on the willingness of respondents to provide the wanted information, the construction of the instrument is of crucial importance. Three essential problems stand out: conceptualization, reliability, and validity.

Consider the final seven delinquency items retained by Short and Nye (1957) from a scale of twenty-three items: driven a car without a driver's license or permit; skipped school without a legitimate excuse; defied his parents' authority; taken little things (worth less than $2.00) that did not belong to him; bought or drank beer, wine, or liquor; purposely damaged or destroyed public or private property that did not belong to him; had sex relations with a person of the opposite sex. This operationalization of delinquency illustrates the difficulty that many researchers have had in defining what they consider as delinquency. Many studies have included in their delinquency scales behaviors unlikely to lead to police or judicial intervention, or have included behaviors related to juvenile status, such as alcohol purchase, getting drunk, cheating on exams, cutting school, and even parental defiance, many of which might be considered deviant but are not delinquent behavior in any legal sense (Cernkovich, Giordano, and Pugh 1985). The main difficulty is that—for most criminologists—infractions of the criminal law, as manifested in official statistics, constitute the frame of reference.

In the case of cross-cultural research, there may be additional problems. Criminal laws in different countries may not encompass identical behaviors, depending on differences in economic, social, and cultural background variables. This makes cross-cultural comparisons more difficult. For example, the Seattle instrument (Hindelang, Hirschi, and Weis 1981) included in its drug index the purchase of beer and cigarettes and the use of beer, wine, and hard liquor, all norm-violating behaviors related to juvenile status that are not addressed in juvenile penal law in a number of other countries. But the essential difference between criminal behavior and mere norm-violating behavior is that in the former the state can intervene and punish the behavior, while in the latter it cannot. Therefore, there should always be some clear distinction between criminal behavior in a legal sense and behavior that infringes on social or moral norms but is not defined as criminal. Some legal infractions in addition are so trivial that they do not present any serious risk of official action. Many of the earlier self-report studies included behaviors of this kind (Short and Nye 1957; Erickson 1972; Elliott and Ageton 1980; Weitekamp 1989). For example, Gold and Reimer (1975) analyzed the follow-up questions of the last three reported events of each offense for the National Surveys of Youth of 1967 and 1972 and found that 22 percent of the reported events were too minor to be considered delinquent acts and provoke any official reaction.

However, the claim that self-reports do not capture "unambiguously violent" behavior has been seriously challenged by the results of the NYS. The measure for a seriously violent offense employed in this survey is restricted to aggravated assaults, robberies, and rapes that involved some injury or a weapon (Elliott 1994a, p. 4). Interestingly, Elliott concludes that base rates for serious violent acts are not exceptionally low in general population studies: the cumulative ever-prevalence for serious violent offenses to age twenty-seven was 30 percent (ibid., p. 18). A consensus appears to have emerged among self-report researchers to conceptualize criminal behavior as behaviors that are infractions of the criminal law or the juvenile penal law and that put a person at significant risk of arrest (Hindelang, Hirschi, and Weis 1981; Elliott and Huizinga 1989).

A slightly different way to approach this question is by a combination of theoretical and empirical means. For example, many researchers define delinquency by a number of serious, nonserious, and additional deviant behaviors in one index, assuming that they all tap one underlying dimension. In an effort to determine whether this assumption of homogeneity is justified, Hindelang, Hirschi, and Weis (1981) used several different statistical techniques, including factor analysis and cluster analysis. They first designated five theoretically homogeneous subscales—official contacts, serious crime, delinquency, drug use, and family/school offenses—and then carried out cluster analyses. Several findings are of interest. First, the subscales showed considerable homogeneity, with internal consistency reliabilities of .67 (family and school offenses) to .91 (drug use). Second, the clusters were also positively related to each other showing considerable versatility in deviant behavior. And third, there was also evidence of high intercorrelations of distinct subsets of items, such as "theft" or "aggression," showing that there seems also to be some specialization in delinquent behavior and homogeneity is not perfect. (But see Klein [1984] for an argument in favor of "cafeteria-style" offending patterns among youth.) Hindelang, Hirschi, and Weis (1981) conclude that if the aim of the research is to present a better measure of prevalence and incidence of delinquency in a specific population compared with official data, trivial nonchargeable events should not be included.

Elliott and Huizinga (1989) claim that the inclusion of minor acts that would not elicit any official reaction can present a serious problem for the face validity of this type of self-report measure. Researchers who want to test theories about the development of delinquent behavior should have greater freedom to define the concept of delinquency. However, the danger is that there would be no clear distinction between potentially independent variables, such as, for example, problem behavior in the family or at school, and the dependent variable "delinquency" (Hindelang, Hirschi, and Weis 1981). For example, truancy and running away from home may be considered as behaviors included in the definition of deviancy/delinquency, or as correlates of both recorded and self-reported delinquency (Hindelang, Hirschi, and Weis 1981; Junger-Tas 1988a, 1988b). To illustrate, repeated national surveys among twelve- to eighteen-year-olds in the Netherlands showed high correlations among truancy, alcohol use, soft drug use, and promiscuity, a cluster that also predicted delinquency (Junger-Tas and Kruissink 1987; Junger-Tas, Kruissink, and van der Laan 1992; Junger-Tas and van der Laan 1995). These behaviors, while illustrating a "deviant" youth lifestyle, were not part of the delinquency concept.

In the ISRD study, agreement was reached on a common core definition of delinquency, which included only acts that are considered as offenses when committed by an adult in all participating countries, thereby allowing for international comparisons.

However, the legally based definition of delinquency also has its limitations. It may make more sense theoretically to include some other deviant behaviors in the definition. Moreover, law varies over time and some behaviors, such as organizational "white collar" crimes and environmental crimes, have long been perceived as immoral acts before being criminalized, while others, such as abortion, have been decriminalized in a number of states. Our position is that the meaning of "criminal and delinquent behavior" should be unambiguous and should exclude behaviors that might be considered serious norm violations but that do not justify police or judicial intervention. We would exclude infractions of welfare statutes from this definition unless these could be punished by a court of law.

However, adopting this approach does not solve the question of face validity, that is the relation between the definition of delinquency and its operationalizations. For example, problems arise in making a selection among the large number of possible offenses that figure in the law. In one early Dutch study comparing recorded and self-reported criminality in an adult city population, the researcher wanted a representative sample of all possible offenses figuring in the penal law, but this proved impossible (Veendrick 1976). Offenses that are very rarely committed were excluded: crimes committed in wartime or crimes committed in the navy or the air force; economic offenses that were formulated in an extremely complex and unclear way; crimes against specific moral standards, such as abortion or euthanasia, which are the subject of intense public and political debate; crimes where both the act and the offender are probably known to the authorities, such as manslaughter or murder; offenses related to specific professions; and crimes with high moral taboos attached to them that would probably threaten the validity of the answers, such as sexual offenses. Veendrick finally decided on twenty-six offenses, including some "white-collar" crimes, such as tax fraud, bribery, blackmail, and illegal withdrawal of goods from a bankrupt firm. This illustrates how most researchers operate: they select those offenses that appear most frequently in the police statistics. Other ways to increase face validity include conducting pilot studies among the sampling population and letting them judge the items in the questionnaire on their relevance (Bruinsma 1985), or surveying juvenile court judges, juvenile police officers, youth social workers, teachers, and psychology undergraduates (Moffitt 1989). Some researchers simply rely on standard questionnaires widely used in self-report research (Riley and Shaw 1985).

IV. Validity Problems

The validity of the self-report methodology is determined by the extent to which the instrument measures delinquent behavior as it has been defined. There are different ways to deal with the issue of validity. Some studies simply compare whether their results are roughly comparable with those of other self-report studies (Hindelang, Hirschi, and Weis 1981; Horney and Marshall 1992; Junger-Tas, Ter- louw, and Klein 1994; Marshall and Webb 1994). Another way of get- ting at the validity of measures is through assessing how the variable in question ought, theoretically, to relate to other variables (construct validity). Several other validity concepts are also used, such as concur- rent (or convergent) validity, predictive validity, and external validity. Concurrent validity assesses whether self-report results are consistent with results from other sources of knowledge about delinquent behav- ior. Predictive validity examines to what extent self-reports predict later behavior. Predictive validity is based on the relation between self- report scores and one or more criterion variables, such as future crimi- nal involvement, arrests, or convictions. Finally, external validity refers to the generalizability of the sample's self-report results to the research population. We agree with Maxfield and Babbie (1995, p. 110) that tests of construct validity are less compelling than tests of predictive (criterion) validity. Yet, in the case of self-report surveys of delin- quency, there is no doubt that results have been consistent with the predictions of a variety of criminological theories (social control the- ory, social learning theory, strain theory, integrated theory). Thus the weight of the evidence is in favor of the validity of the self-report method of delinquency. A strong case has been made by Farrington et al. (1996) for using a combination of data sources: their use of addi- tional information of mothers and teachers in a longitudinal delin- quency study substantially improved predictive validity. And finally, one would expect that if self-reports indeed do measure delinquency, then we should find significantly higher levels of self-reported of- fending among incarcerated populations than among the general pop- ulation (i.e., discriminant validity). This is indeed the case (see, e.g., Hindelang, Hirschi, and Weis 1981; Cernkovich, Giordano, and Pugh 1985; Marshall and Webb 1994).

Some factors related to extent and seriousness of criminal behavior appear to affect validity. People must be willing to admit to the act and they must be able to answer truthfully (i.e., they must remember, and they must remember correctly). People may be more willing to admit to nonserious acts, even those committed with high frequency (which is supported by the observation that these types of items generally lead to high overreporting when compared with official data), but there may be questionable validity with regard to details and accurate timing of events, most probably because such events are easily forgotten. However, serious- and low-frequency offenses have more salience and thus may lead to more accurate reporting; yet, because of their more serious nature, respondents may be more inclined to deny their involvement in such offenses.

However, these effects may be confounded by official recording of offenders: if respondents are officially recorded for the same behaviors that they are questioned about, they may feel threatened and this may introduce serious response bias. This is especially true in the case of adult respondents who are not institutionalized. Incarcerated persons usually do not have much difficulty in admitting offenses. Their situation is clear and they have little to lose in admitting criminal acts. Defendants, however, differ from prison and jail inmates in regard to the circumstances in which they are asked to participate. Inmates have been convicted and sentenced in the past and typically do not have court actions pending concerning their cases; defendants in criminal cases, however, are ordinarily cautioned by their attorneys not to reveal any information that might be harmful to their cases (Chaiken and Chaiken 1990, pp. 70–71).

The validity of self-reported criminal offenses in adult samples is generally lower than in juvenile samples. Adult respondents are more eager to present a prosocial image; they are aware of the social importance of such an image, have more to lose, and have a higher stake in conformity than do juveniles. An exception in this respect are institutionalized or incarcerated populations, among whom prosocial and conformist self-presentation is less an issue than among respondents in the community. There, the problem may be exaggeration rather than underestimation. Generally speaking, the self-report method appears more suitable for juvenile populations than for adults.

Three important threats to validity are discussed below: respondent variables, including respondent motivation and selfpresentation; task-variables referring to the questionnaire and its context, such as cognitive processing of information in order to give accurate replies; and method of administration, such as social background variables, social context, and interviewer effects (see Wentland and Smith 1993; Sudman, Bradburn, and Schwarz 1996). It is clear that there may be interactions among these variables. Moreover, their effects differ according to whether questions are of a nonthreatening or sensitive nature. Because one primary goal of self-report studies is to provide alternative ways to measure incidence and prevalence of offending, we focus on factors related to the measurement of offending or deviant behavior, while recognizing that self-report questions include a large variety of other variables, often with distinctive validity problems.

A. Respondent Effects

Self-report surveys on criminal behavior include sensitive questions about socially undesirable behaviors that may threaten the self-presentation of respondents and which can influence both willingness to participate and response validity. (But see Hindelang, Hirschi, and Weis [1981], p. 124, for a different view.)

Are some respondents' answers more valid than those of others? Respondent characteristics that appear to be related to differential response validity include age, ethnicity, nature and frequency of the behavior, seriousness and saliency of the event, and earlier involvement with the authorities. Concurrent validity may be assessed by several methods, such as asking respondents about their delinquent acts and their contacts with official agencies (Christie, Andenaes, and Skirbekk 1965; Elmhorn 1965), checking one or both sources with official records, or asking other people, such as parents, teachers, and peers, about the delinquent behavior of respondents (Hindelang, Hirschi, and Weis 1981). Most studies use official data to check self-reports. One may wonder why a measure developed as a correction of official measures uses officially recorded data for validation (Nettler 1974). The answer is that most researchers assume that offenses recorded by official agencies have taken place and thus provide a reference point (Erickson and Empey 1963; Antilla and Jaakkola 1966; Erickson 1972; Elliott and Voss 1974; Hindelang, Hirschi, and Weis 1981; Junger 1990).

Sobell, Sobell, and Ward (1980) studied seventy men who participated in an alcoholism treatment program. Answers to questions about public drunkenness arrests and "driving while intoxicated" (DWI) arrests were compared with official data. Only 39 percent of the respondents accurately reported the number of public drunkenness arrests that appeared in official figures, while about 60 percent reported many more arrests than appeared in official data. By contrast, 63 percent of the responses related to DWI arrests were accurate according to police data, but 37 percent of respondents underreported such arrests. Different factors operate to influence differential validity for these two types of events. First, frequent and relatively nonserious behaviors lead to considerable overreporting according to official data. Second, DWI arrests are more serious and salient events than public drunkenness arrests, and therefore will be more correctly remembered and reported. However, questions relating to official contacts with the authorities for this behavior may be perceived by respondents as threatening and thus may not be reported. This example illustrates that interpretation of lack of consistency between self-reports and official records is treacherous. The conventional reasoning asserts that respondents prefer to deny, omit, or cover up undesirable facts about themselves. Based on a review of the literature up to 1980, Marquis et al. (1981) challenge the hypothesis that survey responses about arrests and conviction histories will contain a negative bias. Their conclusion is that in most well-designed studies, contrary to conventional expectations, arrests and convictions have been reported without a negative response bias. Validity studies that are designed and analyzed properly usually find that the average response bias has a positive sign (ibid., p. 2): respondents usually reveal more arrests and convictions in questionnaires or interviews than can be found in official records. It is possible that respondents may report more convictions because they are confused by multiple court appearances for the same event or series of events.[3]

Angenent (1984) studied 222 adult males who either had experienced earlier arrests (50) or had, in addition, been convicted (172) for a criminal offense. Only 32 percent of those who had experienced arrest and 34 percent of convicted men were willing to participate. Considering only those who had been convicted for a crime and checking whether these specific crimes were reported, considerable underreporting of recorded property crimes and violent offenses was found. This was relatively less so in the case of traffic offenses. However, comparison of the total number of reported and recorded crimes

---

[3] Marquis et al. (1981, p. 3) distinguish between "full" and "incomplete designs." Partial record check designs may lead to misleading conclusions. The most common partial design evaluates answers only if records indicate an arrest, conviction, or other official action for a particular person. No evaluation of answers given by persons who do not have a formal record is made. Such a design detects only the respondent's apparent failure to report something already known about him. From such results, researchers sometimes infer that self-reports contain a negative response bias (e.g., denial, omission, lying, cover-ups). However, these inferences may be incorrect. This kind of partial design will miss any positive response biases, so the direction of the average response bias may be incorrect. It will cause random errors made by respondents, records, transcribers, coders, and data entry personnel—either on the main question or on items to link answers and records—to appear as a negative response bias. Thus the size of the bias will be overestimated (ibid.). Full designs select respondents independently of their record values and check answers of all respondents, regardless of whether the records indicate any official action. This allows estimates of errors in both directions and makes it possible to distinguish random errors from net biases (ibid.).

showed that three times as many aggressive crimes and more than four times as many traffic offenses were reported as were officially recorded. The exception was property crime where only about 40 percent of recorded crimes were reported. Angenent speculates that property offenses may be more easily forgotten because of the frequency with which they are committed and their relatively less serious nature. However, the extremely low response rate casts doubts on the generalizability of Angenent's findings.

Veendrick (1976) conducted a study of self-reported crime in a random sample of the male population, ages fifteen to sixty-five, in a middle-sized Dutch city. Comparing self-report data with the city's police records he found considerable underreporting of burglary, assault, joyriding, and hit-and-run offenses. Eight times as many burglary arrests, four times as many assault cases, and twice as many hit-and-run offenses were recorded by the police than were reported by respondents. Offenses that showed equal numbers in self-report and police data were driving without a license, fencing, and extortion. For the other offenses concerned (seventeen out of twenty-four), including property offenses, fraud, swindling, and illegal disposal of dangerous chemicals, considerably higher frequencies were self-reported than were recorded by the police.

These studies support two apparently contradictory conclusions. People tend to report committing far more offenses than are officially known. However, the more frequent the behavior, the higher the risk that some of it will be forgotten, which explains part of the discrepancy between self-reported and recorded offenses. As long as the resulting response error is not systematic, it would not necessarily invalidate the self-report method. However, reporting tends to be selective: concern about the disclosure of behavior that might threaten self-presentation influences willingness to report it. This is particularly the case when the crimes are serious and when they have come to the attention of the authorities.

An even clearer validity problem is illustrated by self-report research on tax evasion. The payment of taxes is generally considered a private matter that people do not discuss with others. In this context, the issue of self-presentation and giving socially desirable answers may be especially relevant. In a study comparing a group of tax evaders—identified by tax collectors on the basis of irregularities in two consecutive years—with a group of nonevaders, several problems appeared (Elffers, Weigel, and Hessing 1987; Hessing and Elffers 1995). First, response was extremely low: 25.4 percent of the evaders and 28.2 percent of the nonevaders completed the questionnaire sent them by mail. Second, only 20.2 percent of the evaders and 23.8 percent of the nonevaders admitted to failing to report income or to adding unjustified deductions. The rate of about 24 percent of admissions of tax evasion in the nonevaders group is not so surprising given that so much deviant and delinquent behavior remains undetected. However, the exceptionally high rate of denials in the evader group, a rate considerably higher than usually found in self-report research on more "common" crimes, does require some explanation. Three suggestions are put forward by Wentland and Smith (1993). The first is that the questions on behavior were preceded by questions on attitudes concerning tax evasion: persons who hold attitudes condemning tax evasion in general will be inclined to present a consistent and prosocial image of themselves, implying the accurate payment of taxes instead of deliberately cutting taxes. A second explanation may be that the tax evasion was accidental and not intentional: this is not very likely because the infraction was noticed by the tax collector in two consecutive years. A third suggestion is that tax collectors' and evaders' definitions of tax evasion differs. This might well be the case. The subject of taxes—their amount and the rules governing their application—are highly controversial and there is certainly considerably less consensus about the seriousness of this offense than there is about "common" criminal behaviors such as burglary or assault.

Validity checks using formal records have been done by researchers involved in criminal careers research using self-reports for adult incarcerated males (Chaiken and Chaiken 1982). Marquis (with Ebener 1981) evaluated measurement error (i.e., how closely the observed values from the questionnaires correspond to the values observed from the official records) for the Second Rand Inmate Survey (arrests and convictions). In addition to standard validity tests, a series of checks were made of the internal quality of responses (inconsistency, omission, and confusion) (Chaiken and Chaiken 1982, p. 9).

The Rand researchers compared prisoner respondent answers on fourteen topics with their official records (which often were incomplete), resulting in a "data quality score." Most respondents had three or fewer disparities, under 7 percent had six or more; none had more than nine (Chaiken and Chaiken 1982, p. 223).

Similar validity checks were made in replications of the Rand study (Mande and English 1987; Horney and Marshall 1992), calculating individual "data quality scores" representing the degree of mismatch between the respondent's self-reported items compared with the corresponding officially recorded items. About 72 percent of respondents in the Nebraska Inmate Survey had two or fewer inconsistencies between self-reports and official records, compared with 42 percent for the Colorado Inmate Survey and 41 percent for the Second Rand Survey.

In order to test whether respondents who seemed confused or untruthful influenced any important results, the Rand researchers carried out key analyses two ways: one, including all respondents, and the second excluding respondents for whom they had any reason to be suspicious of their truthfulness. They found no meaningful differences in the results (Chaiken and Chaiken 1982, p. 9). Marquis (with Ebener 1981, pp. 20–21) undertook an exploratory analysis of variables, such as self-concept, which might identify liars and other error-prone respondents, with little success. Inmates identifying themselves as "family men" had a higher data quality score than those identifying themselves as "players." However, Farrington (1973) found that inconsistent respondents on self-reports tended to have high "lie" scores on personality questionnaires.

Disheartening as it may be, this extensive effort, aimed to shed as much light as possible on the believability of self-reported crime commission rates, "does not directly assess their validity" (Chaiken and Chaiken 1982, p. 9). It is possible that neither official records nor self-reported responses provide a true measure of the extent of respondents' criminal involvement. Why self-reports of having been arrested so often disagree with police records of arrest has been demonstrated by Klein, Rosensweig, and Bates (1973). Based on examination of juvenile arrest definitions and operations in forty-nine police stations in southern California, they concluded that "the meaning of a juvenile arrest was found to vary widely and to reflect poorly the statutory requirements" (p. 78).

A number of scholars have urged efforts to increase validity by using ratings of informants who know the respondent well, such as parents and teachers (Loeber et al. 1989; Sampson and Laub 1993; Farrington et al. 1996). In the Cambridge Study in Delinquent Development, 411 London males were regularly interviewed between eight and thirty-two years. Trying to improve concurrent validity, the study added parent interviews, teacher ratings, and peer ratings (Farrington and West 1981; Farrington 1989). Farrington also examined the predictive validity of self-reports: whether they predicted future convictions among currently undetected males. He found that self-reports of burglary, theft of vehicles, and drug use significantly predicted future convictions for the same type of offense, while none of the twenty-three males who denied all offenses were later convicted of any offense, suggesting they spoke the truth.

Loeber et al. (1989) cite a meta-analysis of 119 studies (Achenbach, McConaughy, and Howell 1987), finding a correlation between self-reports and teacher ratings of .20, and between self-reports and parent ratings of .25. Correlations were higher for problems of lack of self-control, such as aggression, hyperactivity, and delinquency, than for problems of withdrawal and anxiety. In the Pittsburgh Youth Study, a combined scale was used that included information from boys, mothers, and teachers (Farrington et al. 1996). The combined scale did not improve concurrent validity over the self-report scale, but did improve capacity to predict future arrests or convictions of boys that were not recorded at the time of the interviews. Predictive validity was increased for both Caucasian and African-American boys. In one sample, in which the average age of the boys was 16.6 years, the additional information was crucial in identifying serious delinquents (ibid., p. 507).

Research on drug use provides a unique opportunity for cross-validation of self-report answers. In addition to comparisons with official records and responses from informants, urine testing has been used as cross-validation ("collateral source comparison"; see Fendrich and Johnson 1995) of self-reports. A longitudinal survey among 323 male addicts following a compulsory drug-treatment program for narcotic-dependent criminal offenders under court order was conducted by Anglin, Hser, and Chou (1993) in 1974–75 and again in 1985–86. Urinalysis was used to validate survey results. They tried to maximize accuracy of responses by assuring confidentiality and using face-to-face interviews. Participation and furnishing of a urine sample after the interview were voluntary. Respondents were paid for participating. At the first interview, about 40 percent of the respondents failed to report recent drug use as ascertained by urinalysis, while this percentage was only 13 percent at the second interview, which took place ten years later. Comparison of those who provided urine samples at the first wave with those who did at the second wave showed that at the time of the first interview more respondents were under legal supervision than at the time of the second interview and this probably influenced their willingness to report socially undesirable behavior. Respondents will be less likely to admit to illegal behavior while under legal supervision, even when promised confidentiality, because the potential costs if found out are much greater than for those who do not face possibly dire consequences. This may explain the more accurate reporting in 1985–86 than in 1974–75.

Many of the studies used to illustrate validity issues to this point involve male and adult populations, some of which have come to the attention of the authorities, and many of the behaviors involved are relatively serious. The self-report method has also been extensively used with young people and with regard to minor, more common, crimes (Messner and Rosenfeld 1997). It is clear that juveniles have less to lose in admitting rule infractions than do adults and are generally more open to such questioning. Adults tend to present a more conforming self and to give consistently more socially desirable answers than young people (Angenent 1984).

Available evidence suggests higher validity for juvenile respondents than for adults. Comparing self-reports of official convictions with official records in a sample of 400 fourteen- and fifteen-year-old white, lower-class London males, Gibson, Morrison, and West (1970) found that 83 percent of those with official records admitted it. Erickson and Empey (1963) showed that all juvenile respondents who had gone to court in their study admitted it. In a later study, Erickson (1972) found that "self-reported delinquency predicts 'estimates of future violations' considerably better than court records" (p. 394). The association between self-reports of delinquent behavior and court contacts was strong. Farrington (1973) compared self-reports of thirty-eight delinquent acts with official convictions. Convicted boys admitted to considerably more delinquent acts than did nonconvicted boys, suggesting the concurrent validity of the self-report scale. The scale also had predictive validity. An index of the variety of deviant acts admitted significantly predicted official convictions. Farrington (1973) concluded that the concurrent validity was higher than the predictive validity. In their Pittsburgh Youth Study, Farrington et al. (1996) examined concurrent and predictive validity of a self-reported delinquency seriousness scale with respect to juvenile court petitions. They found substantial concurrent validity in relation to past juvenile court petitions and significant predictive validity concerning future petitions, although—with the exception of criminal delinquency, the most serious behavior category—concurrent validity was considerably higher than predictive validity. Combining information of boys, mothers, and teachers on serious delinquency did not improve concurrent validity but significantly improved predictive validity. Elliott and Voss (1974) followed two thousand students from the ninth grade and compared delinquency of those who dropped out and those who continued their education. Comparing self-reports of students with police records, they found that 78 percent of the recorded acts were reported. Validity was much lower in the case of more serious offenses, a finding also shown in studies of adult respondents.

In one large Dutch self-report study (two thousand respondents) of juveniles ages twelve to eighteen, 19 percent of those with a police record did not mention an offense figuring in the record (Junger-Tas, Junger, and Barendse-Hoornweg 1985). However, 42.5 percent of that group was interviewed at the police station or at the prosecutor's office, which might have had a negative effect on response validity. A follow-up two years later compared reports about delinquent acts and police contacts in both studies. With respect to offending behavior, about 12 percent of the recorded group gave inconsistent answers: at time 1, they reported having committed at least one offense and did not report this at time 2. The comparable figure in Farrington's study of London boys was 25 percent. This varied with the type of act: it was about 50 percent for most violent and property crimes, but only 11 percent on average for status offenses such as drinking in pubs under age eighteen (Farrington 1973). As these inconsistencies could also be the result of memory effects, the conclusion was that response validity was reasonable. There were more reservations as far as police contacts were concerned. One-third of those with earlier police contacts and 41 percent of those with prosecutor contacts did not mention them. These results suggest that young people are considerably more willing to talk about their offending behavior than about contacts with the authorities. The latter may be perceived as more shameful and stigmatizing than the former.

B. Ethnicity

In almost every Western country, some minority racial, ethnic, or immigrant groups have higher official crime rates than others or than comparable groups of the majority population (Marshall 1997*b*; Tonry 1997). For example, in the United States, African Americans and Hispanics usually have higher arrest and incarceration rates than do white and Asian population groups. In England, it is the West Indians. In the Netherlands, the Surinamese, Moroccans, and Antilleans have higher rates than the rest of the population. Some ethnic groups show large discrepancies between self-reported prevalence rates and official rates, whereas others often show only slightly higher, similar, or even lower delinquency rates than the rates of the population of origin (Hirschi 1969; Williams and Gold 1972; Gold and Reimer 1975; Junger-Tas 1977; Junger 1990). Many studies have found no relationship between race or ethnicity and self-reported delinquency. For example, Hirschi's Richmond data (1969) showed more police records for black boys than for white boys (42 percent vs. 18 percent), but little or no difference between blacks and whites in the number of boys who reported one or more delinquent acts. The same is true for a study of a sample of Brussels (Belgian) youths, including south European and Arab boys (Junger-Tas 1977). More recent studies in a variety of countries seem to reveal similar patterns (Junger-Tas, Terlouw, and Klein 1994; Tonry 1997; Marshall 1997*b*). For instance, Elliott (1994*b*, p. 197) reports that NYS self-report participation rates in serious violence of white and black respondents are very similar by age thirty: the black-white ever-prevalence ratio is close to 1:1.

Several explanations have been offered for the apparent discrepancies between self-reports and official records for some minority groups. A possible explanation is the lower validity of responses among ethnic minorities. A number of factors may influence response validity of ethnic groups, depending on crime-related variables such as the frequency and seriousness of delinquent behavior and on their social, economic, and cultural situations. Factors found to lower validity among ethnic minorities include lack of language skills, low socioeconomic status (Kleck 1982), strong traditional values, and, for recent immigrants, length of residence in the host country (Junger 1990).

The survey participation rates of some minority groups may be lower than for the rest of the population: the resulting sample may be biased if only the less delinquent members of these ethnic groups are surveyed. A few studies comparing achieved samples with desired samples showed no differential response rates between ethnic groups (Hirschi 1969; Junger 1990), but this does not rule out sample bias. Others have explained these discrepancies by selectivity in police practices: either by patrolling more frequently in neighborhoods with high concentrations of ethnic minorities, or by making more arrests for minor infractions, police practices may artificially inflate the crime figures of some minority groups.

Whether "differential processing" versus "differential involvement" is the more powerful explanation of ethnic differences in police, court, and prison statistics has been a central concern in North America and in several European countries; a detailed discussion is beyond the scope of this essay (see, e.g., Junger 1990; Tonry 1995; Junger-Tas 1997; Marshall 1997b).

We limit our discussion to several studies that have explicitly focused on differential validity of self-reports for different ethnic groups (Hindelang 1978; Hindelang, Hirschi, and Weis 1979; Elliott and Ageton 1980; Hindelang, Hirschi, and Weis 1981; Huizinga and Elliott 1986; Junger 1989, 1990; Farrington et al. 1996). These studies underscore the importance of careful study of individual delinquency items instead of total self-reported delinquency when investigating ethnic (and social class and gender) differences in delinquency. Self-report studies do indicate a greater involvement of minorities in delinquent acts as their seriousness increases. On more careful analysis of individual delinquency items, racial differences do occur, as is shown by Hirschi's study in which the theft scale revealed no racial differences, but the violence scale, including items such as using a weapon, strong-armed robbery, and being involved in a gang fight, showed consistent race differences with a black-white ratio of 2:1 (Hirschi 1969). Similarly, Hindelang, Hirschi, and Weis (1979) concluded that there are no race differences in self-reported petty crime, but considerable differences in serious, violent crime. Brussels' data show comparable results: although Belgian youths reported more theft items than the southern European (mostly Italian) and Arab boys, the latter reported more threats with violence and more violent acts against the person (Junger-Tas 1977).

Comparison of official rates with self-reports and victimization data showed considerable consistency between the latter two data sources (Hindelang, Hirschi, and Weis 1979). Young black offenders under age eighteen accounted for almost half of reported personal victimizations although they represented about 15 percent of the juvenile population. There was no difference between black and white offenders who were reported in less serious victimizations, but black offenders accounted for two-thirds of the most serious victimizations.

Considering that clearance rates for serious and violent crime are usually higher than for property crimes, this might explain the higher official crime rates of some ethnic groups. However, most self-report measurement instruments are heavily skewed toward the nonserious end of the delinquency continuum, which would explain the absence of relationships between ethnicity and self-reported delinquency in earlier studies. Elliott and Ageton (1980) have tried to solve the issue and improve the validity of self-report measures in the National Youth Survey. First, they have included in their self-report measure every act involving more than one percent of juvenile arrests in 1972–74, thus adding a number of relatively serious offenses. Second, they used open-ended frequency responses. Both improvements showed that more black than white juveniles reported committing serious offenses and they committed these in considerable higher frequencies than did white juveniles.

The ethnicity/validity link becomes more complicated when one considers studies explicitly concerned with individual cross-validation of self-reports with formal records (and coinformants), as well as checking out predictive validity. Because of the central importance of race and ethnicity in contemporary society, it stands to reason that this factor influences responses to research; yet, the picture is not as clear-cut as is commonly assumed. While the Seattle self-report data showed only slightly more delinquency among blacks than among whites (Hindelang, Hirschi, and Weis 1981), a reverse record check with police and juvenile court records found considerably greater underreporting of known offenses for blacks. For example, while 19 percent of white boys failed to report a recorded act of auto theft (including joyriding), 57 percent of black boys failed to report such an act (p. 173). However, in the Rand inmate surveys, race and ethnicity were not significantly related to inconsistency between self-reported offending and official records (Chaiken and Chaiken 1982). Comparable results were also found for the Nebraska and Colorado inmate surveys.

Farrington et al. (1996, p. 496) mention that correlations between official records and self-reports are generally positive and statistically significant, and they tend to be higher for whites than for blacks. In the Pittsburgh Youth Study, concurrent and predictive validity of a self-reported delinquency scale were studied both for whites and blacks (Farrington et al. 1996). There was no difference between the two groups in predictive validity but higher concurrent validity for whites. However, with respect to reporting arrests by the police, concurrent validity was higher among African Americans. Farrington et al. (1996) conclude that, in the Pittsburgh Youth Study, a self-reported delinquency seriousness scale had concurrent and predictive validity in relation to juvenile court petitions. No differences in predictive validity related to ethnicity were found. They conclude that ethnic differences in official delinquency were partly attributable to ethnic differences in delinquent behavior, and not to differential ethnic attrition or differential validity of measures of delinquent behavior.

However, the question may be asked whether these results are generalizable to recent immigrant populations and to Europe. In a study of a random sample of twelve- to seventeen-year-old boys in three recent immigrant groups—Surinamese, Turks, and Moroccans—in the Netherlands, Junger (1990) measured reported delinquent acts and police contacts ("ever" and "last year") and used as a validity criterion that boys known to the police admit at least one offense and one police contact. Discrepancies between police records and self-reports were considerably greater for self-reports of police contacts than for self-reports of delinquent acts, confirming findings in an earlier Dutch study (Junger-Tas, Junger, and Barendse-Hoornweg 1985) that more boys had difficulty in admitting police contacts than in admitting delinquent behavior. However, discrepancies varied according to ethnic group. For example, the "delinquency ever" scale showed discrepancy for 37 percent of the Moroccan boys and 44 percent of the Turkish boys, but only 13 percent among the Dutch and Surinamese boys. Factors that appear to be related to these discrepancies are traditionalism, that is strong attachment to the traditions and values of the homeland, and lack of knowledge of the Dutch language. With respect to the latter factor, Junger's findings confirm to some extent Hindelang, Hirschi, and Weis's (1981) findings that there were lower rates of nonreporting in face-to-face interviews than in questionnaires requiring reading skills. One interesting finding is that—although many Surinamese youth are black—discrepancy between self-reports and police data was as low among these boys as among the Dutch ones, emphasizing that police discrimination based on skin color is not the determining factor here.

Ethnicity or race is an ambiguous concept, which has many different meanings according to the economic, social, and cultural context of a country. The question may be asked whether it makes much sense to compare findings of long-term resident minority populations having the nationality of the host country, such as African Americans in the United States, West Indians in England, and Surinamese in the Netherlands, with recent immigrant populations from Asia or (North) Africa without taking into account these factors.

C. Task Variables

Task variables refer to the cognitive processes related to answering survey questions. Respondents have different tasks to perform. First, they must understand the questions, which must be as unambiguous as possible; second, they must be able to retrieve the needed information from memory in a limited time; and third, they must be able to formulate an accurate response. As Sudman, Bradburn, and Schwarz (1996, p. 63) note, a major assumption that governs conversations in everyday life is that speakers are truthful, relevant, informative, and clear. If we consider a survey interview as a special form of social interaction, as a conversation, then it is obvious that the outcome of the exchange depends on the clarity of the questions, the kinds of response alternatives, the context of particular questions, the kinds of previous answers given, and the functioning of the memory of the participant.

1. *Questionnaire Content.* There are a number of pitfalls in the selection of the questionnaire items. We have mentioned the question of the representativity of items. In addition, one may question the wisdom of constructing a delinquency scale made up only of one category of delinquency items. It seems advisable to include a variety of delinquent acts, some of which are rather serious as suggested, for example, by Elliott and Ageton (1980). The items must also be appropriate to the sample: focusing on too many trivial behaviors when surveying a high-risk group is likely to undermine the survey's credibility in the eyes of respondents. Fagan et al. (1996) eliminated trivial offenses from the original forty-seven-item NYS self-reported delinquency scale because they were working in high-crime neighborhoods; they refined questions dealing with weapons use, specification of victims (i.e., teacher, student, other adult), and eliminated such items as "ran away from home" or "made obscene phone calls." The modified and retained items were serious crimes that harm, injure, or do damage (p. 101). Cernkovich, Giordano, and Pugh (1985, p. 47) have also argued that a number of characteristics of self-reported delinquency scales mitigate against adequately measuring the behavior of the small numbers of chronic offenders who are included in general youth samples. They identify five problems that have contributed to inaccurate measurement: lack of item representativeness (i.e., too trivial), item overlap, nonactionable items (i.e., items that do not warrant official action), nonspecifiable items (lacking sufficient detail for classification as status offense, misdemeanor, or felony), and response format and coding conventions (p. 47).

Elliott and Ageton (1980) give as an example of item overlap the items "theft of an item under $5" and "theft of an item of $5–50," which might occur in one and the same event. One criminal event may include a number of delinquent acts; another problem is that counts of the same event may be duplicated. It is also important to ensure that the answers given fit the question, and are appropriately classified. In an effort to check whether the offenses reported in the NYS surveys of 1979, 1980, and 1983 were nontrivial and appropriate, a number of follow-up questions were used (Elliott and Huizinga 1989). Inappropriately reported behaviors did not logically fall into the class of behaviors tapped by the delinquency questions, such as placing bicycle theft in the category "theft of motor vehicle." Delinquency items that led to high numbers of inappropriate classifications were motor vehicle theft (40 percent), fraud (19 percent), and robbery (11 percent). Moreover, half of offenses classified as sexual offenses, 37 percent of fraud offenses, and 24 percent of acts of vandalism were so trivial that no official action would have been taken. It is clear that taking the item responses at face value would have led to serious overestimates of the volume and seriousness of delinquency. Whatever the causes of such overreporting error, it shows the importance of adding detailed follow-up questions to the simple delinquency items. However, a problem with follow-up questions is that respondents soon grow tired and learn that denial shortens the interview. One solution that we used in the ISRD study was to introduce "screening" questions on offenses committed "ever" and "last year."

Question wording is of great importance as even slight changes may alter meaning and trigger different answers (Sudman, Bradburn, and Schwarz 1996). This problem is particularly serious in the case of international comparative research in which questionnaires are translated into different languages. In a small experimental study among seventeen- to nineteen-year-old boys, Villetaz (1994) tried two different versions of a self-report delinquency scale. In the first version, the delinquency items were worded in a nonserious, trivializing manner, such as "taking away" or "pinching" in stead of "stealing." The second version used more serious legal terms like "theft at school" or "fencing." Statistically significant differences were found for questions on theft at school and theft at work, showing lower prevalence of the behavior in the case of the more serious "legal" definitions. A similar tendency was found for theft of or from cars and for fencing. However, where the meaning of the question was unambiguously clear in the particular cultural setting of the working-class boys, the wording made no difference. This was the case for questions on shoplifting, theft of money, bicycle theft, and pickpocketing.

Of course, the respondent has to understand the literal meaning of the question, but should also be able to grasp the researchers' intended meaning. Lexical ambiguities are inherent in language: many words have multiple meanings, and sometimes the meaning of a word changes over time. In many cases the meaning must be determined by information provided by the context (Sudman, Bradburn, and Schwarz 1996). Some meanings are related to cultural differences between regions or countries, a particular problem for cross-cultural research. For example, in countries that have a youth protection system instead of a juvenile court—such as the Scandinavian countries—juveniles cannot be arrested but are handled by the youth board and consequently use of the word "arrest" does not make sense (Clinard 1960). In that case different questions may be needed to obtain comparable measures of a specific concept.

Response alternatives strongly influence the respondent's perception of the question's meaning. For example, a low frequency scale makes the respondent think that the question refers to major events, while a high frequency scale suggests reference to minor events (Schwarz et al. 1988). Moreover, to the extent that questions are not clear and unambiguous, respondents will search the context in order to be able to distill the researcher's intended meaning, or respondents may fall back on answers they have given before. Frequently used formats like often, sometimes, occasionally, never are subject to a wide range of interpretation by respondents and are imprecise (Cernkovich, Giordano, and Pugh 1985, p. 47). Formats such as never, once or twice, three times or more are inexact and fail adequately to measure variation at the high-frequency end of the delinquency continuum (Cernkovich, Giordano, and Pugh 1985, p. 47). It should be recognized, however, that obtaining accurate estimates of numbers of acts from young children will probably always be a great problem (see also Scott 1997). An important choice is between open-ended questions and categorical scales. A given set of response alternatives may seriously limit the respondent's answering possibilities; if respondents cannot identify an answering category that reflects their behavior then they will most probably not report it.

2. *Memory Effects.* A major problem in most self-report studies is that they are retrospective. Our memory is essentially unreliable. Even

assuming a willingness to answer questions, the issue of ability accurately to answer questions about the past remains (Loftus, Fienberg, and Tanur 1985). Our memory is not a passive registration machine; remembering events is more a reconstructive than a reproductive process. Some events are completely forgotten, missing parts are filled in, "new" facts—that may be invented—are added (Crombach and Merckelbach 1996). In addition, there are problems of memory storage, forgetting, deleting, and recalling (Sutterer and Karger 1994, p. 119). This is particularly problematic when survey questions ask respondents for quantitative facts about events in their past (Bradburn, Rips, and Shevell 1987, p. 157). Accurate estimates of prevalence and incidence of crime and precise temporal sequencing of events (a primary concern in etiological studies), requires ability to enumerate specific autobiographical episodes accurately. Insights from cognitive psychology have taught that respondents are limited in their ability to recall, and thus they resort to inferences that use partial information from memory to construct a numeric answer (Bradburn, Rips, and Shevell 1987, p. 157). Recalling an event depends on understanding the question, so that memory can be searched: if events are coded in a different way, this may lead to either under- or overreporting. Information contained in wording, specific images, or emotions may act as retrieval cues. Recall is improved when the retrieval cues better match the representations stored in memory (Wagenaar 1986).

In self-report practice, the two main dangers that threaten validity of estimates of delinquency (besides deliberate deception) are that people simply forget certain events, or report events that have taken place outside the reference period (these are also problems for victimization surveys). With respect to forgetting, time is a critical factor: in one study after five years, although the events themselves were recalled, 60 percent of the essential details were irretrievable (Garofalo 1977; Wagenaar 1986). In particular, frequent events often are forgotten, while rare and recent events are more easily retained. In general, people need "cues" to be able to retrieve memories. These can be specific locations, social occasions, or records of past events (saving accounts, hospital records). Memories are organized in meaningful clusters, such as cause and effect, work, school, family, and they are affected by socially determined time periods, such as the beginning and end of school terms, holidays, calendar years.

Because "assessing the frequency of repeated experienced events, or time dating of events, are probably among the most difficult tasks that we present subjects" (Strube 1987, p. 94), researchers have experimented with ways to improve the quality of retrospective data. A memory cue of growing popularity in crime and delinquency research is the Life History Calendar (LHC), which may be used to collect retrospective event-history data (Freedman et al. 1988). It has been shown that the Life History Calendar may yield accurate retrospective reports over a three- to five-year-period on questions on education, employment, and living arrangements (Caspi and Amell 1994). Caspi and colleagues used the LHC in longitudinal research to record central events that can occur in a respondent's life. Two large-scale studies conducted in New Zealand and the United States of young adults making the transition from adolescence to adulthood attested to the validity of retrospective information gathered with LHC's (Caspi et al. 1996). The Second Rand Inmate Survey used a rudimentary form of such a calendar to establish the reference period, and Horney and Marshall (1991) used a more detailed calendar in the manner suggested by Freedman et al. (1988) to help respondents relate, both visually and mentally, to the timing of several kinds of events. Anecdotal evidence from interviews indicates that the calendar was effective in cueing recall (Horney and Marshall 1991, p. 490).

Memory problems also play a key role in the dating of particular events. Studies on reports of income (Whitey 1954) and of alcohol, tobacco, and marijuana use (Collins et al. 1985) found that answers were greatly influenced by the respondent's income or consumption habits at the time of the interview, showing that most people assume a high degree of stability in their lives and underestimate changes (Sudman, Bradburn, and Schwarz 1996). If the purpose of the survey is to arrive at an estimate of prevalence or incidence of offending over a particular reference period (e.g., a year), then it is important that incidents are not recalled as occurring more recently than they actually did (forward telescoping) or as occurring in the more distant past (backward telescoping; O'Brien 1985, p. 51). This problem is especially troublesome if self-reported misbehavior is moved forward into the reference period, or backward out of the reference period (ibid.). Some telescoping may also occur because specific memories are especially vivid, salient, and accessible. Errors in dating also increase over time. Again, some type of memory aid may improve the accuracy of dating events. For instance, the Second Rand Inmate Survey used a simple twenty-four-month calendar to help the inmate visualize the recent past, and to demarcate the "window period" (i.e., reference period). Elliott and Hui-zinga (1989) propose the use of "anchor points" (such as Christmas, New Year's day, the end of the school year, the first day of the summer vacation) to set off the reference period. Naturally, the longer the reference period, the larger the number of reported events. "Ever" questions must elicit higher frequencies than "last year" questions; "last year" questions in turn must result in higher frequencies than "the last six months" questions. The researcher has to weigh efficiency against minimizing error related to telescoping.

Elliott and Huizinga (1989) observe that for purposes of studying rare events, a three-month reference period requires approximately four times the sample size of a study using a twelve-month reference period, if one wants the same number of events reported. This assumes, however, that telescoping is not a problem; that is, that there are no errors in accurately recalling the events, resulting in over- or underreporting of these events in the reference period. Elliott and Huizinga (1989, p. 165) argue that a twelve-month reference period for self-report epidemiological studies is better than a shorter reference period because recall errors are not substantially greater than for a six-month period and the advantages are better comparability with official crime measures and being able to use a smaller sample size. More specifically, they suggest use of "bounding," a technique most suitable in panel studies: data from a preceding interview are used to make respondents remember behaviors they have reported before. However, the length of the reference period remains controversial and, given that all self-report questions are retrospective, it would seem that answers concerning a short time span, such as the past six months, would be more accurate than answers concerning longer time periods. But, of course, this is an empirical question that must be solved by experimental comparisons. Sudman, Bradburn, and Schwarz (1996) recommend the shortest possible time period, adding that one should not ask respondents to remember dates accurately. Both suggestions are meant to make the respondent's memory tasks as simple as possible.

Another difficult memory aspect in counting relates to accurately estimating high-frequency behaviors. Reporting frequencies of specific activities over a period of past years is a complicated cognitive task. The Rand researchers found that results depended heavily on how questions were asked (Peterson et al. 1982). Contrary to expectations, however, in an experimental comparison of two ways of asking about criminal offending, Horney and Marshall (1992) found that a modified month-by-month reporting method did not result in significantly different estimates of individual offending frequencies.

Another issue is the matter of open versus closed questions. The range of response alternatives has a substantial effect on reports (Sudman, Bradburn, and Schwarz 1996, p. 219). The effect is robust and can be found in multiple domains, such as media consumption, shopping behavior, doctor visits, and medical complaints. Interestingly, the more the respondent knows about the behavior, the less he will be influenced by the response alternatives. If the behavior is regular, the respondent will be able to recall it more easily, but if the behavior is irregular—often the case with delinquent behavior—he will frequently rely on response alternatives.

Successful memory retrieval takes time and effort, and respondent motivation to make these efforts is generally higher at the beginning of the questionnaire than at the end, which may mean that answers to the first items are more accurate than responses to the last (i.e., respondent fatigue). Most real-life issues are quite complex, while survey questions are necessarily simple. Respondents may not have immediately adequate answers to behavioral questions and most of the answers are generated at the moment of the interview in a particular setting (Sudman, Bradburn, and Schwarz 1996). Considerable attention should therefore be given to the setting in which the interview takes place (Marshall 1997a). Face-to-face interviews have a clear advantage over self-administered surveys and telephone interviews in obtaining accurate quantitative assessment of past events.

D. Instrument Administration

The manner in which the survey is administered is usually viewed as of paramount importance. Two things, in particular, are assumed to influence the response: the method of administration and the characteristics of the interviewer. The empirical evidence on these questions is not as convincing as is commonly thought. Whether one specific method of administration—self-administered questionnaires completed by the respondents themselves, either individually or in groups, face-to-face interviews, phone interviews, mail-in surveys, CATI interviews, or some combination—is superior to others, remains an unsettled issue. The advantages and drawbacks of different methods are well known.

A self-administered survey is in some ways superior to an interview because it is more economical, there is less chance of interviewer bias, and anonymity and privacy may encourage more candid responses on sensitive issues (Maxfield and Babbie 1995, p. 240). However, for lower-class and minority respondents, there may be serious problems as a consequence of low reading and writing skills and a lack of understanding the questions. Because reading difficulties and delinquency are highly correlated, self-administered questionnaires seem especially ill-advised for the study of delinquency. This method has been shown to result in larger amounts of missing or misunderstood questions, and ambiguous answers (Hindelang, Hirschi, and Weis 1981; Horney and Marshall 1992).

The advantages of an interview survey over a self-administered questionnaire are that there are fewer incomplete questionnaires and fewer misunderstood questions, generally higher return rates, and greater flexibility in terms of sampling, types of questions that may be asked, and special observations (Maxfield and Babbie 1995, p. 240).

The main advantages of the phone interview are speed and economy; phone interviews when combined with computer technology allow greater flexibility, standardization, and researcher flexibility (Taylor 1994, p. 237). However, refusal rates are likely to be high and there is little control over the identity of the respondent.

The research evidence on the merits of one method compared with another is inconclusive. Hindelang, Hirschi, and Weis (1981) tested different methods of administration under anonymous and nonanonymous conditions and found that no one method was generally superior to any other method. It appears that there is no one best way to interview in surveys that deal with sensitive topics. Sometimes results are better by phone and sometimes by face-to-face interviews with partly self-administered questionnaires (Morton-Williams 1993, pp. 197–98). Self-administered questionnaires do not always result in more valid reports of socially unacceptable behavior (DeLamater with McKinney 1982, p. 32). Hindelang and colleagues suggested back in 1981 that "sensitivity" may not be an important factor in self-report measurement; the conventional research assumption that measuring delinquent behavior (among youth, or among institutionalized adults) raises socially sensitive issues may be wrong. However, they suggest that face-to-face interviews might improve validity, especially for minority respondents. In the ISRD international study, some countries used face-to-face interviews, some questionnaires were self-administered (primarily in the school-based samples), or a combination of methods was used. Although there is no systematic way to evaluate whether one method produced superior results over another (in terms of response rates, missing data, and levels and patterns of self-reported delinquency), that the ISRD results do not show large discrepancies (Junger-Tas 1994) between countries suggests that the method of administration may be less important than is the use of a well-designed and pretested questionnaire. Unfortunately no validity studies were included in the ISRD.

New questioning techniques are now being developed. One such technique is CASIQ (Computer Assisted Self-Interviewing Questionnaires). Respondents read the questions from a screen and type in the answers, circumstances supposed to increase privacy. A meta-analysis by Weisband and Kiesler (1996) concluded that CASIQ increased self-disclosure and thus validity (cited in Van der Heijden et al. 1997) compared with self-administered questionnaires. However, validity may be threatened if respondents have reading or language problems. In a trial study, Turner et al. (1998) introduced a computer program including spoken survey questions administered through headphones (Audio Computer-Assisted Self-Interviewing technique). Selecting a random 20 percent of a sample of 1,672 fifteen- to nineteen-year-old boys, they compared their answers with those to a traditional self-completed questionnaire. When using CASIQ, Turner et al. found considerably more positive answers to questions about behaviors such as violence, drug use, and illegal sex than with the traditional procedure, while nonresponse to individual items was greatly reduced.

Another technique, which may be combined with the former, is Randomized Response (RR). Originally developed by Warner (1965) to increase the validity of answers to sensitive questions, it is based on a choice between alternatives, where some randomized device such as use of dice determines the question to which the respondent must give an answer (Fox and Tracy 1986). Recently, Van der Heijden et al. (1997) compared face-to-face interviewing and CASIQ with two different RR procedures, in a population being identified as having committed social security fraud. Overall the RR techniques resulted in higher validity than either face-to-face interviews or CASIQ, although the proportion of respondents admitting fraud was still low, varying between 19 percent and 49 percent.

If interviews are viewed as social interactions, it makes sense that the interviewer's demeanor, dress, ethnicity or race, gender, age, appearance, body language, and communication style, all the attributes which influence day-to-day interactions between people, will have an effect on the responses of the subject. Anything that influences the responses (above and beyond what the questions are supposed to measure) produces measurement error and undermines the validity of the answers. The problems of interviewer effects are well known. Researchers have experimented with interviewers of different sex, age, and ethnic origin. Most research on the effect of ethnicity of interviewer on response has been done in the United States focusing on black and white respondents and interviewers; systematic research among other ethnic groups is less common (van Heelsum 1993). The effect of the ethnicity of the interviewer depends on the topic (i.e., is the topic related to ethnicity or race?). Although randomized experiments would be needed to settle the issue, common experience suggests that it may be best to match interviewers with subjects based on their ethnicity, although the literature indicates that professional task-oriented interviewers achieve the best results in terms of valid information, regardless of the ethnicity of the interviewer (Nederhof 1985).

V. Reliability Problems

Reliability may be defined as the "level of precision of an instrument, that is the extent to which a measuring instrument is producing identical scores if it were used to make multiple measures of the same object" (Huizinga and Elliott 1986, 293–327). Or, to put it slightly differently, "the absence of non-systematic, random error, that is the extent to which the outcomes are stable when the instrument is administered by a) a different researcher; b) at a different moment; c) under different conditions" (Swanborn 1994, p. 435). While the validity of self-report measures remains much debated, the reliability of self-report scales is much less controversial. A reliable instrument may not be valid, but a valid instrument will always be reliable. It is thus not surprising that reliability has taken a backseat to the validity question. Furthermore, there appears to be a general consensus (with a few exceptions, see Bruinsma below) that self-report items "appear to behave with notable consistency. If self-report measurement is flawed, it is not here, but in the area of validity" (Hindelang, Hirschi, and Weis 1981, p. 84).

What would be the best method to test reliability? Farrington (1973) compared the percentage of boys admitting an act at two ages (fourteen and fifteen, sixteen and seventeen), and found that after a two-year interval a quarter of all initial admissions turned into denials (p. 109).

Huizinga and Elliott (1986) argue that the test-retest estimate is the best method of assessing reliability and many researchers use such a procedure. (According to some, test-retests should only be used by tests where memory does not play a role, for instance perceptual and motor skills [van der Heijden, personal communication, September 1996].) In this procedure, the product-moment correlation between test and retest scores is usually taken as the reliability coefficient. Bruinsma (1994) conducted a test-retest assessment of the reliability of the ISRD questionnaire by drawing a random sample of 87 from the original random sample of 620 young people, and administered the same questionnaire again one month after the first time. He found that, depending on the strictness of the criteria used, using the test-retest method, reliability may vary a great deal. For example, many respondents were unable to mention similar behavior frequencies at the two measurements, in particular in the case of frequent behaviors such as truancy (27 percent), alcohol use (30.5 percent), going out with a weapon (22 percent; a knife mostly), driving without a license (39 percent), vandalism (37.5 percent), and theft from school (23.5 percent), home (22 percent), or work (37.5 percent). Combining the behaviors into separate indexes and cross-tabulating the results of the first and second measurement showed that respondents who had given high behavior frequencies the first time gave lower frequencies the second time and the reverse, a statistical phenomenon that is known as "regression to the mean" (Nijboer 1995; Swanborn 1996). Bruinsma found that reliability was better for "ever" questions and for rarely committed offenses, and he concluded that the self-report method has low reliability.

Bruinsma's critical stance is an exception rather than the rule. Researchers do not usually perform reliability tests on individual items (as Bruinsma did) but on the scales that are based on those items and they generally calculate the correlations between the scales' sum scores at time 1 and time 2 (van der Heijden, Sijtsma, and 'H. 't Hart 1995). Assuming that ordinal or interval scales are used, the question that is really of interest is whether the rank ordering of respondents on the scale is comparable or similar at time 1 and time 2 (Swanborn 1996). Whether, using a self-report questionnaire, respondents give exactly the same answers at time 1 and time 2 is not particularly interesting because the answer may depend on a number of potentially disturbing factors, including changed behavior, changed circumstances, memory effects, the number of response categories, and the frequency distribution. The use of the correlation coefficient, measuring at time 2 whether the rank order of respondents on an interval scale is similar to the one at time 1, is preferable (Moffitt 1989).

Another widely used measure is Cronbach's alpha, a measure that tests the internal consistency of a delinquency scale. Cronbach's alpha depends on the number of items and on the average interitem correlation; its value is the lower limit of reliability. Van der Heijden et al. (1995) argue that realizing test-retest reliability in self-report research is very difficult because it is almost impossible to be certain that no change has occurred in the skills or characteristics of the respondents between time 1 and time 2 (they might have committed a number of offenses in between), and, of course, memories of answers given at time 1 may influence answers given at time 2 (Feldt and Brennan 1991, p. 100; see also Lord and Novick 1968). That is why they prefer the use of Cronbach's alpha, based on a one-time internal consistency test of the measurement instrument. If one wants to test the internal consistency of a delinquency scale, that is, to check whether different behaviors intercorrelate and load on one general factor (e.g., general delinquency, or serious criminality, drugs criminality, or violent crime), then it would be advisable to calculate an internal consistency measure, such as Cronbach's alpha or the Kuder-Richardson-20 coefficient (Moffitt 1989).

A different but equally important question is whether accuracy or reliability of frequency scores is greater in the case of open-end questions than in the case of categorical response sets. Elliott and Huizinga (1989) did not find any consistent difference between the test-retest reliabilities of open-end questions and categorical scales. Both have disadvantages. For example, in the case of high frequency offenses, such as shoplifting, it may be very difficult for respondents to remember exactly the number of incidents and thus to answer an open-end question correctly. Response categories such as "never," "once a month," or "once a week" show a tendency among respondents to give only mean frequency answers (Bachman and O'Malley 1984). However, the open-end response sets in the National Youth Survey were very skewed, which had a strong impact on analysis of relationships between variables, such as regression analysis. Thus in 1977 for "general delinquency," the explained variance was three times as high with the categorical measures as with the open-end measures and in 1980 it was five times as high (Elliott and Huizinga 1989, p. 176). Therefore the authors advise some transformation of raw frequency scores: one can always rescore raw frequency scores, while the reverse procedure is difficult. The problem is that this distorts the nature of delinquency, which in reality is highly skewed. They decided to use open-end frequency measures in epidemiological studies, when they want general frequency rates, and categorical scales in etiological studies (Elliott and Huizinga 1989, p. 176). Sudman, Bradburn, and Schwarz (1996), who assert that respondents who do not find a response-category that corresponds to their behavior may not answer the question at all, recommend use of both open-end and filter questions as precursors to more detailed questions, in order to improve reliability.

In sum, in most cases the reliability of self-report scales is reasonable and does not present major problems.

VI. Conclusions

The self-report method is used all over the world to study opinions, attitudes, and behaviors concerning a great number of issues in the fields of health, education, employment, culture, leisure, and crime. In this respect, the controversial saying that "if you want to know something about people, just ask them" appears to have more truth in it than is commonly believed (but see Nisbett and Wilson 1977 for a critical note on the limits of respondents' verbal reports on mental processes). In particular, when applied to sensitive topics in crime research, there are some complications, a number of which we have discussed in this essay. In addition, the self-report method in criminology has its particular goals: notably, to achieve prevalence and incidence rates that have higher validity than official delinquency measures, and to search for correlates of offending in order to test etiological theories and to evaluate interventions. Here we summarize first the main problems treated in this essay and offer suggestions for improving the self-report method. We then examine the goals—or pretensions—of the method and conclude by discussing what—to us—is the value and the contribution of this method to criminology.

A. Sampling

The sample in any particular study will depend on the objectives of that study and the questions that will be asked. One objective may be to produce a measure that can be compared with police figures and victimization surveys in order to obtain a better and more complete view of the crime picture. In that case a national probability sample would be needed. Moreover, if data are to be broken down by such variables as ethnicity or geographic area, the sample size should be relatively large. However, because of financial constraints and other logistical problems, many researchers look for other options, such as local probability samples or high school samples. Such samples suffer from underrepresentation of respondents expected to score high on criminal and deviant behavior, either because they are hard to locate and contact, or because they refuse to participate. It is, thus, important to realize that sampling problems can be confounded with the dependent variable, delinquency. Ways to remedy this problem include stratified disproportionate random sampling, which allows oversampling of specific SES-strata, high-risk groups, ethnic groups, or samples of known offenders. The advantages of working with samples of known offenders—that is, the guaranteed presence of the "rare" events of serious offending—should be weighed against its drawbacks—limited or no generalizability. Offender-based sampling is currently the primary way in which the self-report method is used on adults.

Research on factors improving participation rates includes guaranteeing confidentiality and careful preparation and explanation of the survey to potential respondents. The logistical and practical problems of obtaining parental consent—a fast-growing obstacle to obtaining a representative sample—deserve more careful study. Since a large number of factors related to participation (societal factors, attributes of the study, and characteristics of potential respondents) are beyond the investigator's control, our advice is to focus on those factors that are open to manipulation (i.e., issues related to obtaining consent, reward, confidentiality). Furthermore, the investigator should invest more time and resources in gaining an awareness and understanding of the special attributes and unique situation of potential respondents. Sometimes, this may mean use of such nonorthodox measures as inviting particular members of the hard-to-reach group of respondents to work as coresearchers, unfortunately with the potential risk of compromising the validity of the responses obtained (see Bernard 1994). It means putting more effort into convincing potential respondents that participation will be potentially rewarding for members of the group. Not only will such approaches reduce the amount of sample bias, they also will force survey researchers to be more cognizant of their social responsibilities to their study subjects.

The problems of partial nonresponse (item nonresponse) and missing data are not approached by researchers in any uniform way. Particularly in cases where estimates of prevalence of delinquency are made, decisions whether to interpret a missing response as a denial of involvement ("no"), to exclude this respondent from the calculations altogether, or to retain him as a specific case ("missing") are important. Although there is little research in this area, partial nonresponse may be selective and should be given much more systematic attention by researchers than has been the case in the past. It often is unclear how this problem has been solved.

No one method of sampling is superior to all others. It depends on what one wants to do with the data. However, researchers should report more extensively on what exactly they have done, why they have taken certain decisions, and what the consequences of these decisions are in terms of the objectives of the study. More systematic reporting in this respect will improve survey designs.

B. Construction of the Instrument

From its inception, the self-report method has struggled with the definition of delinquency, which often was very loose and included many norm-violating behaviors that, if known to the police, would not provoke any official action. This made comparison with official police data very hard if not impossible. There now is some consensus among researchers on defining as criminality only those behaviors that are infractions of the criminal law or juvenile penal law and put a person at significant risk of arrest and that in principle could lead to conviction (so-called "actionable offenses"). Operationalization of this definition occurs in different ways: by selecting those behaviors that figure most prominently in police files, by asking the judgment of respondents in pilot studies, or by consulting experts in the field. Again the specific content of the measure depends on the objectives of the particular study.

C. Validity

The validity of self-reports of delinquency is threatened by a number of factors; it may be affected by age, ethnicity, earlier involvement with the criminal justice system, nature and frequency of the criminal acts, seriousness, and saliency of events. Concurrent validity is checked by different methods, including reverse record checks or using information sources such as parents, peers, or teachers. Official records are the socially constructed products of organizational processes and thus are of questionable worth as indices of crime, a factor that limits their power as a cross-validation source. A strong case has been made for validating self-report measures by "proxy reporting" (Farrington et al. 1996; Sudman, Bradburn, and Schwarz 1996). These reports are highly correlated with self-reports although measurement error is higher for proxy reporting than for self-reports. However, for many behaviors proxy reporting is not significantly less accurate than self-reports with information from parents being more valid than from teachers (Sudman, Bradburn, and Schwarz 1996, p. 243).

Available evidence suggests greater validity in the case of young people than in the case of adults. Prosocial self-presentation and a higher stake in conforming to society's norms have considerable impact on answers given by adult respondents. Earlier involvement in the criminal justice system has an impact on willingness to participate in self-report studies as well as on validity. However, both are also influenced by the setting in which the research takes place, for example, a school room, a youth club, or an institutional setting (Marshall 1997a).

Firm conclusions are hard to draw about the relative validity of responses about nonserious, frequent behaviors compared with those about rare and more serious behaviors because of the complexity of the issues involved. Motivation plays an important role, as do willingness to be truthful, willingness to spend the psychic and mental energy needed to formulate the answers, and ability to recall events accurately. Compared with official data, nonserious and frequent offending tend to result in high overreporting in self-report studies, while more serious crime tends to be underreported. There is a certain reluctance to admit having committed serious crimes, in particular when respondents fear official intervention (unless the respondent knows that his criminal involvement is known to the authorities anyway). However, rare and more serious events tend to have a higher saliency for the respondent than do more frequent and less serious delinquencies, which increases the likelihood of accurate recall and valid answers.

Almost any salient social demographic attribute is bound to influence the manner in which one responds to a survey, and ethnicity is no exception. The research indicates that the impact of ethnicity on the validity of self-report answers is contingent on a multitude of variables: it depends on what ethnic groups are involved in the study, their length of residence in the country, and their social and legal status. Conflicting evidence suggests that blanket statements about generally lower validity of responses of ethnic minorities should be rejected.

Task variables are related to the cognitive processes involved in answering survey questions, such as the meaning of questions, response alternatives, response errors, and memory effects. We agree with Wentland and Smith's (1993) conclusions in their study on survey responses: "inaccurate reporting is not a response tendency or a predisposition to be untruthful," but depends on the instrument's content, clarity, meaning, and sensitivity, on ease of recall, on the research setting, and on the interviewer.

Important issues in the construction of the questionnaire are the selection of items, item overlap, question wording, clarity of questions, and the use of open-end questions or response categories. Of the many sources of response error discussed in this essay, the task variables are most amenable to researcher manipulation and control. An extensive body of research-based literature provides guidance on how to reduce response error by printing instructions, placing questions on a separate page, using a self-administered questionnaire (which gives the respondent more time for recall; or using a face-to-face interview that allows for more probing and checking for accuracy of answers), randomizing question ordering, and using computer-assisted interviewing (Sudman, Bradburn, and Schwarz 1996).

If these concerns are well known, less attention has been given to memory effects, which are related to the retrospective nature of self-report surveys. The main problems are forgetting events and telescoping events that have not occurred in the reference period. People need "cues" for retrieving specific memories, such as special locations, social events, or records. Face-to-face interviews have advantages over telephone interviews in this respect, because they allow more time for retrieval of memories. Ways to reduce telescoping are the use of limited reference periods (six to twelve months), "anchor points" (Christmas, summer holidays), and detailed event calendars.

A major concern is whether respondents are able to count accurately and to provide quantitative estimates of events. The range of response alternatives has considerable impact on answers given. In many cases, open-end questions are to be preferred. Depending on the length of the recall period and whether the event to be remembered is rare (under ten times), the respondent will be able to count, but if the frequency is high he will make an estimate. This has been a central concern in criminal careers research, with a primary interest in estimating "average annual individual offending frequencies" (or lambda) of incarcerated offenders. One experimental study (Horney and Marshall 1992), comparing two different ways of asking questions about offending frequencies, suggests that inmates' estimates of offending (in particular among high-frequency offenders) may be more robust than previously thought. Although the results do not establish that the answers are valid (i.e., true measures of offending), they suggest that we may have underestimated human ability to make quantitative estimates. Other research suggests that questions should be as specific as possible and expressions such as "sometimes" or "frequently" should be avoided, because the meaning may be unclear and invite subjective interpretation.

The evidence on effects of method of administration is mixed. No one method seems vastly better than others; all have advantages and drawbacks. However, recent studies on computer-assisted techniques, either by reading the questions from the screen or by hearing them through headphones hold definite promise.

Some problems with self-report surveys may be due to the use of untrained, poorly prepared interviewers. Although it would be useful to record interviewer characteristics, the sociodemographic characteristics of the interviewer are probably less important than the interviewer's sensitivity, ability to establish rapport with the respondent, and professional orientation. Professional task-oriented interviewers achieve the best results in terms of valid information (Nederhof 1985).

D. Reliability

Reliability is not to be assumed but should be routinely assessed: first, by using a statistical measure to calculate internal consistency of the delinquency (sub)scales and, second, by applying the test-retest method under different conditions. If possible, the instrument may be administered again to the same sample after some time lag, but it is important to give some consideration to the length of time between the two administrations. If that period is too long, events may be forgotten or new criminal acts may have been committed. If too short, respondents may remember the answers given the first time. Test-retest reliability tests suffer from the statistical "regression to the mean" phenomenon. Therefore, what should be measured is whether the second time respondents can be rank-ordered in the same way as the first time. Reliability is generally quite reasonable, according to prevailing social science standards.

E. Final Assessment

The self-report method of measuring criminal involvement has long been seen as inadequate in a number of respects: as having a too low base rate for serious offenses, as measuring only insignificant norm-violating behaviors, and as having low validity and reliability. Compared with police and victimization data, and despite its frequent use, the self-report method has long been viewed as a kind of "second rate" measure and a poor substitute for more robust and valid measures.

This is unjustified. The self-report method has outgrown its childhood diseases; it is now a true-and-tried method of research. Of course, it has its drawbacks, but so do other measures. The limitations of police data are well known, while victimization measures share a number of problems with self-reports. All measures are imperfect, all have particular strengths and suffer from—sometimes serious—limitations. That is why one should use them all and not ignore the contribution of one of them.

Self-report measures can be and must be improved. Much has been achieved in this respect and, compared with other data sources, reliability and validity are entirely reasonable. Self-report research has matured considerably over the past fifty years. Most of the problems in design and inference presented by studies of self-reported delinquency listed in Reiss's (1975) classic critique of self-reports of delinquency have been dealt with satisfactorily. We have learned from our mistakes and have become more modest in our claims of what self-report research is capable of measuring. However, we have also grown more confident about the strengths of the self-report approach. We have made great strides in establishing the conditions under which the self-report method probably will "work" for a particular target population. Isolated technical improvements are always needed, although we are convinced that much more is gained by a "total survey error" approach to self-report methodology. Systematic errors rather than random errors are the most serious threat. Research efforts for improving survey design, sampling methods (including high-rate offenders), instrument design (including serious offenses), question wording (improving recall), survey setting, and instrument administration should continue. We should continue to carry out methodological research on how to improve the self-report method: by experimental or quasi-experimental methods, by pretesting questionnaires as suggested by Alwin (1992), Presser and Blair (1994), and Groves (1996), by continuing experimentation with the Randomized Response Method (Umesh and Peterson 1991), by using focus groups, and by examining more carefully the implications of incorporating notions of measurement errors in our statistical models.

We agree with Fowler that, at this point, "there is no excuse for question design to be treated as an artistic endeavor. Rather, it should be treated as a *science*" (1995, p. 154; emphasis added). A scientific approach to self-report methodology calls not only for systematic empirical research, but also requires more explicit consideration of the insights of theories on motivation and cognition, and theories about interpersonal dynamics and group processes (e.g., Reder 1987; Esser 1990; Dovidio and Fazio 1992; Tanur 1992).

The self-report method is a viable and valuable way to measure criminal involvement, to test theory, and to identify correlates of individual differences in delinquent participation. It deserves more recognition than it has so far had.

REFERENCES

Achenbach, T. M., S. H. McConaughy, and C. T. Howell. 1987. "Child/Adolescent Behavioral and Emotional Problems: Implications of Cross-Informant Correlations for Situational Specificity." *Psychological Bulletin* 101(2): 213–32.

Akers, R. L. 1964. "Socio-economic Status and Delinquent Behavior: A Retest." *Journal of Research in Crime and Delinquency* 1:38–46.

Alvazzi del Frate, A., U. Zvekic, and J. J. M. van Dijk, eds. 1993. *Understanding Crime: Experiences of Crime and Crime Control.* Publication no. 49. Rome: UN Interregional Crime and Justice Research Institute.

Alwin, D. F. 1992. "Information Transmission in the Survey Interview: Number of Response Categories and the Reliability of Attitude Measurement." *Sociological Methodology*, edited by Peter V. Marsden, 22:83–118. Oxford: Blackwell.

Angenent, M. 1984. "Medewerking aan Enquêtes over Niet-geregistreerde Criminaliteit." *Tijdschrift voor Criminologie* 6:345–55.

Anglin, M. D., Yih-Ing Hser, and Chih-Ping Chou. 1993. "Reliability and Validity of Retrospective Behavioral Self-Report by Narcotic Addicts." *Evaluation Review* 17:91–109.

Antilla, I., and R. Jaakkola. 1966. *Unrecorded Criminality in Finland.* Helsinki: Kriminologinen Tutkimuslaitos.

Aromaa, K. 1994. "Self-Reported Delinquency in Helsinki, Finland." In *Delinquent Behavior among Young People in the Western World*, edited by J. Junger-Tas, G.-J. Terlouw, and M. W. Klein. Amsterdam: Kugler.

Bachman, J. G., L. D. Johnston, and P. M. O'Malley. 1992. *Monitoring the Future.* Ann Arbor: University of Michigan.

Bachman, J. G., and P. M. O'Malley. 1984. "Yea-Saying, Nay-Saying and Going to Extremes: Black-White Differences in Response Styles." *Public Opinion Quarterly* 48:491–509.

Balvig, F. 1988. *Delinquent and Not-Delinquent Youth—a Study on Self-Reported Delinquency among Youth in a Metropolitan Suburb in Denmark.* Copenhagen: University of Copenhagen.

Barberet, R., C. Rechea-Alberola, and J. Montanes-Rodriguez. 1994. "Self-Reported Juvenile Delinquency in Spain." In *Delinquent Behavior among Young People in the Western World,* edited by J. Junger-Tas, G.-J. Terlouw, and M. W. Klein. Amsterdam: Kugler.

Bartusch, Dawn, R. Jeglum, Donald R. Lynam, Terrie E. Moffitt, and Phil A. Silva. 1997. "Is Age Important? Testing a General versus a Developmental Theory of Antisocial Behavior." *Criminology* 35:13–48.

Bennett, R. R., and J. P. Lynch. 1990. "Does a Difference Make a Difference? Comparing Cross-National Crime Indicators." *Criminology* 28:153–82.

Bernard, H. R. 1994. *Research Methods in Anthropology: Qualitative and Quantitative Approaches.* Thousand Oaks, Calif.: Sage.

Boers, K., M. Class, and P. Kurz. 1994. "Self-Reported Delinquency in Germany after the Reunification. In *Delinquent Behavior among Young People in the Western World,* edited by J. Junger-Tas, G.-J. Terlouw, and M. W. Klein. Amsterdam: Kugler.

Born, M., and Cl. Gavrey. 1994. "Self-Reported Delinquency in Liège, Belgium." In *Delinquent Behavior among Young People in the Western World,* edited by J. Junger-Tas, G.-J. Terlouw, and M. W. Klein. Amsterdam: Kugler.

Bowling, B., J. Graham, and A. Ross. 1994. "Self-Reported Offending among Young People in England and Wales." In *Delinquent Behavior among Young People in the Western World,* edited by J. Junger-Tas, G.-J. Terlouw, and M. W. Klein. Amsterdam: Kugler.

Bradburn, N. M., L. J. Rips, and S. K. Shevell. 1987. "Answering Autobiographical Questions: The Impact of Memory and Inference on Surveys." *Science* 236(April 10, 1987):157–61.

Brezina, T. 1996. "Adapting to Strain: An Examination of Delinquent Coping Responses." *Criminology* 34:39–60.

Bruinsma, G. J. N. 1985. *Criminaliteit als Sociaal Leerproces.* Arnhem: Gouda Quint.

———. 1989. "Scaling and Reliability Problems in Self-Reported Property Crime." In *Cross-National Research in Self-Reported Crime and Delinquency,* edited by Malcolm W. Klein. Dordrecht: Kluwer.

———. 1991. "De Test-hertest Betrouwbaarheid van de Selfreport Methode." *Tijdschrift voor Criminologie* 33(3):245–56.

———. 1994. "De Test-hertest Betrouwbaarheid van het Meten van Jeugdcriminaliteit." *Tijdschrift voor Criminologie* 36(3):218–35.

Buikhuisen, W., R. W. Jongman, and W. Oving. 1969. "Ongeregistreerde criminaliteit onder studenten." *Nederlands Tijdschrift voor Criminologie* 11(2):69–90.

Canela-Cacho, Jose, Alfred Blumstein, and Jacqueline Cohen. 1997. "Rela-

tionship between the Offending Frequency of Imprisoned and Free Offenders." *Criminology* 35:133–76.

Caspi. A., and J. Amell. 1994. *The Reliability of Life History Calendar Data.*
DPPP Technical Report no. 94–01. Madison: University of Wisconsin.

Caspi, A., T. Moffitt, A. Thornton, and D. Freedman. 1996. "The Life History Calendar: A Research and Clinical Assessment Method for Collecting
Retrospective Event-History Data." *International Journal of Methods in Psy-
chiatric Research* 6(2):104–14.

Cernkovich, S. A., P. C. Giordano, and M. D. Pugh. 1985. "Chronic Offenders: The Missing Cases in Self-Report Delinquency Research." *Journal of
Criminal Law and Criminology* 76:705–32.

Chaiken, Jan M., and Marcia R. Chaiken. 1982. *Varieties of Criminal Behavior.*
Santa Monica, Calif.: Rand.

———. 1990. *Redefining the Career Criminal: Priority Prosecution of High-Rate
Dangerous Offenders.* Washington, D.C.: U.S. Department of Justice, National Institute of Justice.

Christie, N., J. Andenaes, and S. Skirbekk. 1965. "A Study in Self-Reported
Crime." In *Scandinavian Studies in Criminology*, vol. 1, edited by Nils Christie. London: Tavistock.

Clinard, M. B. 1960. "A Cross-Cultural Replication of the Relation of Urban-
ism to Criminal Behavior." *American Sociological Review* 25:253–57.

Collins, L. M., J. W. Graham, W. B. Hansen, and C. A. Johnson. 1985.
"Agreement between Retrospective Accounts of Substance Use and Earlier
Reported Substance Use." *Applied Psychological Measurement* 9(3):301–9.

Cordray, S., and K. Polk. 1983. "The Implications of Respondent Loss in
Panel Studies of Deviant Behavior." *Journal of Research in Crime and Delinquency* 20:214–42.

Council of Europe. 1995. *Draft Model of the European Sourcebook on Criminal
Justice Statistics.* Strasbourg: Council of Europe.

Crombach, H. F. M., and H. L. G. J. Merckelbach. 1996. *Hervonden Herinner-
ingen en Andere Misverstanden.* Amsterdam: Uitgeverij Contact.

DeLamater, John, with assistance of Kathleen McKinney. 1982. "Response-
Effects of Question Content." In *Response Behaviour in the Survey Interview*,
edited by W. Dijkstra and J. van der Zouwen. London: Academic Press.

Dijkstra, W., and J. van der Zouwen, eds. 1982. *Response Behaviour in the Survey Interview.* London and New York: Academic Press.

Dovidio, J. F., and R. H. Fazio. 1992. "New Technologies for the Direct and
Indirect Assessment of Attitudes." In *Questions about Questions: Inquiries into
the Cognitive Bases of Surveys*, edited by J. M. Tanur. New York: Russell Sage
Foundation.

Elffers, H., R. H. Weigel, and D. J. Hessing. 1987. "The Consequences of
Different Strategies for Measuring Tax Evasion Behavior." *Journal of Economic Psychology* 8:311–37.

Elliott, D. S. 1994a. "Presidential Address: Serious Violent Offenders—Onset, Developmental Course, and Termination." *Criminology* 32:1–23.

———. 1994b. "Longitudinal Research in Criminology: Promise and Practice." In *Cross-National Longitudinal Research on Human Development and*

Criminal Behavior, edited by E. G. M. Weitekamp and H.-J. Kerner. Dordrecht: Kluwer.

Elliott, D. S., and S. S. Ageton. 1980. "Reconciling Race and Class Differences in Self-Reported and Official Estimates of Delinquency." *American Sociological Review* 45:95–110.

Elliott, D. S., S. S. Ageton, D. Huizinga, B. A. Knowles, and R. J. Canter. 1985. *The Prevalence and Incidence of Delinquent Behavior: 1976–1980.* National Youth Survey Project, Report no. 26. Boulder, Colo.: Behavioral Research Institute.

Elliott, D. S, and D. Huizinga. 1989. "Improving Self-Reported Measures of Delinquency." In *Cross-National Research in Self-Reported Crime and Delinquency,* edited by Malcolm W. Klein. Dordrecht: Kluwer.

Elliott, D. S., D. Huizinga, and S. Menard. 1989. *Multiple Problem Youth: Delinquency, Substance Use and Mental Health Problems.* New York: Springer-Verlag.

Elliott, D. S., and H. Voss. 1974. *Delinquency and Dropout.* Lexington, Mass.: D. C. Heath.

Elmhorn, K. 1965. "A Study in Self-Reported Delinquency among School Children in Stockholm." In *Scandinavian Studies in Criminology,* vol. 1. London: Tavistock.

Erickson, M. L. 1972. "The Changing Relationship between Official and Self-Reported Measures of Delinquency: An Exploratory Predictive Study." *Journal of Criminal Law, Criminology and Police Science* 63:388–96.

Erickson, M. L., and L. T. Empey. 1963. "Court Records, Undetected Delinquency and Decision-Making." *Journal of Criminal Law, Criminology and Police Science* 54:456–70.

Esser, H. 1990. " 'Habits,' 'Frames,' und 'Rational Choice,' die Reichweite von Theorien der Rationalen Wahl (am Beispiel der Erklarung des Befragtenverhaltens)." *Zeitschrift für Soziologie* 19:231–77.

Fagan, J., J. Weis, and Y. Cheng. 1990. "Delinquency and Substance Use among Inner-City Students." *Journal of Drug Issues* 20:351–402.

Farrington, D. P. 1973. "Self-Reports of Deviant Behavior: Predictive and Stable?" *Journal of Criminal Law and Criminology* 64:99–110.

———. 1989. "Self-Reported and Official Offending from Adolescence to Adulthood." In *Cross-National Research in Self-Reported Crime and Delinquency,* edited by M. Klein. Dordrecht: Kluwer.

Farrington, D. P., R. Loeber, M. Stouthamer-Loeber, W. Van Kammen, and L. Schmidt. 1996. "Self-Reported Delinquency and a Combined Delinquency Seriousness Scale Based on Boys, Mothers, and Teachers: Concurrent and Predictive Validity for African Americans and Caucasians." *Criminology* 34:493–517.

Farrington, D. P., and D. J. West. 1981. "The Cambridge Study in Delinquent Development." In *Prospective Longitudinal Research,* edited by S. A. Mednick and A. E. Baert. Oxford: Oxford University Press.

Feldt, L. S., and R. L. Brennan. 1991. "Reliability." In *Educational Measurement,* 3d ed., edited by R. L. Linn. New York: Macmillan.

Fendrich, M., and T. Johnson. 1995. "Investigating the Validity of Drug Use

Reports Using a Cognitive Frame Work: Implications for Research Design." Paper presented at the forty-seventh annual meeting of the American Society of Criminology, Boston, November.

Fowler, F. J., Jr. 1995. *Improving Survey Questions: Design and Evaluation.* Thousand Oaks, Calif.: Sage.

Fox, J. A., and P. A. Tracy. 1986. *Randomized Response: A Method for Sensitive Surveys.* Beverly Hills, Calif.: Sage.

Freedman, Deborah, Arland Thornton, Donald Camburn, Duane Alwin, and Linda Young-DeMarco. 1988. "The Life History Calendar: A Technique for Collecting Retrospective Data." In *Sociological Methodology,* edited by Clifford C. Clogg. San Francisco: Jossey-Bass.

Friday, P. C. 1974. "Research on Youth Crime in Sweden: Some Problems in Methodology." In *Scandinavian Studies in Criminology,* vol. 5. London: Tavistock.

Garofalo, J. 1977. "Time: A Neglected Dimension in Tests of Criminological Theories." In *Theory in Criminology,* edited by R. F. Meier. Beverly Hills, Calif.: Sage.

Gatti, U., G. Fossa, E. Lusetti, et al. 1994. "Self-Reported Delinquency in Three Italian Cities." In *Delinquent Behavior among Young People in the Western World,* edited by J. Junger-Tas, G.-J. Terlouw, and M. W. Klein. Amsterdam: Kugler.

Gersao, E., and M. Lisboa. 1994. "The Self-Reported Delinquency Study in Portugal." In *Delinquent Behavior among Young People in the Western World,* edited by J. Junger-Tas, G.-J. Terlouw, and M. W. Klein. Amsterdam: Kugler.

Gibson, H. B., S. Morrison, and D. J. West. 1970. "The Confession of Known Offenses in Response to a Self-Reported Delinquency Schedule." *British Journal of Criminology* 10:277–80.

Gold, M. 1966. "Undetected Delinquent Behavior." *Journal of Research in Crime and Delinquency* 3(3):27–46.

———. 1970. *Delinquent Behavior in an American City.* Belmont, Calif.: Brooks/Cole.

Gold, M., and D. Reimer. 1975. "Changing Patterns of Delinquent Behavior among Americans 13 through 16 Years old." *Crime and Delinquency Literature* 7:483–517.

Graham, J., and B. Bowling. 1995. *Young People and Crime.* Home Office Research and Planning Unit, Report no. 145. London: H. M. Stationery Office.

Groves, R. M. 1996. "How Do We Know What We Think They Think Is Really What They Think?" In *Answering Questions: Methodology for Determining Cognitive and Communicative Processes in Survey Research,* edited by N. Schwarz and S. Sudman. San Francisco: Jossey-Bass.

Groves, R. M., R. B. Cialdini, and M. P. Couper. 1992. "Understanding the Decision to Participate in a Survey." *Public Opinion Quarterly* 56:475–95.

Hagan, F. E. 1993. *Research Methods in Criminal Justice and Criminology,* 3d ed. New York: Macmillan.

Hagan, J. 1989. *Structural Criminology.* New Brunswick, N.J.: Rutgers University Press.

————. 1992. "The Poverty of a Classless Criminology." *Criminology* 30:1–19.

Hardt, R. H., and G. E. Bodine. 1965. *Development of Self-Report Instruments in Delinquency Research: A Conference Report.* Syracuse, N.Y.: Syracuse University, Youth Development Center.

Hessing, D. J., and H. Elffers. 1995. "De Validiteit van de Self-report Methode in Onderzoek naar Regelovertredend gedrag." *Tijdschrift voor Criminologie* 37:55–71.

Hindelang, M. J. 1978. "Race and Involvement in Common Law Personal Crimes." *American Sociological Review* 43:93–109.

Hindelang, M. J., T. Hirschi, and J. G. Weis. 1979. "Correlates of Delinquency: The Illusion of Discrepancy between Self-Report and Official Measures." *American Sociological Review* 44:995–1014.

————. 1981. *Measuring Delinquency.* Beverly Hills, Calif.: Sage.

Hirschi, Travis. 1969. *Causes of Delinquency.* Berkeley: University of California Press.

Horney, J., and I. Haen Marshall. 1991. "Measuring Lambda through Self-Reports." *Criminology* 29:471–95.

————. 1992. "An Experimental Comparison of Two Self-Report Methods for Measuring Lambda." *Journal of Research in Crime and Delinquency* 29:102–21.

Horney, J., D. Wayne Osgood, and I. Haen Marshall. 1995. "Variability in Crime and Local Life Circumstances." *American Sociological Review* 60:655–73.

Huizinga, D., and D. S. Elliott. 1986. "Reassessing the Reliability and Validity of Self-Report Measures." *Journal of Quantitative Criminology* 2:293–327.

Janson, C.-G. 1982. *Delinquency among Metropolitan Boys.* Stockholm: University of Stockholm.

————. 1984. *Project Metropolitan—a Presentation and Progress Report.* Stockholm: University of Stockholm, Department of Sociology.

Jensen, G. F. 1996. "Violence among American Youth: A Comparison of Survey and Agency Images of Crime over Time." Paper presented at the forty-eighth annual meeting of the American Society of Criminology, Chicago, November.

Jensen, G. F., and D. C. Rojek. 1992. *Delinquency and Youth Crime,* 2d ed. Prospect Heights, Ill.: Waveland.

Jongman, R. W. 1971. "Verborgen Criminaliteit en Sociale Klasse." *Nederlands Tijdschrift voor Criminologie* 13(4):141–54.

Jongman, R. W., and G. J. A. Smale. 1972. "Ongeregistreerde Criminaliteit onder Vrouwelijke Studenten." *Nederlands Tijdschrift voor Criminologie* 14(1):1–12.

Junger, M. 1989. "Discrepancies between Police and Self-Report Data for Dutch Racial Minorities." *British Journal of Criminology* 29:273–83.

————. 1990. *Delinquency and Ethnicity.* Deventer and Boston: Kluwer Law and Taxation.

Junger-Tas, J. 1972. *Kenmerken en Sociale Integratie van Jeugddelinquenten.* Brussels: Studiecentrum voor Jeugdmisdadigheid.

————. 1977. "Hidden Delinquency and Judicial Selection." In *Youth Crime and Juvenile Justice—International Perspectives*, edited by Paul C. Friday and V. Lorne Stewart. New York and London: Praeger.

———. 1988*a*. "Patterns in Delinquent Behavior." In *Juvenile Delinquency in the Netherlands*, edited by J. Junger-Tas and Richard L. Block. Amsterdam: Kugler.

———. 1988*b*. "Causal Factors: Social Control Theory." In *Juvenile Delinquency in the Netherlands*, edited by J. Junger-Tas and Richard L. Block. Amsterdam: Kugler.

———. 1990. *De Ontwikkeling van de Jeugdcriminaliteit—periode 1980–1988*. The Hague: Ministry of Justice, Research and Documentation Center.

———. 1994. "Delinquency in Thirteen Western Countries: Some Preliminary Conclusions." In *Delinquent Behavior among Young People in the Western World*, edited by J. Junger-Tas, G.-J. Terlouw, and Malcolm W. Klein. Amsterdam: Kugler.

———. 1996. "Youth and Violence in Europe." *Studies on Crime and Crime Prevention* 5:31–58.

———. 1997. "Ethnic Minorities and Criminal Justice in the Netherlands." In *Ethnicity, Crime, and Immigration: Comparative and Cross-National Perspectives*, edited by Michael Tonry. Vol. 21 of *Crime and Justice: A Review of Research*, edited by Michael Tonry. Chicago: University of Chicago Press.

Junger-Tas, J., M. Junger, and E. Barendse-Hoornweg. 1985. *Jeugddelinquentie II—de Invloed van Justitieel Ingrijpen*. The Hague: Ministry of Justice, Research and Documentation Center.

Junger-Tas, J., and M. Kruissink. 1987. *De Ontwikkeling van de Jeugdcriminaliteit*. The Hague: Ministry of Justice, Research and Documentation Center.

———. 1990. *De Ontwikkeling van de Jeugdcriminaliteit: Periode 1980–1988*. The Hague: Ministry of Justice, Research and Documentation Center.

Junger-Tas, J., M. Kruissink, and P. van der Laan. 1992. *Ontwikkeling van de Jeugdcriminaliteit en de Justitiële Jeugdbescherming—periode 1980–1990*. The Hague: Ministry of Justice, Research and Documentation Center.

Junger-Tas, J., Gert-Jan Terlouw, and Malcolm W. Klein, eds. 1994. *Delinquent Behavior among Young People in the Western World*. Amsterdam and New York: Kugler.

Junger-Tas, J., and P. van der Laan. 1995. *Jeugdcriminaliteit—1980–1992*. The Hague: Ministry of Justice, Research and Documentation Center.

Kangaspunta, K. 1995. *Crime and Criminal Justice in Europe and North-America*. Helsinki: European Institute for Crime Prevention and Control.

Killias, M., P. Villetaz, and J. Rabasa. 1994. "Self-Reported Delinquency in Switzerland." In *Delinquent Behavior among Young People in the Western World*, edited by J. Junger-Tas, G.-J. Terlouw, and M. W. Klein. Amsterdam: Kugler.

Kish, L. 1965. *Survey Sampling*. New York: Wiley.

Kleck, G. 1982. "On the Use of Self-Report Data to Determine the Class Distribution of Criminal and Delinquent Behavior." *American Sociological Review* 47:427–33.

Klein, M. W. 1984. "Offense Specialisation and Versatility among Juveniles." *British Journal of Criminology* 24:185–94.

————, ed. 1989. *Cross-National Research in Self-Reported Crime and Delinquency.* Dordrecht: Kluwer.

Klein, M. W., S. L. Rosensweig, and R. Bates. 1973. "The Ambiguous Juvenile Arrest." *Criminology* 13:78–91.

Kreuzer, A., Th. Görgen, R. Krüger, V. Münch, and H. Schneider. 1993. *Jugenddelinquenz in Ost und West—Vergleichende Untersuchungen bei Ost- und Westdeutschen.* Bonn: Forum Verlag Godesberg.

Le Blanc, M., and M. Fréchette. 1989. *Male Criminal Activity from Childhood through Youth. Multilevel and Developmental Perspectives.* New York: Springer-Verlag.

Lee, R. M. 1993. *Doing Research on Sensitive Topics.* Newbury Park, Calif.: Sage.

Le Poole, F. 1977. "Law and Practice Concerning the Counterparts of 'Persons in Need of Supervision' in Some European Countries with a Particular Emphasis on The Netherlands." In *Beyond Control: Status Offenders in the Juvenile Court,* edited by L. E. Teitelbaum. Cambridge, Mass.: Ballinger.

Lindström, P. 1993. *School and Delinquency in a Contextual Perspective.* Stockholm: National Council of Crime Prevention.

Little, R. J. A., and D. B. Rubin. 1987. *Statistical Analysis with Missing Data.* New York: Wiley.

Little, R. J. A., and N. Schenker. 1995. "Missing Data." In *Handbook of Statistical Modeling for the Social and Behavioral Sciences,* edited by G. Arminger, C. C. Clogg, and M. E. Sobel. New York and London: Plenum.

Loeber, R., M. Stouthamer-Loeber, W. B. van Kammen, and D. P. Farrington. 1989. "Development of a New Measure of Self-Reported Anti-social Behavior for Young Children: Prevalence and Reliability." In *Cross-National Research in Self-Reported Crime and Delinquency,* edited by M. W. Klein. Dordrecht: Kluwer.

Loftus, E. F., S. E. Fienberg, and J. M. Tanur. 1985. "Cognitive Psychology Meets the National Survey." *American Psychologist* 40:175–80.

Long, S. B., and J. A. Swingen. 1991. "Taxpayer Compliance: Setting New Agendas for Research." *Law and Society Review* 25:637–89.

Longshore, D., S. Turner, and J. A. Stein. 1996. "Self-Control in a Criminal Sample: An Examination of Construct Validity." *Criminology* 34:209–28.

Lord, F. M., and M. R. Novick. 1968. *Statistical Theories of Mental Test Scores.* Reading, Mass.: Addison-Wesley.

Lyberg, L., P. Biemer, M. Collins, E. de Leeuw, C. Dippo, N. Schwarz, and D. Trewin, eds. 1997. *Survey Measurement and Process Quality.* New York: Wiley.

Mande, Mary J., and Kim English. 1987. *Individual Crime Rates of Colorado Prisoners.* Denver: Colorado Department of Public Safety.

Marquis, K. H., with the assistance of P. A. Ebener. 1981. *Quality of Prisoner Self-Reports: Arrest and Conviction Response Errors.* Santa Monica, Calif.: Rand Corporation.

Marquis, K. H., N. Duan, M. S. Marquis, and J. M. Polich, with J. E. Meshkoff, D. S. Scwarzbach, and C. M. Stasz. 1981. *Response Errors in Sensitive Topic Surveys: Estimates, Effects, and Correction Options.* Santa Monica, Calif.: Rand.

Marshall, I. Haen. 1997*a*. "The Self-Report Method: A First Step to a Rational Approach." Paper presented at the forty-ninth annual meeting of the American Society of Criminology, San Diego, Calif., November.

———, ed. 1997*b*. *Minorities, Migrants, and Crime: Diversity and Similarity across Europe and the United States.* Thousand Oaks, Calif.: Sage.

Marshall, I. Haen, and V. J. Webb. 1994. "Self-Reported Delinquency in a Midwestern American City." In *Delinquent Behavior among Young People in the Western World,* edited by J. Junger-Tas, G.-J. Terlouw, and M. W. Klein. Amsterdam: Kugler.

Maxfield, M. G., and E. Babbie. 1995. *Research Methods for Criminal Justice and Criminology.* Belmont, Calif.: Wadsworth.

McQuoid, J. 1994. "The Self-Reported Delinquency Study in Belfast, Northern Ireland." In *Delinquent Behavior among Young People in the Western World,* edited by J. Junger-Tas, G.-J. Terlouw, and M. W. Klein. Amsterdam: Kugler.

Mednick, S. A., W. F. Gabrielli, and B. Hutchings. 1984. "Genetic Influences in Criminal Convictions: Evidence from an Adoption Cohort." *Science* 224:891–94.

Meeus, W., and H. 't Hart. 1993. *Jongeren in Nederland, Een Nationale Survey naar Ontwikkeling in de Adolescentie en Intergenerationele Overdracht.* Amersfoort: Academische Uitgeverij.

Meloen, J. D., and J. Veenman. 1990. *Het is Maar de Vraag—Onderzoek naar Responseffecten bij Minderhe Densurveys.* Lelystad: Koninklijke Vermande BV.

Messner, S. F., and R. Rosenfeld. 1997. *Crime and the American Dream,* 2d ed. Belmont, Calif.: Wadsworth.

Moffitt, T. E. 1989. "Accommodating Self-Report Methods to a Low-Delinquency Culture: A Longitudinal Study from New-Zealand." In *Cross-National Research in Self-Reported Crime and Delinquency,* edited by Malcolm W. Klein. Dordrecht: Kluwer.

Morton-Williams, Jean. 1993. *Interviewer Approaches.* Brookfield, Vt.: Dartmouth.

Natalino, K. W. 1981. "Methodological Problems in Self-Report Studies of Black Adolescent Delinquency." In *Sociology of Delinquency,* edited by G. F. Jensen. Beverly Hills, Calif.: Sage.

National Institute of Justice. 1996. *1995 Drug Use Forecasting: Annual Report on Adult and Juvenile Arrestees.* Washington, D.C.: U.S. Department of Justice, National Institute of Justice.

Nederhof, A. J. 1985. "Methods of Coping with Social Desirability Bias: A Review." *European Journal of Social Psychology* 15:263–80.

Nettler, G. 1974. *Explaining Crime.* New York: McGraw-Hill.

Nijboer, J. 1995. "Het Meten van Delinquentie door middel van Self Report." *Tijdschrift voor Criminologie* 37:273–81.

Nisbett, R. E., and T. DeCamp Wilson. 1977. "Telling More than We Can Know: Verbal Reports on Mental Processes." *Psychological Review* 84:231–59.

O'Brien, Robert. 1985. *Crime and Victimization Data.* Beverly Hills, Calif.: Sage.

Oppenheim, A. N. 1992. *Questionnaire Design: Interviewing and Attitude Measurement.* London and New York: Pinter.

Pease, K., and K. Hukkula, eds. 1990. *Criminal Justice Systems in Europe and North-America.* Helsinki: Helsinki Institute for Crime Prevention and Control.

Peterson, M. A., J. M. Chaiken, P. Ebener, and P. Honig. 1982. *Survey of Prison and Jail Inmates: Background and Method.* Santa Monica, Calif.: Rand.

Porterfield, A. L. 1946. *Youth in Trouble.* Fort Worth, Tex.: Leo Potisham Foundation.

Presser, S., and J. Blair. 1994. "Survey Pretesting: Do Different Methods Produce Different Results?" *Sociological Methodology* 24:73–104.

Reder, L. M. 1987. "Strategy Selection in Question Answering." *Cognitive Psychology* 19:90–138.

Reiss, A. J., Jr. 1975. "Inappropriate Theories and Inadequate Methods as Policy Plagues: Self-Reported Delinquency and the Law." In *Social Policy and Sociology,* edited by N. J. Demerath, O. Larsen, and K. F. Schuessler. New York: Academic Press.

Reiss, A. J., Jr., and J. A. Roth, eds. 1993. *Understanding and Controlling Violence.* Washington, D.C., National Academy Press.

Reuband, Karl-Heinz. 1989. "On the Use of Self-Reports in Measuring Crime among Adults: Methodological Problems and Prospects." In *Cross-National Research in Self-Reported Crime and Delinquency,* edited by M. W. Klein. Dordrecht: Kluwer.

Riley, D., and M. Shaw. 1985. *Parental Supervision and Juvenile Delinquency.* Home Office Research and Planning Unit Report no. 83. London: H. M. Stationery Office.

Rutenfrans, C. J. C., and G. J. Terlouw. 1994. *Delinquentie, Sociale Controle en 'Life Events.'* Arnhem: Gouda Quint.

Rutter, M., and H. Giller. 1983. *Juvenile Delinquency—Trends and Perspectives.* Harmondsworth: Penguin.

Sampson, R. J., and J. H. Laub. 1993. *Crime in the Making—Pathways and Turning Points through Life.* Cambridge, Mass.: Harvard University Press.

Sarnecki, Jerzy. 1989. "Self-Reported and Recorded Data on Drug Abuse and Delinquency on 287 Men in Stockholm." In *Cross-National Research in Self-Reported Crime and Delinquency,* edited by M. W. Klein. Dordrecht: Kluwer.

Schwarz, N., F. Strack, G. Müller, and B. Chassein. 1988. "The Range of Response Alternatives May Determine the Meaning of Questions: Further Evidence of Informative Functions of Response Alternatives." *Social Cognition* 6:107–17.

Schwarz, N., and S. Sudman. 1994. *Autobiographical Memory and the Validity of Retrospective Reports.* New York: Springer-Verlag.

———, eds. 1996. *Answering Questions: Methodology for Determining Cognitive and Communicative Processes in Survey Research.* San Francisco: Jossey-Bass.

Scott, J. 1997. "Children as Respondents: Methods for Improving Data Quality." In *Survey Measurement and Process Quality,* edited by L. Lyberg,

P. Biemer, M. Collins, E. de Leeuw, C. Dippo, N. Schwarz, and D. Trewin. New York: Wiley.

Shaw, Clifford. 1930. *The Jack-Roller*. Chicago: University of Chicago Press.

Short, J. F., and F. I. Nye. 1957. "Reported Behavior as a Criterion of Deviant Behavior." *Social Problems* 3:207–14.

Smith, C., and T. P. Thornberry. 1995. "The Relationship between Childhood Maltreatment and Adolescent Involvement in Delinquency." *Criminology* 33:451–82.

Sobell, L., M. Sobell, and E. Ward. 1980. *Evaluating Alcohol and Drug Abuse Treatment Effectiveness: Recent Advances*. Oxford and New York: Pergamon.

Stouthamer-Loeber, M., and W. Bok van Kammen. 1995. *Data Collection and Management: A Practical Guide*. Thousand Oaks, Calif.: Sage.

Strube, G. 1987. "Answering Survey Questions: The Role of Memory." In *Social Information Processing and Survey Methodology*, edited by Hans-J. Hoppler, Norbert Schwarz, and Seymour Sudman. New York: Springer-Verlag.

Sudman, S., and N. M. Bradburn. 1974. *Response Effects in Surveys: A Review and Synthesis*. Chicago: Aldine.

———. 1982. *Asking Questions*. San Francisco: Jossey-Bass.

Sudman, S., N. M. Bradburn, and N. Schwarz. 1996. *Thinking about Answers—the Application of Cognitive Processes to Survey Methodology*. San Francisco: Jossey-Bass.

Sutterer, P., and T. Karger. 1994. "Methodological Annotations on Retrospection in Criminological Research. In *Cross-National Longitudinal Research on Human Development and Criminal Behavior*, edited by E. G. M. Weitekamp and H. J. Kerner. Dordrecht: Kluwer.

Swanborn, P. G. 1994. *Methoden van sociaal-wetenschappelijk Onderzoek*. Meppel and Amsterdam: Boom.

———. 1996. "Argumenten en Misverstanden rondom de Kwaliteit van Self-Report Data." *Tijdschrift voor Criminologie* 38:284–89.

Tanur, J. M., ed. 1992. *Questions about Questions: Inquiries into the Cognitive Bases of Surveys*. New York: Russell Sage Foundation.

Taylor, R. 1994. *Research Methods in Criminal Justice*. New York: McGraw-Hill.

Terlouw, G.-J., and G. J. N. Bruinsma. 1994. "Self-Reported Delinquency in the Netherlands." In *Delinquent Behavior among Young People in the Western World*, edited by J. Junger-Tas, G.-J. Terlouw, and M. W. Klein. Amsterdam: Kugler.

Tonry, M. 1995. *Malign Neglect—Race, Crime, and Punishment in America*. New York and Oxford: Oxford University Press.

———, ed. 1997. *Ethnicity, Crime, and Immigration: Comparative and Cross-National Perspectives*, edited by Michael Tonry. Vol. 21 of *Crime and Justice: A Review of Research*, edited by Michael Tonry. Chicago: University of Chicago Press.

Turner, C. F., L. Ku, S. M. Rogers, L. D. Lindberg, J. H. Pleck, and F. L. Sonenstein. 1998. "Adolescent Sexual Behavior, Drug Use, and Violence: Increased Reporting with Computer Survey Technology." *Science* 280:867–73.

Umesh, U. N., and R. A. Peterson. 1991. "A Critical Evaluation of the Randomized Response Method: Applications, Validation, and Research Agenda." *Sociological Methods and Research* 20:104–38.

Van der Heijden, P. G. M., K. Sijtsma, and H. 't Hart. 1995. "Self-Report Schalen zijn nog Steeds Betrouwbaar." *Tijdschrift voor Criminologie* 37:71–77.

Van der Heijden, P. G. M., G. van Gils, J. Bouts, and J. Hox. 1997. *A Comparison of Randomized Response, CASIQ and Direct Questioning—Eliciting Sensitive Information in the Context of Social Security Fraud.* Methods Series no. MS-97-4. Utrecht: University of Utrecht, Department of Methodology and Statistics.

Van Dijk, J. J. M, and P. Mayhew. 1992. *Criminal Victimization in the Industrialized World: Key Findings of the 1989 and 1992 International Crime Surveys.* The Hague: Ministry of Justice.

Van Dijk, J. J. M., P. Mayhew, and M. Killias. 1990. *Experiences of Crime across the World.* Boston: Kluwer Law and Taxation.

van Heelsum, A. J. 1993. "De Invloed van de Etnische Afkomst van Interviewers in een Interview." *Migrantenstudies* 9(2):16–34.

van Kerckvoorde, J. 1995. *Een maat voor het Kwaad?* Leuven: Universitaire Pers Leuven.

Veendrick, L. 1976. *Verborgen en Geregistreerde Criminaliteit in Groningen.* Groningen: Universiteit Groningen, Criminologisch Institut.

Vetere, E., and G. Newman. 1977. "International Crime Statistics: An Overview from a Comparative Perspective." *Abstracts on Criminology and Penology* 17:251–604.

Villetaz, P. 1994. "Le libellé des items de délinquance: Son effet sur les réponses." *Bulletin de Criminologie* 20:100–133.

Visher, Christy A. 1986. "The Rand Inmate Survey: A Reanalysis." In *Criminal Careers and "Career Criminals,"* vol. 2, edited by Alfred Blumstein, Jacqueline Cohen, Jeffrey Roth, and Christy A. Visher. Washington, D.C.: National Academy Press.

Wagenaar, W. A. 1986. "My Memory: A Study of Autobiographical Memory over Six Years." *Cognitive Psychology* 18:225–52.

Warner, S. L. 1965. "Randomized Response: A Survey Technique for Eliminating Evasive Answer Bias." *Journal of the American Statistical Association* 60:63–69.

Warr, M. 1996. "Organization and Instigation in Delinquent Groups." *Criminology* 34:11–38.

Weis, J. 1986. "Methodological Issues in Criminal Career Research." In *Criminal Careers and "Career Criminals,"* vol. 1, edited by A. Blumstein, J. Cohen, J. A. Roth, and C. A. Visher. Washington, D.C.: National Academy Press.

Weis, J. R., R. Crutchfield, and G. S. Bridges, eds. 1996. *Juvenile Delinquency.* Thousand Oaks, Calif.: Pine Forge Press.

Weisband, S., and S. Kiesler. 1996. "Self Disclosure on Computer Forms: Meta-analysis and Implications." In *CHI'96 Electronic Proceedings, ACM,* edited by R. Bilger, S. Guest, and M. J. Tauber.

Weitekamp, E. 1989. "Some Problems with the Use of Self-Reports in Longitudinal Research." In *Cross-National Research in Self-Reported Crime and Delinquency*, edited by Malcolm W. Klein. Dordrecht: Kluwer.

Wells, E., and J. Rankin. 1991. "Families and Delinquency: A Meta-analysis of the Impact of Broken Homes." *Social Problems* 38:71–90.

Wentland, E. J., and K. W. Smith. 1993. *Survey Responses—an Evaluation of Their Validity.* San Diego, Calif.: Academic Press.

Whitey, S. B. 1954. "Reliability of Recall of Income." *Public Opinion Quarterly* 18:31–34.

Williams, Jay R., and Martin Gold. 1972. "From Delinquent Behavior to Official Delinquency." *Social Problems* 20:209–29.

Zvekic, U. 1996. "The International Crime (Victim) Survey: Issues of Comparative Advantages and Disadvantages." *International Criminal Justice Review* 6:1–21.

Zvekic, U., and A. Alvazzi del Frate, eds. 1995. *Criminal Victimization in the Developing World.* Publication no. 55. Rome: UN Interregional Crime and Justice Research Institute.